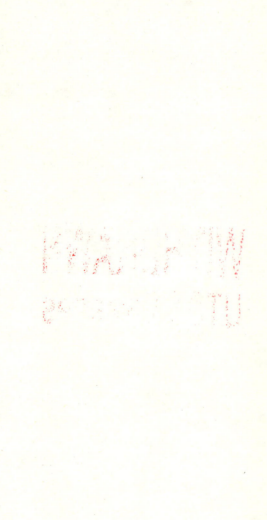

THE
OXFORD HISTORY
OF AUSTRALIA

THE
OXFORD HISTORY
OF AUSTRALIA

General Editor Geoffrey Bolton

Volume 1   Aboriginal Australia Tim Murray
Volume 2   1781–1860 Jan Kociumbas
Volume 3   1860–1900 Beverley Kingston
Volume 4   1901–1942 Stuart Macintyre

THE
OXFORD HISTORY
OF AUSTRALIA

VOLUME 5
1942–1988
THE MIDDLE WAY

GEOFFREY BOLTON

MELBOURNE
OXFORD UNIVERSITY PRESS
OXFORD AUCKLAND NEW YORK

OXFORD UNIVERSITY PRESS AUSTRALIA

Oxford   New York   Toronto
Delhi   Bombay   Calcutta   Madras   Karachi
Petaling Jaya   Singapore   Hong Kong   Tokyo
Nairobi   Dar es Salaam   Cape Town
Melbourne   Auckland
and associated companies in Berlin   Ibadan

OXFORD is a trade mark of Oxford University Press
© Geoffrey Bolton 1990
First published 1990

National Library of Australia
Cataloguing-in-Publication data:

Bolton, G. C. (Geoffrey Curgenven), 1931–
The Oxford history of Australia. Volume 5, 1942–1988: the middle way.

Bibliography.
Includes index.
ISBN 0 19 554613 X.

1. Australia—History—1939–1945. 2. Australia—History—1945–
I. Title. II. Title: The middle way.
III. Title: History of Australia. Volume 5, 1942–1988: the middle way.

994.05

Edited by Angela Gundert
Designed by Guy Mirabella
Typeset by Solo Typesetting, South Australia
Printed by Impact Printing, Melbourne
Published by Oxford University Press
253 Normanby Road, South Melbourne, Australia

CONTENTS

And even I can remember
A day when the historians left blanks
   in their writings,
I mean for things they didn't know,
But that time seems to be passing.

Ezra Pound, 'Canto XIII',
The Cantos of Ezra Pound

PUBLISHER'S NOTE

The Oxford History of Australia covers the sweep of Australian history from the first human settlement down to the 1980s. It consists of five volumes, each written by a single author with an established reputation as a productive and lively-minded historian. Each volume covers a distinct period of Australian history: Aboriginal history; white settlement, 1770–1860; colonial growth and maturation, 1860–1900; the Australian Commonwealth in peace and war, 1901–42; the modern era, from 1942 to the present. Each volume is a work of historical narrative in its own right. It draws the most recent research into a coherent and realized whole.

Aboriginal Australia is treated in its entirety, from the dramatically recast appreciation of early prehistory to present-day controversies of place, identity and belief. Colonial Australia begins with the establishment of tiny settlements at different times and with different purposes on widely separated points on the Australian coastline. From these fragments of British society sprang the competing ambitions of their members and a distinctly new civilization emerged. As the colonists spread over the continent and imposed their material culture on its resources, so the Old World notions of class, status and gender were reworked. The colonists came together at the beginning of the twentieth century and fashioned new institutions to express their goals of national self-sufficiency, yet they were tossed and buffeted by two wars and the dictates of the international economy. The final volume therefore reflects the continuity of Australia's economic and political dependence, and new patterns in the quest for social justice by women, the working class and ethnic minorities.

In tracing these themes, the Oxford History's authors have held firmly to the conviction that history needs to interpret the past as an intelligible whole. The volumes range widely in their use of source material. They are informed by specialist research and enlivened by vivid example. Above all, they are written as narrative history with a clear and dramatic thread. No common ideological orthodoxy has been imposed on the authors beyond a commitment to scholarly excellence in a form which will be read and enjoyed by many Australians.

ACKNOWLEDGEMENTS

In writing this book I have run up more obligations than can conveniently be acknowledged. The libraries at Murdoch University, the University of Queensland, and the University of Western Australia have all been consulted extensively, as has Australia House Library in London and the oral history section of the National Library of Australia. Thanks are also due to the Institute of Commonwealth Studies, London. Christine Owen and Howard Smith were a great help as research assistants in the early planning of this book, and I am aware of not having followed up all the promising leads which they discovered. My students at Murdoch University in 1982 and 1986–87 were stimulating in discussing many of the issues covered here, and I also owe many debts to the support of my colleagues Michael Durey, John Hooper, Pat Jalland, Lenore Layman and Bob Reece, not forgetting the full-time and part-time tutors and postgraduate students. They shouldered many burdens cheerfully, and upheld lively and creative standards of scholarship without adequate appreciation. It is a source of pride to have worked with them.

This is probably one of the last books to be written before the completion of the word-processor revolution and, while I did a fair share of my own typing, I am also most grateful for the skilled typing of Jan Kelly and Ros Golding, and particularly for the unfailing support of Genelle Jones as secretary. I have also benefited greatly from the criticisms—some kind, some stringent

—of those who read this work in manuscript: Fred Alexander, Raymond Evans, Ross Fitzgerald, Stuart Macintyre, Heather Radi and Kay Saunders. Stuart in particular has my thanks for quiet support at a moment of crisis. Carol Bolton has lived for too long for what became known in the family as 'the bloody book'. I cannot sufficiently acknowledge her strength and consistency; but it pleases us both that this book should be dedicated to those two products of contemporary Australia, Patrick and Matthew Bolton.

Geoffrey Bolton

NOTE ON MEASUREMENTS

This book employs contemporary units of measurement. Equivalent measures and conversion to metric units are given below.

currency

12d (12 pence) =	1s (1 shilling)	
20s (20 shillings) =	£1 (1 pound) =	$2
21s =	1 guinea	

weight

	1 pound =	.453 kilograms
14 pounds =	1 stone	
8 stone =	1 hundredweight	
20 hundredweight =	1 ton =	1.02 tonnes

length

	1 inch =	25.4 millimetres
12 inches =	1 foot	
3 feet =	1 yard	
22 yards =	1 chain	
10 chains =	1 furlong	
8 furlongs =	1 mile =	1.61 kilometres

area

4840 square yards =	1 acre =	.405 hectares
640 acres =	1 square mile	

capacity

	1 pint =	.568 litres
8 pints	1 gallon	
8 gallons =	1 bushel	

INDIAN

OCEAN

Darwi

Broome

N O
T E

WESTERN
AUSTRALIA

Yalgoo

Kalgoorlie
Coolgardie ● ●
Boulder

Nullarbor Plain

Northam ● Nangeenan
Perth
● Blackboy Hill
Rottnest Is ● Fremantle

Frankland R

Albany

King George S

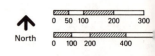

North

| 0 | 50 | 100 | 200 | 300 |

| 0 | 100 | 200 | 400 |

To Patrick and Matthew Bolton

Part I

The Brink of Self-Discovery 1942–1951

For a few years after World War II it seemed possible that Australia was on the brink of self-discovery. As in so many other countries it was an extraordinary time. Past darkness and future brightness came together in startling contrast, and for a moment there was a lapse from passion and prejudice and a glimpse of moral courage and hope.

Bruce Grant, *The Australian Dilemma*

1

THE PEOPLE AT WAR

FOR A CENTURY AND A HALF it looked as if the unlikely experiment would work. Having seized the largest land mass in the South-West Pacific from its Aboriginal inhabitants the British controlled Australia from a distance of 16 000 kilometres and peopled it with their own stock. Ninety-seven per cent of Australians claimed British origins, but they were still few in 1941: fewer than one for each of the continent's 7.6 million square kilometres, and mainly concentrated in several seaboard cities. Troubled at the emptiness of their continent, Australians reacted uneasily as the 1930s brought them into closer contact with a potentially threatening outside world. Poised at the meeting of the Pacific, Indian and Southern Oceans, Australia lay across the paths of expansion which must be taken by Britain's strongest competitors, the United States and Japan, in their quest for greater economic and political power.

It was not just that Japanese militarism and the prospect of conflict for South-East Asian markets struck a note of menace; even the United States seemed a force for cultural imperialism as the talking pictures brought about a superficial familiarity with the American way of life. Most Australians of the older generation still saw themselves as closely allied with and dependent upon Britain: 'If it had not been that we were an offshoot of the great old Mother Country who had money to lend', exclaimed a South Australian farmer–politician in 1945, 'this would still have been blackfellows' land'.[1] British capital and British culture had brought about the change; but the days were numbered when Australia could survive as a far-flung outpost of British imperialism. Australia's dependency on Britain would be followed by dependency, perhaps less formal but no less pervasive, on either the United States or Japan. How far this dependency would be tempered by a mature sense of national identity and nationally determined social and economic self-interest remained one of the great questions for the future.

Some glimpsed these questions, especially the younger poets and artists who were already urging Australians to trust the national experience. A. D. Hope, in an often quoted poem, looked for the time when Australians would turn their backs on 'that chatter of cultured apes / Which is called civilization over there'. Guidance lay not in the cities ('five wounds') but in the deserts from which traditionally prophets came. Russell Drysdale's paintings forsook the softer blues and greens of the pastoral south-east for the arid inland against which human figures were isolated and dwarfed. The most highly acclaimed novel of the 1940s, Eleanor Dark's *The Timeless Land*, reached its most effective moments in early chapters describing the Sydney region when it was all 'blackfellows' land'. Some young poets founded the Jindyworobak movement, which sought a little too self-consciously to graft Aboriginal imagery onto the writing of contemporary verse.[2]

It was far too soon for such movements to find a response among educationalists, but already the British influences which lay so heavily on school curricula were yielding a little ground. If school readers included Tennyson's *Brook* and extracts from *John Halifax, Gentleman* they also introduced children to the Geebung Polo Club, the tragic tale of young Harry Dale the drover, and even to something of *Lasseter's Last Ride* by Ion Idriess. Students might have to learn the location of the coalfields of England and the story of Charles I and his ship-money, but large numbers of them also enjoyed the lively account of their own country and the joky line-drawings by G. V. Portus in *Australia Since 1606*.[3]

For most adult Australians, knowledge of the wider world was mediated by the newspapers, and except in Sydney and Melbourne this meant that one morning daily monopolized the communication of serious news. The coverage of overseas events was more detailed than today, but it was reflected almost exclusively through the prism of agencies based on Fleet Street. Australians knew the rest of the world at a distance. Only 14 per cent were overseas-born, the majority of them in the United Kingdom. Most Australians, especially women, had never been overseas at all. For many men Gallipoli, Egypt and the Western Front was all they had see or would want to seen of foreign travel. Although QANTAS and Imperial Airways offered a weekly service to London in 1939, most of the affluent minority who travelled to Europe went by a sea voyage of four weeks from Fremantle or five from Sydney. Of the men who exercised national leadership in the 1940s neither Arthur Fadden nor Ben Chifley had ever left Australia before becoming prime minister; Chifley was over forty before he left New South Wales. John Curtin travelled abroad once, to an International Labour Organization conference in Geneva in 1924. Robert Menzies was forty before he visited London as attorney-general, at once revelling in the pageantry of George V's silver jubilee and plunging into a round of upper-class contacts whose approval he was delighted to win. He missed experiencing even a student's or a tourist's view of the common life of Britain or of any other country but his own. R. G. Casey owned much of his political reputation because as a rich and well-connected young man in the 1920s he had been Australian liaison officer in London and privy to the secrets of great men. Paul and Alexandra Hasluck were unusual as a young couple in the 1930s in that as well as spending a year in Europe they also visited South-East Asia; during the Vietnam War he was one of the very few Australians in public life who had actually set eyes upon that distracted country.[4]

Although Australia as a trading nation depended on overseas sources for markets and investment, businessmen such as Essington Lewis and W. S. Robinson who moved easily in international circles were still a minority. Many others were narrow and conservative, in some cases because their formative years lay well back in the colonial past. 'It would be rather difficult to find a place where so many old men are in charge', wrote Frederic Eggleston.[5] Sir Thomas Buckland, chairman of the Bank of New South Wales at eighty-nine and a director until his death aged ninety-nine in 1947, made his fortune in the Charters Towers gold-rush of the 1870s. Joseph Mitchell influenced the destinies of Burns Philp until a year before his death in 1967 at the age of ninety-three. Not that the younger generation was necessarily more receptive to new ideas. When E. W. Knox relinquished control of the Colonial Sugar Refining Company at the age of eighty-five in 1932 he was succeeded by Sir Philip Goldfinch who, although nearly forty years younger, shared to the full Knox's implacable hostility to trade unions and social welfare. The majority of Australia's business leaders lived in New South Wales and Victoria, where for a quarter of a century before 1941 they never had to accommodate to a Labor government which lasted for more than two years. Hence conservatism flourished.[6]

Nor were the universities expected to provide new or disturbing stimulation. Many of Australia's finest scholars left the country. W. K. Hancock and Mark Oliphant, respectively the best Australian historian and physicist of their generation, worked at the University of Birmingham, in a city whose only advantage over Sydney and Melbourne must have been its closeness to metropolitan contact. Those who remained in Australia included such influential figures as John Anderson, the formidable and sceptical professor of philosophy at Sydney, and R. M. Crawford, who taught history as a school of morality to a generation of students at Melbourne, but such men were always apt to be vilified by ignorant politicians if they upset conventional thinking. The *Bulletin* sneered at S. H. Roberts, the Sydney historian, for forecasting war with Hitler. 'Communist', then as now, was just a lazy term of abuse for any shred of independent thought. The new radical analysts of Australian society, such as Brian Fitzpatrick and P. R. Stephensen, mostly operated outside the universities. The Australian Broadcasting Commission (ABC), in its first decade already uniquely influential in disseminating Australian culture, was prevented from broadcasting controversial opinions.[7] Shielded from disturbing ideas, ignorant of the clash and compromise of competing ethnic traditions, reliant on British protection and guidance, Australians were at risk of insularity.

This insularity was a little dented by the first phases of the Second World War, from 1939 to 1941. As in the previous world war, Australian volunteers served as Britain's auxiliaries, and in the crisis following the fall of France in June 1940 helped to provide the slim margin of strength which enabled Britain to survive the onslaught of Nazi Germany. Australian airmen manned many of the bombers and fighters denying the Luftwaffe command of English skies. The Sixth and Seventh Divisions, and subsequently the Ninth, soldiered in Egypt and Libya against three large-scale enemy attacks; many of the 'rats of Tobruk', who withstood a seven-month siege, were Australians and New Zealanders. Australians were pitted unavailingly against the German invasion of Greece and Crete in 1941, and more success-fully against the Vichy French in Syria a little later. While these events generated patriotic sentiment back in Australia it was still war at a distance, and business, politics and pleasure on the home front went on much as usual. Australian insularity was abruptly and permanently shattered by Japan's entry into the war in December 1941, and still more by the fall of Singapore in mid-February 1942.

Few Australians were prepared for a disaster of such mag-nitude. The Japanese advance was swift. On 8 December 1941 Australia heard of the bombing of Pearl Harbor. Two days later Britain's major warships in South-East Asian waters were sunk by Japanese aircraft. At Christmas Hong Kong fell amid scenes of rape and pillage which forecast all too vividly the likely be-haviour of victorious invaders. Thrusting through Malaya against inadequately prepared opposition the Japanese reached Britain's key base of Singapore in the first week of February. Singapore was expected to hold out for six months. It fell in ten days. Despite much heroism some Australian units were thought to have given up easily. After the surrender the Australian com-manding officer, Major-General Gordon Bennett, fled in contro-versial circumstances. Among the prisoners were 15 000 Australian servicemen, mostly members of the Eighth Division. They were to face three-and-a-half years of bitter servitude at Changi and on the infamous Burma Railway, during which nearly half their number would die.[8]

'The fall of Singapore opens the Battle for Australia', said the prime minister, John Curtin, on 16 February. Three days later bombs fell for the first time on Australian soil. Morale faltered. The first bombing of Darwin was followed by much looting and a mass exodus that included servicemen. Some of the men were 'nearly hysterical' remarked the cattleman Jack Kilfoyle en-countering them at the pub at Katherine, 350 kilometres from the scene of the raid.[9] During March, Darwin, Wyndham and Broome were raided several times. Meanwhile the Japanese consolidated their hold on the Netherlands East Indies (Indonesia) and the Philippines, and landed in New Guinea and the Solomon Islands. In Australia the army chiefs of staff began to prepare secret contingency plans for invasion. They told the government that if the Japanese could bring down one aircraft carrier and one well-trained division nothing could stop them. At the worst most of the continent must be abandoned outside a line from Adelaide to Brisbane—the famous 'Brisbane Line'.[10]

The government that heard this advice was an untried Labor ministry only four months in office and depending for its majority on two independents. Only one of its members had served in the First World War (three others had been in the Boer War) and only three had briefly held ministerial office. Most of them had concentrated their political energies arguing for the redress of social injustice during the depressed 1930s and few had closely studied the problems of defence, foreign policy or wartime management of the economy. By an irony, Prime Minister John Curtin, a 57-year-old former journalist, had come to the fore as a fervent anti-conscriptionist during the First World War. His potential for national leadership was an unknown quantity, but in six years of unifying the Australian Labor Party's (ALP's) warring factions while leader of the Opposition he had shown patience, guile and a great gift for keeping his own counsel. At least three of his ministers would show a touch of distinction: J. B. Chifley, treasurer, an ex-railwayman whose calm and adroit managerial skills hid a hard core of anger against privilege; H. V. Evatt, attorney-general and minister for external affairs—energetic, ambitious, formerly Australia's youngest High Court judge—gifted with every intellectual quality except political judgement; and J. J. Dedman, a dour representative of those British migrants who tried to wrest a living from marginal farming country until beaten by the Depression, now minister for the war organization of industry. Defence was the responsibility of the loyal and experienced deputy prime minister, F. M. Forde, frequently lampooned for his minor vanities but a competent performer in an office where incompetence would have been disastrous. To these men and their colleagues fell the decisions to be taken as Australia seemed to face invasion for the first time since European settlement.[11]

Australia possessed a home defence airforce of eighteen squadrons, three of them with Malayan experience, and a navy which lost three of its five cruisers during a few months in 1941–42. In January the Sixth and Seventh divisions were recalled from Egypt to defend Java and Sumatra, leaving the Ninth subsequently to play a memorable part at El Alamein. In the face of the rapid Japanese advance the Australian government decided in mid-February that these experienced troops were needed to defend their own country and requested that their convoy should be redirected. The British prime minister, Winston Churchill, tried to divert the Australians to the hopeless Burma campaign, thus prolonging their voyage on the dangerous Indian Ocean, but Curtin insisted on their return, enduring private agony over the decision until their safe arrival.[12] These seasoned troops were reinforced by the Citizen Military Forces (CMF) who, because they were liable to service only in Australian territory, were sometimes scorned as 'chocolate soldiers'. The best were as good as the Australian Imperial Force (AIF), but some of the units stationed in northern Australia were sloppy and half-hearted, and regular officers sometimes despaired of their quality. As a home guard the Volunteer Defence Corps was built up in units ranging from middle-aged veterans of the First World War grown sedentary in city jobs to North Queensland pastoralists who, not without relish, anticipated harassing the enemy as guerrillas hiding among their own gullies and ridges. Thus Australia confronted the victorious professionalism of the Imperial Japanese Army.

Civilians prepared for the emergency. Schools and private households were encouraged to dig slit trenches as a precaution against air raids. In parks and open spaces communal shelters were excavated, boarded with timber and covered with soil or sandbags. Shopfronts were boarded up against bomb blasts. Daylight saving was introduced and a mild form of blackout imposed. Refugees arrived from Malaya and Indonesia to be housed wherever space could be found in flats and hotels. Only 54 per cent of respondents to a newspaper poll in April 1942 acknowledged any risk of an invasion, but perhaps there were more who did not admit their fears. Percy Spender, visiting Palm Beach late in the summer holidays, found all its affluent residents had 'upped and took off for as far west of Sydney as they could go until (apart from . . . the fisherman, the storekeeper and a few others) hardly a soul was to be seen'. Canberra worried about invasion more than most Australian cities; according to the American ambassador, Nelson Johnson, 'Everywhere one got the feeling that Australia was prepared to give up without a struggle; that if it had been possible to leave the country, the people would have gone. For a time the transportation system was clogged'.[13]

Only the United States could be Australia's prop and shield.

A week after the fall of Singapore General Douglas MacArthur, commander of the defeated American forces in the Philippines, was ordered to Australia. In April he became supreme commander of the allied forces in the Pacific with headquarters at Melbourne, moving four months later to Brisbane. Since the majority of troops in the region were Australians, General Sir Thomas Blamey was made army commander but Americans commanded the allied naval and air forces. A youthful-looking 62-year-old, authoritative and crisp (he never sweated even in the most tropical conditions) MacArthur soon won the trust of Curtin and his colleagues, who worked smoothly with the Americans and interfered little in the conduct of the war. It may be true that the Japanese scare suited MacArthur in the rehabilitation of his career and the Curtin government in establishing political credibility, but Curtin took the invasion threat seriously enough to instruct the armed forces in May 1942 to follow a scorched earth policy in the event of a Japanese landing, and MacArthur approved that directive. Meanwhile the experienced troops from the Middle East, reinforced by units of the CMF, were thrust into the New Guinea campaign. As the Sixth Division traversed Australia on a seven-day journey by steam train from Melbourne to Cairns they were welcomed everywhere. 'In Victoria', one soldier remembered, 'the local people gave us chickens and hams; in the Riverina, chops and steak; on the coast, oysters, prawns, and fish; and everywhere, fruit and cakes and puddings to take with us'.[14]

With the return of the troops anxiety subsided, though morale in Sydney was shaken when at the end of May Japanese submarines penetrated the harbour and shelled beachside suburbs, repeating the feat some days later at Newcastle. However, by the end of July censors reported in most parts of the country a receding sense of threat, though it lingered in regions closest to the front line. At Geraldton a register of escape routes was compiled, inland towns were advised to stockpile three months' supply of food, and many women with young children moved to country districts to live in empty shops or farm sheds, yet the municipal council decided not to take responsibility for disposing of the corpses of those killed in air raids. As late as May 1943 J. C. McDonald, storekeeper at Laura in the far north of Queensland, wrote to an English friend: 'I for one do not think Australia is out of the woods yet as far as invasion here by Japan is concerned, but I am sure we will put up a good fight if it is attempted'.[15]

During the emergency, civil rights for dissenters and minorities were at a discount. No fewer than 6780 Australians were interned as potentially dangerous aliens. More than half were of Italian origin, and included naturalized citizens of long standing and the brothers of enlisted volunteers with the AIF. Their farms and businesses suffered from neglect, their wives and children were impoverished and ostracized. In the Innisfail district of Queensland the Education Department closed a small school because board for the teacher was available only with Italian families. Native-born Australians were also interned, sometimes with rough justice. In February and March 1942 the federal authorities rounded up more than twenty members of the 'Australia First' movement who saw Australia's defence as overriding any obligations to Britain or its empire. Two were imprisoned and two others acquitted on charges of sedition brought by a dubious informer. The rest were held without trial for periods ranging from several months to two years. In 1945 a royal commission found that eight had been detained without justification and should be awarded compensation.[16] Similar harassment was meted out to the Jehovah's Witnesses, a religious sect of pacifist leanings whose teaching forbade placing human laws above God's. For these subversive opinions their organization was banned from January 1941 until after a High Court challenge in March 1943. Their children were excluded from Victorian primary schools because their parents did not allow them to salute the flag.[17] The Communist Party of Australia, outlawed in 1940, was not restored to legality until December 1942, nearly eighteen months after the Soviet Union had entered the war as a major ally.

Untroubled by the problems of such minorities most Australians found that, although their worst anxieties about the war were over by mid-1942, restrictions on the home front continued. Between June and August rationing by coupon was introduced for clothing, tea and sugar. In July South Australia banned horse-racing and betting shops, and the other states tried the experiment of suspending racing for one Saturday each month, only to find a resulting increase in drunkenness as frustrated punters took to the pubs. In August Curtin exhorted his fellow Australians to choose austerity as a new way of life. 'By doing so', he said, 'we will be a nation which is spiritually and morally rearmed . . . not only to meet the tasks of war but also the tasks of peace'.[18] A man of peace striving as a war leader to keep faith with his principles,

Curtin willingly embraced asceticism for himself; but although the austerity campaign led to an oversubscribed £100 million war loan, most Australians saw no need to accept such stern morality.

They found plenty to grumble about. Stricter petrol rationing forced motorists to use gas-producers as an unsatisfactory substitute. Interstate travel was restricted. Public transport came under strain, and freight problems led to shortages of unrationed items already in limited supply. Many suburban households reverted to the simpler practices of an earlier generation, digging up their lawns to grow vegetables or keeping a few fowls in the backyard. Hats, waistcoats and double-breasted suits ceased to be an obligatory part of male middle-class uniform, and shirt-tails were shortened. Women's fashions were plain and economical. The wearing of slacks, once a sign of slightly improper modernism, was gradually tolerated because of practicality; and after a submission went all the way to federal cabinet, employers were instructed not to ban young women from going to work without stockings.[19]

Under J. J. Dedman as minister and H. C. Coombs as director-general of rationing, the distribution of resources was generally efficient and fair, although Dedman, a glutton for criticism, was derided as 'the man who killed Santa Claus' when he tried to damp down demand by banning that most popular symbol of advertising for Christmas shopping. For most citizens petty fiddling took the edge off austerity. Even the most respectable grocers and publicans looked after their regular customers, while in Kings Cross and St Kilda black markets flourished. The practice does not seem to have generated as much moral indignation as profiteering in the First World War, perhaps because prices did not rise so steeply. Also, in the 1940s the black market largely covered such popular luxuries as cigarettes, liquor and nylon stockings, whereas the impact of rationing on basic food-stuffs was, for a nation in wartime, remarkably mild. Although rationing was extended to butter in June 1943 and meat in January 1944, in both cases to free supplies for Britain, many families were better fed than they had been in the Depression years of the 1930s.

Government intervention was also required to assure stability for Australia's major exports, especially when the war in the Pacific exacerbated shipping problems. Wool which could not be exported was stockpiled, wheat was purchased for stock feed, and from 1942 all the meat Australia could produce went to feed Britain or the armed forces in the South-West Pacific, for whom Australia was a major supplier under the reverse lend-lease arrangements governing trade between the United States and its allies. Fortunes revived for farmers and graziers, although many did not feel the benefits because they carried debts from the depressed 1930s and were working with rundown equipment. Labour was inadequate although supplemented by the employment of women and many of the 18 000 Italian prisoners of war in Australia. Mining was of less importance. Gold-mining was severely cut and would go to its lowest ebb for a hundred years, but strategic materials were in demand. Some mines, such as that for scheelite production at King Island, operated at considerable loss. To the lasting benefit of Mount Isa Mines, the federal government generously aided the company in switching from lead-zinc production to copper in 1943.[20] All this activity marked the start of a world commodity boom which would last for thirty years and bring easy times and full employment to major suppliers of raw materials such as Australia, but few were bold enough to forecast this openly.

During the war at least there would be no unemployment. In February 1942 an Allied Works Council was set up to secure workers and materials for the construction of the aerodromes, docks, roads, workshops, factories, hospitals and other installations needed by the armed forces garrisoning Australia. Its forceful director-general was E. G. Theodore, once Labor premier of Queensland but now a successful investor and businessman. For its workforce the council recruited a Civil Construction Corps which by mid-1943 numbered over 50 000. Its achievements included the 1500 kilometre bitumen-topped Stuart Highway between Darwin and Alice Springs, a project long deferred in peacetime and now completed in twelve months. Tight industrial discipline was reinforced by fines and the (unused) power of imprisonment. All other civil employment was placed under the autocratic control of a directorate-general of manpower. Men and women were taken from what were seen as inessential jobs and placed in those directed into the war effort. Most domestic servants, for instance, despite the protests of their employers, were transferred to better paid and less onerous work by the end of 1942.[21]

In 1942 about half a million Australians were producing

munitions, aircraft and war supplies, leaving about 200 000 workers for food, clothing and every variety of civil production—less than half the number engaged pre-war. During the war the number of factories increased by 15 per cent, with the government promoting decentralization by situating new plants in country towns such as Stawell and Horsham in Victoria, and Katoomba, Tamworth and Wagga in New South Wales. By June 1943, 90 per cent of Australian men and 30 per cent of women were in either the armed forces, essential civilian jobs or direct war work such as munitions-making. Excluding students and the aged, the remainder were largely housewives, many of them virtually single parents for the duration. Their long hours of hard work and voluntary labour for the war effort were completely ignored by official statisticians assessing the national effort.

Even the Aboriginal community benefited from the labour shortage. During the forty years before the war most Aborigines had either been forced onto reserves, used as ill-paid station hands on outback pastoral properties, or left to eke out a living as impoverished fringe-dwellers on the edge of country towns. Those who managed to remain independent members of the workforce were often hard-pressed during the 1930s Depression. It was not surprising that when the war came some responded like John Egan, who was picked up by the military police for walking along a Geraldton street shouting 'The Japs will do me'. Nine years earlier his family had been forcibly evicted from their home and sent to the notorious Moore River Reserve without their possessions. But the war brought jobs for Aborigines. Some joined the army, although until 1942 they could be excluded. Others found their way to regular work in the inner suburbs of Sydney and Brisbane (they were not then allowed in Perth), thus enlarging urban Aboriginal communities. But it was the influx of armed forces into northern Australia which created the greatest demand for Aboriginal labour and which revealed to thousands of airmen and soldiers, many of whom had previously known no Aborigines, that the stereotype of black Australians as unteachably primitive was utterly false.

The Aborigines were given work carting gravel, digging sanitary sites, spraying for mosquito control, butchering, manning sawmills and unloading ammunition. They received basic pay of 10 shillings a week, were clothed in the same army issue as other Australians and housed in the same kind of waterproof ventilated huts. They ate army rations, and had access to running water, laundries, showers and segregated toilets. They demolished the old prejudices which saw them as ignorant of money and incapable of hygiene. It had been feared that the mixture of tribes could be socially disruptive; the fears proved groundless. They had been called lazy and disorganized; at Mataranka 'The Aborigines worked a ten-hour day and in the opinion of their supervisors worked harder than either soldiers or civilian labour units in the Middle East'.[22] They had been called a 'dying race'. Regular diet and some disposable income, perhaps also the eligibility of some Aboriginal women for child endowment, prompted change. For the first time in a century the Aboriginal birth rate was recognized as rising. There could be no more telling index of the social change, and the change in attitudes and perceptions, generated by the Japanese emergency.

As the Japanese were forced back the conviction grew that Australia had barely escaped invasion. MacArthur fostered this impression by boasting in March 1943, inaccurately but without public contradiction, that it was he who scrapped plans for abandoning northern Australia to the Japanese and insisted on confronting them in New Guinea and the islands to the north. This myth was reinforced from an unexpected quarter in June 1943 when E. J. (Eddie) Ward, a hard-hitting Sydney populist who was minister for labour under Curtin, accused the previous non-Labor government of having decided to order a retreat to the Brisbane Line in the event of a Japanese invasion. It is hard to know why he staked his credibility on such a tale; he never revealed his source, refused to testify before a royal commission on the allegation, and was afterwards demoted to a lower rank in the cabinet. His story was never supported by evidence then or later. Like many an Australian politician before and since, his judgement was probably warped by partisan malice. But the Brisbane Line remained a potent symbol in folklore in Queensland and Western Australia. Most Australians convinced themselves that for the only time in modern history their country had been in danger. This sense of peril encountered and resisted helped to shape much of the thinking about the future.[23]

Recent critics, arguing that the Australian government yielded too readily to American dominance, have pointed out that invasion was in fact unlikely because at an early stage in 1942 those in the Japanese navy who favoured a direct attack on

Australia were overruled by army leaders unwilling to over-extend lines of communication.[24] Even so, the Japanese presence in Australian waters was marked by the sinking of twenty-nine merchant ships between 1942 and 1945, as well as the torpedoing of the hospital ship *Centaur* with the loss of nearly 300 lives in May 1943. It was also feared that the Japanese could isolate Australia by seizing New Guinea, Fiji, New Caledonia and Samoa. The danger receded somewhat after the Battle of the Coral Sea on 4–8 May 1942 when American forces repelled a convoy threatening Port Moresby. In June the Japanese navy suffered a more decisive check at the Battle of Midway. As reinforcements built up in Australia the Japanese saw that they must quickly consolidate their hold on the South-West Pacific. In the last days of August 1942 Japanese troops landed at Milne Bay on the eastern tip of New Guinea, while their main thrust through the Highlands brought them within 80 kilometres of Port Moresby. But they had reached their limit. The Milne Bay landing was extinguished and the advance towards the south coast was stopped. Painfully and gradually a force of 84 000 allied troops, two-thirds of them Australian, turned the Japanese back along the Kokoda Trail. By January 1943 Lae and Salamaua on the north coast of New Guinea were once more in allied hands.[25]

Although the war was to last until August 1945, New Guinea was to be the last major victory for Australia's armed forces. This was partly because members of the CMF were then liable for service only on Australian territory. It was impractical to insist that they should lay down their arms on reaching the border of Dutch New Guinea, but where should the line be drawn? Labor under Curtin was full of men who during the First World War had staked their political lives on the belief that Australians should be conscripted only to defend their own country and never for overseas service. It was not easy for them to admit any compromise. By the beginning of 1943 all but one of Curtin's followers consented to a formula by which the CMF could serve as far north as the Equator and as far east as the enemy-occupied Solomons.[26] In April 1943 Australian forces serving in the South-West Pacific (including Australia) numbered 446 000, as against 111 000 Americans, but during the next eighteen months American numbers built up to half a million and before the end of the war reached a peak of 863 000.

Probably no more than a third of that number were in

Australia at any one time but it was the first time in the history of white Australia that such a concentration of foreigners had entered the country. Although American English was easily intelligible and Hollywood had accustomed Australians to a sanitized version of the American way of life, there remained cultural differences which caused problems. Some American servicemen were black, and care was taken to station many, though not all, of them in remote areas such as the north-west of Queensland where they would not upset too many believers in the White Australia Policy. Americans were scornful of what they saw as leisurely Australian working habits. Yet American servicemen enjoyed amenities which by local standards were luxurious: hotel suites for the officers; beefsteaks and ice-cream for the enlisted men in camp. Their free-spending habits gained favour from night-club proprietors, waiters, publicans, taxi-drivers, good-time girls, and other purveyors of wartime amenities—to the further vexation of 'good' Australians. Their naively patriotic rhetoric was often irksome, particularly when they boasted of saving Australia.

Not surprisingly, brawls broke out. The notorious battle of Brisbane in November 1942 was not entirely, as is often stated, a case of Aussies versus Yanks, but belongs to the annals of anti-police riots. It began when two Australians intervened against an American provost bashing a drunken American private, and ended with a pitched battle in Queen Street, the fatal shooting of an Australian, and the injury of at least twenty others on both sides. But in February 1943 traffic in central Melbourne was blocked for twenty minutes while over 2000 Americans and Australians battled it out, and in the summer of 1944 similar major brawls were reported from Sydney and Perth. Sexual jealousy was a factor. Smoother in their manner than Australian servicemen, better uniformed and twice as well paid, the Americans seemed all too attractive to young Australian women. In March 1942 Brisbane's Archbishop Duhig demanded a ban on marriages between Australian women and American servicemen.[27] In vain! By the end of the war more than 10 000 Australian brides were seeking admission to the United States.

They were not the only Australian–American links for the future. Many later businessmen and politicians, including a Colonel Lyndon B. Johnson, returned home from the war with agreeable recollections of Australia's secure potential for future alliance and investment. Portents of Americanization appeared. The *Reader's Digest* began to circulate in an Australian edition in April 1944. Coca-Cola, bottled under franchise by Australian firms, followed soon after. These were only symbols but they forecast Australia's growing and inevitable involvement with the global economic and strategic interests of the United States. Of the great powers who vied for supremacy in the Western Pacific during the 1939–45 war it was the Americans who seemed the power of the future rather than the weakened British or the defeated Japanese. Such thinking was encouraged by the heightened prominence given to American forces during the later stages of the war. Using sea and air power to save the lives of his troops, MacArthur developed a strategy of 'island hopping'; the allies advanced across the Pacific in a series of leaps, recapturing important bases and leaving behind isolated Japanese garrisons which could be mopped up subsequently or left to languish in the jungles until peace came. While American forces manned the advances and won the headlines, the Australians found themselves relegated to the unglamorous but arduous task of prising the Japanese out of their tenaciously defended hideouts in New Guinea. This took two years. In 1945 the Ninth Division was set to similar work in Borneo.[28]

Reports of this jungle fighting did much to encourage the popular stereotype of Japanese fanaticism, but the great divide between the antagonists concerned the treatment of prisoners of war. Of 22 000 Australian servicemen taken by the Japanese, mainly in Malaya, more than one-third perished from disease and ill-treatment. A number were bayoneted or beheaded. The survivors who returned home after the war were pitifully ill and emaciated. Japanese military tradition held that a captured soldier had lost honour and deserved no pity. The Australians housed their Japanese prisoners in the comparatively humane but utterly alien environment of Cowra, in rural New South Wales. In August 1944 nearly 1100 of them, armed with baseball bats and staves, broke out of camp. More than two hundred Japanese and several Australians were killed before the outbreak was suppressed, and although the matter was hushed up for a while its eventual disclosure brought little sympathy for the Japanese.[29] It seemed that the war would entrench Australian racial prejudices.

The Australian campaigns in New Guinea and Borneo ranked in the media as a relative sideshow compared with the European campaigns which culminated in Germany's surrender in May 1945. Whereas Australians had shared in the vital push on the Western Front which ended the First World War, they took little part in the climax of the Second. When in August 1945 the Japanese in their turn yielded, this was an acknowledgement of the American technological superiority behind the dropping of the first atomic bombs on Hiroshima and Nagasaki. Of this appalling climax Australians were no more than uncomprehending spectators. Relief at the end of six years' conflict overtook all other emotions. The churches in Australian cities were crowded as never since. Young people milled in the streets, singing, dancing and cheering. In Launceston the effigy of the emperor Hirohito on his white horse was burnt in a bonfire. Accepting the enemy surrender at Morotai, General Blamey recalled the atrocities of the past and growled: 'I do not recognise you as an honourable and gallant foe but you will be treated with due but severe courtesy in all matters'.[30] Forty years after this confrontation Japan was respected and courted as Australia's major trading partner and a potent source of investment. The emperor Hirohito, whose image the citizens of Launceston had consigned to the flames, reigned until 1988, and when he died official Australian flags were flown at half-mast.

The war of 1939–45 thus fell far behind that of 1914–18 as an occasion for mythmaking. Neither the siege of Tobruk nor the Kokoda Trail won the same legendary status as Gallipoli. Although 540 000 Australians enlisted in 1939–45, as against 417 000 in 1914–18, they represented a lower percentage of the population, and deaths in action were fewer: 33 826 as against nearly 60 000. It must be remembered, however, that the casualties of 1939–45 came from smaller families than those of the earlier war. In one Melbourne suburban street nine families mourned the loss of an only son in the 1939–45 war.[31] On the other hand, improved medical and surgical techniques undoubtedly saved many more lives, and in Papua New Guinea hundreds of wounded owed their lives to Papuan stretcher-bearers and auxiliaries.

Nor did Australia produce a military leader with the towering reputation earned in 1914–18 by Sir John Monash. Blamey, once Monash's aide and now a seasoned general, had to accept subordination to the charismatic MacArthur. He was too controversial. He quarrelled with some of his senior officers, causing great controversy by the shelving of Lieutenant-General Sydney Rowell just at the moment in 1942 when the Japanese thrust at Port Moresby had been parried. Critics accused him of self-indulgence — 'Falstaff in a scoutmaster's uniform' was one description. He was a very Australian type: shrewd and realistic, but abrasive and careless of appearances. Unlike Monash in his time, and unlike MacArthur and Eisenhower in the United States, he could not be publicized as a man fitter than any career politician to lead his country in peacetime.[32]

Michael McKernan has suggested that the emergency 'galvanised all Australians into action so that servicemen achieved no pre-eminent position'.[33] Another view might be that the war was important for many Australians mainly as providing opportunities to gain improved working conditions while their labour was in keen demand. Memories of the slump which followed the 1914–18 war and the 1930s Depression cut deeply into working-class consciousness. It was unconvincing for employers to demand selfless patriotic zeal from workers whose welfare they had long disregarded. Even after the 1942 national security regulations placed the workforce under strict controls militant unions went on strike. In the crisis month of April 1942, 500 engineers in New South Wales munitions factories stopped work for a fortnight. The waterside workers and seamen, having been ill-used in pre-war years, asserted their rights tenaciously. Much waterside conflict was averted by a Stevedoring Industries Commission chaired by Mr Justice Piper, but in March 1943 a strike protesting against the gang system of pick-up ended only after the federal government threatened to deprive strikers of the reserved status exempting them from military service.

The coal-miners of New South Wales reacted vigorously against a long history of exploitation. Judge E. A. Drake-Brockman, no radical, described industrial relations on the coalfields as 'the rules of the jungle'. In the early years of the war the miners gained improvements in health and safety procedures, paid annual leave and a 40-hour week for underground miners, but only in the teeth of bitter opposition from the mine owners. Although special arbitration tribunals were set up early in 1942, the number of stoppages increased, but the amount of time lost was only 60 per cent of that lost in the last pre-war years. Militancy sprang from the grass roots of the clannish coal towns, in part because employers failed to set up adequate grievance procedures. Alan Walker, a cleric conducting a pioneer socio-logical study of Cessnock during the war years, found a question-ing mood among the miners. 'I can't feel very keen about the war', said one, 'There are too many people making money out of it'. As the Japanese retreated, output fell, and strikes and absentee-ism increased. Such stoppages exasperated the middle class and the Americans, and embarrassed the Curtin government, divided as it was between its Labor loyalties and commitment to winning the war.[34]

Communist union officials were often blamed for stirring up strife. In fact they favoured an all-out war effort in support of the Soviet Union and sometimes had to be pushed into strike action by the rank and file. Capitalist society had done little for the wharfies and the colliers when times were hard and they could see little to gain from considering the convenience of capitalist society. Communist union officials such as Ernie Thorn-ton among the ironworkers, Paddy Troy on the Fremantle water-front, and Wattie Doig of the Wonthaggi coal-miners were elected because of their readiness to spend long hours in the tedious chores of organization, as well as their capacity for confronting the employers and government in articulate and forceful terms. Much hostility was disarmed by admiration for the part played by communists in European resistance movements and by the Soviet Union's massive contribution to the war against Nazi Germany.

There would never be a more favourable season for Australian Marxists than the later years of the war. In the Victorian state elections of 1943 communist candidates polled one-eighth of the vote at Ballarat, between one-fifth and one-quarter in inner suburbs such as Collingwood and Richmond, and nearly 40 per cent in Port Melbourne. Communists also fared well in North Queensland where local populist radicalism throve on the short-ages and disruptions which came of forming part of Australia's front line against the Japanese. In 1944 a communist lawyer, Fred Paterson, was elected to the Queensland legislature as member for Bowen. He was the only member of his party ever to sit in an Australian parliament. In the same year the party purchased a four-storey headquarters in George Street, Sydney, and named it Marx House. By 1945 one of their leading antagonists claimed that half a million workers were communist-influenced, but the party acknowledged only 23 000 paid-up members.[35] The communist achievement in Australia was too easily exaggerated both by enthusiastic comrades and by opponents who for various motives wanted to portray them as a menace to Australian society. Although there was a good deal of admiration for Stalingrad, and even for a time for Stalin, it is doubtful whether the majority of Australians were shifted out of their customary distaste for 'red raggers'.[36]

For the minority who thought of themselves as intellectuals or artists communism had its attraction, offering an easily identifiable rallying point for individuals at odds with the social injustice of the Depression, the brutalizing effects of war, and the common Australian tendency among all classes to scoff at things of the mind. Idealistic students such as Ian Turner found communism 'a profound emotional experience' offering an exhilarating camaraderie. The experiences of the 1930s had already led artists such as Noel Counihan and writers such as Judah Waten to an acceptable discipline in Marxism. Although bodies such as the Contemporary Art Society and the Fellowship of Australian Writers—both hives of creativity in those years—included active communists, they never dominated intellectual debate. Artists such as Albert Tucker and Sidney Nolan, writers such as Max Harris and the editor of the up-and-coming literary quarterly *Meanjin*, Clem Christesen, although able and willing to work and argue with the committed communists, soon went their individual ways. Many Australians nevertheless were fortified in their prejudice against artists and writers as fashionable subversives.

In 1944 two stories broke in the newspapers, both putting creative artists in a ludicrous light. When the respected portrait painter William Dobell won the Archibald Prize a group of conservative artists took legal action on the grounds that his subject, Joshua Smith, was caricatured too grossly for the result to qualify as a portrait. The courts quite properly rejected the case, but not before the public had been regaled by the spectacle of Sydney's leading artists and critics tearing each other's work to shreds. Artistic experiment was further discouraged by the Ern Malley affair. This was a hoax aimed against *Angry Penguins*, a lively journal which boxed the compass from Marxism to surrealism and was edited by the precocious Adelaide writer Max Harris. Feeling that young Harris needed taking down a peg or two, a pair of Sydney sceptics, James McAuley and Harold Stewart, sent him a sheaf of poems deliberately thrown together as nonsense and allegedly the work of one Ern Malley, a telegraph linesman now dead of Graves' disease. McAuley and Stewart were both sound poets and perhaps wrote better than they realized. At any rate Harris devoted a whole issue of *Angry Penguins* to the exciting new find. The hoax was exposed, Harris ridiculed, and *Angry Penguins* soon ceased publication. It was not surprising that some preferred the promise of scientific certainty in social realism and a Marxist line.[37]

In one important respect the Left gave an uncertain call. Women sometimes found even the Communist Party paternalist. One woman graduate who joined the party in Adelaide 'always felt conscious of male superiority . . . if I queried any aspect of policy I was crushed by young men'. In North Queensland the writer Jean Devanny was expelled and smeared by personal gossip when male colleagues found her too assertive. The labour movement was divided over equal pay for women employees, some union officials fearing that wages would be forced down in the process of equalization. In one month, November 1942, the *Sydney Morning Herald* reported the welders as going on strike in support of equal pay for equal work by women, and the moulders at the Commonwealth Aircraft Corporation as threatening industrial action if women were not withdrawn.[38] Women sometimes suspected that male unionists campaigning for equal pay were often less concerned with industrial justice than with making them unattractive to bosses; if an employer had to choose between a male or a female worker for the same money he was likely to pick a man. Employer groups sent up one hostile legal challenge after another against the operations of the government's Women's Employment Board, until by September 1944 it was scuttled by a series of discouraging High Court decisions. In its two-and-a-half years of life the board, chaired by the intermittently radical judge A. W. Foster, edged women's pay in the industries under its scope from 54 per cent to between 60 and 100 per cent of the adult male rate, with 90 per cent a common formula. It never occurred to anyone in power that in some cases women might deserve more than 100 per cent of the male rate. Awards were allegedly measured in terms of efficiency and productivity, often in the face of sexist fault-finding by employers, who attacked absenteeism among women workers without considering whether hours and conditions needed to be adapted for wives and mothers.[39]

Some women learned militancy. In February 1943 textile workers at the Alexandria Spinning Mills in Sydney struck for a fortnight to secure a modest increase in their rate of pay. They faced not only predictable press criticism, but hostility from the officials of the male-dominated union which went to the lengths of sending the names of strikers to the Arbitration Court to be fined for absenteeism. In all, the board's activities resulted in improved working conditions for both sexes but did not noticeably increase women's long-term participation in the workforce. In 1943–44, when female employment was at its wartime peak, women constituted a little less than 30 per cent of the workforce. This was the same figure as in the Depression year of 1932–33, when men were not serving in the armed forces but were unemployed. The figure was not to be exceeded until the late 1960s.[40]

Employers clamoured for more workers, blaming labour problems for shortcomings in productivity. By mid-1943, with increasing American forces in the South-West Pacific, the Australian government had to decide whether to keep up its army at maximum strength or to release men for civilian employment. Britain needed food, the American armed forces needed supplies, and Australia had the resources and the necessary industrial base to supply them. Overcoming military doubts, the Australian government decided in October 1943 to discharge 40 000 servicemen for industry, but the process was slow and shortages continued. It has been calculated that during the war living standards were never lower than in its last year.[41] Fearing inflation in a period of full employment and insufficient goods, the federal government used its national security powers to clamp down on price and wage increases and impose controls on rents. Despite the black market these controls were largely successful, though dependent on wartime powers which might not survive into peacetime. Enjoying the unaccustomed experience of full and regular pay-packets, unable to spend on housing, cars or other durable consumer goods, emerging from a season of austerity and uncertain of the future, many Australians understandably reacted by spending more on the pleasures of the moment.

These took many forms. Art galleries reported boom sales between 1943 and 1946 as investors, combining culture with a hedge against inflation, snapped up the works of safely popular artists. Cinema audiences reached record numbers, in part because of a lack of competition from live theatre. Attendances at football matches and race-meetings increased. Less innocent pleasures also flourished. Servicemen on leave contributed much of the demand for night-clubs and sly grog which laid the foundations of a number of fortunes in Sydney and Melbourne. Bottled beer and spirits were often in short supply and in an era when New South Wales, Victoria and South Australia still insisted on the closure of pubs at 6 p.m. this added an extra pressure in bars already so crowded and barbaric that women were excluded. There was a good deal of anxious pontificating by prominent citizens about sexual morality. Some were perturbed because the number of divorces doubled between 1942 and 1945. Others took alarm at the spread of venereal disease, although with wider knowledge of contraception and the introduction of penicillin the problem was contained more effectively than in the past. In Queensland, for instance, where infected women could be sent to an isolation hospital in a gaol, policing intensified. This explains why the number of women reported as infected trebled during 1942–43 only to revert to pre-war levels by the end of the war.[42]

It is easy to exaggerate the sensational, less easy to capture the essence of wartime life as experienced by typical Australian families. Penelope Hetherington has given us one sample of a South Australian family in her account of her father and mother, Ron and Liza Loveday, parents of seven children supported by his earnings as a munitions worker at Whyalla:

For the first five years in Whyalla Ron and Liza were anxious about the outcome of the war, seriously overworked, and deeply engrossed in problems outside the family. Yet the family milieu remained central to their lives. Liza's life continued to be dominated by domestic activities. She prepared three substantial meals a day with unbroken regularity, so that to the children certain routines established in the household seemed to be immutable. Ron rode his bicycle to work every morning and home again for lunch every day, regardless of the often tearing headwind. The children, once they were attending high school, also came home for lunch. It was always ready. Liza was always there. She took an interest in the Red Cross organization and the Housewives Association as well as being a committee member at various times of both Primary and High School parents' and friends' associations. The headmaster of these schools learned quickly to heed her complaints, even to treat her coming with some trepidation. But most of these activities were extensions of her role as parent and housewife, anxious to do the best she could with limited resources.[43]

Her husband, like many others, 'came home with his pay packet on Friday nights and gave it to her unopened'. He was secretary of the Whyalla war effort committee, war workers' club, and 'Sheepskins for Russia' campaign, an honorary trade union official, and secretary of the local adult education lecture programme based on Adelaide University.

Family life of the sort embodied by the Lovedays spelt normality for the majority of Australians, and it was a normality denied to many by the demands of war following on the 1930s Depression. When the war ended the *Australian Women's Weekly* came out with a statement of peacetime aims which has since struck feminist critics unfavourably because it saw the returned men as coming back to 'children's laughter and the sight of a small sleepy head upon a pillow—an armchair by the fire and clean sheets—tea in the kitchen and a woman's tenderness no longer edged by unspoken fears'.[44] This dream failed to accommodate those women who had discovered a new independence and self-respect through the employment opportunities thrown up by the war. But it was not surprising that many Australians in 1945, women as well as men, hoped for post-war compensation for the hardships of earlier years and felt drawn towards life as a family unit—Mum, Dad and the kids in a home of their own with job security. During the next twenty years material security for home and family was accepted in mainstream political debate as the great goal of Australian society. For the rest of the 1940s the issue in dispute was whether conditions of stability could be maintained by a modified version of the controls and planning accepted in wartime, or whether Australian capitalism unfettered could be trusted to share its benefits more equitably than in the past.

2

THE PLANNERS

HAVING LED AUSTRALIA through a traumatic crisis the Labor government could confidently claim authority to take decisions on the shaping of post-war Australia, but the aims and instruments of social reform remained to be spelt out. Curtin had promised not to nationalize any industries during the war, and although conservatives feared, and socialists demanded, a great growth in government ownership after the war, Labor's leaders were in general cautious about taking on new commitments. For Chifley especially it was important to give first priority to sound fiscal policies, even at the cost of postponing reforms which appealed to Labor's supporters. A powerful section of the party, strongest in Melbourne, was influenced by Catholic social teaching and sought to entrench the family as the bedrock of Australian society. For the majority of Labor politicians the task was as it had been fifty years earlier: civilizing capitalism.

The ALP's leaders had no wish to eradicate private enterprise, overseas investment or the profit motive. Their opponents, who frequently accused them of introducing socialism and communism, were talking nonsense. Labor was determined, however, to prevent any repetition of the mass unemployment and penury of the 1930s. As Chifley said: 'The ordinary people of Australia wonder what sort of democracy it is which is unmindful of their interests in peacetime, yet in wartime says to them, "Give us of your best in the factory or the fields; give your lives for your country". What happened previously must never happen again'.[1] If the war could be won by systematic planning then planning would be a sound basis for social action in the post-war world.

The Curtin government began with a highly significant extension of federal power in May 1942. Previously the Commonwealth government and the states each imposed income tax. Now Canberra took over the entire responsibility, promising compensatory funding to the states if they refrained from collecting income tax. Most of the states resisted, but the High Court ruled that wartime emergency authority merely reinforced the Commonwealth's existing takeover powers. Uniform taxation, although at first raising only another £5 million annually, was a potent instrument for social planning. The government reduced the rate of minimum liability so as to bring many more working-class households into the tax-paying category, thus fortifying their right to welfare benefits while disarming conservative opposition and damping down the risk of inflation. Usually no admirer of Labor policies, the *Bulletin* crowed: 'So ends the fiction that the States are "sovereign". They are in effect, dying on their feet, mortally wounded by their own selfishness and arrogance'.[2] This was premature to say the least, but although in later years state governments grizzled about their lost privilege, and federal governments offered to return them the right of income tax collection, the arrangement was never seriously challenged. Thus the balance of power tilted away from the states towards Canberra, never to waver until the late 1960s brought the mineral boom to Queensland and Western Australia.

As soon as the Japanese were definitely on the retreat the Curtin government addressed itself seriously to post-war planning. In October 1942 a bill was introduced into parliament to enlarge the federal government's constitutional powers. The following month it was shelved after a federal–state conference agreed to delegate the powers necessary for post-war reconstruction to the Commonwealth for five years after the war ended. Only Queensland and New South Wales honoured this arrangement. Desultory negotiations persisted, but the Curtin ministry was inhibited from venturing too far because the Opposition commanded a narrow majority in the federal Senate and might easily be provoked into hostility. Then in August 1943 it was time for a federal election. It was an unprecedented triumph for Labor who won forty-nine of the seventy-five seats in the House of Representatives and every contested seat in the Senate. The United Australia Party was left with no more than fourteen members in the House, and the Country Party with nine. Three independent members were returned. Almost 15 per cent of the voters, largely previous supporters of the non-Labor parties, favoured independents or mushroom minor parties. Communist candidates received 2 per cent of the vote; they would never do as well again. Fifty per cent voted straight Labor. It was a convincing mandate for change.

Labor began with a frontal attack.[3] Despairing of the states, Chifley and Evatt persuaded their colleagues to agree to a list of fourteen powers which should be retained by the Commonwealth for five years after the war. Against Curtin's better judgement these fourteen points were put to a federal referendum in August 1944 on an all-or-nothing basis. They included uncontentious items such as civil aviation and uniformity of railway gauges as well as more difficult issues such as price control and the production and distribution of goods. But the war was long past its critical phase and Australian mistrust of bureaucracy was as strong as ever. Opposition politicians such as Arthur Fadden painted alarming pictures of endless rationing, mass-produced housing, and heavy-handed compulsion in work; in short, all the worst inconveniences of wartime prolonged indefinitely. The referendum was rejected by over a third of a million votes in a poll of 4.3 million, only South Australia and Western Australia voting in favour. The government would have to make do with the means at its disposal.

In December 1942 the Department of Postwar Reconstruction was hived off from the Department of Labour and National Service. The ministers in charge, Chifley and (from 1945) Dedman, were among the ablest in cabinet and they were supported by an outstanding group of public servants, mainly young graduates. They created policy in an atmosphere of intellectual excitement seldom encountered in Canberra. Some of them were influenced by the ideas of Keynes and Laski. Equally, if not more, potent was the example of the United States president Franklin Roosevelt, whose New Deal legislation and sponsorship of the Tennessee Valley Authority provided a model of purposeful social engineering in a free enterprise capitalist society. The head of the department, H. C. (Nugget) Coombs, a railwayman's son from Western Australia then in his mid-thirties, held a doctorate from the London School of Economics. He combined shrewd hard-headedness and powers of persuasion with a lively social conscience. Coombs and his colleagues were, he wrote, 'stimulated to believe that human communities could, by corporate action, shape the context in which the lives of their members were to be lived'.[4]

More than that; together with ministers such as Curtin and Chifley they believed in full employment as a realistic post-war goal. Throughout 1943 and 1944 a team including many of Australia's ablest economists worked in Postwar Reconstruction on a White Paper (drafted eight times) arguing that full employment could result from a banking policy on Keynesian principles; expansion of private enterprise could be encouraged together with increased activity by the government in funding social services and projects of national development. Few governments outside Australia shared such hopes. On its appearance in May 1945 the White Paper was derided by sections of the press as a pipe-dream which could be achieved only by severe regimentation. But some anti-Labor politicians accepted the goal of full employment, while wanting greater emphasis on productivity and business growth as the means of accomplishing it; Menzies indeed was one of the few public figures predicting a high post-war demand for labour. Even so, most authorities accepted 4 per cent unemployment as a satisfactory definition of full employment. Anything less, wrote two respected economists, would be 'a counsel of perfection that could hardly be realized under a system of private enterprise'. Stan Carver, the oficial statistician, wrote: 'to encourage the belief that it is within the Government's power to maintain a long-term high level of employment was to manufacture political dynamite'.[5] Yet for thirty years Australia was to sustain a rate of unemployment below even 3 per cent.

The Department of Postwar Reconstruction spawned four major planning agencies: the Commonwealth Housing Commission, the post-war Rural Reconstruction Commission, the Secondary Industries Commission, and, a little later, the Commonwealth Reconstruction Training Scheme. Of these, the Rural Reconstruction Commission, recommending measures to remodel Australia's primary industries, had perhaps the least immediate impact because the strong post-war demand for Australian produce meant that for the first time in many years farmers and graziers were facing problems of prosperity rather than debt.

However its reports were significant for the quality of their research and thinking, particularly in stressing the importance of the family farmer and the need to upgrade the amenities of rural life if families were to put down roots in Australia outside the cities—a social issue which despite the lip-service paid to decentralization was largely to defeat the ingenuity of governments during the next forty years.[6]

The Secondary Industries Commission took a narrower view of its mandate by concentrating on the conversion of munitions factories to peacetime uses and ignoring long-term goals. Australia therefore remained committed by default to the protection of industries geared largely for the home market. The implications of this policy and the exploration of alternatives were not seriously considered. In one important respect however the Secondary Industries Commission took a fateful decision. Shortly before the war Australia had developed a motor vehicle industry based on the assembly of parts manufactured overseas, and it was now time to encourage the manufacture of almost entirely Australian-made motor vehicles. In 1940 monopoly rights on the manufacture of motor vehicles were granted to Australian Consolidated Industries, but on the commission's advice this legislation was repealed in 1944. Without waiting for submissions from other interested parties the commission persuaded Chifley to grant production rights to General Motors-Holden's, an American firm with the largest share of the market before the war. As incentives the Australian government offered the right to import capital equipment free of duty and priority in the allocation of foreign exchange. As the parent company refused to invest further capital in its Australian subsidiary the government arranged access to local bank overdrafts; no restriction was placed on the repatriation of profits to the United States. Anxious to secure a manufacturing industry which would generate employment, the Australian government showed itself unequal to negotiating a shrewd bargain with a major overseas investor.[7]

The Commonwealth Housing Commission on the other hand was a success: 'one of the most admired chapters in the history of Australian social welfare policy'.[8] Its report emphasized that 'a dwelling of good standard and equipment is not only the need but the right of every citizen'.[9] Perhaps this was conventional wisdom in Australia but few other nations upheld such a splendidly egalitarian principle; and even in Australia the failure of early schemes of slum clearance, the slump in home-building during the Depression and war years, and shortages of skilled trades-people meant that much needed to be done to achieve the commission's goal. In practical terms the commission's report was mixed. Assuming that the bulk of new housing would be built for owner-occupation, it concentrated on the provision of rental housing for low-income workers. Acting on its recom-mendations, the Commonwealth government set up a Ministry of Works and Housing in July 1945 and in September negotiated an agreement providing federal funding for the state governments to build low-cost rental housing for those who could not afford to buy a house.

This scheme was an early and important example of co-operative federalism, bringing together federal funding and state government authority to create a national housing policy. Most of the states already had their own housing commissions, South Australia having pioneered the policy of providing cheap govern-ment housing to attract industry. Over 200 000 houses were built during the remainder of the 1940s. In one respect, however, the new policy flew in the face of strong tradition. If a state government sold a federally funded dwelling to the occupying tenant, it would be required to reimburse the Commonwealth for the capital cost. Some commentators feared that tenants would be discouraged from saving to buy their own homes. With remarkable tactlessness Dedman informed parliament that 'The Commonwealth Government . . . is not concerned with making the workers little capitalists'.[10]

He never lived down that insensitive phrase. Most Australians saw home-owning as their main chance of accumulating a little capital towards security in their later years. For a home of their own they were prepared to pledge most of their working lives to paying off a mortgage. The uncertainties of the Depression and the war reinforced their view that security lay in becoming 'little capitalists'. Consequently state housing would be relegated to two classes of tenant: newcomers, either young couples or migrants, who sought rented accommodation while they saved diligently for a deposit on their own house, or the under-privileged poor who could not afford to save. As their numbers grew on housing commission estates social problems were to multiply, but little of this could reasonably be foreseen in 1945. The overpowering need was to get houses built, resources were in short supply, and effective state intervention was essential if the less well-off were to enjoy any share of them.

Australians must be adequately housed, and they should be adequately educated. The Commonwealth government stayed steadfastly out of the funding of primary and secondary education because religious antagonisms were still lively enough to prevent rational discussion of the allocation of needs between state schools, private schools catering for the middle class and the more broadly-based Catholic education system. The Commonwealth showed fewer inhibitions about supporting kindergartens and tertiary education: as Chifley said, 'they're for kids before they've got souls and after they've lost them . . .'.[11] Many members of the armed services due for post-war rehabilitation belonged to a generation that had been forced to leave school early because of the Depression. Four per cent of recruits tested in the army in 1943 were found to be functionally illiterate, and some estimates went higher. On the other hand, the army education service, founded in 1941 in an endeavour to build up morale, succeeded beyond the expectation of cynics. Its journal *Salt* discovered a number of talented writers. Nor was it futile to offer serious music or drama; in New Guinea the troops had contributed their own rations to a party in honour of Dame Judith Anderson when with Maurice Evans she performed *Macbeth* for them. Certainly many Australians emerged from the forces with a keener taste for educational opportunity.[12]

Australia's need for a home-grown professional class was clearly increasing. If industry continued to grow, more scientists and technologists would be needed; if the population grew, the services of more doctors, teachers and lawyers would be required; and as the public service grew it was at last dimly recognized that intelligence could be a more valuable quality than either seniority or war service, and that recruitment was proceeding from the ranks of what one Labor politician called 'graduate goats'. By introducing the Commonwealth Reconstruction Training Scheme the federal government provided grants for veterans to take courses at all levels from technical school to university. University scholarships were soon extended to students who had not served in the armed forces. As a culminating feature the Department of Postwar Reconstruction envisaged the creation of an Australian National University at Canberra which might grow into a centre of excellence for advanced research.

Behind the reforms mooted by the Curtin government and the Department of Postwar Reconstruction a paradox lurked. By enabling more Australians to better their educations and buy their own homes a Labor government was enabling families to move out of their working-class origins into a middle-class status where it could no longer be taken for granted that they would retain Labor loyalties. This problem drew little attention at the time. Since the First World War Australia had seen perhaps less social mobility between classes than in earlier years. Far from foreseeing the long boom of the mid-twentieth century, most authorities were expecting to have to insure against recession. It was understandable to think that purposeful government intervention would be required to preserve equity among Australians. Opposition cries of 'creeping socialism' could be set aside as cheap rhetoric; but young intellectuals such as Donald Horne readily agreed with the sceptical Sydney philosopher John Anderson when he wrote that 'the well-intentioned reformer *always* produces results which he did not anticipate',[13] thus endorsing an ingrained Australian cynicism towards politicians and bureaucrats. Undeniably there was a risk that a public service recruited as an agent of reform might fatten into a mandarin caste. Between 1939 and 1951 the number of public servants rose by over 300 per cent to form one of the most influential graduate professional groups in Australian society.[14]

Nor was it helpful that the government's image was shaped by its Department of Information, whose minister, from 1943 the headstrong and inexperienced Arthur Calwell, soon antagonized the press by his maladroit censorship. Undeniably some newspaper managements were irresponsible and sensational in their coverage of the war and politics; in 1944 Calwell was goaded into denouncing 'many examples of unwise, if not vicious, propaganda', and said 'the writers of some of these diatribes are little better than fifth columnists'.[15] He suspended the Sydney *Daily Telegraph* for publishing censored material and the *Sydney Morning Herald* for reprinting it. The *Telegraph* re-appeared with blank spaces on its front page to indicate where stories had been banned by Calwell's department and struck heroic attitudes in defence of freedom of speech. The whole affair petered out in recriminations, but the Curtin government from that time onwards was at odds with a large section of the media. Calwell was for some time caricatured as a malignant cockatoo forever squawking 'Curse the press!'.[16]

Politicians bullied the ABC for not broadcasting their comments on current affairs; Calwell removed control of Radio Australia from the ABC. Early in 1945 the ABC chairman, W. J. Cleary, resigned because he felt he no longer possessed the government's confidence. When his successor Richard Boyer took office Curtin issued a statement affirming 'a position of special independence of judgment and action for the national broadcasting instrumentality'.[17] But this did not stop his colleagues from meddling.

A reputation for heavy-handed interference hindered the Curtin government in its attempts to extend the scope of welfare legislation. There was little opposition in 1942 when the federal government introduced widows' pensions, thus bringing to the whole of Australia a benefit pioneered fifteen years earlier by the state government of New South Wales. But in March 1944 Australia's most influential middle-class professional lobby group, the medical profession, raised the cry of resistance to government interference as their main pretext for opposing a reform intended to benefit wage-earners. Many families feared illness because they could not afford medicine or even the payment of contributory insurance through a friendly society. Accordingly, the Curtin government introduced legislation providing government payment of chemists' bills on a wide range of medicines listed on a pharmaceutical formulary. Although the pharmacists accepted the scheme, the federal council of the British Medical Association in Australia (BMA) broke off negotiations and came out strongly in opposition. Unaccustomed to co-operating with governments over reform legislation, the BMA groundlessly feared the proposal as the first step towards nationalization of the medical profession. They wanted the scheme administered by a statutory corporation with strong medical representation instead of by the officials of the Department of Health; physicians, not bureaucrats, should determine what medicines appeared on the pharmaceutical formulary. The Opposition weighed in with cruder embellishments: the scheme was a plot to nationalize the pharmacies, chemists would be put out of business, it was 'merely another instalment of the dole—something for nothing'.[18] Parliament eventually approved the legislation but it was struck down by the High Court, which ruled in 1945 that the Commonwealth government must not usurp a function belonging to the states. So, not for the last time, the sovereign rights of the states stood in the way of reforms designed for the welfare of the Australian people.

But behind this invocation of state rights lay the power of Australia's middle-class professional pressure groups.

To a surprising extent even conservatives were coming to accept the welfare state. The Institute of Public Affairs (IPA), a small, privately funded research unit generating ideas for the private sector, was trying to cultivate an enlightened self-interest among employers by arguing that the removal of insecurity would reduce industrial unrest.[19] An IPA questionnaire of October 1943 showed 85 per cent of businessmen interviewed as favouring a government social security scheme and 70 per cent supporting government control over monopolies. Such findings influenced Robert Menzies, who soon after the 1943 elections replaced the aged W. M. Hughes as the head of the United Australia Party (UAP) and resumed the leadership of the Opposition from the Country Party's Arthur Fadden. Rejected by his own party in 1941, which in turn was rejected by the voters in 1943, Menzies recovered some credibility during 1944 by leading the successful resistance to the government's fourteen-point referendum. In October 1944 he convened a meeting of reinvigorated conservatives at Canberra who endorsed the formation of a new non-Labor party on a broader basis than the old UAP. Two months later delegates from all states attended a three-day conference — not in the national capital, nor in the rival metropolises of Sydney or Melbourne, but at Albury, a border city between two states, much as Sir Henry Parkes fifty-five years earlier had chosen Tenterfield as the birthplace of federation. Here they launched the Liberal Party of Australia which in time would mount a successful challenge to the vision of a planned social democratic future as propounded by Curtin, Chifley and their colleagues in the federal Labor government.

By reaching back to the name 'Liberal' the architects of the new party were tapping into the prestige of such giants of the Edwardian era as Barton, Deakin, Higgins and Isaacs, politicians who had used the power of government constructively as a force for social reform. The old UAP had not been totally bereft of social conscience, but as a coalition of business interests and Labor renegades hastily cobbled together to meet the opportunities of the 1931 Depression it had never agreed on a coherent philosophy, so that it drifted too easily into a deadlocked *laissez-faire*. Under Menzies the Liberals would pitch their appeal to what he called 'The forgotten people': those members of the lower middle classes—clerks, tradespeople, shopkeepers—who identified neither with the rich and successful nor with the blue-collar workers of the trade unions.

Menzies was also credited with a remarkably sound instinct for what would appeal to women voters. He was a model of the successful scholarship boy who from modest beginnings had risen to the top rank in law and politics. He presented himself as a man with the kind of poise, charm and educated diction that many women would have appreciated in their own menfolk. When in office he had given them child endowment. Where Labor's leaders spoke of the conflicts of the economy and the workplace, realms from which many women were excluded, Menzies spoke of 'the home and the consensual symbols of the domestic sphere'.[20] When strikes occurred and meals were spoilt because of power cuts, or families were stranded without public transport, Menzies appreciated, as the male-dominated trade unions did not, that housewives suffered inconvenience. Powerless themselves to influence the outcome of industrial disputes, many housewives would turn to the political leader who promised to stand up to the trade unions. Thus Menzies offered a formidable long-term threat to the Labor government, but because of his wartime failures he was underrated. In its first two years the Liberal Party made few gains. At the end of 1945, when John Cain senior formed a Labor government in Victoria, the only state in Australia with a Liberal ministry was South Australia, where Thomas Playford held sway with the help of a rural gerrymander.

Labor meanwhile looked increasingly secure in office. Curtin, whose health had steadily grown worse as the war lengthened, failed to survive into peacetime, dying in Canberra on 5 July 1945. As his successor the party passed over his deputy, Frank Forde, as too ineffectual for leadership and instead chose the 60-year-old treasurer Ben Chifley, who had been Curtin's strongest supporter in the wartime cabinet. Where Curtin had looked forward to embarking after the war on a major programme of national public works, Chifley's concern, or so Coombs judged, was 'with financial issues and his close association with Treasury meant that economic viability began to be rated as more important'.[21] During his first year of office several measures were taken to encourage economic stability and growth. A five-year co-operative wool marketing agreement was negotiated with Britain, New Zealand and South Africa. To promote exploration and investment in the mining sector a Bureau of Mineral Resources was set up in 1946. Interstate civil aviation was taken from the hands of an overseas-owned near-monopoly, Australian National Airways (ANA), and entrusted to the government's own carrier, Trans-Australian Airlines (TAA); and although the High Court rejected the ousting of ANA, it allowed TAA to survive in competition. Nor was welfare neglected. The Commonwealth undertook to pay the states a daily subsidy for hospital patients in public wards or an equivalent contribution to those who chose private hospitalization. Once it emerged that these reforms would not overthrow the long-established honorary system, they went unchallenged by the medical profession and were soon supplemented by anti-tuberculosis measures and a pharmaceutical benefits scheme. The Chifley government ensured that Australian families need no longer fear illness as a financial disaster.

The government's record with Aboriginal welfare was less impressive. No attempt was made to consolidate the improvements in Aboriginal well-being opened up by wartime employment. In 1946 Northern Territory Aborigines petitioned King George VI for citizenship rights, but to no avail. The authorities, anxious to expand beef production, did not want to offend pastoral investors by pressing them to improve conditions for their Aboriginal workers and their families. Although in February 1947 standard wages were prescribed for Aboriginal station-hands in the Northern Territory, they fell well short of the minimum pay for non-Aborigines. In the Pilbara district of Western Australia Aboriginal pastoral workers under the inspiration of two Aborigines, Clancy McKenna and Dooley Binbin, and a white stockman, Don McLeod, went on strike for better pay in May 1946. Despite official harassment they secured useful gains during the next two years. Not all returned to work. Some asked McLeod to join them in a co-operative settlement maintaining itself by alluvial mining, and were reinforced in 1949 by ninety Aborigines who walked off Red Hill station under the leadership of a remarkable woman, Daisy Bindi. These developments were largely, though not entirely, ignored outside Western Australia; the *Sydney Morning Herald* for 1946 contained no mention of them. The 'Pindan' movement, as it was called, remained for a time an isolated portent of the ways in which a war might change racial and ethnic stereotypes.[22] Elsewhere change came slowly.

At least New South Wales placed Aborigines on the state's Aborigines Welfare Board; but in Queensland and the Northern Territory Aborigines were specifically excluded from voting, and in New South Wales from 1943 and Western Australia from 1944 they could do so only if they satisfied a magistrate that their standard of living entitled them to be 'no longer a native or aborigine'. With such insensitive wording few bothered to register.[23] It was perhaps only incidentally that the Commonwealth Nationality and Citizenship Act of 1948 stated that in common with all others born in the country Aborigines were Australian citizens. Most of the time the Australian nation continued to present itself exclusively as a white Australia.

Australia was also a colonizing power, and Aboriginal policies were not necessarily a sound guide for Papua and New Guinea. Until the Japanese invasion Australians largely thought of this possession as a land of exotic primitives and impenetrable jungle, the scene of a minor gold-rush in the 1930s. Wartime propaganda made much of Papuan stretcher-bearers as 'fuzzy-wuzzy angels' but without granting Australians much insight into the problems of welding several hundred distinct clans and groups— from barely known highlanders to Motu sophisticates of Port Moresby—into a community which might in time achieve nationhood. As the Japanese were ejected it was proposed that there should be a merger between the old Australian colony of Papua and the mandated territory which had once been German New Guinea, and this arrangement was readily accepted by the United Nations. But who would be in control? In the later stages of the war a bid was made by the Directorate of Research under Lieutenant-Colonel A. A. (Alf) Conlon, an uncouth, talkative but able man in his mid-thirties who, having been a perpetual undergraduate at the University of Sydney, showed during the war a genius for making friends in high places, as with Curtin and Blamey, and a capacity for recruiting talent. The directorate urged such post-war economic and racial strategies for New Guinea as the creation of a colonial development and welfare fund under trusteeship principles. But at the end of the war Conlon was eased out of his power base by permanent federal officials and ended his days as a family doctor in a Melbourne working-class suburb.[24]

Two of the directorate's initiatives survived. One was the School of Civil Affairs for training Australian public servants for work in the Pacific territories; in 1947 it became the Australian School of Pacific Administration, with John Kerr, a young lawyer with a future, as its first principal. The other was the appointment in 1945 of an agricultural scientist, J. K. Murray, as administrator of Papua New Guinea. This was due to the intervention of the minister for territories, Eddie Ward, who during 1945 showed an unprecedented burst of reforming zeal. A 44-hour week was introduced, shortening the average working day by about a quarter; cash wages were increased, although the minimum was only 15 shillings a month; and in October the indenture system was suddenly abolished, thus freeing labourers from roughshod employers who used the knuckle or the boot.[25]

There Ward's initiatives ended. Tireless in battling for his Sydney working-class constituents, he failed like most politicians of his day to develop a continuing interest in the Western Pacific. In six years as minister he visited Papua New Guinea only once. In 1948–49 he was obliged, although personally guiltless, to stand down from the ministry during a royal commission into improper trading in New Guinea timber concessions. Murray meanwhile built on the village as the basis of rehabilitation for Papua New Guinea. In his time village schools were set up, local government councils and co-operatives were created, agricultural education was initiated, and the first indigenes were admitted to the Legislative Council.[26] But he was surrounded by opponents, expatriate businessmen and planters sceptical of Papuan capacity, and he received little support from Canberra. So the opportunity passed for coming to terms quickly with the new principle of racial equality which had been brought to birth by the Second World War. Australians would conserve their reforming energies for use at home.

In the first trial of strength with the new Liberals and their Country Party allies, the general elections of 1946, Chifley scored a convincing victory. Labor commanded forty-three seats in the House of Representatives as against twenty-nine for the combined Opposition and two Labor independents—one of them the 70-year-old J. T. Lang, whose three-year term would be notable mainly for the vituperation which he poured on his former Labor colleagues. In the Senate, because of a simple preferential system, Labor finished up with a landslide, holding thirty-three seats with three Queenslanders as the sole opposition.

For the only time since 1913 a Labor government controlled both houses in the federal parliament and held an unrestricted mandate to put its policies into practice.

The main curb on the Labor government rested with the High Court as interpreters of the federal Constitution. One eminent constitutional scholar has described the years from 1946 to 1949 as 'a period of intense judicial activity, during which government policy was frustrated by judge-made doctrine rather than clear constitutional restrictions to an extent not equalled since the Deakin period'.[27] Of its six members, two were ex-politicians: the chief justice Sir John Latham (formerly an anti-Labor attorney-general), and a Labor appointee, Edward McTiernan. Although opposed on many points both tended to the pragmatic view that changing economic and social conditions sometimes justified the enlargement of federal powers at the expense of the states. Sir Owen Dixon, intellectually the dominant member of the bench, possessed superb powers of analysis but was a little remote from contemporary life; he once observed that no novel written in the twentieth century was worth reading. In his concern that the court's decisions should be consistent with precedent he was an unpredictably independent factor but his temper was habitually conservative. The other three were professional lawyers from the Sydney or Melbourne bars, for although the High Court was a federal instrumentality its judges were hardly ever chosen from the four outer states. In the 1940s two of these judges were well over seventy, having taken their law degrees and formed their ideas in the pre-federal nineteenth century. These men clung resolutely to office until Labor was no longer the party of government, probably fearing that if they went the court would be packed with radicals. But although Evatt was on prickly terms with several of his former colleagues he made no such attempt. The vacant seventh judgeship went to Sir William Webb, who presided over the Japanese war crimes tribunal and whose legal experience was gained in the Queensland public service. Consequently the High Court remained a barrier to government innovation.

This issue assumed some urgency with the coming of peace in 1945. During the war a considerable amount of social and economic control was exercised through the Commonwealth's use of its defence powers, and these would soon cease to be applicable. By rejecting the pharmaceutical benefits scheme in

1945 the High Court threw doubts on the Commonwealth's power of expenditure on social services and research. All the welfare measures introduced during the war—child endowment, widows' pensions, unemployment, sickness and funeral benefits, and a spouse's allowance for invalid and old-age pensioners—were liable to challenge. At the 1946 general election voters were accordingly asked to empower the Commonwealth to provide social services. All major political parties gave their support, and the referendum passed, but even then over 45 per cent of the voters said 'No'. This meant that in 1947 the Pharmaceutical Benefits Bill could be passed. At the same time voters narrowly rejected two other referenda which would have given the Commonwealth power over the marketing of primary products and the conditions of employment in industry. Many Australians seemed to feel that any demand for wider powers by any government, even for the most benevolent purposes, should be mistrusted and denied.

Federal authority grew nevertheless, though slowly and unevenly: by High Court decision, by consent of the states, and throughout by using the financial muscle which came of uniform taxation. The High Court did not immediately terminate the government's wartime controls but judged each example on its merits, usually allowing a transitional period of two or three years to avoid administrative dislocation. Price and rent controls were not disallowed until 1947; Calwell later claimed that while the federal government controlled price stabilization Australian prices rose by only 22.5 per cent, the lowest figure for any non-communist economy.[28] Fearing that the loss of these powers would weaken its capacity to fight inflation, the Chifley government once more tried a referendum in 1948 seeking federal control of rents and prices and was once more rebuffed by the voters (although in practice most of the state governments maintained similar controls in some form until 1954 or 1955).

Nor was the government greatly disadvantaged by its failure to carry the 1946 referendum on organized marketing. During the war, farmers had grown accustomed to the advantages of stable marketing, and although there was strong disagreement on the extent of subsidies and the control of marketing, all political parties had come to accept the principle of pooling. The test case was the wheat industry, which during the 1930s had been a constant source of political strife, and which in 1943–49 was the mainstay of several federal electorates evenly balanced between Labor and the Country Party. In 1946 the government placed the acquisition and marketing of wheat under a board consisting largely of growers' representatives. This board was empowered to accumulate reserves during good seasons which could shore up the return to farmers in poor years, with the government intervening where necessary to ensure a guaranteed minimum price. Despite criticism in detail this arrangement became law and was a model for the marketing of other grain crops. By placing grain sales in the hands of growers' boards the government contrived to distance commercial policy from foreign diplomacy. This was an advantage in later years when the Wheat Board was able to sell crops to communist China while that country was officially unrecognized by Australia.

Paramount in the Chifley government's thinking was the need to maintain a firm hold on the economy. It was no good legislating for the welfare of Australian workers if international financial pressures gave rise to inflation, unemployment, or high interest rates. In the early post-war years inflation seemed the greatest menace of the three. Australian wool and wheat were in keen demand overseas, with export prices rising each year. Trade unionists, having postponed their demands during the war, were eager to seize improved wages and conditions while they could, without thought for the long-term implications for the Australian economy. Consumer demand was insatiable. To restrain these pressures while at the same time moving forward with a programme of social reform and the promotion of new industries required all the powers and the skills that the Chifley government could command. After the dire experiences of the 1930s its members were not prepared to trust the hidden hand of market forces, and even the Opposition, although never ceasing to denounce socialism, did not seek a return to *laissez-faire*. Accordingly the federal government must be armed with new powers.

At the heart of the issue lay control over banking and the financial system. Labor remembered bitterly how the Scullin government in 1930–31 was powerless to resist dictation by the Commonwealth Bank Board and the representatives of overseas 'money power'.[29] Although a bi-partisan royal commission in 1935–36 insisted that the federal government must have ultimate power to control monetary policy, no steps were taken in this direction until the introduction of wartime national security regulations. These enabled the government to hold down interest rates and to set up a mortgage division within the Commonwealth Bank, but stronger powers were required to achieve the aim of a stable economy as a necessary pre-condition of social welfare. Early in 1945 the Commonwealth Bank was restructured to consolidate its position as Australia's central bank. Its tasks were defined as the maintenance of a stable currency, full employment and national prosperity. Most wartime controls on the private trading banks were to continue except for the limitation on profit levels. These banks would be required to operate under licence and to keep a stated proportion of their reserves in a special account controlled by the central bank as a crucial instrument of economic management. In addition the Commonwealth Bank was empowered to compete with them in housing finance and other new fields. Authority over banking was transferred from parliament to the government of the day.

For a reformist and mildly nationalist Australian government a central bank was essential if the economy was to be controlled, business confidence maintained and inflation curbed. Overseas investment had to be encouraged without yielding too much power over Australia's future to Wall Street and the City of London. It was accepted that Australia's economy was most likely to prosper if international capitalism was flourishing. Australia formed part of the sterling bloc, its exports favoured by imperial preference among British Commonwealth countries, although Britain would emerge from the war financially drained. The United States would press its advantages as a creditor by seeking to dismantle imperial preference and building up markets and investment in Commonwealth countries such as Australia. Accordingly Australia had to follow American initiatives for economic co-operation in the non-communist world.

In 1942 the United States formed the International Bank for Reconstruction and Development which after its ratification at an international conference at Bretton Woods in July 1944 became known as the World Bank. At the same time the International Monetary Fund (IMF) was set up to regulate exchange rates and balance of payments. Many Labor stalwarts would have preferred to stay aloof from such creations of American capitalism. Eddie Ward forecast that Bretton Woods would 'enthrone a World Dictatorship of private finance, more complete and terrible than any Hitlerite dream . . . it will undermine and destroy the democratic institutions of this country'.[30] In 1947 Chifley and Dedman persuaded the party (possibly they even persuaded themselves) that membership of the World Bank and the IMF would help to promote full employment. For similar reasons Australia joined the General Agreement on Tariffs and Trade (GATT), sponsored by the United States as a mechanism for freeing international trade and discouraging the erection of high protectionist barriers.

Membership of these organizations has been seen as a surrender to American hegemony.[31] The hard truth was that in the uncertain financial environment of the early post-war years it would have jeopardized Australia's hopes of economic growth to remain isolated from major sources of investment and international economic co-operation. Entry into the IMF and GATT was an acceptable risk provided—and it was an important proviso—that Australia's federal government kept firm control of the economy through the central banking system set up in 1945. But part of that legislation came under legal challenge, and in August 1947 the High Court threw out the section of the 1945 Act requiring local authorities to transact their business exclusively with the Commonwealth Bank. Chifley at once announced that the government would nationalize the entire Australian banking system.[32]

Even friendly commentators have since said that this was an unwise over-reaction.[33] Only the least significant part of the 1945 legislation was invalidated. The judges showed no disposition to strike down the central banking system as a whole, and the private banks were prepared to work within that system, though they failed to provide Chifley with assurances that they would never challenge the critically important requirement to deposit part of their funds in a central special account. On the other hand, having urged Labor to accept membership of the IMF, the Chifley government could afford no doubts about its capacity to control the Australian financial system; Labour in Britain had just taken control of banking; and for the first time in thirty years Labor in Australia had a majority in both houses of federal parliament. Caucus unanimously accepted the plan for bank nationalization. No voice was raised for caution or dissent. The timing of the decision cannot be blamed simply on Chifley's pique at another rebuff from the High Court.

It was a mistake nevertheless. The public was unprepared and the government's announcement of its plans was offhand and unconvincing. Many businesses, small and large, owed their survival from the Depression to competitive private banking. Thus when the Bank of New South Wales threatened to close down the Western Australian timber firm of Bunning Brothers after a fire in 1933 they survived through gaining the confidence of the English, Scottish and Australian Bank.[34] The Bank of New South Wales on the other hand came to the rescue of several pastoralists who could not get credit from stock and station agents such as Dalgety and Elders. Small clients — home-owners, tradespeople — saw the banks in terms of the helpful local manager rather than as faceless agents of monopoly capitalism. Above all, a job as a bank clerk was one of the most respected careers for white-collar workers. Their families did not wish to see them become public servants or restricted in their opportunities. Bank officers accordingly threw themselves with enthusiasm into the determined and well-funded campaign which was at once mounted by the banks in resistance to nationalization.

Despite the clamour the Act passed through parliament and the private banks appealed to the High Court. Evatt insisted on fighting the government's case himself. He was long-winded and abrasive, and he failed. By four to two (Latham and McTiernan dissenting) the High Court held that nationalization was invalid because it interfered with the right of the banks to conduct interstate commerce. From the tenor of the judgments it seemed likely that the Chifley government could have framed modified legislation which would have given it a large measure of effective control over banking without overstepping the High Court's limitations. Instead its remaining two years in office were wasted in an appeal to the Privy Council in London. Evatt harangued the English judges for twenty-two days; his opponent, the up-and-coming Sydney barrister Garfield Barwick, confined himself to nine. The Privy Council upheld the High Court. It served the Chifley government right; as good Australian nationalists they should have accepted the verdict of their own country's judges. Meanwhile the contentious issue was kept alive for more than two years during which the banks poured money into an endless barrage of anti-Labor propaganda. In itself the banks' opposition was not enough to topple the Chifley government, but it was lead in their saddlebags in the race for public favour. During 1947 Labor lost office in Western Australia and Victoria, and the outlook for the 1949 federal elections was unpredictable.

Chifley's priorities were right nevertheless, and this was indicated by the decision of later governments to keep the powers gained during the 1940s. As financial hegemony shifted from Britain to the United States, Australia had to manoeuvre to preserve as much autonomy of choice as possible. If post-war Australia was to mature its own form of civilized capitalism its federal governments would need clear powers of economic decision-making. Without the exercise of such authority Australian governments might for a while benefit from any general upsurge of the world economy but they would abdicate their opportunities of influencing change and innovation; and once again, as in the 1930s, Australia would end up drifting helplessly before every wind of doctrine or advice blown from the world's major financial centres.

While Chifley worked to build up Australia's capacity for economic self-determination the minister for external affairs, Dr H. V. Evatt, strove with greater publicity but less long-term effect to assert self-determination in Australian foreign policy.[35] Inheriting a newly recruited department of able young graduates and amateur ambassadors, Evatt imposed his ideals and prejudices on the conduct of foreign policy as none of his successors could. Piqued at what he saw as the failure of the major wartime allies to consult Australia adequately he began to push Australia's regional interests, and in January 1944 persuaded New Zealand to join Australia in an agreement asserting the right of the two nations to be consulted on the future of the South-West Pacific after Japan's defeat. The most constructive aspect of this Anzac Pact provided for a common trusteeship policy over the advancement of Pacific islands governed from Australia and New Zealand, and led to the creation of the South Pacific Commission in 1947.

Evatt apparently had in mind an antipodean version of the Monroe Doctrine, as he unsuccessfully suggested that Australia should assume post-war responsibility for the New Hebrides (now Vanuatu) and the Solomon Islands and annoyed the Americans by insisting that their possession of bases in the South-West Pacific should not constitute a claim to sovereignty. This led to several years of low-level wrangling about the future of Manus in the Admiralty Islands north-east of New Guinea, site of a strong American base. Opposition spokesmen claimed that such squabbling would alienate the United States, which would leave Australia defenceless; but Manus was not of first-class importance and the Americans eventually agreed to go in 1948, leaving the buildings and fixtures to Australia. Australia did not relish a strong American presence too close to home, but north of the Equator it was justified as a safeguard against Japan, China and the Soviet Union.

Australia willingly provided nearly one-third of the 35 000 members of the British Commonwealth Occupation Force (BCOF) in Japan and the proportion later increased. Even the postage stamps used by BCOF were overprints of Australian issues. During demilitarization in 1946–47 the force rounded up many caches of illegal arms, but by 1948 its routine garrison duties were largely confined to preventing smuggling and illegal immigration and the force was reduced to the Third Battalion of the Royal Australian Regiment. A tough-minded Australian judge, Sir William Webb, presided over the international military tribunal which tried Japanese accused of war crimes, and an Australian was nominated as British Commonwealth representative when in December 1945 it was agreed to set up a four-power Allied Council with its headquarters at Tokyo. William Macmahon Ball, a political scientist at the University of Melbourne, took up the appointment as representative in March 1946.[36]

It was a futile assignment. Since hostilities ended MacArthur as supreme commander had taken complete control of Japan. MacArthur's proconsular style apparently suited the Japanese, and the Allied Council quickly found that its role was purely consultative, and then only when the Americans chose. Their priorities were not the same as Australia's. 'To Australia . . .', wrote Ball, 'the first interest in Japan is undoubtedly a negative one: to assure by every possible means that she shall not regain the power to become an aggressor in the foreseeable future'. This might mean maintaining an army of occupation for twenty-five years. MacArthur however believed that Japan was destroyed as a military threat for at least a hundred years to come. Fearing that communism would triumph if Japan lapsed into internal anarchy, the Americans sought to shore up the emperor Hirohito—overriding the first reaction of many Australians, Evatt included, that he should be tried as a war criminal—and to impose American values on the Japanese while they were pliable and shocked with defeat.

The United States wanted to encourage a strong capitalist

economy based on medium and heavy industry; the Australians believed that external aid should be linked to internal reform and the creation of something like a welfare state, fearing that without such safeguards Japan's reviving economy would fall back into the hands of the Zaibatsu cartel which had supported the militarists in the 1930s. While both favoured the redistribution of land from Japanese absentee owners to the peasantry, the Australians went considerably further than the Americans in wishing to safeguard tenant rights and restrict the size of holdings. In practice Australian influence on the process of reform through local land commissions was considerable, particularly through the work of one of Ball's senior officials, Eric Ward, formerly of the Department of Postwar Reconstruction.[37]

In April 1947, perturbed at the apparent incapacity of the Japanese government to curb inflation or maintain industrial peace without the intervention of the occupying forces, Ball urged price control, the rationing of essential consumer goods, the introduction of a basic wage and progressive income taxation, all of them devices tested by Australian experience. None of these notions found favour with the free-enterprise Americans. Frustrated by MacArthur, Ball resigned in September 1947. He felt inadequately supported by Evatt although both shared a confidence (too seldom held by Australian public figures) that Australian experience could produce ideas and concepts that could usefully be exported for application elsewhere.

By this time the Liberal Democratic Party in Japan was establishing its long hegemony as a businessmen's government. The Australians, meanwhile, were growing disillusioned about their wartime ally, China. Australian aid to China through United Nations agencies was generous—Australia was the world's fourth largest donor to the United Nations Relief and Rehabilitation Administration, and two-thirds of its contribution went to China—but nullified by the failure of Chiang Kai-shek's government to control inflation, inefficiency and corruption. China's delegation to the United Nations attacked Australian racial policies in New Guinea and Nauru. Goodwill towards Chiang Kai-shek's regime faded together with confidence in its capacity to stave off the communist challenge led by Mao Zedong. In 1949, when mainland China fell to the communists, professional opinion in the Department of Foreign Affairs was prepared for Australia to grant recognition to the new regime. Evatt however stalled, fearing a backlash from anti-communists in Australia in an election year. With the defeat of the Chifley government in 1949 the opportunity passed for more than twenty years.[38]

Between China and Japan in the north and Australia to the south there lay the states of South and South-East Asia where European influence had been permanently shaken by Japanese invasion. As former colonies and client states won independence their goodwill gained importance in Australian eyes. Despite the handicap of the White Australia Policy this goodwill soon grew. Australia quickly established friendly terms with India and Pakistan after the British withdrawal of 1947. In 1949, when a mediator was required in the dispute between India and Pakistan over the ownership of Kashmir, Australia's foremost jurist Sir Owen Dixon was readily accepted, and despite his failure to resolve the problem he left an excellent impression. Australia sometimes preferred to enhance its reputation for anti-colonialism at the expense of British Commonwealth loyalties. Thus in 1948 Chifley and Evatt refused a British request for assistance in the Malayan Emergency even though the main anti-colonial movement had fallen into the hands of communist guerrillas. Although the Anglophile Menzies strongly urged intervention in Malaya, he confined himself, once in office in 1950, to sending a Royal Australian Airforce (RAAF) transport squadron of Dakotas.[39]

Closer to home Australia played a significant part in the Indonesian revolt against the restoration of Dutch rule. On 17 August 1945, two days after Japan's surrender, the Indonesian nationalists proclaimed their independence. Five weeks later the Brisbane branch of the Waterside Workers' Federation, after contact with Indonesian evacuees admitted to Australia during the war, imposed a ban on ships carrying Dutch arms for use against the rebels. Given an embarrassed tolerance by the Chifley government, and disregarding the scorn of conservatives at this intervention into foreign policy by working-class unionists, the waterside workers throughout Australia maintained these bans for four years in what the Indonesians saw as a heartening show of solidarity by a people of European origin.[40] In November 1946 the Dutch recognized an autonomous federation of Indonesian states, but the presence of Dutch armed forces led to renewed strife in July 1947 which ceased only when Australia, together with India, brought the question to the United Nations Security Council. A month later Australia was nominated by the Indo-

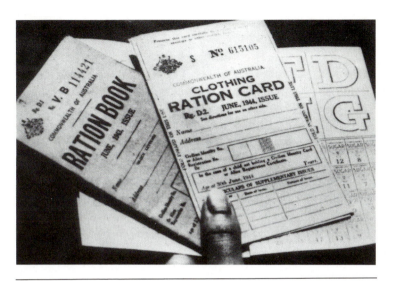

*Ration cards were introduced at the height of the war in 1942,
and remained for several years into peacetime*

*During the war children were encouraged to 'do their bit':
manufacturing a camouflage net, Adelaide 1942*

Women took many new jobs during the war. This picture of a Melbourne bread carter shows the effect of petrol rationing

'Now, Sarah, before you leave us I must know how you peel the eggs before frying them.' (Bulletin, *3 February 1943*)

nesians to the three-nation committee established to offer the United Nations good offices. An uneasy truce was negotiated in December 1947 but despite Indonesian success in putting down a communist revolt in Java the Dutch were not satisfied. In December 1948 they seized control of much of Java but met with sustained guerrilla resistance. Australia continued actively lobbying on behalf of the Indonesians, and in August 1949 both parties came to the conference table. By November an agreement was hammered out under which Indonesian independence was recognized in return for the safeguarding of Dutch investments. The Dutch also retained for the time being the ethnically distinct territory of western New Guinea, West Irian (now Irian Jaya). Because of West Irian's common boundary with Papua New Guinea this suited the Australians, who for several years opposed Indonesian attempts to bring the question before the United Nations.[41]

The Indonesian crisis was probably the most important example of Australia's readiness to resort to the United Nations as an international forum but it was not the only one. Evatt cherished the hope that the United Nations would succeed better than the old League of Nations as an instrument of collective security, and he certainly saw it as a means by which smaller nations such as Australia could exercise restraint on the super-powers. At the April 1945 San Francisco conference setting up the United Nations he came to the fore, overshadowing the nominal leader of the Australian party, F. M. Forde. As the Canadian delegate Lester Pearson recalled years later: 'In a sense he was the outstanding person of the conference, but he rushed around refusing to make compromises and leaving others to make moderating steps'.[42] Australia sponsored many more amendments to the United Nations Charter than any other nation: a later foreign minister acutely observed, 'it was a principal weakness of Evatt to place an extravagant faith in organizations and in the precise text of their constitutional structure'.[43] Evatt had little luck with his campaign to limit the power of veto which the great powers could impose on United Nations resolutions, except for ensuring that discussion could continue on a vetoed issue. However, Australia's special concerns fared better. The United Nations undertook to refrain from matters falling under a member's domestic jurisdiction, such as Aboriginal policy. A charter of women's rights was endorsed—though this owed less to Evatt than to another Australian delegate, Jessie Street—and full employment policies were supported. This set a pattern. Australia could sometimes achieve specific aims relevant to its own concerns but was not powerful enough to influence broader issues in the international polity.

Evatt's own style reinforced this tendency. He had no long-term perspectives beyond seeking leadership among the small and middle powers. In exercising this leadership Evatt drew a model from his legal background. International disputes could be treated as a 'new province for law and order' to be arbitrated with judicial impartiality through the United Nations. Such a concept required an unlikely degree of self-restraint by the great powers. With heroic naïvety, immense energy, and no little personal vanity Evatt sought to impose the Australian notions of equity and the 'fair go' on the battered and suspicious Old World. There had been nothing quite like it since Woodrow Wilson's ill-fated attempt to impose American morality on the Treaty of Versailles, and Evatt's power base was much less significant than Wilson's. Nevertheless he prized his term in 1948 as president of the United Nations General Assembly. And when every allowance is made for the blunders and shortcomings of Evatt's interventions in foreign policy, it remains undeniable that he reminded Australians that they could play a distinctive and independent part in international relations instead of tamely echoing more powerful allies.

Outside the South-West Pacific Australia's initiatives between 1945 and 1949 were chequered in their fortunes. When the Irish Republic finally signalled in 1948 that it regarded itself as completely independent of the United Kingdom, Evatt led the representatives of New Zealand and Canada in ensuring a mild British response which did nothing to curb existing Irish rights of migration and trade.[44] Quicker than Britain to support the independence of Israel in 1948, Evatt nevertheless went against Israeli wishes in seeming to favour the internationalization of Jerusalem. In 1948 Evatt angered the Soviet bloc by vigorous denunciation of the rigged trial of the Hungarian primate, Cardinal Mindszenty. A few months later, during the Berlin airlift which marked the nadir of the cold war, the United States considered him insufficiently hostile towards the Soviet Union.[45] Such impartiality was admirably judicial, but it was hard to maintain as the world polarized into two major power blocs, and the possibility loomed of a post-atomic third world war. Perhaps the impartiality of diplomats like Evatt helped to avert that war.

But it did not make for popularity; and Australian foreign policy in those years was so largely perceived as Evatt's personal creation that his reputation stood or fell by his performance. He was backed by an able staff, largely youngish graduates whom he drove hard. Some found him an insufferable boss, mistrustful and capricious. He was incapable of accepting advice when it differed from his own intensely focused preoccupation of the moment, or of building an administrative structure which would survive his departure from office. Consequently, although Australia gained an enhanced international reputation on which his arch-rival Menzies could build, Evatt failed to entrench his concept of Australia as an independent-minded small nation able to take its own initiatives without undue deference to the super-powers. Perhaps this concept could flourish only in the brief interlude after Japan's defeat and before the rise of communism in China sent Australia scuttling back to the protection of great and powerful allies. It was also easier to take an independent line in foreign policy at a time when Australia's major exports were in keen demand. But Evatt's policies reflected more than Evatt's personality; they represented a short-lived hope in the 1940s that Australia, no longer dependent on Britain, could revert to the nationalist ideals of the federation period and mature into the kind of society which at least to some extent could set a model of equity for the rest of the world.

If such an Australia were to be more than a provincial outpost of British culture it would have to shift from its overwhelmingly British ethnicity. In June 1947 the first census for fourteen years revealed that Australia's population had grown by less than 1 per cent annually during the interim. In some years departures from Australia exceeded arrivals. Although the spate of post-war marriages went some way towards arresting this trend it was commonly accepted that Australia was underpopulated. In a large country of sparse numbers with crowded northern neighbours the fears generated by Japan's thrust in the Pacific war were slow to disperse. Sir Raymond Huish of the Returned Services League of Australia (RSL) spoke of 'the menace of 1500 million starving Asians within 4000 miles of Australia', while in Brisbane the economist Colin Clark forecast: 'if we do not quickly settle all the available land in Queensland to its fullest capacity, somebody else will come and do it for us'.[46] The xenophobia latent in such comments soon spilt over into hostility towards migrants from any source. As put by Arthur Calwell, who was to be the architect of post-war immigration policy, Australians were too prone 'to ostracize those of alien birth and then to blame them for segregating themselves and forming foreign communities'.[47]

Unfortunately Australians were not prolific. Dr J. H. Cumpston, Commonwealth director-general of health, conducted an inquiry in 1944 into the limitation of family size and found that many of the 1400 women who responded gave eloquent testimony to the struggle of maintaining a decent standard of living on the basic wage with the fear of unemployment. 'What do we owe to Australia?', asked one woman, 'It starved us and our children after the last war and it will do the same after this one *If We Let It*. Therefore we have decided that there won't be so many of us to starve this time'.[48] Much of the social policy underlying the Australian government's schemes for post-war reconstruction—improved housing and welfare, better education, the basic goal of full employment—was designed to provide a stable and encouraging setting where male breadwinners and female home-makers could feel secure in raising a new generation of young Australians.

Even before the end of the war it was accepted that natural increase was not enough. Migration, virtually at a standstill since the 1920s, would have to be revived. An official committee looked at the prospects and in October 1944 informed the cabinet that Britain alone could no longer supply all that were needed. A majority of cabinet including Curtin and Chifley agreed, but some led by Ward were swayed by traditional working-class fears that migrants would compete for jobs and bring down wages. However in July 1945, when Chifley became prime minister, he created a separate federal Department of Immigration and placed it under Ward's former ally Arthur Calwell. Coming of Irish-American descent, Calwell was readier than most Australians for an 'open door' migration policy which in time would dilute Australia's primarily Anglo-Celtic stock. Earlier in 1945 he had published a pamphlet calling for a population of 20 million.[49] Immigration was a cause dear to his heart which enabled him to exercise his skills to the utmost.

Britain remained Australia's traditional reservoir of migrants. The times were propitious, since Britain's need to trade its way out of wartime debt meant that post-war rationing was even more austere than at the height of the blitz, and the winter of 1946−47 was uncommonly savage. An agreement came into force early in 1947 under which British ex-servicemen and their families intending to migrate to Australia would receive free passages provided they remained in Australia for two years. Others were accepted on payment of a nominal fee of £10. Because of shipping shortages the scheme could not begin until April 1947, but by July no fewer than 200 000 Britons were registered at Australia House as prospective migrants.

This unexpectedly eager response coincided with an anti-foreign backlash in Australia. A curious mixture of critics in Australia gave tongue—the RSL, the Australian Communist Party, sections of the Sydney press feuding with Calwell—denouncing the proposed influx of foreigners. Anti-Jewish prejudice was particularly strong in those years, perhaps because of anti-British terrorism in Israel. Over half of those questioned in a Melbourne survey of 1948 thought that Jewish migrants should be excluded entirely, and most thought that positive encouragement should be given only to British and perhaps Irish migrants.[50] Calwell ducked in the face of such sentiments. He announced in November 1946 that only one alien migrant should be admitted for every ten British and imposed restrictive quotas on Jewish migration, but through carefully underpublicized administrative procedures these limitations were soon eased.[51]

The demand for labour in Australia was too strong to be filled by any other means. Instead of the feared post-war slump Australia was enjoying full employment. In June 1947 Calwell flew to Europe in search of eligible migrants. On his arrival in London the chief migration officer, Norman Lamidey, persuaded him to sign an agreement with the International Refugee Organization to take 4000 of the displaced persons in its European camps.[52] Most were fugitives from central or eastern European nations which had fallen under communist rule. Calwell hoped to draw migrants from Scandinavia, the Netherlands and France, but finding no interest in those countries decided to make the most of the eastern European refugees. At first preference was given to Balts from the small nations (Estonia, Latvia, Lithuania) absorbed by the Soviet Union in 1940. During the next two years more nationalities were accepted until by mid-1949 any European displaced person under forty-five was likely to find a passage to

Australia so long as he or she was free of physical handicaps or communist sympathies. On arrival such migrants would be required to work for two years under the Australian government's direction. This usually meant manual labour in localities and jobs which established Australians found too unattractive.

In his anxiety to prove that large-scale European migration would not threaten Australian living standards, Calwell administered the White Australia Policy with all the thoroughness of his bureaucratic training. Several hundred South-East Asian refugees from the Japanese invasions of 1942 remained in Australia after the war; Calwell determined that all should be deported. An Indonesian widow who had remarried an Australian citizen named O'Keefe appealed against the minister's refusal to grant her a certificate of exemption, and early in 1949 the High Court ruled that, once admitted into Australia, a migrant should not be subject to this requirement. Oblivious to the ill-will among Australia's northern neighbours, Calwell then persuaded the government to push through legislation authorizing the deportation of all such refugees although by then many had lived in Australia for seven years. Particular comment was aroused by the case of Lorenzo Gamboa, a Filipino sergeant who had taken American citizenship. The Philippines legislature considered the expulsion of all Australians, the consulate in Sydney was closed in protest, and the *Manila Evening Chronicle* spoke of the 'natural sadism that springs from Australia's penal origins'.[53] But Calwell stood firm against the slightest tincture of Asianization in Australia, believing that future security lay in the rapid and successful encouragement of more and more Europeans.

'New Australians' were prominently associated with the Chifley government's greatest scheme for national development, the Snowy Mountains Hydro-Electric Scheme. This plan, which took twenty-five years to complete, involved diverting the headwaters of the Snowy River which, fed by the snows of the Australian Alps, ran unused through eastern Victoria. If a series of tunnels and dams fed these waters into the Tumut–Murrumbidgee system, irrigation in the Riverina would benefit. This was a point which weighed with William McKell, the premier of New South Wales, who had been born in the region and cherished its possibilities.[54] Victoria and South Australia, fearing that water supplies in New South Wales would be enriched at their expense, were less easily persuaded, but in time accepted the scheme because of its potential for generating electric power which could be used by industry. Because the scheme was open to constitutional challenge much of it worked on gentlemen's agreements. Landowners were not threatened with compulsory acquisition. The unions curbed unrest. At the political level there was an unusually heartening example of co-operation between two Labor governments (the Commonwealth and New South Wales) and two Liberal (Victoria and South Australia).

Labour for the Snowy Mountains scheme was largely recruited from 'new Australian migrants' and the undertaking soon gripped Australian imaginations: 'It's the only *visionary* thing I've seen since I've been back in this bloody country', the author George Johnston said (through his largely autobiographical character, Jack Meredith):

The yellow tractors against the glaring drifts of snow, the beards and mackinaws, the polyglot babble of smoke-hazed men's huts, the tingling atmosphere of a collective excitement; these as much as the sheer audacity of the concept had a profound effect . . .[55]

Sir William Hudson, an engineer–administrator in the tradition of C. Y. O'Connor and Sir John Monash, made his reputation through his leadership of the project. Although doubts have been voiced about the safety and medical aspects of the Snowy Mountains scheme, it was a sign of the times that Hudson responded thoughtfully when advised of the environmental implications of all this construction activity on the ecology of the Australian Alps, already under threat from excessive summer grazing. Hudson was to prove an enlightened conservationist, establishing sanctuaries and winning McKell's tribute: 'a lot of Australia, that Australia we knew as children, he has brought back to us'.[56]   The Snowy Mountains scheme could thus stand as a striking symbol of constructive national purpose, with recent migrants contributing to that recurring Australian dream of making the wilderness fruitful and generating power for the service of industry and the well-being of the people. It epitomized many of the themes dearest to the Chifley government: the promotion of national development by wise administrative decision and by co-operation between the states and Commonwealth, the provision of opportunity for disadvantaged newcomers, the vindication in the world's eyes of Australian skill and Australian capacity to plan great designs and execute them. By all rational calculations it should have ranked as a great achievement for the Chifley government and its methods. But rationality seldom triumphs in politics. Projects of national development such as the Snowy Mountains scheme were not the issues which swayed voters to bring down the Chifley government in 1949.

3

PRAGMATISM ASCENDANT

FEAR OF COMMUNISM dominated political debate in Australia between 1945 and 1951 and yet throughout this period membership of the Communist Party of Australia fell from its wartime peak of 23 000, and it was rejected at the polls more consistently than in any other parliamentary democracy outside North America. This paradox has three explanations. The Soviet Union, the standard-bearer of world communism, was expanding unscrupulously into eastern and central Europe, overthrowing not only gimcrack monarchies such as Bulgaria and Romania but parliamentary democracies such as Czechoslovakia in 1948. With each conquest it was harder to believe that the Russians were simply seeking insurance against invasion and easier to fear that they wanted to enforce communism on the rest of the world. Within Australia trade union militancy in support of improved wages and conditions led to frequent strikes and confrontations, and it was consoling for the middle class to believe that this strife was due, not to flaws in the Australian system of social justice, but to communist machinations. Given these two factors it was irresistible for Labor's opponents to combine them by alleging that the pragmatic measures of the Chifley government to control the economy and promote social welfare were a mere preliminary to a communist takeover of Australia, abetted from outside by Moscow's resources and propaganda and from within by radical agitators operating in secret and profiting by the complacency if not the sympathy of Labor. Obligingly, the Russians went deeper into the cold war and several trade unions, defying the Chifley government's policies, continued to use the strike weapon in pursuit of their aims; thus the scaremongering gained credibility.

Probably the strikes made the greatest impression. Tom Sheridan argues that because the Depression and the war had accustomed Australians to shortages 'most people . . . felt less disconcerted by the effects of industrial disputes than does the present Australian community',[1] but this is debatable. Between 1945 and 1947 nearly 5.5 million working days were lost through industrial disputes, a figure previously matched only at the end of the First World War and at the onset of the Depression in the late 1920s. Employers were tough and antagonistic, seeking the restoration of their pre-war authority; unions on the other hand were anxious to make the most of the moment of full employment, expecting a post-war slump such as followed the 1914–18 war. Disputes remained frequent on the New South Wales coalfields. There was a major steel strike at Port Kembla against the Broken Hill Proprietary Company (BHP) in October 1945 over the dismissal of a union official. In September 1946 public transport in Victoria was halted by a railway and tramway stoppage; then it was severely cut after a six-months strike in 1946–47 by the metal trades unions, and household gas went on short rations. It seemed impossible for employers and unions to resolve their differences without head-on confrontation.

The Australian Council of Trade Unions (ACTU) at its congress in 1945 put its weight behind three major industrial demands: a substantial increase in the basic wage, an end to wage-pegging, and a 40-hour week. The ACTU also wanted to abolish the Arbitration Court, which it saw as too dominated by conservative legalism, in favour of industry-based conciliation committees headed by commissioners with suitable industrial experience. In pushing these views the ACTU was reflecting the influence of the Left—seldom greater than at this period—but it was also trying to impose coherence on trade union demands because it knew that the federal Labor government, although headed by Chifley, who had been notably victimized for his part in the 1917 railwaymen's strike, was quietly but implacably opposed to sweeping concessions.[2]

The ACTU considered that its aims could be met by unilateral government action; the Chifley government, aware that reforms granted by one government could be dismantled by another, insisted on going to the Arbitration Court whose decisions could be enforced on grudging employers. The unions saw improved wages and hours as the pay off for restraint during the war; the Chifley government, worried by its failure to secure administrative controls over prices and wages, wanted to impose delays and checks so as to damp down inflation and the risk of unemployment. Union leadership, not wishing to be outflanked on the Left in the loyalties of the rank and file, threatened the use of industrial muscle to speed the coming of concessions; the Chifley government, anxious to maintain Australia's credibility in the harsh world of international finance, did not wish to be seen as anticipating or pre-empting the Arbitration Court. In the end the ACTU won most of its demands, though more slowly than its members hoped, and the Chifley government's procrastination meant that it was easier for the economy to absorb these changes.

Chifley's caution is sometimes seen as reflecting his austere personal tastes, but there was more behind it. High on the list of priorities came the need to support the sterling bloc in the face of pressure from the aggressive American economy. This was not just a question of British Commonwealth loyalty, or of fellow-feeling for another labour government. Britain was still Australia's major source of trade and investment, and although favouring diversification the Chifley government did not want to become an American satellite. In order to assist Britain's economic recovery Australia increased its sterling balances from £199 million in mid-1947 to £452 million in mid-1949 and maintained food rationing for several years. In August 1947 import restrictions reduced the quantity of petrol bought from dollar-currency sources, and rationing continued although the Commonwealth's legal powers might be challenged at any time. Clothing and meat rationing were abolished only in June 1948, butter and tea not until 1950. The Liberal—Country Party Opposition jibed continually at the Chifley government's love of bureaucratic controls, and consumers grew restive.

Meanwhile the ACTU pressed its demands. The 40-hour case came before the Arbitration Court in May 1946 and turned into a 'lawyers' feast', dragging on for nineteen months.[3] By September 1947 the ACTU was threatening a general strike on the issue, but it was not necessary. Before the year ended the court had granted the 40-hour week with reasonable provision for overtime. The basic wage case went more slowly, partly because in 1947 the government legislated to make basic wage inquiries a function of the full Arbitration Court, thus repudiating the ACTU's idea that the court should be dismantled; instead, the court's punitive powers were strengthened. However, detailed industrial negotiations were remitted to a panel of sixteen conciliation commissioners, thus encouraging informality and flexibility. The government also created special tribunals for the coal and waterfront industries.

It was not until 1949 that the basic wage case finally came before the full Arbitration Court. By the time its findings were handed down, early in 1950, the Chifley government was out of office and accelerating inflation took the edge off its award of an increase of £1 weekly, bringing the figure to £7 18s. It was not as good as the £10 claimed by some unions but it was more than employers wanted to give. The success of the basic wage case following on the 40-hour week demonstrated that the mainstream trade union movement was capable of winning gains for the workers from the arbitration system, and this weakened the communist claim that only direct action could secure a better deal. At the same time the standard female wage was confirmed at 75 per cent of the unskilled male rate. Unfortunately, in awarding this increase Mr Justice Foster committed the court to the view that 'the productivity, efficiency, and the needs and responsibilities etc of females were substantially less than that of males in this country',[4] thus setting back hopes of equal pay for nearly twenty years.

Employers could afford higher wages because industry everywhere was booming. After two decades of struggle and heartbreak these were fat years for primary producers. Wool-growers did especially well. Between 1945 and 1950 Australia joined with Britain, New Zealand and South Africa in co-operative wool marketing so that the price was kept up for producers. Stockpiling increased as the cold war worsened, until in 1949–50 wool prices rose by 30 per cent, and the best was yet to come. It was at last possible to afford fencing, improved watering points and other improvements which had been deferred for years because of hard times. Primary producers eagerly snapped up bargains as the army disposed of unwanted material left over from the war, such as lorries and four-wheel-drive vehicles. In a land of big distances the use of aircraft seemed attractive.

The Royal Flying Doctor Service was expanded, and between 1949 and 1953 the Air Beef enterprise attempted to establish it-self in the Kimberleys, eliminating wastage through droving by slaughtering cattle at an inland centre and freighting the car-casses to market by air. Drought ended the scheme, but it was a harbinger of the new technologies available to rural and pastoral Australia.

Though farmers and graziers were once more prospering, their good fortune did not necessarily spill over into the country towns. Many were stagnating because, having been established during the horse-and-buggy era as service centres for farming families within a radius of 20 kilometres or less, they could find no new function once they were by-passed by motor transport. Macdonald Holmes, professor of geography at the University of Sydney and president of the Royal Flying Doctor Service, visited Charleville in the heart of Queensland's wool-growing outback at the height of the pastoral boom in 1950, and was 'astounded at the poverty'.[5] Bernie Fraser, son of an unskilled worker with the New South Wales Electricity Commission, grew up in Junee in New South Wales in the early 1950s in a family that could not always afford boots for his football or books for his schooling— but from these beginnings became within thirty years secretary of the federal Treasury. For most Australians of that generation, however, the opportunities were sought in the cities. The suburbs were resuming their long spread out of Sydney and Melbourne.

Already half of Australia's 7.7 million inhabitants[6] at the 1947 census lived in the five major metropolitan areas: 1.5 million in Sydney; 1.2 million in Melbourne; just over another million shared between Brisbane, Adelaide and Perth. (Forty years later they would boast a million each.) Because of the 1930s Depression and subsequent wartime shortages there was a backlog of houses. The birth rate rose slightly in the later years of the war, and at 24.06 per thousand in 1947 reached a figure unmatched since the early 1920s. As 1946 and 1947 were peak years for marriages it could be expected that the demand for family housing would grow. In Australia as a whole there were about 2 million private dwellings, about 53 per cent of them owner-occupied; home ownership had not yet fully recovered from the effects of depression and war. Among the rented accommodation 86 000 houses were shared by more than one family. There were many more where a young married couple, often with infants or toddlers, co-existed uneasily with the older generation. Others lived in inadequate flats. Most of them wanted to buy or build their own homes as soon as opportunity permitted. Politicians encouraged them. Home ownership, said the Queensland Labor premier V. C. Gair, 'encourages a sense of responsibility in the individual', while for Victoria's Sir Albert Dunstan the person who could afford a deposit for a house was 'invariably an exemplary citizen, a symbol of achievement, purpose, industry, and thrift'.[7]

Difficulties abounded. Materials were in short supply, and skilled tradespeople hard to find. Many couples resorted to do-it-yourself methods, wives and husbands alike learning the skills of the artisan as they laboured during the weekends and the evenings, often with the help of relatives or friends. Some newspapers ran advice columns, and the Melbourne *Age* from 1946 ran a notable 'small homes service' under the guidance of an able young architect, Robin Boyd, who was to have great influence on the way Australians regarded their home environments. Except in Queensland and Tasmania, brick and brick-veneer houses were favoured somewhat more than weatherboard, while fibro-cement and concrete were gaining acceptance as alternatives. Household technology was still backward. Wood-burning coppers and stoves were common. Only a minority enjoyed hot-water systems. Even the Duke and Duchess of Gloucester on arrival at the governor-general's residence at Yarralumla found neither electric kettle nor refrigerator. The water-filter did not work and the house was riddled with vermin: 'Just as Henry was knighting some old gentleman a mouse dashed past with a tabby cat in hot pursuit'.[8]

Gradually shortages gave way to plenty. What this meant to the generation who had lived through the 1930s Depression may be illustrated by the experiences of one couple. In 1939, after thirteen years of paying rent, Frank and Winifred Bolton bought their first home. The only brick-and-tile residence in a street of nineteen houses in a respectable working-class suburb built between 1895 and 1920, their purchase cost them £675, which they largely funded through a loan from the Perth Building Society on which they paid 18s 9d weekly. Frank Bolton was in regular employment as clerk to a firm of motor-cycle retailers, and rose to be country orders manager; he was not called up for military service because of a hernia which he could never spare the time or money to have operated. In 1939 he was earning less than £5 weekly. By 1946 his weekly wage had risen to £7 and by July 1949 to £8 11s 8d. Then came the push of inflation. By February 1951 the figure had risen to £11 18s and by May 1952 to £15 8s 6d. Although these increases were accompanied by rising costs, the Boltons' standard of living was undoubtedly improving, particularly since by 1951 they had finished paying off the instalments on the house at a depreciated rate. This improvement can be seen in their purchases of household equipment. In November 1940, eighteen months after moving into the house, they bought a new gas stove, but the war deterred further purchases, and in 1943 they suffered a financial setback through the prolonged illness of their elder son. But by January 1947 they were able to afford an Electrolux cleaner, and the wage increases of 1951–52 produced a new dinner service, lino for the kitchen and a sitting-room carpet. They never owned a car, but put their two children through university and looked after a widowed parent who lived with them. They were quietly pleased with what they had achieved, but it would not have occurred to them that there was anything unusual about it, nor to question the essential rightness of a political and economic system which allowed couples such as themselves the security of their own home and possessions and opportunities for their children.[9]

Not every Australian was as yet committed to investing in the suburban dream. In 1946–47, 7.5 million Australians put £92 million away in personal savings but they also disposed of £26 million on gambling. At that time the average Australian was estimated to devote 18 per cent of income spent on personal consumption to racing, trotting, two-up, lotteries (though these were still recovering from a wartime decline) and various other forms of legal and illegal gambling. In New South Wales arrests for drunkenness increased massively between 1945 and 1948 despite frequent shortages of beer and a referendum in 1945 which upheld six o'clock closing of hotel bars. Many preferred to find their recreation in the social clubs run by the RSL sub-branches, football teams and other voluntary organizations because their premises usually offered more amenities and comfort than the pubs. The number of private clubs quadrupled between 1945 and 1947, receiving a boost in August 1947 when the Royal Sydney Golf Club successfully appealed to the Supreme Court against a charge of trading outside licensing hours.[10]

Reassuringly, Australian sport in the early post-war years took up almost precisely where it had left off in 1939. Several veterans enjoyed a remarkable Indian summer. In tennis Adrian Quist and John Bromwich, although in their mid-thirties, consistently achieved the finals in the Davis Cup and in 1950 took the doubles title at Wimbledon. Don Bradman and his team thrashed the English cricketers at home in 1946–47 and in England in 1948, thus disposing of the argument that Australia's monotonous victories were due solely to superior rations. After Bradman's retirement Lindsay Hassett captained more victories until 1950–51 when, to the relief even of the Australians, England won one game out of five. It was still part of the Australian tradition that individual excellence could be achieved from unprivileged beginnings—'the boy from Bowral' could become Sir Donald Bradman, receiving the accolade from the hands of King George VI.

Even on the turf the success story of these times combined obscure origins with game performance as a veteran. Bernborough, a rangy 5-year-old stallion that was raced during the war under dubious sponsorship on rural courses in Queensland, was purchased in 1945 by Antonio Romano, a Sydney restaurateur. In one season the newcomer outran the best of the Sydney and Melbourne turf, winning fifteen races consecutively over distances of 6 to 11 furlongs (1.2 to 2.2 kilometres), and lapsing to third only when required to run the 1946 Caulfield Cup under a weight of 68 kilograms. Bernborough's courage and stamina filled a gap in the public imagination dating from the untimely death of Phar Lap fourteen years earlier. But he never won the Melbourne Cup, retiring to stud after an injury. In 1950 that national trophy was won in record time by a hardly less legendary stayer, Comic Court. The House of Representatives postponed a session for three-quarters of an hour in order that members might listen to the race on the radio, and when a new member, Paul Hasluck, protested at this use of working time he was overruled by both Chifley and Menzies. 'I do not think the four million people who listened to the broadcast will have any complaints', said Menzies.[11]

Far fewer than 4 million Australians took pleasure from the attempts of a handful of innovators to find a distinctive national voice in the arts. The most noted Australian film of this period, Michael Balcon's *The Overlanders* (1946) shows a group of working-class Australians ostensibly droving cattle from Western Australia to Queensland during the war, but it also shows ordinary men and women taking decisions and functioning without management. It was a suitable theme for the era of post-war reconstruction and introduced Chips Rafferty to the public, but it had only a few successors during the following decade: *Bush Christmas*, *Sons of Matthew*, later *Jedda*, the first film to feature an Aboriginal star in Robert Tudawali. The international competition was too formidable. In addition to Hollywood, the British were striking form with a succession of comedies such as *Passport to Pimlico* and *Kind Hearts and Coronets*; and for the first time in years Australian audiences could watch masterpieces of the European cinema such as *Les enfants du Paradis* and *Bicycle Thieves*. Australian film would languish for another twenty years. For the arts generally European imports were welcomed after years of wartime isolation as an inspiration for local endeavour. The Australia-wide tour of the Ballet Rambert in 1947 was followed a year later by Sir Laurence Olivier and Vivien Leigh in *Richard III* and *The School for Scandal*. Travelling exhibitions of paintings from the Tate Gallery in 1949 and of French modernist art in 1953 stimulated the ideas of local artists.

Radio on the other hand was at its peak. Listeners could identify with such popular programmes as 'Australia's Amateur Hour' or the 'Quiz Kids' because they gave the impression that any week might see the discovery of a soprano from Launceston or a bright boy from a Brisbane suburban high school who would be launched on the path to success. Unlike television, radio was not the monopoly of the remote élite. Serials such as 'Dad and Dave', which ran under George Edwards's management from 1937 to 1954, may have presented a debased version of Steele Rudd's original characters but they were very popular, not least as providing background for many of the mildly smutty jokes of that time. When the Snake Gully Cup was run—always on the evening of the Melbourne Cup—the actors in 'Dad and Dave' had to be sworn to secrecy because large sums of money changed hands on the result. Such programmes provided welcome employment for Australian actors. Live theatre was still recovering from the dislocation of wartime. The one notable new play of this period, Sumner Locke-Elliott's *Rusty Bugles*, struck a chord with many because of its realistic portrayal of the boredom and the camaraderie of life in a Northern Territory army camp during wartime. Its success was marred by trouble with the New South Wales Vice Squad who objected to characters using coarse expressions such as 'bastardry' and 'bloody'. Questions were asked in parliament. Disenchanted, Locke-Elliot soon left to reside permanently in the United States.

At least Locke-Elliott went unpunished for his realism. In Melbourne in 1946 a novelist, Robert Close, was imprisoned for three months and fined for *Love Me Sailor*, a work of fiction which hinted too vividly at the language and preoccupations of working seamen. He also left Australia for many years. Actors such as Peter Finch and the comedian Dick Bentley found too few opportunities in Australia and left for London or the United States; so did artists such as Albert Tucker and Sidney Nolan, although the latter was already deeply involved in transforming the Ned Kelly myth into new statements about the Australian environment. Yet at the same time some long-term expatriates were abandoning the Old World to try Australia once more, believing like Patrick White that London had become a graveyard, or like Martin Boyd that Australians possess 'great vitality . . . and a general feeling of optimism and appetite for life'.[12] Both were disappointed, perhaps because they made their moves a little too soon. For in the late 1940s pressures against nonconformity and dissent in Australia were intensifying because of a growing fear of communism. Before long the pacifist Boyd found that Melburnians thought him a communist 'as I believed in aristocratic government and the Divine Right of Kings'.[13]

As the cold war deteriorated most of the Liberal–Country Party Opposition urged the banning of the Communist Party. Although Menzies stood out for a while, believing that 'in times of peace . . . the Communists should be left alone',[14] by May 1949 he said he was convinced that the cold war justified such a ban. Well before that date his colleagues were abusing the Chifley government as the dupes or sympathizers of communism. Their philippic reached a new pitch in July 1948 after reports reached the Australian press that the United States refused to pass on atomic secrets to Britain for fear that they would be leaked to the Russians because of Australia's faulty security.[15] At least two British scientists had recently been convicted for communicating atomic information to the Soviet Union, and it was unthinkable that Australia should fall behind the rest of the world, even in the production of traitors. The anti-Labor parties duly turned to the harassment of scientists and academics.

Their first target was Sir David Rivett, the distinguished chairman of the Council for Scientific and Industrial Research

(CSIR).[16] At a graduation address to the Canberra University College in March 1947 Rivett argued that the international scientific community flourished on the free exchange of research findings and ought not be liable to censorship; if scientific research was required for defence purposes it should be conducted in specialist establishments whose scientists understood that their work was subject to security restrictions. As a corollary it was inappropriate for CSIR to engage in secret defence research. When parliament resumed in September 1948 several Liberal–Country Party members denounced this doctrine. Rivett was recklessly smeared, and much was made of the fact that one of the government's appointees to the council had a brother in the Communist Party.[17] Dedman as responsible minister rebutted the attacks, which were groundless; but he determined to bring CSIR under closer public service control as a government department, and was persuaded with difficulty to retain it as a statutory corporation remodelled as the Commonwealth Scientific and Industrial Research Organization (CSIRO). Rivett retired and was succeeded by Ian Clunies Ross, a no less independent-minded and respected veterinary scientist. Chifley and Evatt also set up a federal intelligence agency, the Australian Security Intelligence Organization (ASIO), with a South Australian judge as director-general. This was to provide a rod for Evatt's own back in future years.

Some state governments played rougher. In February and March 1948 the Queensland Labor government under E. M. Hanlon took draconian measures against the Australian Railways Union which, although not communist-dominated, included several communist officials. A strikers' parade in Brisbane on St Patrick's Day was broken up violently by police and among those injured the communist member of parliament, F. W. Paterson, was batoned over the head while standing on the footpath taking notes. He never completely recovered, and in 1950 his seat was redistributed out of existence. Under sweeping emergency legislation of a type which would become familiar in Queensland the state government imprisoned several union leaders for refusing to return to work.[18] The ACTU executive disliked the use of gaol by a Labor government but Hanlon stood firm, and the new Liberal government in Victoria followed his example more mildly when the gas workers went on strike six months later.

The Communist Party reacted to these pressures by declaring

war on Labor. Lance Sharkey, an uncompromising veteran communist, took the lead in denouncing the reformist Labor government as an ally of 'United States imperialists' against the Soviet
Union. Later in 1949 he was gaoled for giving a silly answer to a
silly question: when asked by a reporter whether Soviet troops
entering Australia in pursuit of an aggressor would be welcomed,
he said 'Yes'. This case was a portent of toughening attitudes.
Aware of losing ground, the Communist Party decided that
industrial action must be stepped up. The coalmining industry
offered opportunities. Apart from the traditional legacy of ill-
will between management and men, new causes of contention
could be found in the advance of mechanization. In Hagan's
words, 'A campaign for industrial gains and the nationalization
of the mines would win unity among more workers and differen-
tiate the Communist Party from the timid and fraudulent Labor
Government'. At the end of June 1949 the Miners' Federation
called a strike in support of long-service leave, a 35-hour week,
and a pay increase of 30 shillings weekly.[19]

The Chifley government, supported by the Labor government
of New South Wales, said it would fight back 'boots and all'.
Legislation was rushed through parliament to prohibit the use of
union funds in support of the strike. When union leaders refused
to reveal the whereabouts of their funds several were imprisoned
for contempt of court by Judge Foster, normally counted a Labor
sympathizer. The ACTU recommended a return to work in
exchange for release of the gaoled officials, but the unions
refused. By the middle of July gas was rationed in Sydney to one
hour's use daily and the railways were paralysed. Many people
were thrown out of work. Public sympathy was almost entirely
against the strikers. After four weeks the federal government
sent troops to work open-cut coalmines and ordered the navy to
unload imported coal. On 15 August the miners returned to
work, aggregate meetings of the rank and file overruling the
union leadership. Soon afterwards the miners were granted long-
service leave, but not their other claims. It was probably neither
less nor more than would have been achieved without the
strike.[20]

Some Labor men contended that by turning on a section of the
union movement the Chifley government had antagonized its
traditional supporters and weakened its prospects for the next
elections.[21] This seems unlikely; the militants would never have

voted Liberal and the government's resolute handling of the strike probably won back some swinging voters in the cities who blamed the unions for disruptions to power and public transport services. The importance of the coal strike lies in its rebuff to the communists and other advocates of direct action. Backed by the ACTU the Chifley government also legislated to enable the Arbitration Court to intervene when ballot-rigging or other irregularities had taken place in a trade union election. Using this amendment a moderate candidate, Laurie Short, soon afterwards wrested the secretaryship of the Federated Ironworkers' Association from communist hands, after a 1949 election in which the court discovered 'forgery, fraud and irregularity on a grand scale'.[22] Others followed, showing that the communists were increasingly coming under challenge from a section of the union movement that was prepared to fight fire with fire.

During the later stages of the war industrial groups were formed in a number of unions in New South Wales and Victoria with the aim of combating communist influence. In 1945 the New South Wales branch of the ALP recognized them, and the other state branches followed. The 'Groupers', as they were called, soon saw that the communists owed much of their success to their willingness to spend long hours at meetings, attend to the tedious process of whipping up members and organizing votes, and master every rule in the book—and more—to ensure the success of their policies and candidates. They would use the same tactics. But the communists were also buoyed up by a doctrine, the Marxist faith of dialectical materialism which taught that their cause would eventually triumph because of the working of objective economic laws. Many of the Groupers found a no less compelling ideology in the teachings of the Roman Catholic Church.

Anti-communism was powered by 'the Movement'. Founded in 1942 under the aegis of Archbishop Daniel Mannix of Melbourne, the Catholic Social Studies Movement was specifically set up to oppose the spread of communist influence. Melbourne's inner suburbs, traditionally a breeding ground of Catholic Labor politicians, were more vulnerable to communist wartime progress than any other part of Australia, so it was not surprising that the church in Melbourne took the lead in anti-communist counter-attack. The Movement had a brilliant publicist in the youthful B. A. (Bob) Santamaria. The son of an Italian migrant greengrocer, Santamaria came to the fore as a law student at the University of Melbourne in the late 1930s when the Spanish Civil War was the great focus for debate between Right and Left, attracting Mannix's favourable attention. At first Santamaria was involved in the development of Catholic rural policy and was among those who argued that Australia's hope lay in nurturing a self-sufficient peasantry rather than in the encouragement of protected manufactures. For this reason immigration should be encouraged on a substantial scale from European countries where religion, the family and peasant farming were still strong social forces.

In opposing communism Santamaria and his associates in the Movement became ideological crusaders. Communism was implacably evil, to an extent which easy-going Australians found hard to picture. It must be resisted, and part of that resistance consisted of promoting in Australia a morality based on the family and the Christian faith which would be strong enough to counter the enticements of Marxism. For Santamaria recognized, as many anti-communists did not, that like all great heresies Marxism was most seductive when it appealed to idealism, and specifically to the Australian hope of finding a secure future in a new country. It was no coincidence that many prominent Australian communists came from Catholic or orthodox Jewish backgrounds, exchanging one rule of discipline for another. Together with this readiness to fight communism on ideological grounds, the Movement developed an earthy grasp of tactics. Many priests were sympathetic to the Movement's aims; their advice to their parishioners often went well beyond the convention of keeping church and state apart. By 1949 the Movement was not only gaining influence among industrial groups in the unions but, especially in Victoria, was enjoying some success in the counsels of the ALP and in the pre-selection of parliamentary candidates.[23]

It was possibly because of the coal strike that the Chifley government decided to hold the federal elections in December 1949, the latest possible date. The outcome was unusually difficult to predict because the House of Representatives was enlarged by another forty-eight seats, bringing its membership to 123 (including the members for the Northern Territory and the Australian Capital Territory who could speak and vote only on matters affecting their own constituencies). At the same time the

Senate grew from thirty-six members to sixty, ten chosen from each state by proportional representation. The latter change was favoured by Chifley and Evatt as reflecting public opinion more fairly than the old system; Calwell objected, foreseeing that it gave an opening to independents and minority parties who could hold the balance of power whenever, as often happened, support was divided fairly evenly between Labor and its opponents. He was overruled but he was right, although it took some years for this to become apparent. In the House of Representatives veteran members tended to take the safe seats, leaving new or marginal constituencies to be fought by the younger generation. This meant that whichever party lost the 1949 election would be bereft of bright youngsters, a risk particularly unfortunate for a Labor government which had been eight years in office and whose spokesmen were beginning to sound distinctly old-fashioned.

Menzies and his cohorts attacked the government repeatedly as socialists in love with bureaucratic controls for their own aggrandizement. Enough examples could be cited to lend some plausibility to this in the eyes of voters. Calwell's heavy-handed administration of the White Australia Policy was one example; another was the 1948 broadcasting legislation which funded the ABC from consolidated revenue instead of licence fees and set up the Australian Broadcasting Control Board to oversee technical and programme standards on both ABC and commercial stations. One clause of this Act forbade the dramatization of contemporary political issues, and was directed against 'John Henry Austral', a series of anti-Labor broadcasts lampooning members of cabinet. This meant that the 1940s and the 1950s did not produce any notable political satirists. The Opposition attacked the measures without restraint as 'one step further towards the development of a totalitarian state'.[24] It was not an issue to disenchant many Labor voters. Nor were the controversies over medical benefits and bank nationalization necessarily fatal, though they shook the allegiance of swinging voters among the lower middle class whose respect for the professions was greater than its respect for politicians. But the old stagers of the Chifley government were becoming too much associated with rationing and controls. The spruce young ex-servicemen coming forward in the Liberal Party often projected a greater sense of energy when they talked of the virtues of free enterprise.

Middle-class opposition was also stimulated by Labor's running feud with the medical profession. Having secured acceptance of pharmaceutical benefits and federal subsidies to state public hospitals the Chifley government in 1948 brought in a national health service scheme which provided government payment of one-half of a patient's medical expenses. For the sake of administrative simplicity it was proposed that doctors should make returns of their patients and fees and receive the government contribution direct. The British Medical Association objected that this would invade the privacy of the doctor—patient relationship and argued that it should be the patient who collected the government subsidy.[25] If this had been the only issue at stake it should not have been beyond human wit to negotiate some acceptable compromise. But many other factors, some unspoken, underlay this confrontation. Undoubtedly most doctors were principled and sincere in fighting to preserve confidentiality, though some also resented disclosure of their earnings and more joined the campaign with relish because the foe was a Labor government. Having created a tradition that first-class service could be secured only if a fee changed hands, Australian doctors noted with dislike the recent introduction of a British comprehensive national health scheme providing full government payment of hospital and medical expenses, and feared that the Chifley government would do likewise.

Basically the issue was power. In a country without an aristocracy, such as Australia, senior members of the professional classes stood high on the ladder of prestige and status, the medical profession highest of all. It was hard for such people to bear a challenge to their authority from any quarter, or to accept that their skill in treating patients did not qualify them to decide how the patient's bills should be paid. Accordingly the doctors fought the medical benefits scheme in the High Court, and in 1949 a majority of the court found by a process of reasoning too tortuous for the logical mind of Dixon or the humane instincts of McTiernan that, although the 1946 referendum entitled the Commonwealth to legislate in most areas of social services, it was an unacceptable form of civil conscription to require that doctors must use authorized Commonwealth prescription forms for drugs. Here matters rested during the lifetime of the Chifley government except that as an alternative the medical profession actively promoted the formation and growth of private hospital and medical benefits funds whose contributors paid for insurance to cover many of the costs of illness. Herein lay the possibility of future progress.

The final crisis for the Chifley government, typifying as it did so many of its weaknesses and strengths, was petrol rationing. As the coal strike revealed, questions of fuel and power loomed large in Australian politics, and petrol was a notably sensitive subject. It could be argued that Labor won office in 1941 because at the previous elections Menzies had lost votes by introducing petrol rationing. Between 1944–45 and 1948–49 the number of motor vehicles in Australia increased from 800 000 to 1.25 million. From November 1948 the first Holden sedans were rolling off the assembly line, creating a market so strong that for two or three years buyers paid extra for a recent second-hand model rather than wait months for their turn for a new vehicle. In the face of such vigorous demand it must have been tempting to end petrol rationing, especially when the High Court in mid-1949 declared that the Commonwealth's defence powers no longer authorized its imposition. Instead the Chifley government legislated to restore petrol rationing, ignoring the Opposition's claim that plentiful supplies were available to satisfy Australia's motorists.[26]

To take such a decision on the eve of an election was courageous if not foolhardy, but the reasoning was compelling. Most petrol was imported from sources which had to be paid in American dollars. Since August 1947 Australia had imposed import restrictions against petrol, cars and a number of other dollar commodities in order to safeguard the British and Australian pound. Government policies probably discouraged American investment in Australia. On the other hand Australia's overseas debts had been systematically reduced throughout the 1940s, so that although Chifley had to go to the IMF for a US$20 million loan in October 1949 he could justly claim to have rescued Australia from its vulnerable over-dependence on overseas borrowing. From the perspective of 1930 such an achievement must have seemed meritorious (as it would in the 1980s), but in the years of the post-war boom it was little appreciated. Consumer demand was insistent, fed by the rising value of Australia's exports, especially wool. Inflation was running at 10 per cent. Having denied the federal government powers to curb inflation, the electorate was inclined to blame it for rising prices. Dissatisfaction crystallized around the issue of petrol rationing, and the Opposition made the most of it.

The election was one of the hardest fought in modern

Australian history. Menzies and the liberals knew that if they lost this time their credibility as an alternative party of government would be gravely damaged. Their slogan became 'Put the value back into the pound', though they did not explain how this could be achieved at a time of full employment without government intervention on a scale well beyond anything attempted by Chifley. Instead they spared no effort to chill the voters with prophecies of 'socialist regimentation' if Labor was returned. The fight against Marxism would call for the banning of the Communist Party of Australia and the introduction of compulsory military training. Petrol rationing would go, taxation would be substantially reduced, and child endowment extended to cover the first child in every family. In rebuttal the government fought a lack-lustre campaign. Too much emphasis was placed on the personal qualities of Chifley—'Australia's Abe Lincoln' to some—provoking a vicious attack from old J. T. Lang, who accused him of lending money at usurious rates during the Depression. The press and the cartoonists were generally anti-Labor; Ted Scorfield's savage caricatures of Chifley in the *Bulletin* are among the most merciless of their kind. Much of this mud failed to stick, but about 10 per cent of those who voted Labor in 1946 thought that this time it would be safer to give the other side a chance. At the close of counting in December 1949 Labor retained its majority in the Senate but was beaten decisively in the House of Representatives, retaining only forty-seven members against seventy-four for the Liberal–Country Party coalition. Menzies was back as prime minister.[27]

Several members of the new cabinet had experience of office. The Country Party took the main financial portfolios: its shrewd, earthy leader Arthur Fadden became treasurer and deputy prime minister, with the formidable 'Black Jack' McEwen as minister for commerce and agriculture. The party's founding father, Sir Earle Page, became minister for health, a post where he would end his long ministerial career with his most constructive achievement, a workable national health scheme. Among the Liberals R. G. Casey, treasurer during the 1930s and then minister to Washington, was returning to Australian politics after serving Britain as minister for state in the Middle East and governor of Bengal. Some thought him a potential rival to Menzies but his ambitions were blunted by bouts of self-doubting depression, and he was too gentlemanly; it was said of him that he had the ethical values of Bulldog Drummond.[28] The colleague best able to stand up to Menzies was the aggressively energetic Sydney lawyer Percy Spender, minister for external affairs. The likeliest heir to the prime minister was the affable Harold Holt, minister for labour and immigration at just over forty. He would maintain Calwell's initiatives with more than Calwell's diplomacy. Another Liberal appointee was the first woman to enter a federal ministry, Dame Enid Lyons. Widow of an earlier prime minister, she was given the largely honorific post of vice-president of the executive council; 'They needed someone to pour the tea', she commented.

There would not be a counter-revolution. The Menzies ministry was in no hurry to dismantle the efficient machinery of government inherited from Chifley. Russel Ward relates that on Fadden's first morning as treasurer, having been among the fiercest critics of 'socialized' banking, he telephoned the governor of the Commonwealth Bank, H. C. Coombs, to say: 'That you, Nugget? Don't take any notice of all that bullshit I was talking during the election. We'll be needing you, you know'.[29] Although the Menzies government wanted to restore the Commonwealth Bank Board it would be half made up of officials, with Coombs still governor. This was symbolic of the coalition government's approach. One or two minor government enterprises such as the unprofitable Glen Davis shale-oil workings would be sold off, but major enterprises such as TAA were retained. Social-welfare spending increased from 4.5 per cent of all expenditure in 1948–49 to 5.5 per cent in 1953–54. The government quickly kept its promise to extend child endowment to the first child. Page persuaded the medical profession to consent to a benefits scheme under which the government paid supplementary hospital and medical benefits to claimants subscribing to one of the registered contributory funds set up by friendly societies and similar groups. A number of expensive drugs and medicines would be provided for a nominal fee. It was neither as comprehensive for cases of sharpest need nor as administratively simple as a national health scheme, but it provided the majority of Australians with welcome relief from the costs of illness.

In foreign affairs also the new goverment made a constructive start. Little credit for this could go to Menzies, for whom London was still a lodestar; he tended to feel that Australia should avoid too much enmeshment in South-East Asia in case Australian forces were required to help Britain in Europe or the Middle

East. On the other hand the Department of External Affairs and its minister, Spender, had a lively appreciation of the importance of South-East Asia. Spender was a major architect of the Colombo Plan, formulated in January 1950 to promote education, health and economic modernization in the less prosperous nations of that region. Australia would donate technological aid and expertise to countries such as India, Pakistan and Indonesia, and would admit and subsidize regular intakes of Asian students for Australian secondary and tertiary qualifications. If the scheme was intended partly to counter the appeal of communism, it also marked a bold and imaginative sharing of Australian resources which did something to soothe the effects of the White Australia Policy.

Quiet diplomacy of this kind was overshadowed by the outbreak of fighting in Korea. That country, liberated at the end of the war after thirty-five years of Japanese occupation, had been split at the 38th parallel, North Korea soon becoming one of the most authoritarian communist regimes and South Korea adopting western parliamentary forms under the leadership of a wilful ancient, Syngman Rhee. Late in June 1950 the North Koreans launched an invasion to reunify the country. Injudiciously they chose a moment when the Soviet Union was boycotting the United Nations and was hence unable to veto a resolution denouncing the act of aggression and authorizing American and allied troops to go to the rescue. MacArthur was put in charge of the operation and the Australian garrison in Japan was one of the first available forces to go into action. In September, after nearly the whole of South Korea was overrun, the allies counter-attacked, not only rolling the North Koreans back across the 38th parallel but thrusting deep into their territory. November found them within a short distance of the Chinese border. Unsure of MacArthur's intentions, the Chinese released volunteer forces to aid the North Koreans; MacArthur contemplated atomic attack, but was dissuaded and later dismissed for his refusal to obey civilian orders; and by mid-1951 the battle front stabilized not far from the original border where it remained while two tedious years of negotiation eventually led to a grudging but durable armistice.[30]

The Korean conflict could plausibly be described as Australia's last just war. The part played by the Royal Australian Regiment fell squarely within the tradition of quick support for major allies fighting aggression. In committing troops to Korea Australia reflected the thinking not of Menzies, who was overseas when the decision was taken and was concerned about Australia's British Commonwealth obligations, but of Spender and Fadden who were keen to promote a defence pact in the Pacific with the United States as the essential senior partner. But although the United States had recently made a commitment to a European alliance in the North Atlantic Treaty Organization, Washington saw the Western Pacific as more peripheral and doubted the feasibility of putting together a stable equivalent there. A higher priority was peace with Japan as a preliminary to concentrating on the containment of communism in Asia. Australians were still uneasy about Japan as a potential aggressor. No doubt the United States could have ignored these misgivings, but Spender ably argued the need for a formal security pact, and the Menzies government was a more comfortable ally than Evatt with his schemes for mobilizing the smaller members of the United Nations against domination by the super-powers. Early in 1951 the United States consented to negotiate a regional pact with Australia and New Zealand. This was signed in July and became ANZUS, for a generation a corner-stone of Australian foreign policy. The Americans thus gained a trouble-free acceptance of the Japanese peace treaty signed in September 1951. The British were chagrined at their exclusion from ANZUS, which could be seen as signalling Australia's permanent shift from a London-centred diplomacy to dependence on Washington. The Australian government viewed ANZUS as a valuable piece of insurance, the due reward for a prompt response when Anzacs were needed in Korea, although the words of the pact were not a guarantee of help against invasion; they simply committed each member to 'act to meet the common danger' if one of their number came under armed attack.[31]

Many of the utterances of the Menzies government during 1950 and 1951 suggested a grave sense of threat. Menzies returned from his overseas visit in 1950 forecasting that war would come within three years, but defence preparations were not much upgraded beyond requiring 18-year-olds to undergo six months' basic compulsory military training. It was still believed that Australia's role would comprise the supply of auxiliary troops to great allies. As Casey's brother-in-law, R. S. Ryan, told the House of Representatives: 'Australia is a second-class power and the first plank of its policy must be to choose its friends wisely, and having chosen them to gain their goodwill'.[32] The idea that Australia should assume greater responsibility for its own defence and foreign policies struck most government supporters as unrealistic.

Choosing powerful friends and gaining their goodwill had one great advantage as a defence policy. It was cheap. Labour would not be required at a time of full civilian employment, extra taxation need not be imposed for the defence budget, above all no new pressures would be loaded onto an economy where inflation was overheating. This last consideration was especially important. The Menzies government, as it must have known, could do nothing to put value back into the pound. Instead the Korean War heightened world demand for the stockpiling of wool and drove up prices to unprecedented levels. In 1950–51 wool accounted for nearly two-thirds of Australia's export income, earning over £633 million. Graziers and farmers suddenly found themselves replete with spending money.[33] Reluctantly they accepted Fadden's proposal to sequester 20 per cent of export earnings from wool as a reserve against future taxation, but only after the coalition nearly split asunder over a proposal to appreciate the value of the Australian pound on world currency markets. The Country Party would never agree to any such proposal as damaging to the export competitiveness of Australian primary products, and accepted Fadden's tax as a compromise.[34]

Even so, farm profits poured into the economy precisely at the moment when urban workers were enjoying the £1 increase in the basic wage with subsequent cost-of-living adjustments. Non-farm weekly wages rose by an average of 20 per cent in 1950–51 and by nearly 25 per cent in 1951–52. To this overstimulation of demand the abolition of petrol rationing in February 1950 made its modest contribution by fuelling the demand for motor vehicles and machinery; however, the effect on the balance of payments was not the disaster Chifley had feared because the United States was persuaded to accept from the sterling bloc commodities such as Australian wool in payment for its oil exports. The rate of inflation nevertheless accelerated beyond anything known in the 1940s, and by the early months of 1951 posed a threatening problem for the Menzies government.

The crusade against communism offered a welcome and popular diversion. At the spring session of federal parliament in 1950

Menzies brought forward legislation outlawing the Communist Party and seizing its assets. The Labor Opposition at first used its majority in the Senate to hold up this legislation—less from sympathy with communism than from libertarian views against banning any political party, coupled with a well-founded suspicion that left-wing Labor members would be harassed. Menzies openly threatened Tasmania's Senator Morrow and predicted that Eddie Ward would escape 'only by the skin of his teeth'.[35] Contrary to usual practice, the bill provided that where persons were accused of membership of a communist organization the onus of proof would rest with the defence, not the prosecution. Many who were far from communist in sympathy were disturbed by this; but within the Labor Party the Movement exerted all its influence in favour of the ban, and in October the federal executive instructed the Labor senators to let the legislation pass. The Communist Party, supported by several trade unions, appealed against the legislation to the High Court. Evatt in his capacity as a private lawyer accepted a brief as their counsel, although well aware that this would expose him to abuse as a communist sympathizer. But his arguments fared better than in previous encounters with the High Court. In March 1951 the judges found by a majority of six to one that (despite Korea) Australia was not in a state of war and therefore the federal government was not empowered to outlaw a political party. The only dissentient was Chief Justice Latham, who resigned in the following year and was replaced by Sir Owen Dixon.

Although Chifley was managing to contain the dissension in the Labor ranks over the communist issue it was a point of weakness too tempting to ignore. With difficult economic decisions ahead, Menzies decided to call an election. The federal Constitution provided that when a state of deadlock arose between the Senate and the House of Representatives the governor-general might grant a double dissolution of parliament and fresh elections. The expedient had been used only once, in 1914, and the ministry which tried it was decisively beaten; but Menzies found the omens more hopeful in the autumn of 1951. The governor-general, William McKell, was a former Labor premier of New South Wales, whose appointment in 1947 had been abused unmercifully by the Liberal—Country Party coalition, partly because he was appointed straight from the arena of partisan politics, but mostly because he was neither an English patrician nor a military officer. In office McKell conducted himself with great propriety, and he accepted the prime minister's advice as custom decreed. The pretext for the double dissolution was the Senate's refusal to pass the government's banking legis- lation, but during the election campaign most of the debate was about communism. When the results came in Menzies and his colleagues had their majority in the Senate, and although they lost five seats in the House of Representatives to Labor they were still left with a majority of seventeen.

Some changes in cabinet followed. Spender and Dame Enid Lyons, though each only in their mid-fifties, retired from politics on the grounds of ill-health. (Both subsequently had active and honourable public careers and survived well into their eighties.) Casey was moved to external affairs, where he maintained Spender's Asian interests but was less effectual against Menzies. A new member, Paul Hasluck, was brought in to commence a long and distinguished tenure in the department of territories. Essentially the Menzies government was the mixture as before, fortified by a renewed mandate from the voters. But a rebuff followed. In September 1951 the government submitted to the electorate a referendum seeking power to ban the Communist Party and retaining the controversial 'onus of proof' clause. Menzies campaigned with great eloquence, asserting that without such laws it would be impossible to curb subversion but assuring the public that only genuine communists would be affected. The 'No' case concentrated on the threat to liberty of the individual. There was a good deal of cross-voting as many right-wing Labor supporters were fiercely anti-communist and many habitual Liberal voters mistrusted any growth in government power. Besides, the Korean War had shown that communist military might was not unbeatable. By a margin of no more than 53 000 in a poll of 4.7 million voters—less than the number who contrived, even on so simple a question, to vote informal—Australia voted 'No'. Menzies was disappointed, but not much distressed. The Communist Party survived, and remained a useful bogey in political rhetoric, but grew every year less substantial.[36]

Three months before the referendum Australia turned to ceremonies which spoke of a more unifying influence: the fiftieth anniversary of the Australian Commonwealth. In Canberra the celebrations included a procession in which amateur actors got themselves up to impersonate prominent personalities of the

Wartime leaders: Prime Minister John Curtin and the US General Douglas Macarthur

Chifley, McKell, and a colleague at the inauguration ceremony for the Snowy Mountains hydro-electric scheme, 1949

Army volunteers for the Korean War, Victoria, 1950

Prefabricated housing factory, Manjimup, Western Australia, 1951:
one of many responses to the postwar housing shortage

federation era; Billy Hughes, the sole survivor in federal parliament of that distant period, took to his bed in disgust at seeing his likeness attempted by a self-confident parliamentary employee. The climax of the celebrations was a state ball conducted with much glitter and formality on the evening of 13 June 1951. Chifley, who was not a dancing man, retired to the Hotel Kurrajong to work on some papers. He had a heart attack and died within the hour. The festivities were interrupted at their height when a sombre Menzies informed the guests that they must go home; a fine Australian had died.

Five years later, at a memorial lecture in Chifley's honour, Heinz Arndt, one of those young European intellectuals who found refuge in the Australia of the 1940s, described Chifley's death as a great divide. He saw the heyday of Curtin and Chifley as a time when Labor was governed by principled aims: not socialism, but the quest for equality, security and democracy.[37] Five years on and L. F. Crisp, a sometime official of the Department of Postwar Reconstruction, wrote a biography in which he characterized Chifley as a sagacious practical reformer whose ideals had been denied by an Australian electorate too easily beguiled by appeals to self-indulgence.[38] Since then the Labor leaders of the 1940s have enjoyed a good press from the historians, except for one or two iconoclasts of the New Left who blame Curtin and Chifley for working within the framework of capitalism and for deliberately refusing to enrich the working class through wage rises and low taxation, preferably at the expense of company profits.[39] Such criticisms probably take an unrealistic view of the options that were open to any reformist social democracy during and just after the Second World War. The question remains: if the Labor governments between 1941 and 1949 were so constructive in their purposes why did they fail to endure?

Some blamed the hostility of the press. Relations between Labor and the media were never good after Calwell's interventions, and the Labor front bench seldom paid great attention to the style and content of their communications with the wider public. But the state Labor governments of New South Wales, Queensland and Tasmania flourished untroubled despite the press, and the federal party triumphed over media hostility in 1946. A survey in 1951 found much anti-Labor bias in editorial comment but very little in news reporting.[40] Nor could an adequate explanation be found in the coalition's free enterprise doctrines, since in practice the Menzies government was scarcely less interventionist than its predecessors. Keynesian thought still guided economic policy, social welfare was maintained, the arbitration system was upheld as the proper arena for resolving industrial problems. The communist issue loomed large because it was one of the few sharp divergences between the policies of the two parties, Labor's leadership believing that communism could be contained at home and abroad without extraordinary measures and the coalition insisting on a crusade. But this was largely a dispute over rhetoric and tactics rather than an indication of strong disagreements about the ultimate validity of Australian capitalism. The continuities before and after the 1949 election were greater than the changes.

Labor's thinking was doubly conditioned by the 'depression mentality': not only the crisis of the 1930s but, in cases such as Curtin and Chifley, memories of the hardship caused by the bank failures of the 1890s. In their eyes social justice could be achieved only if governments took power to regulate the workings of capitalism within Australia and to protect as far as possible Australia's position in the international world of trade and finance. The experience of the 1930s suggested that Australia was too dependent on a handful of primary exports and must diversify its productivity; that Australia must reduce its dependence on overseas borrowing and overseas technology and develop the capacity to generate its own capital and its own industrial skills; that Australia was underpopulated and must expand its domestic market; that Australia was too closely tied to Britain and must cultivate a variety of trading and defence partners rather than relying on a single protector; in short, that Australians must possess the collective self-confidence to take informed decisions about national priorities and aims, looking first to Australian interests.

Could such self-confidence have been fostered in the 1940s? The shock of war momentarily stilled the competing demands of state loyalties and created an environment favourable to Canberra's leadership. But Australians were not called upon to defend themselves from invasion. Instead they were obliged to accept American protection, reinforcing the belief that Australia was incapable of standing alone in an unfriendly world. By 1949 this sense of isolation was strengthened as traditional fear of

Asian 'hordes' was fused with fear of militant communism. In such circumstances it was easy for Australians to doubt their capacity for autonomy. They were also spared the stimulus of economic hardship. In the world of post-war recovery Australia's traditional exports were keenly sought. When the economy brought profits to employers and high wages to workers there was no incentive for change and no call for creative national planning. The Labor government had been preparing for a recession which was delayed for a generation. Australians thus grew sceptical about the merits of planning; it seemed too often like interference with the enjoyment of good things which were at last abundant. As Australians prepared to ride the boom they saw the politician's art as resembling the surfer's: unable to foresee or control the underlying waves and currents, and distinguished mainly by the ability to stay upright and look convincing.

Part II

The High Summer of Robert Menzies 1951–1965

The wise therefore rule by emptying hearts and stuffing bellies,
by weakening ambitions and strengthening bones,
If people lack knowledge and desire
then intellectuals will not try to interfere.
If nothing is done, then all will be well.

Lao Tsu, *Tao Te Ching*, 3 (tr. Gia-Fu Feng & Jane English)

4

GETTING AND SPENDING

SIR ROBERT MENZIES remained in office for sixteen years, finishing in January 1966 as the only Australian prime minister since the First World War to retire at a time of his own choosing. This is a mark both of his political skill and the disarray of his Labor opponents, but more than either it reflects the economic buoyancy of the 1950s and the 1960s when political change came seldom. (Apart from Western Australia no state government lost office between 1947 and 1965 except as a sequel to a split in the ranks of the ruling party.) In political and economic terms Australia was a model of stability in a fast-changing world. To the extent that the Menzies government presented a reassuring image of resolute anti-communism and fidelity to great and powerful allies it could claim credit for creating an attractive environment for large-scale investors of overseas capital. But it must be noted that Australia's progress was matched by most advanced capitalist nations. Some did better. Nevertheless the Menzies era enjoyed in retrospect a nostalgic reputation for prosperity with only a few to cry it down as a time of 'limited personal affluence and public squalor'.[1]

The fact is that when Menzies retired in 1966 most Australians, recently migrant or otherwise, seem to have thought themselves better off than they were fifteen years ago, and by most measures of material progress they were right. During each year of Menzies's prime ministership the average weekly earnings of the

Australian worker increased by about 4 per cent in real terms. This represented roughly five times the annual average rate of advance in living standards between 1901 and 1940.[2] Critics have argued that 'the increased ownership of consumer durables and housing was at the expense of increased leisure and was achieved by substantial increases in indebtedness',[3] and indisputably too many Australians, not all of them Aborigines, missed out on the good things of life. When Ronald Henderson discovered in 1966 that at least 4 per cent of Melbourne families lived below the poverty line he was describing nothing new.[4] But the comparable figure for the United Kingdom was 14 per cent and for the United States nearly 20 per cent, and unemployment was lower than at any period in Australian history, standing at 1.2 per cent in 1950 and at precisely the same figure in August 1965. In the years between, the figure climbed no higher than 3.2 per cent in late 1961 and early 1962. That was the only moment to shake the stability of the Menzies regime. It was understandable that in 1964, when Donald Horne published *The Lucky Country*,[5] many readers took the name at face value and failed to notice the sardonic implication that Menzies's economic success was the result of good fortune rather than good management.

Australia's good fortune during the 1950s and the 1960s was founded on a continually expanding world trade and a stable international monetary system, both largely the result of measures initiated by the United States to safeguard western capitalism. Between 1952 and 1965 Australian gross domestic product rose annually at a little less than 5 per cent, a rate somewhat greater than that of the United States or Britain, but barely half the performance of Japan or the German Federal Republic (both recovering from wartime loss with American aid). Britain remained Australia's major trading partner and largest source of investment, providing more than half the overseas capital for Australian enterprises until 1960—61. During the next five years the United States drew level, each country then providing over 40 per cent. Coincidentally with Menzies's retirement British investment slumped to 23.3 per cent in 1966—67, reflecting a sterling crisis in which Harold Wilson's government restricted capital exports from the City of London, giving preference to Third World nations in need of development. Even this was not much of a turning point. Britain was to bounce back as Australia's major supplier of investment capital in the late 1960s and again in the late 1970s. The ties between Australia and Britain depended on much more than Menzies's sentimentality about the royal family.

Export growth was fostered by a vigorous demand for Australia's traditional rural products; they generated more than three-quarters of Australia's export income until 1956–57, and over two-thirds until 1965–66. Metals and minerals accounted for no more than 10 per cent of exports, rising to 13.8 per cent in 1965–66 with the departure of the first shipments of iron ore and open-cut coal. Britain's share of Australia's exports reached a post-war peak of 41.3 per cent in 1952–53 but then fell steadily. The shape of the future was sketched in 1961–62 when Britain sought unsuccessfully to enter the European Economic Community (EEC), for although few foresaw how far European farm subsidies would eventually oust Australia from traditional markets it must have been evident that Britain would increasingly look for trading partners among its near neighbours.

The quest for new export markets dominated Australian trade policy during the 1950s and 1960s when John McEwen as minister was backed by two very able public servants, Sir John Crawford and Sir Alan Westerman. Australian exports to the United States remained constant at between 8 and 10 per cent, leaving an unfavourable balance of trade which was rectified by probing new markets in South and East Asia. Even China, officially scorned as a pariah that might at any moment plunge the region into a major war, was trusted as a buyer of Australian wheat who could be granted easy terms. Japan, having embarked upon the Pacific war in 1941 partly to force open new markets and sources of raw material denied by the United States and Britain, now found itself welcomed as a customer. Trade with Australia resumed in 1949, and in 1957 the two countries signed a formal agreement under which Japan promised to admit Australian wool and cotton at favourable rates and Australia agreed to impose no discriminatory tariffs against Japanese goods without prior consultation. By 1965–66 Japan was taking 17 per cent of exports and would shortly overtake Britain as Australia's best customer.[6]

Wool, more than any other single industry throughout the 1950s and 1960s, was the great mainstay of Australia's export trade. Pastoralists and graziers benefited enormously from successful experiments in 1950 by CSIRO scientists in introducing myxomatosis, a lethal infection which wiped out a large proportion of Australia's rabbit population. Spared this competition for good grazing, sheep numbers grew unprecedentedly. Between 1950 and 1965 they rose from 113 to 171 million, and wool production from 518 000 to 819 000 tonnes. Yet behind this expansion a nagging doubt lurked. The needs of wartime had accelerated the production of artificial fibres such as rayon and nylon which competed with wool on world markets. Drought, industrial disputes (a long shearers' strike in Queensland in 1956), and the uncertainties of the auction market could all have unpredictable effects on the price and quality of the wool clip, whereas the synthetics could be costed and quantified more reliably. Thoughtful authorities in the wool industry began to seek a more orderly system of marketing. In 1953 the federal government set up the Australian Wool Bureau to promote wool sales at home and overseas. Inveterate individualists, Australia's wool-growers were unwilling to co-operate further in marketing their product and, in 1965, despite the earnest advocacy of the industry's most prominent leader, Sir William Gunn, rejected a scheme for imposing a minimum price on wool sold at auction. Thus a major Australian export remained perilously dependent on the health of overseas markets.[7]

The profitability of wool nevertheless encouraged many wheat farmers to convert arable land into pasture. Of more than 5 million hectares under wheat during the late 1940s more than a quarter was put to other uses during the 1950s. The governments of South and Western Australia reacted by opening up light lands in marginal rainfall areas to attract new settlers. By the end of the decade wheat was recovering favour because of international price agreements. In 1960 China was opened as a market which by 1962–63 was taking half of Australia's exports. Production leaped, reaching a maximum of 307 million bushels in 1962–63. But the old dream of a small-farming yeomanry was dead. The new breed of wheat-growers were agrarian capitalists working large acreages and investing heavily in labour-saving machinery. Their clearing was done by bulldozers and hi-ball units, and their crops cultivated by large disc ploughs and harrows. The sugar industry of Queensland and northern New South Wales produced its own yeomanry because producers were restricted to quotas which kept farms small. Mechanization at first took the form of bulk handling for sugar, introduced at five major ports between 1957 and 1964. It was only in the 1970s that cane-harvesting machinery was designed cheaply enough to do away with the traditional gangs of itinerant cane-cutters. Meanwhile, protected by a British Commonwealth sugar agreement lasting from 1953 to 1971, the Queensland growers enjoyed a minor boom when the United States boycotted Castro's Cuba in 1960. But the long-term prospects for the industry were limited.

British readiness to end post-war food shortages by long-term agreements also benefited Australia's meat producers. Between 1952 and 1967 Australian beef and mutton found a guaranteed minimum price in the United Kingdom. From 1959 the United States surpassed the United Kingdom as an importer of Australian beef, and this market was secured by an agreement in 1964. The strongest demand was for hamburger beef as the open-range conditions of northern Australia's cattle stations did not produce beasts of gourmet quality. Despite some American investment and the acclimatization of Brahman-cross cattle, the 1950s and 1960s saw little improvement. Dairy cattle, on the other hand, improved steadily in quality and yield, but Australia's butter and milk exports were vulnerable to overseas competition, and numbers stabilized in 1957 at around 5 million while farmers awaited Britain's negotiations with the EEC. Smaller rural industries—forestry, fruit-growing, cotton—showed no great potential for export growth, and some products such as flax and tobacco were in trouble despite substantial government aid. Other expedients would have to be sought if Australia's export trade was to diversify.

Many looked to mining as Australia's economic saviour. Admittedly the traditional leader, gold, was going through a period of decline, but the ten years after the end of the war saw a boom in demand for base metals and strategic materials, private enterprise following the exploratory work of the Bureau of Mineral Resources. Foremost among the exploring companies was the Zinc Corporation (later Comalco), whose director of exploration, Maurice Mawby, promoted investigations into oil, silver-lead, pyrites, phosphate, scheelite and bauxite, as well as the company's established concerns with lead and zinc.[8] No mineral in the early 1950s seemed to hold out so much promise as uranium, and no shadow of doubt clouded the quest for it. Radiation was little feared at a time when compulsory X-rays were standard practice and Australia's major allies were building nuclear power plants. Labor politicians hailed nuclear energy as a clean source of technology which might eliminate the need for underground coal-miners; the veteran radical Leslie Haylen hoped that uranium would make Australia prosperous enough to support a population of 50 million and had to be reminded that Australia could not afford her own reactor for ten years.[9] The Bureau of Mineral Resources actively promoted uranium exploration. Geiger-counters ticked across northern and central Australia, and between 1949 and 1954 finds were announced at Radium Creek (South Australia), Rum Jungle (Northern Territory) and Mary Kathleen (Queensland). The federal government entrusted development to major mining firms and arranged for uranium sales to the Anglo-American Central Development Agency.

Meanwhile Britain, anxious to keep step as a great power, wanted to develop its own atomic weapons. Since the British Isles are too crowded for convenient testing Australian space was requested. The Australian government took advice from a recently arrived Englishman, Professor Ernest Titterton, who had made his reputation as a physicist serving the Anglo-American atomic tests and brooked no doubt about the safety and value of nuclear energy. Thus fortified, Menzies consented without consulting cabinet or parliament, though both later unanimously accepted the necessary legislation when Menzies assured them there could be 'no conceivable injury to life, limb, or property'.[10]

The tests were carried out between 1952 and 1957, with smaller-scale sequels until 1963. For the first tests the Monte Bello Islands off Onslow (Western Australia) and Emu Field (South Australia) were used. The rest took place at a custom-built test-site at Maralinga, 35 kilometres north of the transcontinental railway near Ooldea (South Australia). Throughout, the tests were an exercise in futility. Britain was not enabled to become an independent nuclear power. Australia gained very little useful scientific information or technical assistance. At Maralinga the local Aborigines were ousted from their traditional lands without compensation and reduced to the status of fringe-dwellers on alien ground; some became contaminated by radiation. Several tests exceeded the set maximum in fallout levels and were inadequately monitored against the spread of radioactive fallout over inhabited parts of Australia. In 1956, after tests at the Monte Bello Islands, the wind shifted to the mainland, and it is claimed that the acting prime minister, Sir Arthur Fadden, cabled London: 'What the bloody hell is going on, the cloud is drifting over the mainland?'. It would not have been out of character but, because of the strict secrecy imposed on the tests, there was no outcry. Smoothly Titterton continued to reassure the public: 'Australia has great desert areas and also some little-used seas about her shores . . . We are glad to have the opportunity of helping the Commonwealth defence effort in the development of weapons which are a threat to no-one'.[11] In 1957 the Menzies government tried to buy some atomic bombs for Australia, but Britain would not sell.

Titterton's senior colleague at the Australian National University, Mark Oliphant, was left out of the tests. He was an iconoclast about nuclear weapons and official secrecy. Instead he concentrated on a valiant but ill-starred effort to put together a giant particle accelerator of world status. To many Australians in those years Oliphant was 'Mr Science'. There is a photograph of him and his team at the synchrocyclotron receiving a visit from H. C. Coombs and other public servants; the scientists look like a delphic priesthood receiving homage at a shrine. In some ways Oliphant was to Australian science what Evatt was to foreign policy: a talented nationalist seeking to promote his country's standards by the exercise of personal skills and will-power, but doomed to failure because the resources to back his dream simply were not available. Eventually Oliphant's team had to settle for a more modest construction and by that time the United States had gained a lead in the production of cheaper and more efficient methods.[12]

Meanwhile an Australian Atomic Energy Commission was set up in 1957 under the chairmanship of Philip Baxter, another keen advocate of nuclear power who wanted Australia to develop its own atomic bombs. The Commission's headquarters were at Lucas Heights, south of Sydney. From 1958 radio-isotopes were produced for medical and technological purposes. The commission's long-term aim was the generation of electricity through nuclear power, as many politicians hoped that nuclear power stations using advanced forms of fast-breeder reactor would encourage decentralization and reduce Australia's dependence on oil imports. But, as the minister for development, Sir William Spooner, said, 'the use of nuclear power will depend very largely upon a hard-headed business appraisal by the State electricity commissions'.[13] A nuclear power station required heavy capital outlay, and electricity could be generated more cheaply by coal and hydro-electricity. So, more by accident than design, Australia was spared controversy about the uses of nuclear power. Meanwhile overseas demand for uranium fell below early expectations. By 1964 all but one mine producing yellowcake had ceased operation.

Base metals held the key to the future. In 1960 the Commonwealth government decided to raise the embargo on iron-ore exports imposed in 1938 in the mistaken belief that Australia's reserves were limited. Improved shipping and railway technology meant that deposits previously thought inaccessible could be worked for profitable export. The raising of the ban was followed by the revelation of several immense deposits in the Pilbara district of Western Australia. International capitalists were soon attracted to the scene, and Japan came to the fore as an eager but canny customer. By 1965 Western Australia's capable minister, Charles Court, had negotiated agreements with four major consortia for the construction of towns, railways, and port facilities to handle the promising export trade which began in that year.[14]

Nor was this all. Bauxite was developed at Weipa in North Queensland following its rediscovery there in 1955, and at various places along the Darling Range of Western Australia in the early 1960s. The search for oil and natural gas, having survived the disappointment of a momentary excitement at Rough Range in Western Australia in 1953, was rewarded by small finds in Queensland, first of natural gas at Roma, then in April 1964 of commercial quantities of oil at Moonie. Hopes were high for further finds. Meanwhile coal remained Australia's staple fuel. The underground coal-mines of New South Wales, benefiting from improved mechanization and greater industrial tranquillity, remained the leading producer, and from 1959 they were to be substantially reinforced by developments in central Queensland. Here open-cut coal-mining came to be dominated by two multinationals, the Utah Development Company based in San Francisco, and a consortium in which the largest American coal company, Peabody, held a majority shareholding with Japanese and Australian junior partners.[15] Both firms found Japanese customers for long-term contracts at low prices. The Queensland government provided support in the form of railways and port facilities. Gladstone, pushed as the major port for coal exports, was also selected in 1964 as the site of an alumina plant to refine Weipa bauxite. All these developments were to bring Queensland, like Western Australia, into much greater prominence for overseas investors, and before long were to strengthen the muscle of these two states within the federal system. Freely welcoming multinational company investment, and alert to the promise of Japan and other Asian markets, these states would chafe at the different priorities of a Canberra which they saw as too much dominated by the interests of Victoria and New South Wales who had already enjoyed industrial growth. In the mid-1960s these changes were not fully foreseen. Australia's mineral developments and exports were only a foreshadowing of the future.

Wool, wheat and minerals ensured a favourable balance of trade for Australia in most years between 1949–50 and 1965–66. During that time Britain remained Australia's major source of imports, though declining from 52 to 26 per cent. Meanwhile the American share rose from 10 to 24 per cent and Japan's from small beginnings to nearly 9 per cent. In 1951–52, as the wool boom receded, imports temporarily exceeded exports by over 50 per cent and inflation soared to 20 per cent. The Menzies government reacted by imposing comprehensive import restrictions in March 1952. They were a rather blunt instrument for fine-tuning the economy and were held responsible for a sharp temporary increase in unemployment, but they stayed throughout the 1950s as a protection for Australian jobs. In fact it was estimated that no more than a quarter of Australia's imports could be seen as competitive with local products, and no more than 20 per cent consisted of consumer goods.

Australian manufacturing was largely geared to the needs of a thriving home market. According to the 1961 census 10.5 million Australians were housed in slightly fewer than 2.8 million dwellings. For these households Australian manufacturers produced in the five years from mid-1958 to mid-1963 a million refrigerators, a million electric or gas stoves, a million petrol-driven lawn-mowers, half a million vacuum cleaners, two million wireless sets, and a million and a half television sets, as well as large quantities of clothing and furniture. About a million and half motor bodies were produced, slightly more than the number of new vehicles registered during that period. Most of these products were protected against competitive imports. About 60 per cent of Australian secondary industry was covered by tariffs. Spokesmen for manufacturing interests such as Sir Charles McGrath of Repco or the electrical goods magnate Sir Arthur Warner were deep in the counsels of the Liberal Party. Although Menzies tried to keep his distance from the sectional interests that had used him when younger, the government seldom listened to Tariff Board recommendations to cut protection. Trade unions saw the tariff as creating jobs, and were at one with employers in defending it.[16]

In February 1960 the Menzies government ended import licensing as a check to inflation, only to find Australian trade under new international pressures. In 1961 the United States sponsored the Kennedy Round of tariff revision which was designed to free international trade by persuading members of GATT to cut duties by 50 per cent on a wide range of manufactured goods. At the same time Britain sought to join the EEC, a move favoured by the United States as strengthening anti-communism but mistrusted by Australian and New Zealand exporters. McEwen was able to secure Australian exemption from the Kennedy Round but had no luck in negotiating with the Europeans for special treatment if Britain joined the EEC. As he later said: 'We were never able to shake off the image of a rich country that was able to look after itself'.[17] Because of this image problem McEwen insisted that Menzies drop a junior minister, Leslie Bury, from office for claiming that Australia would not be much harmed if Britain entered the EEC. Australia was reprieved early in 1963 when the French vetoed Britain's application.

McEwen took advantage of the breathing space by pushing tariff protection yet higher. He overruled the Tariff Board whose chairman, Sir Leslie Melville, vainly pointed out that tariff protection often diverted Australia's scarce resources of capital into high-cost industries which made relatively little contribution to the national income. This left the highly profitable mining and pastoral industries dependent on foreign investors whose dividends went out of Australia.[18] A growing mutter of concern was also arising from mineral exporters and the governments of Queensland and Western Australia who feared that the Japanese would resent a consistently unfavourable balance of trade unless their access to Australian markets improved. But while McEwen dominated trade policy there would be no concessions.

The strengths and weaknesses of McEwen's approach could be seen in the motor vehicle industry. General Motors-Holden's, although largely dependent on imported technology and exporting big profits to an overseas parent company, was a prime example of an 'Australian' business protected by tariffs. Between 1953 and 1971 the firm commanded at least a third, and in some years such as 1958 one-half, of the domestic market for cars. Some of the benefits of protection trickled down to the consumer. In 1948 an employee on the basic wage would have needed to save 94 weeks' pay to afford a new Holden sedan; by 1965 it would have taken less than half that time.[19] Encouraged by General Motors-Holden's success four competitors set up Australian factories, so that by the early 1960s the industry employed between 80 000 and 100 000 workers, at least four-fifths of them migrants who worked hard and monotonously to accumulate money for an independent start elsewhere. In addition over 150 000 Australians made their living servicing the motor vehicles on Australian roads. With five manufacturers competing there were too many models for too small a local market, and the factories were not geared to practise economies of scale or to ensure consistent standards of workmanship. In 1964, seeking to appease local manufacturers of spare parts and components, the Menzies government decreed that Australian-built motor vehicles could contain no more than 5 per cent imported parts, and in 1966 the tariff on motor vehicles was raised from 35 to 45 per cent. Thus protected, the motor-vehicle industry lapsed into lethargy instead of using the respite to improve and cheapen its product. Instead, car design aped American standards of opulence. Similar stories could be told of other heavily protected industries. Menzies and McEwen gave them a suspension of competition without insisting on improved performance in research and technology or a more aggressive quest for new markets.

Applied research was left to the CSIRO and the universities. Under the leadership of Sir Ian Clunies Ross and Sir Frederick White the CSIRO made numerous advances in rural and commercial technology, among them the introduction of myxomatosis, the eradication of pleuro-pneumonia in cattle, the development of pasture plants such as Townsville lucerne and Siratio, the acclimatization of the dung-beetle, the first experiments in artificial rain-making, the identification of cobalt deficiency in South Australian soils, the improvement of self-twisting yarn in wool-spinning, and the surveys which led to the prawning industry in the Gulf of Carpentaria.[20] But the CSIRO was regarded mainly as a support for primary industry, which provided 20 per cent of its funding. Secondary industry contributed virtually nothing. When attempts were made around 1960 to foster chemical engineering the petrochemical companies gave minimal support, preferring to base their plans on overseas developments. Sections of the mining industry on the other hand were consistently research-minded; for example Consolidated Zinc, as well as supporting its own metallurgical scientists, maintained liaison with the CSIRO in industrial chemistry and tribophysics.

University research during the 1940s depended almost entirely on the interests and energy of senior staff. Universities were often starved of funds; at the University of Tasmania 'some laboratories in the old building closely resembled representations of alchemists' laboratories found in books on the early history of chemistry'.[21] The war pushed university scientists into many unpremeditated forms of research such as the adaptation of sulpha drugs and penicillin, the exploitation of low-grade mineral, timber and agricultural resources, the improvement of synthetic foodstuffs and materials, and the exploration of the uses of radar in radio astronomy and physics. Following a lead given by the University of Melbourne in 1948 the PhD came to be recognized as an increasingly essential qualification in research training. Research blossomed, particularly after the Menzies government adopted the recommendations of the Murray Report in 1957 and initiated Commonwealth funding of universities. The Australian National University achieved excellence in at least two of its sections, the John Curtin School of Medical Research and the observatory at Mt Stromlo under the leadership of Richard Woolley and Bart Bok. Through the latter's collaboration with the CSIRO division of radio physics Australia acquired a radio telescope at Parkes and an interferometer at Narrabri, thus by 1960 winning a high reputation in astronomy.

Respected scientists urged the need for a purposeful research strategy. Sir Frederick White of the CSIRO argued that Australian scientific research was excessively fragmented. In a presidential address to ANZAAS (the Australian and New Zealand Association for the Advancement of Science) in 1962 Bok urged the creation of an Australian National Science Foundation. He was concerned at the increasing age of Australia's scientific leadership: 'Surprisingly little responsibility is given to the younger Australian scientists', said Bok, 'Far too often the approach is: "He is still young, he can wait"'. And he criticized the slowness of Australian universities to enter the computer field. His university had only just been persuaded to buy its first IBM for astronomy—three years after the Bank of New South Wales and Mount Isa Mines, at least five after the first academic application of computing by Harry Messel, professor of physics at the University of Sydney and a recent arrival from North America.[22] It was 1962 before the Australian Bureau of Census and Statistics introduced computers.

Private enterprise was laggardly. Of 629 scientists who took higher degrees in chemistry between 1945 and 1963 only 13 per cent were employed in industry, 27 per cent had gone overseas, and nearly half were employed by the government or universities.[23] Whereas in 1953 nearly half the patents taken out in Australia were of Australian origin, by 1961 the Australian number had declined slightly, while overseas patents had nearly doubled.[24] Investigating Australian manufacturing in 1963, S. H. Bastow of the CSIRO found that of seventy-five firms, only eight were sympathetic to innovation, and only one could claim to be a world leader. Very few held scientific libraries. Bastow, like Bok, complained that management was dominated by older men who thought 'in terms of what they remember of their own understanding of technology twenty or thirty years ago'.[25]

Bastow and Bok spoke out at one of the rare moments when they might have secured a receptive audience. For the Menzies government was alarmed at its narrow escape from electoral defeat after the economic downturn of 1961, and in a repentant mood set up a five-man committee of inquiry into the economy. Chaired by the general manager of Colonial Sugar, Sir James Vernon, and including among its members McEwen's veteran adviser J. G. Crawford, the committee was set impossibly wide terms of reference but represented an Australian government's first major effort since the Royal Commission on Banking of the 1930s to seek an impartial and authoritative overview of economic problems. When the Vernon Committee submitted its report to the prime minister in 1965 one of its recommendations drew attention to the inadequacy of industrial research and development in the private sector and urged its encouragement by federal support. It would be twelve precious years before anything was done about this recommendation.

The Vernon Report was in no sense a radical document, and some of its detailed findings were disputed by economists, but it represented a consensus by five experienced observers and merited serious attention.[26] In brief, it set Australia a target of 5 per cent annual economic growth, advocated the orderly development of Australia's resources, cautioned against large increases in government spending, and predicted a shift into services and tertiary industry which could create a stronger demand for the employment of women. The Vernon Committee opposed the massive inflow of outside capital, fearing that this would upset Australia's balance of payments and run up unacceptably high levels of overseas debt. Instead Australia should accumulate capital through boosting exports and encouraging local investment. To monitor the fluctuations of the economy a qualified federal advisory council to the Commonwealth government should be set up along lines already adopted by conservative governments in Britain and de Gaulle's France.

As it was the fate of the Trojan priestess Cassandra that her prophecies were never believed, so Menzies abruptly rejected the findings of the Vernon Committee. It would create, he pontificated, a coercive influence on governments. By this he really meant that if a government was known to be receiving considered advice on economic management from a panel of experts it would be harder to take unsound but popular decisions for short-term political advantage, thus depriving governments like his own of opportunities for beguiling the electors. He was also influenced by the Treasury, which feared loss of influence if a federal economic council came into being, and probably also by McEwen who was discomfited by the Vernon Committee's criticisms of aspects of his high tariff policies. So, at a point when Australia's affairs were prospering and long-term economic decisions could be taken in an atmosphere unusually free from crisis, the opportunity was wasted. Donald Horne was right. Australia would simply count on remaining 'the lucky country'.

National economic planning and technological innovation were undervalued in an Australia whose voters believed themselves to be prospering under the established order of things. This belief was not grounded in the use of Australia's wealth to provide comprehensive social welfare for its citizens. Despite the leeway created by the Curtin and Chifley governments, Australia in 1950, although one of the richest of advanced nations, spent less than most on social security—in terms of gross domestic product only three-quarters of that spent by the United States, barely half that of the United Kingdom and less than half that of New Zealand.[27] The Menzies government brought in few new measures of social security. After extending child endowment to first-born children and introducing Page's medical benefits scheme, its initiatives were confined to care of the aged. In December 1954 federal funding became available for churches and other non-profit groups interested in building retirement villages for the elderly, an important safeguard of independence for retired people who might otherwise have to choose between loneliness and moving in with their married children; and in 1962 special hospital benefits were introduced for pensioners. But during the 1950s and 1960s the proportion of national expenditure devoted to social welfare steadily fell. Maternity allowances and child endowment were not indexed against inflation and were never raised. To the Menzies government and the voters who regularly supported it, there was no need to increase government welfare spending at a time of full employment and rising living standards.

The trade unions, which in those years included about 57 per cent of all wage and salary earners, were behaving less militantly than they had in the 1940s. After 1951, and especially after 1955, strikes were shorter and fewer. Communist union leaders, with their emphasis on the class struggle, lost ground to more prag-matic officials who concentrated on pay and conditions and often used a short stoppage as a warning to management of an issue in need of resolution. The coal-miners remained the greatest mili-tants during the 1950s, but production improved steadily. Sir Ian McLennan of BHP gave the credit to the Menzies government for funding housing on the coalfields, thus removing an old source of grievance and facilitating the employment of migrants.[28] Employers learned from wartime experience the value of per-sonnel management; by 1949 nearly half of Australia's large manufacturers had personnel officers, and in 1959 BHP took on an industrial chaplain. Greater attention was also paid to industrial safety. A national conference in Canberra in 1958 was followed by the formation of industrial divisions in the state branches of the National Safety Council. By the mid-1960s training schemes for industrial safety officers were in operation, and in accident-prone areas such as the timber industry casualty rates fell sharply as a result.

At the same time employers were also turning to automation,

though still lagging by international standards. In 1957 the Peak Frean biscuit company in Sydney claimed that in three years productivity had been increased threefold and labour costs halved as a result of automation.[29] Workers were unenthusiastic about such changes because some lost their jobs and others found less scope for the exercise of their skills and judgement. With less to satisfy them in the workplace, Australian workers sought greater leisure time and improved conditions. Between 1951 and 1958 the states, beginning with New South Wales, introduced long-service leave. Paid annual holidays, originally introduced for one week in the late 1930s, were extended to three weeks between 1959 and 1963, again with New South Wales in the lead. The quest for improved conditions turned white-collar unions into vigorous lobbyists; thus the bank officers, who since the nationalization debate of 1947–49 had nearly all voted Liberal, mended their links with Labor in the process of campaigning for the 5-day working week which their Tasmanian colleagues had enjoyed since 1945. Between 1958 and 1963 all the mainland states legislated to allow Saturday closing.[30]

Despite these successes the unions experienced uneven fortunes over the central issue of wages. In September 1953 the Commonwealth Arbitration Court ceased its thirty-year-old practice of granting automatic quarterly adjustments to the basic wage, belatedly bowing to claims by the government and employers that such increases had fuelled the inflation of 1950–51. Between 1953 and 1959 the real value of the federal basic wage fell by 5 per cent as a result. The stronger unions responded by putting their efforts into negotiating for special awards, especially for margins for skill over and above the basic wage. Between 1953 and 1967 the metal trades unions established a reputation as ringleaders, partly because their employers were mainly large, prosperous corporations such as BHP which could absorb extra costs because they enjoyed tariff protection. Where the metal trades unions established a precedent other unions and even professional staff could follow. Ultimately the Arbitration Court's policy on margins was inflationary because an industry's capacity to pay higher wages was counted twice, once as a forecast for estimating margins and again retrospectively in assessing basic wage rates. But while inflation remained gentle and manufacturers were protected by tariffs, employers on the whole were prepared to go along with these increases. Wage rates came to be governed by an ever more complicated accumulation of case law, calling for increasingly sophisticated arguments by trade unions and employers' organizations, and gradually to the recruitment, on both sides, of economists and professional research staff. It was as the academically qualified research officer to the ACTU that the young Bob Hawke gained his first foothold in national politics.[31] These developments fostered a growing post-war tendency towards the consolidation of trade unions into larger units.

The Menzies government responded by reshaping the federal arbitration system to allow for greater specialization of function. The matter became pressing in March 1956 when in response to an appeal by the Boilermakers' Union the High Court ruled by a four to three margin that the Arbitration Court did not possess judicial authority and could not impose fines or penalties. The Menzies government set up an Industrial Court possessing these powers, and a Conciliation and Arbitration Commission which among its other duties determined wages. Although wage-fixing was no longer part of the judicial process, the commission continued to see its main function as the containment of industrial disputes, and employers often criticized it for paying more attention to the cost of living than to productivity or the economic consequences of its decisions. Eventually, at the 1967 national wage case, the commission yielded to employer pressure and imposed a 'total wage' instead of conducting separate hearings for the basic wage and margins.

The emphasis on margins disadvantaged unskilled workers. Between 1950–51 and 1965–66 average weekly earnings in money terms increased by 250 per cent, but the basic wage and the adult female minimum only doubled. All wage levels consistently rose somewhat faster than prices, but the poor benefited least. One Victorian estimate computed that between 1957 and 1964, while average weekly earnings rose by 18.3 per cent, earnings of the professional classes were up by between 27 and 38 per cent, with dentists securing an increase of 61 per cent.[32] Women were also disadvantaged because their wages were pegged to a percentage of the basic male rate. The post-war trend of moving women out of the workforce did not last beyond 1952, when the female share of trade union membership stood at 17.3 per cent. Then gradually numbers rose again. Perhaps the recession of 1952–53 sent married women out to work. Certainly a significant part was played by migrant wives prepared to accept comparatively poor wages and conditions as part of the struggle to become established. It remained difficult for educated women to enter the professions because in many quarters marriage was thought to lead to permanent incapacity. In 1956 the Victorian Education Department admitted married women to the teaching service, but it was more than ten years before all Australian universities followed this precedent, and 1966 before the Commonwealth Public Service did so. Sex prejudice was also strong in private enterprise. Until 1966 General Motors-Holden's never authorized a woman to run a rural agency. But there was no industrial equivalent of the public service bar on marriage, and married women found a niche in some areas of the private sector.

Migrants were not blocked by law, but their advancement in the workforce did not come easily. About 2 million post-war migrants had arrived by the end of 1963. After the supply of refugees from the Second World War began to dwindle the Australian government in 1951–52 signed migration agreements with seven European countries (Spain in 1958 became an eighth), but by the 1960s as prosperity returned to continental Europe the bulk of assisted passages went to British settlers. Fewer than half the migrants were British. Of the others Italians formed the largest group; then came the Greeks, Dutch, Yugoslavs, Germans, Poles and a score of others. Fewer than a quarter of the non-British newcomers were qualified as skilled workers. Regardless of their previous qualifications they often had to take work as factory hands or labourers. They received little protection from trade unions, for although their pay and conditions were covered by awards they suffered from various discriminatory practices and were usually the first to be laid off in times of economic downturn.

Assimilation was the great goal of migration policy. It was taken for granted that there was a prototype Australian—a male home-owner with one wife, three children, a mortgage at the bank, a Holden in the garage, Fosters in the fridge, and Collingwood or St George to cheer on winter afternoons. Lithuanians, Greeks, Germans and Portuguese would abandon most of their cultural baggage and conform to these Australian folkways. 'We must have a single culture', asserted Bill Snedden, minister for immigration in the late 1960s and formerly a migration officer in Italy:

if immigration implied multicultural activities within Australian society, then it was not the type of Australia wanted. I am quite determined we should have a monoculture, with everyone living in the same way, understanding each other, and sharing the same aspirations. We don't want pluralism.[33]

Despite the efforts of such officially-backed voluntary organizations as the Good Neighbour Council there were no deeply considered guidelines about what was involved in being Australian. The conventional wisdom could be found in John O'Grady's popular novel *They're a Weird Mob*.[34] This purported to be the memoirs of a 'New Australian' from Italy. As a 'Dago', Nino Culotta might have expected to meet prejudice. Fortunately he is no swarthy peasant southerner but a blond Piedmontese male journalist. Despite early difficulties with Australian slang he is soon accepted by the rough-and-ready Sydney workers as a mate and an equal, learns to enjoy beer and football, and ends up by happily marrying a local girl and shaking his head over his compatriots who persist in conversing in their mother tongue. The popularity of this novel suggests that most Australians expected assimilation to work in this way. A survey in Perth in the early 1960s found that nearly two-thirds of those interviewed thought that migrants should be naturalized as soon as possible and discouraged from speaking their native tongues in public.[35] Nino and the like would be absorbed effortlessly into the Australian democracy.

It was seldom so easy. Giovanni Sgro arrived as a penniless youth in 1952 and for the first six months lived with an Aboriginal family at Cobram in the Murray valley. Thirty-four years later, having become deputy president of the Victorian Legislative Council, he still complained of police harassment and colleagues who called him 'wog' behind his back.[36] Migrant hostels were uninviting. Food was mass-produced, monotonous and Anglo-Saxon. Tom Hungerford, who worked at Canberra's Eastlake in the 1950s, wrote of the migrants' quarters: 'They weren't given a great deal to cherish—a bare and impersonal unshielded light globe hanging from the centre of the ceiling. Bare boards in rooms and corridors; an ice-chest in winter and an oven in summer, and usually a noisy drunk in the room next door'. Such conditions encouraged inmates to find work quickly and leave, but in periods of recession there were few jobs for foreigners, and discontent grew. Italian migrants demonstrated at Bonegilla camp in north-eastern Victoria in July 1952 and again in 1961, both times of economic downturn. In 1952 there was also a hunger strike at Melbourne's Maribyrnong camp and demonstrations at Sydney central railway station and at Amberley in Queensland. These outbreaks were played down by the press, and as prosperity returned migrants were gradually absorbed into the labour force.[37]

Some of course, especially those with professional backgrounds or sporting prowess, adapted ably and secured the glittering prizes. Several Hungarians did notably well. Peter Abeles, son of a steel merchant, left his native land when it became communist in 1947 and arrived in Australia two years later with a useful nest-egg of £4000. After experience as a bookseller and salesman for a knitting mill he and a partner formed their own transport firm with two ERF trucks. The firm grew, amalgamated in 1967 with the older and bigger company Thomas National Transport, spread its operations overseas, and by 1988 had 50 000 employees in Australia, Europe, Canada and Brazil, as well as a half-share in Australia's major private domestic airline.[38] Bela Strasser, a Hungarian lawyer who spent two-and-a-half years in a Nazi forced labour camp, was able to borrow £25 000 in 1956 and to build up a finance and construction complex including Parkes Development and the Project Development Corporation until by 1971, like Abeles, he was a knight and a millionaire.[39] Andrew Mensaros, another Hungarian lawyer, founded a more modest construction business in Perth before entering politics in 1968—the first post-war European migrant to do so—and becoming Western Australia's minister for energy. Julius Kovesi, who was originally employed as a gardener at the University of Western Australia, put himself through a philosophy degree, secured a scholarship to Balliol College, Oxford, and became associate professor at the campus where he had once wheeled compost.

Others were less fortunate. The middle-aged Hungarian potter Francis Kotai found little demand for his skills in the 1950s. He 'had to make such things as vases shaped like grape leaves, which he had to spray yellow, green, and pink. He hated such work but there was no market for any other kind of item'.[40] Appointed acting head of the department of applied arts at Fremantle Technical College for a decade, he lost his job in 1970 for want of formal qualifications and died of a heart attack soon after.

Yet despair apparently overtook few. Although a survey in 1963 found that suicide was more commonly attempted by migrants than by the Australian-born, those who did so came mainly from Britain and the United States. Nor did migrants display those forms of social maladjustment which swell the crime statistics. On the contrary, European migrants (except for Croats driven to violence by political feuds) were more law-abiding than Australians or New Zealanders. In Cooma, base town for the Snowy Mountains scheme, 2500 of the 4000 inhabitants in 1951 were migrants of recent origin, with a high proportion of single men, but in the five months between August and December the police laid just ninety-four charges, of which only nineteen involved migrants.[41]

As the 1950s progressed male migrants who had made good sent for the wives they had left behind in Europe, or asked the parish priest or some trusted intermediary to arrange a matrimonial introduction. In addition, government policy moved towards the encouragement of married couples as promising greater stability for the future. But adaptation was often traumatic. An Abruzzi woman who arrived in Sydney in 1959 recalled: 'At first I had to sleep on a couch in the house of friends. Then we had a garage at Kirrawee for two months. I cry every day. Every day I am cranky with my husband. Then we had another house, more dirty than the garage. For six years I cry every day until at last we bought a house'.[42] Banks and building societies were slow to grant loans to uninfluential migrants, and successful borrowers often carried heavy burdens of interest. Some European governments provided credit facilities to expatriates buying homes in Australia, a scheme initiated by the Netherlands in 1958 and followed by Italy in 1960. The Australian government did nothing.

Even when the migrant family acquired a home the neighbours were sometimes unwelcoming and at best indifferent. This forced families back onto the society of their own compatriots. Those who went out to work at least learned enough English for social conversation, but migrant housewives were often cut off by the language barrier and had to rely on their children at school for communication with outsiders. Yet many migrants stayed, finding that the compensations of Australian life outweighed the problems. Even the absence of an extended family or village network could be seen as an advantage. A woman from the Treviso region in northern Italy who followed her fiancée to Brisbane in 1958 put it thus: 'I don't like being in a city. I would like to have a farm. But in spite of that I feel freer than my sister. I am my own boss in the house, there isn't the gossip and the fighting that we had in the cortile. I can please myself about what I do and whether or not I give the children ice-cream'.[43] Most migrants of low social and economic status saw successful adjustment in terms of achieving social acceptance, reasonable fluency, and a level of economic well-being. It was as yet too demanding to take part in politics or public community activities.[44]

It might therefore have seemed that migrants were conforming to Bill Snedden's expectations when he said: 'We ask particularly of migrants that they be substantially Australian in the first generation and completely Australian in the second generation'.[45] For the second-generation Australian Snedden this simple creed was easy to accept. Son of the deserted wife of a Scottish migrant, he had grown up under-privileged during the 1930s Depression to find that the post-war opportunities open to hard work, mediocre abilities, sporting prowess and an unaffected genial personality could bring him access to the highest places in Australia. But by the early 1960s a European contemplating migration could find job opportunities in booming economies much closer to home than Australia. On the other hand Australia, having enjoyed an easy prosperity in the two decades after 1945, was committed to an economic conservatism which was already resulting in a slower growth rate than that of most other advanced nations. Migrants who sought their fortunes in Australia would find it more difficult to secure those material rewards which might enable them to establish themselves as home-owning Australian families. Nor was it certain that the inhabitants of the country whose prime minister was Robert Menzies had yet arrived at a satisfactory consensus on what it meant to be Australian.

BEING AUSTRALIAN

MOST AUSTRALIANS born during the Menzies era emerged into the artificial light of a public hospital labour ward, rather than being born at home or in a small midwife-controlled nursing home as their parents and grandparents had been. About 13 per cent of all children were conceived out of wedlock, but in two-thirds of such cases the parents married before the baby was born. The child would probably have been one of three, living with both parents in a suburban house in a city or substantial country town. He—or she—(a majority of Australians aged under sixty were male) would have been breast-fed for several months. His grandmothers, who probably regarded lactation as a partial safeguard against pregnancy, would have advised at least nine months, but a younger generation, better served by patent baby foods and contraceptives, began weaning earlier. For advice on this and many other aspects of 'scientific' parenting mothers took their babies, dressed in their smartest clothes, to one of nearly 1800 infant welfare clinics established since the 1920s. Victoria and Tasmania were the best provided states, but throughout Australia in the 1960s half a million infants under the age of two paid an average of seven visits annually for the critical inspection of the 'Baby Health Sister'. Most mothers were schooled to believe that they should subject their children to toilet-training at the earliest opportunity, but a more relaxed attitude was growing as Dr Benjamin Spock's ideas gained currency during the 1950s and early 1960s. This relaxation of attitude was facilitated after 1955, when convenient, disposable nappy-liners became available. In the cities, beginning with Melbourne in the early 1950s, mobile 'nappy wash' services were on hand for those who could afford them.[1]

Up to the age of five, children looked to their mothers for upbringing and nurture, and learned to regard their fathers as the playmate and chauffeur of weekends and the important bread-winner who at other times left home during daylight hours to provide for the family. Mothers usually decided whether children would be received into a religious faith, and whether they would become one of the minority who attended playschool or kinder-garten. Mothers took the diffident 5-year-olds to their first day at school, and left them there. After this rite of passage children could expect to spend at least nine years acquiring the skills thought necessary in a productive and conforming member of society. School was an essentially homogenizing experience. Although one-quarter of Australian children went to private schools, mostly Catholic, the state education departments laid down the content of teaching. 'The primary syllabuses have an emphasis on basic subjects like reading, writing, and arithmetic, social studies, and oral language', stated a standard work of reference, adding hopefully, 'but the teacher has some freedom to modify courses to suit local circumstances and the varying abilities of his students'.[2] (Or, presumably, *her* students, as most primary school teachers were female.)

Morality was also shaped at school. W. D. Borrie wrote in 1953: 'It is doubtful if in the majority of homes there is any longer deliberate inculcation of children with an ethical code . . . parents are tending to leave to the school an increasing share of the task of moral training'.[3] In state schools local clergy con-fronted, once weekly, large and apathetic classes of mixed ages. Catholic schools interspersed the teaching day with prayers at stated intervals and imposed a stronger discipline. This did not always have the desired effect. Jack Mundey, a boarder at St Augustine's, Cairns, thought the children were compelled 'to get the right answers by endless study, without trying to get them to develop their intellects';[4] when he grew up he joined the Com-munist Party. Josie Arnold at St Joseph's, Northcote, found that being a boy, and therefore potentially a priest, gave special privileges in the eyes of God. Girls were inferior.[5] Greater flexibility may have crept in as the dominance of teaching orders such as the Marist Brothers, the Christian Brothers, the Sisters of Mercy and the Dominican convents gave way to a more centralized Catholic education system, but for many youngsters the church schools left a lasting impression.[6] Apart from the small Jewish community no other group of young Australians was so marked out by the externals of its religion.

Catholic children slept and woke under the sorrowful gaze of Pellegrini prints of the Madonna or the Sacred Heart of Jesus. They did not eat meat on Fridays, and were not allowed to enter non-Catholic churches, even for weddings. Although the anti-Catholic scandal and scurrility of the Queensland periodical *The Rock* may have appealed only to a minority, most outsiders saw Catholics as bossed by their priests. Marriage outside the faith was strongly discouraged, since Catholic teaching insisted that the children must be brought up within the church, and Protestants feared that Catholicism spelt endless fecundity. In rural dioceses such as Sandhurst (Bendigo) and Goulburn, and where aged archbishops survived, such as Mannix of Melbourne and the more politic Duhig of Brisbane, these distinctions took on something of a tribal character (Irish against English), but the entrenched positions of the past were yielding under the influence of Catholic migrants from different backgrounds—Polish, Italian or Spanish—even before the Vatican councils of 1962–63 forced the pace of change.[7]

For Catholic and Protestant boys alike sport was probably the main teacher of morality. To play by the rules and obey the umpire, within reason, meant more in the here and now of young Australians than any amount of Sunday preaching. Boys were encouraged from their earliest years to barrack for the local football team: rugby in Queensland and most of New South Wales, Australian rules elsewhere, with Canberra aptly sited in the debatable land between the two codes:

> When children are born in Victoria
> they are wrapped in the club colours,
>   laid in beribboned cots
> having already begun a lifetime's
>   barracking.
>
> Carn, they cry, Carn . . . feebly, at first . . .[8]

Cricket was a little less prominent than in earlier decades because, despite the well-publicized patronage of Menzies, Australian elevens were not doing so well. Tennis on the other hand flourished under the cunning coaching of Harry Hopman, slave-driver to a generation of youthful recruits (Sedgman, Hoad, Rosewall, Laver) who dominated their world in the 1950s. They were not products of a privileged élite, one writer suggests, but 'a gauge of national virtue' who by beating the Americans showed that the United States was not a hegemonic master but a friendly rival.[9]

As part of the folklore of sport the young learned that anyone with the necessary prowess could win fame, no matter from what origins. Though most Aboriginal boxers might end up poor and brain-damaged, would not one of their number, Lionel Rose, win through to the world bantamweight championship? Were not the achievements of Ilsa and John Konrads proof that young migrants could make good as swimming champions? But even swimming champions were expected to behave like 'a gauge of national virtue'. Dawn Fraser, although three times an Olympic gold medallist between 1956 and 1964, was debarred from competition sport for ten years by the Australian Swimming Federation on the grounds of allegedly larrikin behaviour.[10] Sporting heroes had to set a good example for the next generation.

Schools were under less pressure to promote excellence. After the war only Queensland and Western Australia retained scholarship examinations at the end of primary school, and these went in 1959. These scholarships had offered children from families of limited means a chance of moving into the professional middle class through such schools as Fort Street in Sydney, MacRobertson and University High schools in Melbourne, and Perth Modern School. In the post-war era they were seen as creating élitism. High schools, it was thought, should be comprehensive, democratically recruiting from a given neighbourhood students of every range of ability. In practice this simply meant that a school reflected the class and ethnic character of its surroundings. Affluent neighbourhoods supported better schools—except in New South Wales where a succession of Labor ministers for education favoured working-class suburbs and where, following the Wyndham Report of 1957, specialized streaming of students was allowed within high schools and an extra year added before university.[11]

Pressure of numbers placed many schools under great strain. This was a particular grievance with taxpayers with children at church schools denied government funding because of nineteenth-century sectarian squabbles. In Goulburn, a strongly Catholic rural district in New South Wales, overcrowding led in 1962 to a financial crisis which provoked the diocese into closing all its schools and throwing nearly 7000 new enrolments on the state system. This soon persuaded state and federal governments to reverse the policies of eighty years and fund church schools. It was a blow to the waning forces of sectarianism, but also meant stronger competition for funds for the scarcely less hard-pressed state schools. These were still catching up with the stagnation of the 1930s and 1940s; in Queensland, for instance, no new state high schools had been built between 1924 and 1952. Overcrowding went with a decline in the qualifications of teachers. Between 1944 and 1966 the proportion of graduates teaching in state secondary schools fell in New South Wales from 85 to 41 per cent, and in Queensland to 20 per cent.[12]

In reaction many parents decided that the social and career opportunities of their children were best served by sending them to private schools. Three-quarters of Victorian students matriculating in 1948 came from independent schools, and although government high schools caught up with them during the next fifteen years, the private schools were seen as offering better career prospects. According to one estimate more than 10 per cent of the men appearing in *Who's Who in Australia* in 1962 were educated at Victoria's six leading independent schools.[13] Shrewd headmasters such as Melbourne Grammar School's Brian Hone aimed at producing a meritocracy. It was no longer enough to belong to an old or even a moneyed family; the independent schools were as open to the newly affluent as to established wealthy or professional families. Although most of these schools claimed some vestigial allegiance to one or other branch of the Christian church, they seldom saw it as their task to exalt the humble and meek from working-class backgrounds.

In not a few private schools there still lingered a hankering after the values of English public schools and a preference for English headmasters. This could be beneficial when the appointee was a discriminating idealist such as Dr James Darling, who in thirty years at Geelong Grammar School taught privileged boys a sense of social responsibility and tolerance of dissent; but it also fostered the cultural cringe. At Barker College, on the death of a long-serving 'legendary' headmaster, a genial thug who beat boys for bed-wetting, he was replaced by an English nonentity whose sole qualification over local candidates was a mediocre record in Test cricket. Competitive sport was usually compulsory because it was seen as character-building, partly as absorbing the excessive energies of adolescence, but largely because it was a school of teamwork for youngsters who had already developed commitments to private ambitions rather than collective goals.[14]

Girls' private schools sometimes encouraged greater individualism, especially under the inspiration of head teachers such as Dorothy Ross of Merton Hall, Olga Hay of Clyde, or Winifred West at Frensham. Of Catholic schools Germaine Greer has written: 'Convent girls are inducted into life by a rare and eccentric brood of women, who reject the servility of marriage and with it all the paraphernalia of middle-class acquisitiveness', adding, 'If it hadn't been for the nuns I might well have gone to secretarial college, had streaks in my hair, and married a stockbroker'.[15] Too many girls emerged from school with no more than a little culture and the modest skills required to fill their time usefully until marriage relieved them of the prospect of a career. At Lithgow High School in 1956 the senior girls made a bonfire of school uniforms and sang:

> We're leaving school to earn a crust,
> If the devil doesn't take us then
> a husband must.[16]

Going to university was a third option, but country girls were not often encouraged in that direction. Growing up in the Eyre Peninsula of South Australia, Jill Roe found: 'In my experience country people value educational achievement highly, but they expect it to have a practical outcome . . . because income-earning women with skills are an asset, not a drain, in rural communities where liquidity is often a problem. But the idea of girls aiming for the university was something new'.[17] Although by the early 1960s the proportion of women among university graduates was slowly increasing, they made up fewer than a quarter of the total, and of them over 60 per cent graduated in arts and music. By 1962–63 the number of women taking their degree in those fields had overtaken the men, but males still dominated science and the more obviously vocational fields such as medicine, dentistry,

law, agriculture, engineering, veterinary studies, and commerce/
economics. Between 1959 and 1963 only three women graduated
in engineering, one in forestry, and none in surveying or divinity.
Increasingly the professions looked to the universities to provide
credentials for admission to their ranks. Awareness of international standards and demand from Colombo Plan and other
overseas students fostered this trend; so did the beneficial effect
of graduate status on salary levels. The maintenance of university
standards was encouraged by the formation of learned academies,
membership of which was held to reflect scholarly distinction.
First came the Australian Academy of Science in 1954, followed
by the humanities and the social sciences.

The quality of individual academics and the reputation of
particular courses played little part in determining a student's
choice of university, since there was only one option in every
state except New South Wales (where a University of Technology
was founded in 1949 and the first non-metropolitan university,
the University of New England, won autonomy in 1954). By the
mid-1950s demand for places was straining resources and accommodation at a number of universities. Menzies, mindful of his
own debt to the scholarship system, numbered the advancement
of university education among his few enthusiasms. He commissioned a report on tertiary education from the British authority Sir Keith Murray, who in 1957 showed that years of
reliance on state governments had left Australian universities
seriously under-provided. Federal funding would have to be
substantially increased to make good the leeway.[18] Coming at a
moment when the Soviet Union's launching of Sputnik alerted
the western world to the value of education as investment in
human capital, the Murray Report won speedy acceptance.
Menzies's later years were a halcyon period of university growth.
By 1961 Melbourne had a second university, Monash, and university colleges were set up at Newcastle, Wollongong and
Townsville. So Menzies facilitated the rise, if not of an intelli-
gentsia, at least of a much enlarged white-collar professional
caste, recruiting increasing numbers from families, many of them
migrants, who had not previously seen tertiary education as
accessible.

Not that the universities seemed designed to radicalize their
students. Politics loomed less conspicuously on the campus than it
had in the previous decade. Students tended to show interest in

issues such as the easing of the White Australia Policy, campaigning through groups such as the Australian Student Christian Movement more than the established political parties. Staff appointments were made with an eye to protecting young minds from contentious views. In 1955 there was a major row over Sydney Sparkes Orr, who was dismissed from the chair of philosophy at the University of Tasmania following allegations of sexual misconduct with a female student. Orr had been a notable controversialist and troublemaker, and many academics felt that he had not been accorded justice.[19] Whether or not he was wronged, the repercussions for the University of Tasmania were severe. Sometimes universities refused appointment to able but controversial academics. In 1956 the historian Russel Ward was refused employment by the New South Wales University of Technology because he was once a member of the Communist Party.[20] Six years later the University of Sydney rejected the right-wing emigré Frank Knopfelmacher for an academic post on the grounds of his contentiousness. In both cases the ensuing protests gained support from both Left and Right, although Ward and Knopfelmacher were diametric opposites in their beliefs. Such episodes were few and spasmodic, but they gave no encouragement to vigorous teaching.

Then, as always, most young Australians were less interested in political and philosophical ideas than in social life and the rituals of courtship. In the 1950s socially conscious parents still went through the rites of launching their daughters as debutantes, the most privileged under vice-regal auspices, others being presented to a bishop or eminent local dignitary. Many young women managed without these formalities. Some formed their social links through church youth fellowships, for many of the churches were going through an optimistic phase in attracting young people.[21] At the other end of the social scale were the sharply dressed 'bodgies' and 'widgies'. Usually factory or office workers, these youngsters dressed to stand out from the majority. Where most women's fashions were influenced by Parisian *haute couture*, after 1948 dominated by Dior's full-skirted New Look, widgies wore round-necked sleeveless blouses with split gaberdine skirts, bobby socks and flat shoes. The young men spurned the double-breasted suits and short-back-and-sides haircuts favoured by Australian males of most ages in favour of single-breasted drape jackets in grey or powder blue, with 'snakeproof' trousers, baggy at the knees and tight at the ankle. These fashions were practical for dancing to the American swing which monopolized commercial radio at that time. Good clothes were among the expanding range of consumer goods in demand in an era of greater affluence. The bodgies and widgies were blamed for an increase in shoplifting, but this may have been due to prejudice among their elders; the bodgie gangs were apparently relatively conservative when it came to drugs and sex. Fashions changed in the later 1950s. Girls moved into flared skirts and matador trousers. Some adopted beehive hairdos, others stayed with pony-tails. Many youths imitated the hair-style, lumberjacket, narrow ties, and taciturnity of Elvis Presley. This reflected the coming of rock-and-roll as presented by such stars as Presley and Bill Haley. It was not long before Australia developed its own rock-and-roll idiom with a performer in Johnny O'Keefe, of whom it was said: 'You could hear the streets of Sydney in that voice'.[22] In the late 1950s also Aboriginal stockmen were fusing country-and-western rhythms with their own melodic traditions to create a distinctive style. Australians may have borrowed their pop music from the Americans, but they soon made it their own.

The most authentically Australian aspect of teenage culture was the beach. All Australia's major cities were within easy reach of the sea, and some offered surfing. Until the 1950s this meant mostly body-surfing. The more competent young men won admiration as members of the trained and disciplined surf life-saving teams. With the increase in motor vehicles the young no longer had to confine themselves to the popular patrolled beaches accessible by public transport, and the introduction of lightweight Malibu surf-boards in the 1960s brought about a transformation. The regimentation of surf life-saving lost its appeal for many. Surfers as a peer group became intensely anti-authoritarian and individualistic.[23] It was a portent of a coming revolution in the attitudes of youth, just as more and more young women, despite the combined disapproval of church leaders, influential women's magazines and the majority of parents, were abandoning more comprehensive swimwear in favour of the bikini with its scope for suntans. Increasingly the young were trusting their own judgements.

This independent-mindedness was fostered by the steadily growing custom of enjoying a spell of overseas travel. With the thaw in foreign relations which followed the death of Stalin in

1953 and the end of rationing in Britain in 1954 Europe resumed all its old attraction. During the 1950s steamships were generally less expensive than air travel, but the gap closed in the early 1960s even before the second and more disruptive blockage of the Suez Canal in 1967. For young women it was sometimes a consolation for their lack of career that they could spend two tax-free years based in the United Kingdom before settling down to domesticity. They frequented the Down Under Club which in those years was beginning to form the nucleus of an Australian precinct in London's Earls Court; they hitch-hiked throughout Western Europe; they roughed it in youth hostels and turned their hands to any job which enabled them to stretch their finances further. They experienced some of the world's finest theatres, art galleries and concert halls. And then they went home and married, retaining memories of a world beyond Australia with which they might at some time in the future fire their children's imaginations.

Most young couples, whatever their religious beliefs, decided on a church wedding with the bride wearing white. In 1962 over 88 per cent of all Australian marriages were solemnized in a church. The proportion was highest in Queensland with nearly 96 per cent, and lowest in the Australian Capital Territory with its large number of university graduates. The wedding was usually preceded by a formal engagement with all its rituals. Young women planned a trousseau and had 'shower teas'; young men endured the ribaldry of a bucks' party. By the early 1960s the average age at which couples married for the first time was about twenty-four for women and twenty-seven for men. Since the end of the war there had been a slight but steady drift towards earlier marriage, probably reflecting the affluence which enabled couples to save for a car and a block of suburban land or the minimum deposit on a mortgaged house. This meant that couples committed themselves to an economic and political status quo whose stability they hoped would last during the twenty-five or thirty years before they gained the clear title to their property and with it security in retirement.

New wives often chose to remain at their jobs for another year or two, contributing to the household savings until the first pregnancy came. As few couples wished for unlimited fertility, family planning was increasingly adopted. Approaches varied considerably. Catholic teaching forbade all forms of artificial contraception, leaving abstinence or the 'rhythm method' as the only alternatives. Many couples of Southern European origin preferred *coitus interruptus*. Those whose beliefs permitted the use of artificial devices may have been inhibited by laws which prohibited pharmacies from advertising contraceptives (until the 1950s some family chemists refused to stock them), but with each decade acceptance grew. During the Second World War perhaps one half of fecund couples practised some form of birth control; by the late 1950s three-quarters did. This probably meant that fewer married women resorted to backyard abortionists, while the unmarried and those whose unwanted pregnancies were the result of extra-marital sex, could often find a qualified medical practitioner to perform termination. Then at the end of 1960 the contraceptive pill came on the market. It won speedy acceptance, especially among city-dwellers. It was calculated that by 1964, 30 per cent of married women were taking the pill, and the number went on rising for the rest of the decade.[24] At this time the pill was seen mainly as a tidy and efficient device for family planning, more reliable and more aesthetic than its competitors. Its capacity for changing sexual morality and women's self-concept was at first unrecognized.

Sooner or later—in 70 per cent of cases within two years—wives became mothers. Usually this meant leaving the paid workforce and defining themselves, as so many of that generation did, as 'just a housewife'. To some this was a welcome and natural destiny, and with their husbands and children they created the nuclear family unit which many asserted to be the foundation of Australian society. For others it was less easy. Husbands who found fulfilment in the workplace often did not have much to communicate to wives whose energies were absorbed in home-making. Often the environment of a new suburb offered hard work and little solace. Peter Spearritt has calculated that in 1952 half the new houses in New South Wales were owner-built, but by 1957 the proportion had fallen to one-third. Neither owner-builders nor tradesmen showed much sensitivity to design; they could seldom afford to. Many householders, wrote an observer in 1957, 'paid rates for street lighting which was almost non-existent, and for street maintenance even though they were not likely to see kerbing and guttering for the next fifty years'.[25] In Melbourne's outer suburbs the residents were expected to pay a substantial lump sum when eventually the authorities laid a bitumen road and footpath outside their front fence. Sewerage lagged behind new growth. In 1960 only two-thirds of Sydney's houses were sewered; in the whole of Australia the figure was below 55 per cent. Brisbane had less than half the mileage of sewers or number of properties connected as Adelaide, although the two cities had comparable populations. Many unsewered houses used septic tanks, although even in quite affluent middle-class suburbs the traditional nightcart was still plying its rounds in the early 1960s.

The streets of new suburbs were often planned in the traditional grid pattern of Australian cities, but by the 1960s an increasing number of new developments attempted to escape monotony by experimenting with the crescents and culs-de-sac favoured by the National Capital Development Commission in Canberra. Unfortunately developers usually tried to simplify their work by bulldozing all the trees and shrubs left standing on a subdivision—if indeed the land had not been cleared decades before for farming—and it was only towards 1960 that some recognition was given to the attraction of treed localities such as Blackburn and Mount Waverley in Melbourne and St Ives in Sydney. Even after that date the retention of native trees tended to be yet another of the amenities distinguishing middle-class housing from the less affluent. Some of the western suburbs of Sydney and Melbourne created in those years were soon to house families as disadvantaged as any of the 'social problem' areas surviving from the nineteenth century in the inner cities.

The Australia of the 1950s and 1960s was increasingly suburban. Rural Australia accounted for only 14 per cent of the population at the 1966 census, compared with 31 per cent in 1933. Only 8 per cent lived on farms. A La Trobe University survey of a sample of Melbourne residents in 1971 found 55 per cent who claimed to have worked on farms or in country towns, but among those under forty the proportion dropped to 23 per cent. Traces of depopulation were evident even in the most productive regions. In 1920 more hay passed through the railway station at Crookwell than through any other in the New South Wales rail system; forty or fifty years later a visitor to the district found abandoned farmsteads, decayed churches, disused schools and derelict pubs.[26] Country towns declined as the closing of railways, the automation of telephones and the centralization of police and administrative services closed off job opportunities for young locals. Farmers and country businesspeople sent their children to city boarding-schools. When they built new farmhouses they often spurned the wide-verandahed idiom of an earlier generation in favour of incongruous replicas of the brick-and-tiled smartness of modern suburbia. Rural Australia was yielding to suburban Australia.

Few Australian intellectuals of that generation gave suburbia a good name. Patrick White, while producing the novels whose transcendental themes would fit him for a Nobel Prize, turned aside to create the imaginary suburb of Sarsaparilla, a community of clownish vapidity through which the Australian petty bourgeoisie was gibbeted. Of a younger generation, Barry Humphries made an early reputation as comedian and social commentator through his meticulously faithful ear for the speech patterns and treasured clichés of neighbourhoods such as Moonee Ponds. As time passed his affection for his subject-matter withered, and in later years he came to spend the remnant of his talent informing British audiences that in Australia they would find a society even more philistine than their own. Another young writer who sought refuge as an expatriate was Germaine Greer, who remembered her home town of Melbourne as a place of completely home-grown ugliness, and Australia as 'a huge rest home, where no unwelcome news is ever wafted on to the pages of the worst newspapers in the world'.[27] To such critics Australia seemed uniquely awful beyond the average of western capitalist democracies.

One lonely voice who crusaded against derivative mediocrity and in favour of a self-confidently Australian idiom was the architect Robin Boyd, who after pioneering the *Age* small homes service went into private practice from 1947 until his early death in 1971. Australia, he wrote, was 'the constant sponge lying in the Pacific', following the fashions of overseas and minimally confident in home-produced original ideas. In a nation of home-buyers Boyd thought that change could best be promoted by improving Australian concepts of the built environment.[28] As part of an apparently inexhaustible clan of creative artists, he nourished an easy confidence in his own taste and standards. His approach was continually experimental. At one time he designed the light aluminium Stegbar window-frame, at another he was exploring the techniques of prefabrication, and after a visit to Japan he preached the virtues of open-plan housing and the use of screens. He was always willing to experiment with unpopular materials and, when he designed Menzies College for La Trobe University with interior walls of rough bricks, was astonished that the reputedly radical students complained. He poured out his views in a series of witty and well-informed books. His special scorn was reserved for featurism, that love of useless artifice for its own sake: the china ducks in flight across the sitting-room wall above the piano, the multi-coloured roof tiles, the plaster Aboriginal in the front garden. Australians enjoyed his wit, gave him a CBE, and largely ignored him. Perhaps the economics of home-buying were against him. His last, posthumous, book *The Great, Great Australian Dream*, was filled with bitter outrage against the incapacity of Australians to think creatively and independently about themselves and their environment.

A few observers of Australian life stood up to defend the suburbs. Craig Macgregor, a young journalist with a sharp eye for the trends of fashion, saw suburban life as a satisfactory solution to the needs of migrants seeking land, but admitted that 'the Australian's concentration upon his home and his family . . . represents a turning away from the wider community and the world of politics, commitment and social participation'.[29] Hugh Stretton, coming from the Melbourne and Balliol traditions of applying intellect to social problems to live in the best planned of Australia's cities, Adelaide, was much preoccupied with urban design. Finding no publisher for a seminal book, *Ideas for Australian Cities*, he eventually produced it himself in 1970, at once earning substantial royalties for the urban social services of the Brotherhood of St Laurence. In this book, Stretton argued that:

Australia's 60' x 150' suburbia—sparser than much English suburbia, closer than much American—does at least permit three societies to coexist. Child, family, and adult life can use overlapping territories without too often getting in each other's hair. There can be subtle gains in the generations' consciousness of each other . . . There are also ranges of perfectly tolerable behaviour (child and adult) which however can't be tolerated either indoors or on public land: building, carpentering, metalworking, digging, hosing, basking, horsing about . . .[30]

'Plenty of dreary lives are indeed lived in suburbs', asserted Stretton, 'But most of them might well be worse in other surroundings'.

But families in new suburbs faced no end of financial demands. While state governments and the Catholic system were seldom tardy in building primary schools with basic furnishings, beyond that it was up to the parents and citizens. Sporting facilities, library books, even chalk and dusters had to be provided by fund-raising activities and working-bees. Such weekend chores not only stocked the schools with much-needed amenities, but also did much to break down any sense of isolation by bringing together families from a wide variety of backgrounds. So did the other organizations for growing children: kindergarten, scouts, guides, sporting teams. In Melbourne the new suburbs were parcelled out to old-established League football teams, and it was wonderful how quickly children forgot their family's traditional allegiances and barracked for the 'little league' team to which their neighbourhood was allocated. Municipal loyalties, however, were weak. Most of the new suburbs sprang up in what had been large semi-rural shires suddenly propelled into 'city' status and stretching to the utmost the skills of the small businessmen who tended to be elected to councils.

Nor could the churches serve as a major focus for community life as they had in older suburbs, where church choirs, parish councils, mothers' unions, Sunday schools and youth fellowships absorbed the energies of many. While Australians were never such ostentatious church-goers as Americans, 95 per cent in 1949 and 87 per cent in 1969 professed a belief in God, although only a minority of these attended church more or less regularly. When a census was taken on a representative Sunday only 2 per cent of Western Australia's nominal Anglicans had been to church.[31] Even for the largest denominations, the Anglicans and Catholics, the building of new churches placed a great strain on financial and human resources. When they were built it was often found that migrants, perhaps influenced by the traditions of their homelands, were more staunchly supportive than the native-born. In such new suburbs itinerant evangelists hoped to make their harvest. Often they represented sects of American origin: the clean-cut, neatly dressed young Mormon men who travelled in pairs, or the Jehovah's Witnesses, no longer branded as subversive.

Men with a taste for community service often found the churches less attractive than clubs such as Rotary and its imitators the Lions, Jaycees and Apex, again largely organizations of American origin. To some extent they replaced the lodges which had claimed the allegiance of an older generation. Although many older Australian men gained some satisfaction from lodge membership, they said little about these rituals. The most widespread and the oldest of the benevolent societies, the Freemasons, were the least communicative of all. It was estimated in the 1950s that one Australian man in sixteen was a Mason, but the movement was to decline from a peak of 341 000 members in 2415 lodges in 1961 to half that number by 1989. Membership of a Masonic lodge was considered helpful in business or in certain branches of the public service. Some government departments were noted for a preponderance of Masons, while others seemed to favour Catholics. These matters have been largely ignored by scholars, and in the absence of evidence a historian who is not a member of the organization can do no more than record the prevalence of such folklore and surmise that for many middle-class Australian males of that generation Masonry was a powerful binding influence. Women, of course, could not be Freemasons and seem to have had neither the time nor the inclination for similar rituals of their own.[32]

For many housewives in new suburbs their isolation was enforced by poor public transport. In many homes it was taken for granted that the husband would need the family car to drive to his job, leaving his wife, often encumbered with small children, to walk in all weathers for the family shopping or friendly visiting. Housewives, schoolchildren and the elderly were the main customers for the public transport services whose provision they were seldom politically powerful enough to influence. Between 1958 and 1961 all state capitals except Melbourne and (for another decade) Brisbane disposed of their trams, which were considered too slow and inflexible for the longer distances to the outer suburbs. Cheap petrol encouraged reliance on bus services, so the suburban railways were nowhere expanded to cope with growing demand.

Increasingly, people travelled to work by private car, thus reducing the patronage for public transport so that financial losses accumulated, services were duly cut, and inconvenienced commuters turned ever more to the use of private cars.[33] Little thought was given to the possibility that a heavily subsidized public transport system might incur a smaller social cost than the waste and inconvenience of overloading the road system with more cars than it was designed to take. The human carnage alone was grievous: in five years from July 1958 to July 1963, 12 340

Australians were killed in motor vehicle accidents and over 300 000 were injured. No Australian city except Canberra was planned with the car in mind, although Perth partially retrieved the situation in 1954 by adopting the Stephenson–Hepburn plan with its early provision for freeways. In larger cities such as Melbourne and Sydney freeways could be created only by purchasing and devastating parklands and housing in old-established inner suburbs.

Reliance on the private car dominated the quality of suburban life. Shopping was transformed. Before the war, grocers, greengrocers, icemen, butchers and bakers all delivered their wares to suburban households, thus mitigating the isolation of the elderly or mothers with small children. The war put an end to nearly all such deliveries. After 1945 retailing became less labour-intensive. Consciously following North American examples, a chain of grocery shops in northern New South Wales introduced self-service, with the customer loading a shopping trolley from open shelves of goods and paying for them at a checkout point. Soon independent shopkeepers gave way to chain stores that could purchase wholesale in bulk.[34] The old suburban string of small shops along a main street was found to create parking problems and impeded the smooth flow of traffic. Developers came to favour the North American model of the multi-purpose supermarket, a complex of shops dominated by one major retailer and surrounded by a bitumen desert of parking space. The Myer centre opened at Chadstone in the eastern suburbs of Melbourne in 1957 and was much talked of as a prototype for such developments. Supermarkets were appreciated by, among others, the writer Nancy Keesing, who remarked that in the 1930s: 'Food poisoning was more prevalent than it is now. So were flies, cockroaches, rats and mice. The milk saucepan on which unpasteurized milk was scalded was a daily horror to wash up. Three cheers for the bright, clean, health-regulated Supermarket'.[35]

Those who lamented the passing of the small shopkeeper complained that it was less easy to secure redress for products of faulty design or quality, while others were dissatisfied with high-pressure methods of salesmanship. Few remedies were available to shoppers until an initiative was taken by two state parliamentarians: Ruby Hutchison from Western Australia and Edna Roper from New South Wales. Under their inspiration the

Australian Consumers' Association was set up in 1959, operating first from a suburban flat at Coogee. The association produced a periodical, *Choice*, in which with striking candour it published the results of scientific and technical tests on samples of anonymously purchased consumer goods, indicating which was the best buy. By concentrating in its early stages on widely used items such as electrical goods and children's shoes, *Choice* soon secured a wide public response which forced manufacturers and retailers to improve their standards.[36] Grass-roots action of this kind did more to protect the consumer than the government's Trade Practices Act of 1965, the belated fruit of an attempt by Sir Garfield Barwick, while attorney-general, to legislate against collusive price-fixing and other practices aimed at restricting competition among wholesalers and retailers.[37] The need for consumer protection reflected the growing complexity of suburban life in a modern capitalist economy. It was noteworthy that even the able and energetic Barwick, alert to the needs of a constituency in the western suburbs of Sydney, found it hard to check traders from enriching themselves at the expense of consumers.

Suburban Australians were also consumers of entertainment, and here too the car brought lasting changes. During the 1930s and 1940s every suburb had its own cinema, usually a theatre whose architecture and name—the Regal, the Roxy, the Ritz— vaguely evoked the opulence of Hollywood, and often with an adjacent open-air garden and deck-chairs for summer nights. From the early 1950s, following an American model, drive-in movies began to appear in the newer suburbs. Instead of belonging to a collective audience, the viewers sat in individual cars, noisily if there were children in the party, decorously if they were middle-aged couples, amorously if younger. But the effect of the drive-in in privatizing what had previously been a communal activity was as nothing compared with the impact of television.

Compared with the United States and Britain, Australia was slow to embark on television, partly because of debate about the correct balance between government and private ownership, but largely because the economy and the cold war were higher priorities for both the Chifley and Menzies governments. Under pressure from the electronics industry and other interest groups the Menzies government in 1953–54 appointed a royal commission chaired by Professor George Paton, vice-chancellor of the University of Melbourne, whose report reflected majority public opinion in recommending a dual system of ownership, with the ABC running a national system and private competitors selected and regulated by the Australian Broadcasting Control Board. There was opposition from the Labor Party, which favoured either an exclusively national system or no television at all, as well as from some rural anti-Labor politicians who considered it just another luxury for the urban middle class. The Menzies government accepted the Paton commission's report, setting the Melbourne Olympic Games of 1956 as target date for television's debut. To nobody's surprise the commercial licences went to existing newspaper and radio interests, foreign participation being limited to 15 per cent of the issued capital of any proprietorial company. On the other hand Actors Equity failed to secure a minimum quota for Australian-produced content in programmes, so the way was open for the media owners to import large quantities of cheap and undemanding American material. Such a bonanza did much to consolidate the handful of companies monopolizing Australia's major media.[38]

On 16 September 1956 Bruce Gyngell introduced the first television programme broadcast on TCN9 Sydney. Six weeks later the ABC followed with an opening night of great confusion in a studio so blindingly illuminated that the dignitaries present all had to close their eyes as if asleep. By the time the Olympics opened on 22 November two channels were available to viewers in Melbourne and three in Sydney. Between that date and 1960 Canberra and the remaining state capitals were brought into service, and by the end of 1963 so were major provincial centres such as Launceston, Newcastle and Rockhampton. By 1965, 2 million Australian households were licensed for television. At least two-thirds of all Australians might now choose to spend their evenings at home absorbing the output from the black-and-white screen. It is impossible to judge how far the quality of Australian life was enriched by staying home together to watch 'My Favorite Martian' or 'I Love Lucy'. Certainly the new medium broke down any remaining sense of Australian isolation from the rest of the world. Families in their living-rooms watched the feats of the first astronauts, Wimbledon, the funeral of Marilyn Monroe, the assassination of President John F. Kennedy. In other respects television may have taken people away from old habits of communal interaction. Even the churches altered their hours of service to avoid conflict with favourite programmes. A Western Australian branch of the Democratic Labor Party passed its resolutions during the commercial breaks between shows.[39] Between 1957 and 1965 more than half of Sydney's cinemas closed and were converted into supermarkets, skating rinks, or (another American import) ten-pin bowling alleys.[40] It was the same everywhere else. Television also doomed many of the circulating libraries which for threepence or sixpence a week hired out fiction, travel and biography to the suburban reading public, although these small businesses were also under challenge from the relative cheapness of paperback books. Besides, between 1944 and 1955 each of the state governments had set up a central Library Board which through subsidies and other encouragements stimulated the establishment of municipal libraries.

Television also competed with the hotels. With the increasing emphasis on family entertainment publicans came under pressure to improve their standards. This in turn encouraged state governments to defy the dwindling 'wowser vote' and legislate for conditions which would create more civilized drinking. (In South Australia, a state with 6 p.m. closing, diners in hotels were permitted to take the excellent local wine with their meals until 9 p.m., at which stage the glasses were relentlessly removed from the table.) Migrant influences counted for reform, both the British with their tradition of a small pub as a community centre transcending class and gender, and the Europeans for whom wine was a mainstay of private and public culture. In 1954 New South Wales abandoned the 'six o'clock swill' after a referendum narrowly favouring the extension of hotel trading hours to 10 p.m., but retained for several years a one-hour closure to allow drinkers the opportunity of going home for a meal instead of drinking on an empty stomach. To attract custom on summer evenings publicans converted their yards into open-air beer gardens, where men and women could drink together without subjecting themselves to the plastic gentility of the ladies' lounge. More strait-laced Victoria adhered to 6 p.m. closing at a 1956 referendum, and succumbed to later hours only at the beginning of 1966, though at the same time pioneering a measure which was soon imitated by all the other states—making it a criminal offence to drive a car with a high blood-alcohol level. Even under these constraints Australians relished their liquor. During the 1950s the annual average consumption of beer for every man, woman and child in the Commonwealth rose from 16.9 to 22.7 gallons (76.7 to 103 litres), before stabilizing for several years.

In the 1950s Australians spent 10 per cent of their household outgoings on alcohol and tobacco, although from 1956–57—the year television was introduced—there was a slow but consistent fall which persisted throughout the 1960s and 1970s. Cigarette smoking, not yet under attack as a cause of lung cancer, was promoted skilfully as the old-established near-monopoly of British Tobacco was challenged after 1953 by the advertising campaigns of Rothmans, Philip Morris, and other competitors specializing in filter-tipped cigarettes.[41] Before 1953 filter-tips commanded barely 5 per cent of the Australian market; by 1963 the figure was 80 per cent, after which the market tended to stagnate as the rising young middle class discovered the virtues of physical fitness and clean palates for the enjoyment of wine.

Gambling also stood high among the classic Australian vices. Because private clubs complained of the competition from extended hotel trading hours the New South Wales government permitted them to instal poker machines. Their success was immediate. In the first year of operation, 1956–57, 5596 'pokies' came into operation, taking nearly 25 per cent of all money invested in legalized gambling in New South Wales. By 1969 the proportion was over 40 per cent, with nearly 30 000 machines. Most of the takings went to providing members of clubs and their friends with amenities, furnishings and entertainments which grew more sumptuous every year, adding new dimensions to the living standards accessible to ordinary citizens. The New South Wales government took between 15 and 20 per cent of the total profit for the Hospitals Commission and other welfare purposes. By 1969–70 this lucrative source of voluntary taxation netted $30 million in revenue.[42]

Except in South Australia, where the puritan conscience of the Playford government kept temptation at bay, all other states profited from gambling either through the legalization of off-course betting or through lotteries. Britain, with five times the population, spent only twice as much on football pools.[43] The Queensland Golden Casket and the Western Australian Charities Consultation recovered from their wartime slump, and in 1954 the Victorian government scored a coup by persuading the old-established Tattersall's lottery to move from Hobart to

Melbourne. (This struck a blow at the Tasmanian economy which was only partly offset in 1969 by the licensing of Australia's first casino at Wrest Point.) Not to be outdone, New South Wales upgraded its state lottery in November 1954, and from 1957 initiated a series of mammoth lotteries to help fund the rising costs of the Sydney Opera House. This ambitious project, designed by the Danish architect Joern Utzon, was planned to grace Sydney's harbourside with an edifice of cosmopolitan magnificence, but it entailed engineering and acoustic features for which there was no known method of construction, and it was to take nearly three years of computer calculations to arrive at a solution. The original completion date of Australia Day 1963 came and went without much to show except a deepening debt. Thus the gambling instincts of ordinary Australians were harnessed to underpin an architectural and cultural gamble of monumental proportions.

Perhaps this was the only way in which high culture could be securely implanted as part of the Australian way of life. It had been left to the ABC to develop symphony orchestras in each of the state capitals. By 1950 each had a resident conductor. Sydney for some years enjoyed the services of the eminent Sir Eugene Goossens until he resigned after an unfortunate encounter with the customs regulations; Melbourne's Sir Bernard Heinze, though less technically excellent, gained wide recognition for his work in musical education. Perhaps an even stronger force for bringing classical music to a wider public was Dr A. E. Floyd, who until his ninety-fifth year hosted a listeners' choice programme on the ABC on Sunday afternoons. Commercial radio, unlike some of its equivalents in the United States, saw no need to bring its listeners anything more demanding than the hit tunes of the day, or at the most the sentimental ballads which appealed to the older generation. It accurately reflected public taste, for over 80 per cent of radio listeners habitually tuned in to the commercial stations in preference to the ABC.

Cinema and television were usually held to have killed popular drama, but actors found some encouragement in the activities of unsubsidized repertory societies, among which Doris Fitton's Independent Theatre in North Sydney stood pre-eminent. Radio drama performances, especially those given by the ABC, were also a nursery of talent. In the immediate post-war years Australians still looked overseas for new drama. Highly acclaimed in its time, Christopher Fry's *The Lady's Not for Burning*, first produced in London in 1948, reached Perth by 1953 and St Barnabas's Hall at Ravenshoe in the north of Queensland in 1959. The move to a home-grown tradition was stimulated by the visit in 1950 of the Anglo-Irish producer Sir Tyrone Guthrie. Following his recommendations to the federal government the Australian Elizabethan Theatre Trust was set up in 1954. Subsidized by government and private funding, the trust's charter not only required it to present drama, ballet and opera throughout Australia, but also to encourage the production of works by local artists.

Soon it was no longer necessary for those with ambitions in the performing arts to leave Australia. The trust helped in setting up the National Institute for Dramatic Art at the University of New South Wales as a training ground for young actors, producers and technicians. It also sponsored the Australian Ballet, which commenced its first season at the end of 1962. Here the trust was building on the foundations of dedicated private enthusiasts, notably the Czech-born impresario Edouard Borovansky, who during an often hand-to-mouth career before his death in 1959 had brought forward many young Australian dancers such as Kathleen Gorham and Marilyn Jones.[44] In encouraging local dramatists the trust scored an early success with Ray Lawler's *Summer of the Seventeenth Doll*, a study of two cane-cutters on holiday, which beneath its proletarian high spirits made some searching observations on male–female relationships. From its first production in 1956 the *Doll* was applauded, soon winning acceptance for staging by Britain's National Theatre. Controversy surrounded the trust's second hit, Alan Seymour's *The One Day of the Year*. Rejected by the Adelaide Festival of Arts in 1960, the play drew fire on its production in Sydney in 1961. Seymour had been bold enough to explore differing attitudes towards the celebration of Anzac Day ('one generation looks upon it reverently as a day to be cherished; the other sees in it nothing more than an excuse to stop work and get drunk').[45] This upset returned servicemen who disliked the play's questioning of their values. It was a long time before Seymour recovered his stride as a dramatist.

Whenever the generations conflicted during the Menzies era it was usually the middle-aged who won out over the young, and they were not given to subtleties. 'He was often wrong', said

Arthur Fadden in 1956 in what he meant as a tribute to a deceased colleague, 'but he was never in doubt'.[46] Returning to Adelaide in the early 1950s, the young lawyer Don Dunstan found that 'Unorthodox opinion or behaviour could bring penalties both in employment and in social acceptance:

Dress was carefully prescribed . . . Men and boys were required to wear suits and collars and ties, clerks in Messrs. Elder Smith & Co's offices and the Public Service must wear collars, ties, and jackets *done up* in the streets on days when the temperature exceeded 40°C . . . On Sundays everything closed . . . During the other days of the week there was little entertainment after dark.[47]

Adelaide was regarded as a little strait-laced even by the standards of Hobart or Perth, but the comments would have been valid for any of Australia's cities at that time. As Frederic Eggleston had remarked years previously, and as Geoffrey Dutton (another Adelaide iconoclast) wrote in *Nation* in 1963, 'institutionalized old men'[48] dominated Australia. Burly from the ingestion of too many carbohydrates, buttoned into their gracelessly cut suits, they glare at us from the official photographs of that era, ranging from the dogmatically pompous to the genially ill-at-ease. Sometimes they are flanked by their wives—corseted, hatted, gloved, inscrutable. It was the men who appeared to exercise leadership in public situations and who pontificated about politics and football. But ultimately, though covertly and indirectly, it was the women who had the authority.

In 1957–58 David Adler, a Canadian sociologist, questioned over 1300 primary schoolchildren, average age twelve, on the patterns of decision-making in their homes. He found that in Australia, even more than in that legendary shrine of motherhood the United States, women took the major responsibility for deciding on family activities and seeing that they were carried out. Australia, he said, was a matriduxy.[49] In every aspect of decision-making about household duties, spending and recreation mothers took more initiatives than fathers: 50 per cent of mothers, and only 2 per cent of fathers, involved themselves in all aspects of home routine. This meant that when the children grew up and left home there was often not much for wives and husbands to communicate about. This problem was little discussed in the 1950s and 1960s, but a woman who had been a wife and mother of four during those years felt driven in later life to write to the

Australian Women's Weekly about her problem. Her husband, she said, was basically a good man, 'has a steady job, is never mean with material things, puts time to voluntary work, especially church projects, and does not drink or smoke'. But all he needed in life was his job, the newspapers and television: 'he makes it fairly clear that all he needs to put into our marriage is the steady housekeeping money, his fidelity, and reputation as a good-living man. He states flatly that he is not interested in entertaining, in outings or in my friends'. Lonely, uneasy, and feeling at fault, she found herself with 'the responsibilities of wife and partner, without the freedom of a widow'.[50] Numerous readers responded to her story. One or two sympathized with a husband who, as they saw it, wished to be left in peace ('Nothing', wrote a Toowoomba woman, 'can make up for a good, solid, unexciting life with a faithful husband'[51]), but the majority supported the wife's complaint. Apparently there were many husbands, dutiful as providers, sober and sexually faithful, who did not know how to begin sharing their feelings and concerns with their lifetime partners.

This incapacity to communicate was nothing new; indeed it was most marked among the older generation, especially returned servicemen who had undergone the traumas of the First World War. Of Sir Ernest White, successful real estate developer and founder of the Australian–American Association, his obituarist wrote: 'Few of his family and friends ever knew how fond he was of them. He had difficulty sharing his emotions'.[52] Another example of the communication difficulties within marriage can be found at the opposite end of the political spectrum in the militant trade unionist Paddy Troy and his wife Mabel:

Essentially, Mabel wanted more of Paddy for herself and resented the absorption of so much of his energy in enthusiasms which she did not share. For his part, Paddy relied heavily on Mabel's support but underestimated the load she carried. Since he emptied his pay packet straight into her purse, taking out only his daily expenses, he left to her the task of balancing the budget. She suffered on and off from an asthmatic condition that was aggravated by stress . . . She did not share his pleasure in going out to meetings and found it difficult to participate in the discussions . . . And let anyone say a word against her husband within her hearing and the sparks would fly.[53]

This emotional inarticulateness was hardly less common among younger men, according to the Catholic psychiatrist Ronald

Conway, whose professional experience during the late 1950s and 1960s convinced him that Australian men were stunted by a 'great taboo on tenderness'.[54]

Women who found this great taboo on tenderness in their menfolk often contrived to build up emotional support systems among accessible neighbours and relatives. When their husbands retired from work and sat at home all day they often found themselves obtrusive in these feminine circles. Suddenly, after years of seniority or at least continuity in the workplace, they had no special status and nothing to do. Many fell ill or died within a year or two of retirement. They may have been suffering from chagrin.

Women certainly survived longer. Of nearly 900 000 Australians over the age of sixty-five at the 1961 census, 57 per cent were women; of those over seventy-five, 60 per cent. As women were usually younger than their husbands it meant that most faced the experience of widowhood. Security in old age was thus a vital concern for many women, and the margins were often narrow. About a quarter of Australia's workforce benefited from some form of superannuation on retirement, but for most the mainstay was the old-age pension, non-contributory but subject to a means test. Gough Whitlam noted that during the 1950s and 1960s the old-age pension failed to improve proportionately to the increase of gross national product, with the largest rises tending to occur in federal budgets presented shortly before an election. One of his colleagues in 1964 challenged Menzies's minister for social services:

if he would like to get up early one morning and go to Paddy's Market or the general City Markets area of Sydney he would see many pensioners going through rubbish heaps to pick out food scraps with which to supplement their meals. You will see pensioners buying second-hand clothing because it is cheap. You will see other pensioners trying on spectacles. Spectacles are not included in social services benefits and the pensioners go to Paddy's Markets because glasses may be bought there for one or two shillings a pair. I have seen age pensioners in the market trying sets of false teeth which are sold there.[55]

Of course many pensioners were better off, particularly those who owned their own homes or had supportive families, but it was usually necessary to be careful. Yet despite the emergence of pensioners' leagues which lobbied for improved conditions the old were among the most reliable voters for the Menzies government.

Whether battling for survival in an inner-city slum or enjoying the bowls and golf of the middle-class suburbs, the old generally found their activities narrowing, their illnesses increasing, more and more of their friends 'passing on'—for death, like cancer and the genitals, was not to be named outright. Heart disease would claim most victims in the end, killing nearly one-third of those who died in the early 1960s. Deaths from this cause were three times as common as they had been fifty years earlier, but this did not imply that life was three times as stressful. It simply meant that people were not taken earlier in life from miners' phthisis and other forms of tuberculosis, septicaemia, childbirth, typhoid or diptheria; diagnostic methods were also better. Cancer in its various forms took another 15 per cent. Lung cancer was seven times more common among men than among women, its link with smoking as yet undemonstrated, although in Adelaide the veteran pathologist Sir John Cleland was already voicing suspicions based on a lifetime of observation. The main reason for the increase in deaths by cancer was the gradual ageing of the Australian population, a process slowed during the 1950s and 1960s by immigration.

When Australians died in old age their families and mourners placed notices in the local newspaper, sometimes with an annotation—'Formerly 10th Light Horse' or 'an old colonist'—more often with a stylized piece of verse:

> As God put His arms around you,
> And whispered 'Come and rest',
> He must have loved you dearly
> As He only takes the best.

When it came to the last rites an interesting change was taking place. Cremation had been available in Australia's cities since the earliest years of the century, but until the Second World War most Australians were buried. For many families it was a ritual to visit the parental graves with flowers on anniversaries and Mother's Day. Then cremation gradually took over. In 1951 fewer than 20 per cent of funeral services were cremations; in 1961 a third, with a steady increase following the Vatican councils of 1962–63 when the Catholic Church lifted its embargo on the practice. Nobody seems to have enquired why so many

Australians favoured this change in tradition.[56] Possibly they were rebelling against those Sunday afternoons of family duty visiting the cemetery; possibly they saw cremation as somehow more hygienic; possibly the massed headstones of large metropolitan graveyards reminded them too strongly of the suburban conformity of which they had been accused too often during their lifetimes. It was at any rate a departure from generations of Old World ritual in which bodies returned to the earth from which they and their ancestors had sprung. But it was their choice.

6

THE POLITICS OF AFFLUENCE

THE MENZIES GOVERNMENT of 1949—66 was characterized by great stability. Apart from Menzies himself, whose second prime-ministership lasted sixteen years, and McEwen, who held the trade and commerce portfolios for twenty-one years, other senior ministers enjoyed a continuity in office which contrasted markedly with the fluctuations of the post-Menzies era. There were only two treasurers under Menzies: Fadden for nine years and Holt for seven. Hasluck was minister for territories for twelve years. Casey was at foreign affairs for over eight years, and although Menzies with ill-judged confidence took the position on as a pendant to his prime-ministership during 1960 and 1961 his successor, Sir Garfield Barwick, left it after two years only to become chief justice. Hasluck then followed him for five years. Such ministers developed experience, competence and some sense of proprietorship towards their departments.

Senior public servants enjoyed a similar stability in office and grew accustomed to Liberal—Country Party hegemony. Even Coombs, a major architect of post-war reconstruction under Curtin and Chifley, served the Menzies government peaceably, albeit with diminished panache. In general the machinery of government worked smoothly, although in some cases complacency led to intellectual stagnation. It is hard to resist the thought that if (as so nearly happened) a Labor government had held office even briefly in the early 1960s it would have benefited the temper of Australian politics considerably, since a new generation of Labor front-benchers would have gained experience of the practice of government and the Liberal–Country Party coalition would have been stimulated to useful re-thinking. As it was, Menzies and his colleagues could be seen as a fixture against which their opponents battled in vain.

There was little about the performances of the Liberal–Country Party government in the early 1950s to suggest that it would secure office for thirty of the next thirty-three years. Its handling of economic problems was undistinguished. Faced with Australia's worst post-war rate of inflation the Menzies government's first thoughts were of increased taxation, a 25 per cent cut in immigration, a severe reduction in public works, and the dismissal of 10 000 public servants. The 1952 budget avoided such measures but it was harsh enough to alienate many voters. Flinders, a Victorian constituency which deserts the Liberals only *in extremis*, went to Labor at a by-election, and Labor governments won office in Victoria in 1952 and Western Australia in 1953. At the Senate elections of 1953 Labor secured over 50 per cent of the vote; the party has never done as well since. Against expectations, Evatt as leader of the Opposition was managing to hold together Labor's volatile factions. He confidently led his party into the House of Representatives poll in May 1954. But although Labor won more votes than the coalition, the Menzies government held more seats: 64 against 57. The rural constituencies stood firm for the Country Party, and Labor failed to make enough headway in the Sydney and Melbourne suburbs.

Gough Whitlam, then a very new Labor back-bencher, later observed that in his anxiety to win votes Evatt promised too much for credibility: 'I am bound to say that in the aftermath of Menzies' inflation the extravagance of Labor's policy speech in 1954 was unacceptable to the electors. It cost us the election'.[1] Menzies was also helped by the prolonged tour of the young Queen Elizabeth II and the Duke of Edinburgh in February–March 1954. It was an occasion of great popular enthusiasm, the first visit to Australia by a reigning sovereign, and Menzies showed himself an accomplished and avuncular courtier. But Labor folklore has followed Evatt in attributing Menzies's win to his skill in producing a new twist to the old anti-communist issue with the announcement in the dying days of the old parliament of the defection of an official from the Soviet embassy, Vladimir

Petrov. A few days later Petrov's wife Evdokia, returning under escort to the Soviet Union, was rescued at her own request in a dramatic confrontation at Darwin airport. More than her husband's original defection, this well-publicized drama confirmed for Australians all they had ever heard of Russian espionage and Russian coercion. Diplomatic relations with the Soviet Union were broken for five years. But none of this was quite enough to lose the election for Labor; as Whitlam remarked, 'It was not just Petrov'.

Petrov may not have lost the election for Labor but he soon smashed the Labor Party. Before the election Menzies, with Evatt's concurrence, had set up a royal commission to inquire into the evidence which the Petrovs had brought with them of Russian activities in Australia. Of the three judges nominated to the commission all were conservative, and the chairman, Owen of New South Wales, was a disappointed cynic who had done social favours for Menzies.[2] During the election campaign Menzies himself made little political capital out of the Petrovs, though he did not restrain colleagues who taunted Labor with being soft on communism. But in July the royal commission questioned Evatt's press secretary and other members of his staff whose names were mentioned in the Petrov documents as contacts. During August and September Evatt appeared before the commission as counsel for his staff. His performance was courageous but intemperate. He claimed that the Petrov affair was a conspiracy, abetted by forgery, designed to discredit him as leader of the Opposition. The royal commissioners barred him from their hearings. It was almost the only occasion on which their conduct of the inquiry showed purpose or direction.

Far too much of the royal commission's time was spent in probing the activities of various minor radicals and acquaintances of radicals without care for the hurt to their reputations. Bruce Milliss relates how his father, a Katoomba businessman who had converted from Catholicism to communism in the 1930s, was cross-examined in a fruitless attempt to find a sinister twist to his community activities years previously in organizations such as the 'Sheepskins to Russia' movement and the anti-tuberculosis campaign.[3] The commission paid too much attention to Documents H and J in Petrov's cache, two compilations of small-town gossip about Canberra put together by some journalist. It was becoming simply an exercise in scandal-mongering.

The great victim was Evatt. It is unlikely that Menzies set up the Petrov affair in order to destroy his rival, but he understood too shrewdly the divisive potential of the communist issue for Labor and he liked Evatt too little to deflect in any way the nemesis which would shatter both party and leader. Brooding over the electoral defeat of May, rebuffed by royal commissioners of lesser stature than his own as judges, Evatt saw himself as hemmed round by conspiracies. He identified his enemies as the largely Catholic 'groupers' of the Victorian right-wing whom he had been doing his best to conciliate for the past three years. On 5 October 1954 he lashed out in a press statement, threatening to use the next federal party conference to discipline what he called 'a small group' for repeated disloyalty. This group, he said, was 'largely directed from outside the Labor movement. The Melbourne "News Weekly" appears to act as their organ'.[4] Later he defined the group as 'an outside semi-Fascist body' financed by big business and Liberal politicians. It was adding fuel to the fire. From this moment the great schism of the Australian Labor Party was inevitable.

Evatt's outburst could have been an early portent of the complaint which in his last decade was to cloud his intellect and eventually drive him from public life; but the hardening arteries of a 60-year-old are no adequate explanation of the self-destructive spirit which then possessed the ALP. Evatt's views offended many Catholics who were not groupers and many groupers who were not Catholics. The controversy was nowhere fiercer than in Victoria, where ten years earlier Santamaria, with the blessing of Archbishop Mannix, had first organized resistance to the temporary wartime popularity of communism in the inner suburbs. Against the Movement and the groupers were ranged not only some who were their traditional enemies on the Left and more who were moved by old-fashioned anti-Catholicism, but others who saw Labor as a coalition of factions and disliked the ascendancy of any element, Right or Left, whose commitment to ideology got in the way of the power-broking required for the smooth running of the party machine. During the summer of 1954–55 Labor in Victoria was racked by the bitterness of a civil war. In February 1955 the strife spilt over into the party's federal conference at Hobart. Two delegations claimed to represent Victoria, one manned by partisans of the old grouper-dominated state executive, the other sent by their opponents. By the narrowest of margins the federal conference approved the credentials of the anti-grouper delegation, thus ensuring that at the national level the party would side with Evatt against his foes.[5]

The rift widened inexorably. In Canberra seven Victorian Labor members of the House of Representatives and a Tasmanian senator seceded to form the Anti-Communist Labor Party. Throughout the 1955 parliamentary session Menzies and his colleagues enjoyed the spectacle of the two Labor parties savaging each other. When eventually the report of the Petrov Royal Commission was laid before parliament in September 1955 it contained no startling revelations and might have passed into the limbo of anti-climax but for Evatt's ineptitude. He informed parliament that in order to ascertain whether Petrov's evidence was genuine he had written to the Russian foreign minister, Molotov, and accepted his denial.[6] His foes derided. His followers squirmed. Menzies could no longer resist the temptation of calling a general election in December. The Anti-Communist Labor Party set a trend for the future by directing its supporters to give their second preferences to the coalition against Labor. More than one Labor voter in ten shifted allegiance to the new party. In the Senate the Anti-Communist Labor Party won two of the sixty seats; in the House of Representatives the Menzies government improved its majority from seven to twenty-eight. Kinder than a later generation to defeated leaders, Labor retained Evatt at its head only to suffer a slightly bigger hiding at the 1958 elections.

The split claimed other victims. Early in 1955 Victoria's Labor government under John Cain senior fell when over one-third of its members in the Legislative Assembly went over to the breakaway party.[7] At the ensuing elections the two Labor parties butchered each other so effectively that the Liberals were able to form a government in their own right under Henry Bolte, thus stabilizing the local political scene after thirty years of fragile coalitions and minority governments. Labor's downfall was accompanied by an upsurge of sectarianism. Official Catholic doctrine held that a member of the faith might vote in good conscience for any political party except the communists; but several bishops and many parish clergy encouraged their flocks to put Evatt's brand of Labor beyond the pale and to work actively in support of the Anti-Communist Labor Party. His deputy

Calwell had to leave his parish church of St Brendan's in Flemington to avoid provoking attacks from the pulpit. When he accompanied his godchild, the son of Italian parents, to the boy's first Mass the family and Calwell were ostracized by the rest of the congregation.[8] Such bitter divisiveness could only weaken the church in the long run, but at the time it became, at least in Victoria, a powerful antagonist for Labor.

The new party renamed itself the Democratic Labor Party (DLP). Outside Victoria it enjoyed chequered fortunes. In Tasmania and Western Australia it gained influence out of proportion to its numbers, not only because of the conservative political temper of those states but because of their smaller populations; where Labor and its opponents were fairly evenly balanced it would not require the shift of many allegiances to bring about a change of government. The right-wing Labor governments of both states survived the initial challenge in 1955–56 but Labor lost ground federally in both. South Australia with its largely Protestant background was stony soil for the DLP. In New South Wales J. J. Cahill's right-wing Labor government, veterans who remembered the barren years when J. T. Lang divided the party, managed to hold many of the industrial groupers to their loyalty. Sydney's Cardinal Gilroy gave no encouragement to the breakaways, who failed to make much headway.

In Queensland too it looked as if the critics could be contained by another right-wing Labor regime; but after twenty-five unbroken years in office the Queensland Labor Party was little more than a playground for rival bullies jockeying for power. The ministry under V. C. Gair squabbled with its central executive and both were at odds with some of the unions. After a series of manoeuvres tedious to all except the participants the Gair ministry defied the central executive by refusing to introduce legislation for three weeks' annual leave for workers. In April 1957 Gair and nineteen followers, including all but one of his cabinet, were expelled from the ALP and set up their own Queensland Labor Party. As in Victoria the two Labor factions savaged each other, and in August 1957 a jubilant Coun-try–Liberal Party coalition found itself in power after seeming permanently becalmed in opposition by an unjust electoral system. Naturally the coalition soon changed the system so that the injustice worked to their advantage in future.[9]

The Queensland Labor Party joined forces with the DLP in 1962 after a lengthy courtship, and although it dwindled to extinction in state politics after 1963 it shared the honours with Victoria as a major source of strength for the party federally. There was usually enough support in those states for the party to pick up one or two seats in the Senate, although its share of the national vote peaked at 9 per cent in 1958 and 1961 and was never enough to earn them a seat in the lower house of any parliament outside Queensland (except once by accident in New South Wales when a sitting Liberal member forgot to nominate). Nearly 90 per cent of DLP voters habitually gave their second preferences to Liberal or Country Party candidates, and this bonus was seen as a vital margin of strength for the coalition. It probably gave them victory in the 1959 elections in Western Australia, leaving New South Wales and Tasmania as the only surviving Labor governments.

The hope persisted in some Labor circles that the separated brethren might rejoin the fold. Under Vatican pressure the Movement loosened its links with the church after 1957 and developed into a secular organization. Its driving force, Santamaria, still preached anti-communism tirelessly through radio, television and the *News-Weekly* journal, but his contacts with Labor never quite ceased. The possibility of reunion was canvassed in 1960 when Evatt was at last persuaded to quit politics and was succeeded by his deputy Arthur Calwell, a Melbourne Catholic, but without result. Probably it was an illusion to think of reconciliation.[10] The DLP's supporters came largely from old Labor families who were moving out of the working class into the lower middle class: clerks, shopkeepers, artisans, primary schoolteachers who ceased to share the outlook of industrial workers but were not yet ready to claim alliance with the largely Protestant professional and business families who were the backbone of the Liberals. The DLP was an acceptable half-way house for the socially mobile, and its political rhetoric reflected this. While never ceasing to proclaim the menace of international communism, the DLP turned more and more to championing the family and denouncing permissiveness in all its forms. Thus it touched closely on the hopes and fears of aspiring home-owners and church-goers who sensed that the family values which they found of central importance were somehow threatened by the modern forces of change.[11]

Labor, on the other hand, faced with the slow erosion of its traditional working–class base, had to look for support among the more idealistic or radical members of the professional middle classes: voters for whom politics mattered less as a means for controlling industry and the economy than as an instrument for social reforms such as the improvement of health and welfare services, a fairer deal for Aborigines, or a more enlightened immigration policy. It was a significant shift in 1960 when as Calwell's deputy the party rejected the veteran Sydney radical Eddie Ward by a narrow margin in favour of a lawyer from a younger generation, Gough Whitlam. The university graduates were beginning to move into the ALP. Power still lay, however, with older trade unionists who had cut their political teeth during the 1930s Depression. F. E. (Joe) Chamberlain, federal secretary of the party from 1955 to 1963, was an epitome of the breed, a grimly uncompromising chieftain who would sacrifice the ablest of politicians and the fairest chances of electoral victory for the sake of the purity of the party line, but was not above doing deals with the Country Party for some temporary advantage. Such dinosaurs could not easily convince the sympathies of voters who had migrated to Australia or had come of age since 1949.[12]

Yet Labor almost won in December 1961. Since the communist threat was nearly worn out as an election issue the Menzies government depended heavily on its record for sound economic stewardship. During 1960 and 1961 public faith was weakened by a phase of inflation and unemployment largely caused by the termination of most import controls followed by an ill-judged credit squeeze. Perhaps after twelve years of office the coalition was over-complacent. At the election Labor captured fifteen seats from the coalition, eight of them in Queensland. If a ninth had fallen, as appeared at one time likely, Labor and its opponents would have sent equal numbers to the House of Representatives and a second election would then have followed. Only Victoria was unmoved; after the 1955 split it would be fourteen years before Labor recovered a seat there. The Victorian branch of the Labor Party, thoroughly purged of its right-wing, was the most socialist in character and the least interested in winning elections.

Advocates of change such as Whitlam were frustrated by the party's time-honoured structures. Its top councils, the federal conference and the federal executive, were dominated by paid

Mollie Dunn, member of the Pilbara Aboriginal co-operative, yandying for wolfram, c. 1950

Migrant family, victims of an earthquake in the Ionian Islands, Greece, arriving in Australia, 1953

Immigrant fruitpickers arriving at Mildura, Victoria, in the summer of 1956

The migrant dream: the Holden and the tiled-roof house, probably Perth, mid-1950s

officials of the party or the trade unions. Even the leader and deputy leader of the parliamentary party could be present at meetings of the federal executive only by invitation. The absurdity of this situation became notorious early in 1963 when a sharp-eyed press photographer caught Calwell and Whitlam glumly standing at midnight under the streetlights outside Canberra's Hotel Kingston while inside closed doors a special federal conference debated Labor's policy towards American strategic installations at North West Cape. The sight of Labor's leaders awaiting decisions from 'thirty-six faceless men' of the federal conference was a godsend to the Liberals, and the damage was done although Labor subsequently admitted the leader of the party and his deputy to meetings of the federal conference and executive in a non-voting capacity. Labor could be portrayed as the creature of irresponsible union functionaries and unfit to hold the middle ground.

Dominated by Chamberlain and salaried party officials, the Labor Party's federal executive could be crushingly insensitive to the issues which won and lost elections. When the question of state aid for church schools resurfaced in 1963 the New South Wales state government, mindful of Labor's precarious hold on rural seats such as Goulburn, wanted to modify the party's traditional ban on such subsidies, but was firmly vetoed by the federal executive. The conservative Menzies had no such inhibitions about reversing a tradition as old as the Commonwealth. In 1963 he announced federal funding for science blocks in state and independent schools alike, citing Australia's technological needs as justification. Nor was Menzies reluctant to borrow from Labor's platform when it came to stimulating the economy by deficit budgeting. Aided by the timely easing of a major drought and overseas investment in the coal and iron-ore industries, unemployment dropped by 1963 to its previous low level. Foreign policy also served the government's turn. Mistrust of Sukarno's Indonesia and uneasiness over communist penetration in South Vietnam could encourage Australians to play safe with the experienced professionalism of the Menzies government. In contrast to the vacillations of Labor the Menzies government welcomed the American naval communications station at North West Cape as proof of the continuing strength of the American alliance.

By November 1963 Menzies felt confident enough to call an

election for the House of Representatives. During the campaign Archbishop Mannix died, four months short of his hundredth birthday, and President John F. Kennedy of the United States was assassinated. Both events probably sharpened a hunger for stability. At the election the Menzies government gained ten seats from Labor in New South Wales and Queensland, thus recovering the comfortable majority which was coming to be seen as the normal pattern in Australian politics. The gloom was a little relieved for Labor early in 1965 when South Australia rejected the Liberal government of Sir Thomas Playford, who held office for nearly twenty-seven years by a mixture of managerial competence and unblushing rural gerrymander, and was to some extent victim of his own success in promoting South Australian industry.[13] This success was offset a few weeks later when the Liberal–Country Party coalition won power in New South Wales for the first time in twenty-four years under the leadership of Robert Askin, a crude version of Victoria's Henry Bolte. Labor's defeat was due partly to the federal executive's intervention on state aid for church schools, but the lesson was slowly learnt. Although in 1965 the ALP federal conference agreed to accept existing measures of state aid, Chamberlain in February 1966 persuaded the federal executive to challenge such legislation in the High Court, and when Whitlam as deputy leader publicly came out against this move Chamberlain and Calwell sought his expulsion from the party. They failed narrowly, and the idea of a High Court challenge was dropped after a special party conference ruled in favour of the status quo. But the dispute weakened Labor for several years and once again showed Menzies's skill for picking issues which would divide his opponents.

Menzies was often presented as a statesman of international stature, yet the sweep of his sympathies was restricted. He travelled often to Britain, less frequently to the United States and Europe, and seldom to South-East Asia. This more accurately reflected his personal tastes than Australia's interests. Belief in the threat of a third world war was fading after Stalin's death in March 1953 because the Soviet Union, although now known to possess atomic weapons, seemed content to strike a 'balance of terror' with the United States based on the tacit understanding that neither great power would interfere openly in the other's sphere of interest. This threw regional diplomacy into sharper focus. The United States wanted to contain the spread of communism in South-East Asia where anti-colonial nationalists often borrowed the rhetoric of Marx. The fear arose, and was shared in Australian official circles, that if opportunity offered China would take over one after another of the nations to the south: Taiwan, Vietnam, Cambodia, Thailand, Malaya, Indonesia, and so to the edge of Australia like the Japanese in 1942. An American defence presence therefore must be maintained in the Western Pacific and encouragement given to local opponents of communism, no matter how dubious their credentials in other respects.

These policies led to the formation of the South-East Asia Treaty Organization (SEATO) at a conference in Manila in September 1954.[14] It followed a rebuff in Vietnam where the French had been unable to suppress nationalists led by the communist Ho Chi Minh and were obliged to accept the partition of the country into a communist-dominated North Vietnam and an uncertainly democratic South. There was a precedent in the formation of the North Atlantic Treaty Organization of 1948 when the United States, Canada and several western European nations agreed to pool military resources to protect Europe against further communist inroads. Australia applauded this aim. The ANZUS treaty of 1951 had been supplemented by ANZAM, under which military representatives of Australia, New Zealand and Britain consulted about the defence of Malaya. But a stronger regional pact including Britain and some of the autonomous Asian nations would increase Australia's security. SEATO met this requirement only partially as its terms were scarcely more precise than ANZUS, but Menzies and Casey spoke of it as a cornerstone of Australian policy, matching the unity of the communist powers and greatly preferable to the consortium of non-aligned powers who assembled at the Bandung Conference of 1955.

Until 1956 it seemed feasible for Australia to enjoy the patronage of both Britain and the United States, but in that year the two loyalties clashed. The Suez Canal was the catalyst.[15] For three generations Australian passengers and goods plying to and from Europe had passed through the canal, owned by an international company in which the British government held a substantial shareholding. Successive Egyptian governments endured this arrangement, knowing that in 1968 the contract must be re-negotiated. But in 1953 Egypt came under the leadership of a republican nationalist of uncertain temper, Colonel Gamal Abdel Nasser, who cultivated both the West and the Soviet Union. Smarting at an American refusal to fund an important dam on the Nile, Nasser nationalized the Suez Canal at a stroke in July 1956. The major users of the canal, Britain and France, were outraged. Australia loyally echoed them, especially after an Egyptian mob in a paroxysm of patriotic fervour tore down the Anzac monument at Port Said. The United States was perturbed but decided against strong measures after a series of talks with interested parties including Menzies, who happened to be in Washington at the time.

A consortium of user nations sent a delegation to treat with Nasser in September, and Menzies was asked to head it. The mission failed, perhaps expectedly. Menzies and Nasser were culturally and personally antipathetic. Their concepts of economic nationalism were poles apart. To quote Menzies:

I pointed out that many countries in the world had willingly granted concessions to foreign enterprises to explore and develop national resources, and that so far from thinking that these represented foreign domination, the nations granting such concessions granted them willingly because they were convinced that their own resources and position would be thereby strengthened.[16]

The story of Australia in a nutshell, but Egyptian nationalism was more sensitive. Menzies blamed the failure of the talks on a statement by the American president, Eisenhower, seeming to rule out any involvement by the United States in the coercion of Egypt. This was ironic, as Washington's attitude was shaped partly by Menzies's opposition in July to the use of force; but since then Menzies had fallen in with the British prime minister Sir Anthony Eden in regarding Nasser as a second Hitler whose potential for aggression must be resisted from the start.[17] The crisis persisted until late October when the outbreak of hostilities between Israel and Egypt gave Britain and France a cooked-up pretext for sending troops into the Suez Canal. Within a few days it was evident that this piece of gunboat diplomacy commanded very little support from the rest of the non-communist world. Under American pressure a truce was negotiated. A few weeks later the British and French forces withdrew, to be replaced by a United Nations peace-keeping contingent.

Australian reactions to the crisis smacked of colonial immaturity. Except for Casey, whose sense of ministerial solidarity and personal acquaintance with Eden forbade him to speak out, the federal cabinet was persuaded by Menzies's simplistic views, stifling their doubts in the belief that British judgement must be trusted.[18] Voting on the issue followed party lines. Unlike Britain, where debate was vigorous and cross-voting noticeable, no Australian Labor politician suggested intervention and no conservative had enough independence of judgement to question the wisdom of belligerence. Little concern was expressed about the strain on British Commonwealth relationships when Canada and India pointedly dissociated themselves from the intervention. Menzies never ceased to plume himself on the part he played in great-power diplomacy over Suez. He sedulously kept every favourable press-cutting about his role in the crisis, and as an old man long in retirement he wrote to Eden on his pride at having stood shoulder to shoulder with him.[19] Yet all his forecasts were wrong. The Suez Canal soon re-opened under Egyptian control. Apart from the special case of Israel, no nation's ships were excluded. Egyptian administration and pilotage proved perfectly competent. By the time another war with Israel closed the canal in 1967 the bulk of Australia's trade in any case was shifting away from Europe and passengers were taking to the quicker and cheaper airlines. But with only the crumbling Evatt to oppose him Menzies's reputation for statesmanship went unchallenged.

Menzies's later interventions as Britain's admirer were equally unfortunate. In 1960 relations between the United States and the Soviet Union took a turn for the worse when an American intelligence aircraft was forced down on Russian soil. At the United Nations General Assembly a number of intermediate nations were promoting a motion urging the two super-powers to resume negotiations on the limitation of nuclear arms. Menzies came up with an amendment urging the addition of Britain and France to make it a four-power conference. The proposal was ignominiously defeated, Menzies took a scolding from Nehru of India, and the waters were sufficiently muddied for the idea of a summit conference to lapse. Perhaps that was what Menzies intended. He was never happy with the performance of Asian and African nations in international diplomacy, and viewed their increasing prominence in the British Commonwealth as a disquieting presence in a gentleman's club. When South Africa became a republic in 1961 and withdrew from the British Commonwealth to avoid expulsion it was Menzies who tried hardest to square the circle of accommodating a regime dedicated to apartheid in a multi-racial organization.

There was something curiously undeveloped about Menzies's concept of the British Commonwealth, which at times seemed to go little further than an intense personal loyalty to Queen Elizabeth II as head of the Commonwealth. During the royal visit of 1963 the veteran statesman welcomed his sovereign with an Elizabethan madrigalist's lines: 'I did but see her passing by / And yet I love her till I die'. In the same year his Scottish ancestry was recognized by a knighthood of the Thistle, the highest order of chivalry awarded to any Australian, though later surpassed by the award of the Garter to the governors-general Casey and Hasluck. Until the very end of his regime Menzies insisted that only an Englishman could serve as the Queen's representative in Canberra. Between 1952 and 1965 three Englishmen served as governor-general — Slim, Dunrossil and De L'Isle — the first of them with considerable success. It was only in 1965 that an Australian was chosen in Casey — and he was a member of the House of Lords. (Menzies was not alone in his preference for the English. During these years no Australian was appointed as an Anglican archbishop, or editor of the *Sydney Morning Herald*.)

It would be easy to dismiss Menzies's affection for Britain and Britain's sovereign as an idiosyncracy shared, perhaps less fulsomely, by many of his generation, but it was all of a piece with his thoroughgoing Burkean view of politics. Believing in a legal system based on precedent as a defence against barbarism, living in an era when western civilization was challenged by competing ideologies, Menzies valued the continuities of communal thought and association built over many generations. Post-Aboriginal Australia was too new to accommodate such slowly evolving traditions and must draw on its British background until a decent period had elapsed for maturation. Holding such opinions, Menzies was always apt to regard most major forces for change with doubt, if not outright hostility.

In one area at least, respect for British precedent enlightened the performance of the Menzies government. Britain was a model of a colonial power relinquishing authority gracefully. Compared with the violence of the French exodus from Algeria, or the chaos into which the Congo fell after the Belgians withdrew in 1960, the British recipe of exporting the Westminster parliamentary system seemed at that time a hopeful experiment, from which Australia might take example as the colonial power administering Papua New Guinea. Responsibility for policy was largely in the hands of two men, Paul Hasluck as minister for territories from 1951 to 1963, and Donald Cleland, administrator from 1952 to 1966. Both were able and hard-working and took a close and systematic interest in their duties. Their first priorities were social and economic rather than political: the provision of medical facilities, hospitals, primary schools, and better agriculture leading to the development of a cash-crop economy. In a country subdivided by its rugged geography into numerous clans and tribes it was at first easy to predict that the evolution of a unified nation must be decades in the future.

Official thinking on this score began to shift after 1960, the year in which seventeen African countries gained independent status, when Menzies and Hasluck returned from a conference of Commonwealth prime ministers accepting that Papua New Guinea must move more swiftly towards independence. Even then, the deadline was seen as falling in the late 1980s or 1990s. Democracy was proving a frail flower in exotic climates, with power soon falling either to the military or to an élite minority of university graduates. Hasluck in particular believed that universal primary education must be assured before an élite was groomed. In 1962, however, a commission was set up which led to the foundation of the University of Papua New Guinea in 1966, and in 1963 a capable director of education, Les Johnson, organized a programme to train senior educational administrators. Among the indigenous ex-teachers who graduated from this regime Michael Somare, Oala Oala Rarua and Vincent Eri were to ride to high public office after Papua New Guinea gained autonomy. Meanwhile the United Nations was beginning to prod Australia into setting a timetable for staging Papua New Guinea towards independence, a pressure unwelcome to Hasluck and even more to his successor, the conventionally-thinking Country Party grazier C. E. Barnes (minister from 1963 to 1972). In 1964 the Legislative Council was replaced by a House of Assembly in which the majority of members were elected by direct vote. Over a million voters were identified for a common electoral roll. Nation-wide political parties had not yet begun to emerge, and most candidates concentrated on bread-and-butter issues.

Thirty-eight indigenous members were returned, from whom a number were attached as under-secretaries to government departments as a training in ministerial experience. It nevertheless aroused considerable controversy when Gough Whitlam, speaking at a Goroka seminar in 1965, advocated independence by 1970. Some Australians wanted to retain Papua New Guinea as a buffer against Asian hostility, and even spoke of it as potentially a seventh Australian state. Others feared that an autonomous Papua New Guinea would be swallowed up by an expanding Indonesia. Having almost absent-mindedly become a colonial power, Australia faced the challenge of relinquishing Papua New Guinea as an orderly state in what many perceived as an increasingly disorderly Third World.[20]

Throughout its sixteen years in office the Menzies government's defence and foreign policies were dominated by the threat of foreign communism. In 1957 R. G. Casey warned that 'There is no more dangerous term than "conciliation" when we are grappling with the Communist threat of expansion and their aim of subjugation of the non-Communist world', but he conceded that because of the superior retaliatory capacity of the United States and Britain, 'the Communists see more advantage in maintaining an uneasy status quo than they could ever hope to enjoy by direct aggression'. A simpler and probably commoner view was voiced as late as 1965 by Sir John Cramer: 'there is one thing that remains constant in our present world. It is the desire of Communism for world domination. This is one thing we must never forget'.[21]

Despite this constant sense of threat the Menzies government took a surprisingly relaxed attitude towards defence provision. Cynics supposed that the rhetoric about the Red menace was designed for the consumption of such groups as the DLP, the RSL, and the migrant vote, but all the evidence suggests that most ministers sincerely held a stark view of Russian and Chinese intentions. Yet the calls of publicists such as B. A. Santamaria for conscription and a greatly increased defence expenditure went unheeded. Much as Menzies and his followers feared the communists, they feared even more the electoral unpopularity which might follow increased taxation and workforce planning. By an unswervingly faithful adherence to great and powerful allies—originally the United Kingdom, but increasingly the United States, Australia might win protection on the cheap without diverting resources from economic growth and social welfare. It was an unheroic policy which by its nature could not be openly admitted; but until the moment when something like a genuine crisis developed on Australia's doorstep it worked.

After the Korean War annual defence spending was allowed to drop below 3 per cent of gross national product (GNP), one-half of the proportion allotted in the United Kingdom, one-third of that in the United States. The most sustained thinking about future defence planning came from a committee of inquiry under General Sir Leslie Morshead, set up after a series of critical articles in the *Sydney Morning Herald* in November 1957.[22] The Morshead Committee recommended the integration of the three armed forces, but this advice was not followed. Instead, in the same year national service trainees ceased to be recruited for the Royal Australian Navy and the RAAF and were scaled down for the army. At first it was intended to select the army's intake by lot but in 1958 national service was abandoned entirely. This was meant to coincide with a shift to professionalism. Small, highly trained, very mobile forces would be equipped with supplies standardized to those of the United States armed forces with whom it was anticipated Australia would act. As would later become apparent over the TFX fighter-bombers contract, this meant that defence expenditure would tend to benefit American suppliers rather than stimulating Australian secondary industry or reviving trade with Britain.

But who would be the enemy? The cold war between the super-powers was gradually thawing, so that by 1965 Paul Hasluck, then minister for external affairs, could assert that the United States and the Soviet Union were further from a deliberate choice of war with each other than at any time in the past two decades.[23] China, under Mao Zedong, was more generally feared as 'an imperialist aggressor . . . with the power and the will to extend her empire throughout Southeast Asia until it laps the shores of Australia'.[24] Much thus depended on the stability of the Asian nations that stood between Australia and China. With its nearest neighbour, Indonesia, Australia's relations were correct but lacking in empathy, particularly after Casey's retirement in 1960. The Indonesian leader, Sukarno, was not much interested in Australia. As Bruce Grant described him, 'His tastes are sensual rather than intellectual, and the Australian technological assault on its land mass has no parallel to interest him in modern

Indonesia'.[25] Still it was disturbing when Sukarno dissolved parliament to make room for a National Front mobilizing 'the revolutionary forces of the people', banned such westernized organizations as Rotary and the Masonic lodges, and in 1961 entered into a $1000 million arms agreement with the Soviet Union.

Worse followed. Indonesia showed an appetite for territorial increase, pressing for the return of the last Dutch possession in the region, the ethnically distinct western half of New Guinea (West Irian). This would give Indonesia a common land frontier with Australian-occupied Papua New Guinea and, although Sukarno never made explicit territorial claims against Australia, such a volatile neighbour caused uneasiness among many who remembered Japanese expansion and feared Sukarno's increasing readiness to give patronage to the PKI (the Communist Party of Indonesia). Despite Australia's coolness towards Indonesia's demand for West Irian the United States, when asked to act as mediator in 1962, negotiated the transfer of West Irian to Indonesian rule. There were promises that the local inhabitants would be consulted by referendum at a future date, but nobody seriously believed these. This decision served notice that the United States, although Australia's patron and senior ally, could not always be counted on to serve Australia's interests. Accordingly, Australia grew more concerned to secure American commitments in South-East Asia and the South-West Pacific.

Scarcely was the West Irian issue settled than Indonesia began another campaign of sabre-rattling, this time against the newly created Federation of Malaysia. When in 1961–62 the plan was mooted of joining the former British colonies of Malaya, Singapore, Sarawak and Sabah into one political unit Indonesia at first made no objection, but following a Filipino claim to a portion of Sabah, Indonesia refused to acknowledge Malaysia and in January 1963 embarked on a policy of confrontation. Australia's minister for external affairs, Barwick, was among those who urged Malaysia, Indonesia and the Philippines to compose their differences—at first with some success. Then in July 1963 confrontation resumed, accelerating after the proclamation of Malaysia in September. During the next two years Indonesian patrols and irregulars, later reinforced by paratroops, infiltrated Malaysia's borders and were met by Malaysian and British forces. Indonesia spurned the western powers who favoured Malaysia and drew closer to China and the Soviet Union.

This gave a new urgency to the task of upgrading Australia's armed forces. Menzies had an election to win and the Liberal–Country Party coalition thought it enjoyed a reputation for being sounder than Labor on defence and foreign policy. In September 1963 Menzies in parliament promised Australian military assistance for Malaysia. A month later, ignoring the rival claims of British manufacturers, the Menzies government sent the minister for defence, Athol Townley, to Washington to negotiate the purchase of twenty-four TFX (later F-111) fighter-bombers. 'The "negotiators" must have got stuck into the claret or something', commented one of his cabinet colleagues.[26] Townley committed Australia to an open-ended agreement which helped the Menzies government to decisive victory at the polls, but the progress of the F-111 from drawing-board to delivery met with repeated delays while costs escalated, and it was ten years before Australia benefited from Townley's bargain. Fortunately no invader came meanwhile.

Nor was the Royal Australian Navy at its peak. In January 1964 it was authoritatively described as comprising 'an anti-submarine carrier which cannot protect itself except in a limited way . . . nine escort ships and three elderly British submarines attached'.[27] Morale was further damaged in February when during manoeuvres the aircraft-carrier *Melbourne* collided with and sank the destroyer *Voyager* with a loss of eighty-two lives. After prodding from government back-benchers two lengthy public inquiries followed, laying the responsibility first on one ship's captain, then on the other. The effect on public opinion was unimpressive. As for the army, it seemed improbable that in an era of full employment enough volunteers would come forward to make up an expeditionary force in defence of Malaysia. Yet the crisis continued to fester. Following a resolution of the United Nations Security Council supporting Malaysia's complaint of aggression, Australian troops were sent into action against Indonesian infiltrators in Malaya in October 1964 and in Borneo in February 1965. Meanwhile the United States cut off aid to Indonesia, and in January 1965 Indonesia withdrew from the United Nations. There were substantial reports of Indonesian interest in acquiring its own atomic bomb.

Breaking fatefully with half a century of tradition the government decided in November 1964 to introduce compulsory military service with liability to overseas duty. To the military authorities this made good sense, because in the circumstances of modern warfare the distinction between national servicemen and others was often messy and inefficient besides having an adverse effect on morale. The new form of national service (the blunt term 'conscription' was officially discouraged as too evocative of past controversy) operated through a somewhat ill-starred innovation foreshadowed during the last phase of the earlier national service scheme of 1950—58. The Australian armed forces were not geared to cope with a very large intake of raw recruits, nor was it desirable to dislocate the economy by withdrawing the labour of many young male adults. It was decided that all men should be required to register when they reached their twentieth year. A lottery would be conducted every six months at which a certain number of birth dates were drawn from a barrel. When enough birthdays had been drawn to provide the required number of recruits—allowing for those rejected on grounds of ill-health or permitted to defer because of study or other commitments— those with nominated birthdays would do two years' service. No demands would be made on the rest. Some thought it unfair that chance should determine whether one man would have his career disrupted for two years while another stayed at home. The RSL predictably demanded national service for all. An anti-conscription movement sprang into being within days of parliamentary approval of the bill. While Indonesia was perceived as the main threat to Australia the debate remained fairly low-key. But after the conscription debates of the two world wars the question of compulsion could raise the strongest of feelings, particularly if national servicemen found themselves in a campaign about which opinion at home was divided.

So it fell out. Before any conscripts could be sent to serve against Indonesia Sukarno's regime was shaken at the end of September 1965 by a coup and counter-coup which resulted in the seizure of control by the army and the massacre of large numbers of communists. Sukarno was reduced to a figure-head and the new rulers of Indonesia began to mend their fences with the West. But by this time Australia was committed to another and much more contentious theatre of war—Vietnam. Less immediately dangerous to Australia's interests, less clear-cut in the moral issues which it presented, Vietnam was a subject on which Australians could have widely differing views. It was an unhappy laboratory for experimenting with the use of conscripts overseas.

Doubts on this score were not evident in the thinking of the Menzies government. The situation in Vietnam seemed in many respects a replica of the Korean conflict, which had won almost unanimous support. As was the case in Korea, Vietnam was divided since 1954 between a communist North and a South which at least paid lip-service to parliamentary traditions. South Vietnam was weakened by quarrels between the dominant Diem family, who were Christians, and the Buddhist majority, providing scope for a guerrilla movement, the Viet Cong. Their aim was reunion with the North under the Marxist nationalist hero Ho Chi Minh. After the formation of the National Liberation Front in November 1960 the Americans built up an armed force in support of South Vietnam, and in 1962 the Australians sent in military advisers. After several Buddhist monks had burnt themselves to death as a gesture of protest the Diem government was overthrown in November 1963. Its successors were unstable, and the United States was drawn increasingly into building up its forces in Vietnam. In February 1965 American aircraft began bombing North Vietnamese territory with a fire-power which stopped short of nuclear weapons but came to include napalm and a variety of powerful defoliants. Domestic and international criticism sharpened. It was becoming important for President Lyndon B. Johnson's domestic policies that the United States should not be seen as standing alone against the communist advance.

Some have argued that Australia pushed the United States into raising the stakes in Vietnam.[28] This exaggerates Australia's influence, but there can be no doubt that the Australian government applauded and encouraged American initiatives, thankful that despite the West Irian decision the United States was not going to relinquish its allies in the Western Pacific. Contrary to the advice of his government's strategic planners, Menzies claimed that a communist takeover of Vietnam formed part of a direct military threat by China towards South-East Asia and Australia. What became known as the 'domino theory' gained currency: if South Vietnam fell, Thailand would shortly follow, then Malaysia and Indonesia, until before long the enemy would be at the gates of Australia. This theory was plausible enough to an Australian government whose members remembered the Japanese advance of twenty years earlier, who believed South Vietnam to be the victim of unprovoked aggression, and who were not in the habit of forming opinions independently of Washington. Australia's influence might have been thrown against the escalation of the Vietnam conflict. The United States might have heeded the advice of one of its most faithful allies. Instead, Australia pressed for a stronger commitment and was willing to share part of the cost.

On 29 April 1965 Menzies informed the House of Representatives that an infantry battalion, like all other units a mixture of regulars and national servicemen, would be sent into action in Vietnam. He said this decision had been taken in response to a request from the South Vietnamese government, but in fact the message arrived several hours after his announcement. Most of the press supported the decision unquestioningly, sharing the *Bulletin*'s view that the loss of Vietnam 'would inevitably be followed by the Communisation of the rest of South-East Asia'. Only the *Australian*, newly established by the young Rupert Murdoch as Australia's first attempt at a truly national daily newspaper, seemed sceptical. Intervention, its editorial argued, would only stir up Asian opinion without helping the Americans. It was 'a reckless decision . . . which this nation may live to regret'.[29]

Nine months later, in January 1966, Sir Robert Menzies retired. He had long claimed that a man should leave high office after the age of seventy. Like Curtin and Chifley before him, he had not enriched himself in office, and in the Australia of the 1960s this was not considered surprising. Having been created a Knight of the Thistle in 1963 and Warden of the Cinque Ports in 1965, he looked for leisure to enjoy these honours, varying retirement in a comfortable Melbourne suburb with visits to the United Kingdom and the United States as a respected elder statesman. He looked every inch the part; his instructions to his tailor at the age of sixty-eight gave his size in hats as 7½ (7⅝ for academic headgear), his chest measurement as 48 inches (122 cm), his waist as 51 inches (130 cm) and his size in shoes as 8½ (43).[30] Beneath the proconsular bulk of the statesman there still lurked the nimble feet of the politician.

In retrospect the Menzies era has taken on the nostalgia of a golden age compared with the troubled times which followed, so that his statesmanship appears in a favourable light. But even conservatives have questioned Menzies's performance. Sir Walter Crocker has asked:

How many measures during his two decades of rule can be singled out for their constructive or their enduring qualities? An even harsher criticism must be that he did not give enough of the intellectual, or moral, leadership Australia needed; he raised up no group of successors; and far too much of his rule was a thing of expedients and feints.[31]

Like Sir Robert Walpole before him, Menzies was 'content to meet daily emergencies by daily expedients'[32]—the stock-in-trade of a politician of consummate professionalism who places a low value on ideology. In his younger years Menzies had been an unabashed élitist, but the adversities of the 1940s had tempered him so that there was little that was doctrinaire about his conservatism. Apart from selling the government's shares in the Commonwealth Oil Refineries in 1952 the Menzies government did not unscramble the work of its predecessors by privatization of state assets. In 1951 and again in 1957 legislation was passed maintaining TAA as competitor against a private operator, originally ANA and subsequently Ansett. Although theoretically other private competitors could have come into being, the two-airline policy was upheld by government regulation throughout the coalition's term of office.[33] In the same way the ABC and QANTAS were maintained as a guard against monopoly and to set competitive standards.

Innovation was not the hallmark of the Menzies regime. Commonwealth subsidies for homes for the elderly were introduced in 1954 by William McMahon, then the responsible minister, with bipartisan support, but there is no evidence that Menzies took the lead in promoting the scheme. On the other hand, the appointment of the Murray Committee in 1957 and the federal government's powerful reinforcement of university education owed everything to Menzies; as he once told two vice-chancellors, 'When I go into the cabinet room, I'm the only friend you've got'. But though substantial, this is a solitary achievement. The introduction of an Australia-wide divorce law in 1959 was the work of Sir Percy Joske and Sir Garfield Barwick, and it was Barwick who made the running with the mildly contentious trade practices legislation introduced in 1962. McEwen and his advisers were the architects of Australia's trade policy, just as Hasluck dominated Aboriginal policy and Papua New Guinea. It would be tempting to suggest that Menzies simply surrounded himself with colleagues who would not dispute his ultimate authority, and left those with ability to get on with their jobs and the less energetic to stagnate.

But it might be misleading. Particularly during his last years in office Menzies indulged his authority, and his prejudices, in ways which sometimes seemed merely old-fashioned and reactionary, but more than once had a curiously radicalizing effect on Australian political discourse. It was, for instance, Menzies who broke through the century-old barriers against government funding of church schools, and if this was only capitalizing on a trend already evident in Tasmania and New South Wales it undoubtedly laid to rest a major sectarian grievance as well as embarrassing the Labor Party. It was eventually Menzies who agreed to drop the convention that only an English gentleman was fit to be governor-general, thus paving the way for a renewal of the vice-regal authority. With less enthusiasm he consented to the decimalization of the Australian currency, though this was introduced only a few weeks after his retirement and symbolized another break with British tradition in that the new unit of money would be known as the dollar, and not the 'royal' as Menzies wished. More balefully, he jeopardized Australia's long-term economic prospects by his cavalier rejection of the Vernon Report which, however debatable in detail, would have provided the basis for a more systematic and enterprising management of the Australian economy. But his boldest initiative overthrew the convention that young Australian men should not be compelled to face death in wars fought far from home. He left his successors with Vietnam as the debatable ground on which the acceptability of this change would be tested. Ultimately Vietnam would become the symbol of all those forces of change and innovation which by 1972 would bring down the Liberal ascendancy created under Menzies.

Part III

The Search for New Directions
1966–1975

History fails to treat kindly those individuals who raise popular expectations far above their own capacity to perform.

G. Whitlam, *The Whitlam Years*

7

THE FAITHFUL ALLY

THE VIETNAM WAR, although a limited conflict like the Korean War, was a major catalyst for Australian society; yet it involved far fewer Australians personally than war had involved the hundreds of thousands who served in 1914–18 and 1939–45. Between 1964 and 1972 the Australian Regular Army's numbers increased from 22 000 to 39 000, peaking at 44 000 in 1970. During the same period 63 700 national servicemen passed through the ranks, selected by ballot from a pool of four times that number. Of these national servicemen slightly under a quarter served in Vietnam: 15 542 as against 26 395 regulars. Originally forming part of the 173rd Airborne Brigade, the Australians in 1966 were given sole responsibility for the Phuoc Tuy province south-east of Saigon with headquarters at Nui Dat, where they remained until their withdrawal in December 1971. An initial commitment of one infantry battalion was increased under American prompting to two in February 1966 and three in October 1967. These numbers were the minimum sought by the United States and the maximum compatible with continued popularity for the Australian government at home.

Partly because the ballot made recruitment simply a matter of lottery, the Vietnam War never seems to have generated as much acceptance among young Australians as the two world wars. Terry Burstall was one who volunteered for Vietnam. He was a country youth who had worked as a horse-breaker, drover, rodeo-rider and builder's labourer before buying a small farm near Ballarat. With a father killed in action in New Guinea and a stepfather who had been a prisoner of war on the Burma Railway, he knew what army life was about, but could still find pity for the national service recruits:

The training at Kapooka was hard and relentless and must have seemed brutal in its disrespect for many of them. For those forced into the system it must have been hard to realise that society not only condoned this treatment but backed it with the law. The weather was cold and wet, and the Nissan huts of Second World War vintage and crammed with twenty men, were not comfortable, warm or hygienic.[1]

Of the Australians sent to Vietnam about one in nine were casualties: 475 killed and 4307 wounded. The proportion of national servicemen killed and wounded was somewhat higher than these numbers would suggest because most were privates and therefore front-line troops. There is no evidence that they were singled out for dangerous assignments. Morale was generally good. Unlike the Americans or the Vietnamese on both sides, the Australians were hardly ever the centre of accusations about the deliberate massacre or maltreatment of civilians, although like the AIF before them, they got up to some roughish larrikin behaviour when on leave in Saigon. Although the Australians had some reservations about the Americans as jungle fighters, very few questioned the value of the alliance or the necessity of their presence in Vietnam.[2] But it was different on the home front.

The thinking behind Menzies's Vietnam policy was endorsed by his Liberal successors in the prime-ministership, Harold Holt (January 1966 to December 1967), John Gorton (January 1968 to March 1971) and William McMahon (March 1971 to December 1972). The domino theory held that 'expansionist' powers must be deterred from invading their weaker neighbours because otherwise one act of aggression would follow another until war reached Australia's shores. 'Resistance to such aggression does best promote our national security', said Gorton in April 1970, 'because we must strive to ensure that history is not repeated and that invasion and aggression is not allowed to be successful'.[3] The government refused to see the conflict in Vietnam as a civil war, too readily regarding the North Vietnamese as stooges of the communist Chinese despite the long tradition of Vietnamese mistrust of its big neighbour. South Vietnam at least paid lip-service to political democracy, and it was better to fight the enemy at a distance than to await the invasion of Australia. Besides, an American commitment in Vietnam was reassuring evidence that the Americans were not tiring of their role as Australia's protector in the Western Pacific. Accordingly Australia was often among the first of the United States's allies to applaud escalation of the war and the last to welcome an easing of hostilities.

Yet there was a limit to gratitude. Wiser in their generation than President Lyndon Johnson, who came to grief in endeavouring to combine the expense of the Vietnam War with expanded welfare programmes in the United States, Australia's leaders refused to build up Australia's military commitment in Vietnam to the point where it would have required heavier taxation or the cutting of civilian social services. Most Australians initially supported the government over Vietnam. In July 1965 a Morgan Gallup poll showed that 59 per cent approved of Australia's involvement and 27 per cent opposed it. Their views at this time were not informed by adequate media coverage. Only two Melbourne papers had full-time correspondents in South-East Asia, and *The West Australian* had a journalist in Tokyo; otherwise the Australian press depended largely on syndicated material from overseas tailored for North American or European readers. Special correspondents occasionally visited the Vietnam front but none stayed for long. Consequently Australians got a patchy and limited picture of a very complex conflict. Editorial comment, with the notable exception of that of the *Australian*, tended to reflect the Australian government's line uncritically, and the public followed.[4]

Some clergy and academics asked questions. When nearly half the Anglican bishops wrote a public letter to the prime minister in 1965 doubting the wisdom of the escalation of the war they received short shrift from Menzies. Seeking a wider discussion of the issues academics at several universities, the Australian National University, Queensland, and Monash, organized teach-ins, along the lines developed at some American campuses. During these open forums, held in the winter of 1965, audiences of several hundred heard a range of arguments, including the government's case. Paul Hasluck, since 1964 minister for external affairs and a staunch advocate of intervention, spoke at Monash. Soon the protest movement grew more militant. In October an anti-Vietnam group disrupted Sydney's Friday afternoon rush-hour traffic by sitting down in Martin Place. In December a rally at the Sydney Town Hall attracted three thousand people. Throughout 1966 a succession of demonstrations ('demos') followed.

Perhaps inevitably, the forms of protest followed American models as faithfully as the Australian government followed American policy. Women from the Save Our Sons movement held hour-long silent vigils. One student group burned a fiery cross beside the state war memorial in Perth, infuriating the RSL. The Labor leader Arthur Calwell, a veteran warhorse of the anti-conscription movement, stumped the country vigorously. A new and shocking element touched Australian politics in May 1966 when at the close of an anti-war meeting in the Sydney suburb of Mosman Calwell was shot and slightly wounded. Fortunately it was an isolated incident. His assailant, diagnosed as a 'borderline schizophrenic', later rehabilitated himself and became a poet. Nevertheless the protest movement tapped a vein of violence in its opponents. Confronted by anti-Vietnam demonstrators as he drove with President Johnson through the streets of Sydney in October 1966, the state premier, Robert Askin, was reported as saying: 'Drive over the bastards'.[5] This may have passed for ferocious jocularity, but there was nothing jocular about the New South Wales president of the RSL, Sir William Yeo: 'A baton behind the bloody ear—there's nothing will calm the bloody ardor quicker than that'.[6] A more thoughtful response came from the prime minister's wife, Dame Zara Holt, who, although shaken by the anger of the crowds confronting her husband, could comment:

I can respect the feelings of people who demonstrate against things in Australia if they're dedicated. Possibly it is the only way they can get a public hearing. They can't get on TV. They can't get into the papers. They can write letters but they'd probably never be printed. Perhaps demonstrations are the only way that they can get a hearing, but I don't understand their logic when they are demonstrating against violence, to be violent themselves.[7]

The gap between the governing classes and the protesters could not be put more clearly.

To some extent the anti-Vietnam campaign grew from a broadly-based peace movement which, taunted throughout the 1950s as little more than a communist front, had achieved a limited amount of public acceptance in the early 1960s. In 1962 a petition supporting Calwell's proposal for a nuclear-free Southern Hemisphere had attracted over 200 000 signatures, and in 1963—64 the first of many protests against French nuclear tests in the Pacific gained respectable sponsorship. But when Calwell's policy of withdrawal from Vietnam was tested at the elections of December 1966 there came a daunting rebuff. Labor was thrashed more thoroughly than at any poll since 1931. Although the coalition under Holt was clearly the beneficiary of prosperous times, Vietnam contributed to the coalition's victory because many swinging voters and many recently enfranchised migrants were moved by issues of national security. Calwell resigned the leadership of the Opposition, to be replaced by his deputy Whitlam. The anti-Vietnam movement tasted the bitter bread of defeat. As one member wrote: 'Seemingly, no matter how much we petition, march or demonstrate, our protests make little impact upon our Governments and the war proceeds to escalate regardless'.[8]

Encouraged by victory, the government sought to bind the American alliance still closer by the grant of sites for the tracking and communications stations required for the United States's world-wide nuclear weapons systems. By 1967 Australia was the largest single centre for American missile and space operations outside the United States. As Robert Cooksey observed, 'with its technological and logistic facilities, its political stability and external security it is the most suitable piece of real estate for such operations in the southern hemisphere'.[9] In September 1967 the North West Cape Naval Communications Station was formally opened by Harold Holt, in whose honour the station was renamed after his disappearance and presumed death a few months later. Space-tracking stations were also established near Canberra at Honeysuckle Creek and Tidbinbilla. Of greater significance was the installation between 1966 and 1968 of what was termed a 'joint defence space research facility' on about 2500 hectares of semi-desert at Pine Gap, south-west of Alice Springs. The main purpose of this installation was the detection and interception of Russian and possibly Chinese missiles, but this was shrouded in obscurity since the project was never submitted to parliamentary debate. Labor, smarting over its self-inflicted wounds over the North West Cape issue in 1963, was not eager to stir up the matter. A few critics worried that Pine Gap might make Alice Springs a nuclear target, and a few more complained that an allegedly independent Australia had no say in the control of Pine Gap, but they went unheeded. Instead another space communications station was built at Nurrungar, near Woomera in South Australia. If Australia gave only a limited workforce to the American alliance, it made its contribution as 'a suitable piece of real estate', and during the Vietnam years all major political parties entirely accepted the American alliance.

Protest was meanwhile side-tracked into the self-indulgent issues of student politics. Encouraged by the examples of campus radicals in the United States and France, movements sprang up during 1967 and 1968 at several Australian universities, where the Vietnam question was joined to a variety of demands. Some sought an alliance of students and workers to bring about the immediate downfall of capitalism; others simply wanted a stronger student voice on university committees. Each group varied in its aims and tactics, for despite conservative alarm there was little effective nation-wide direction to student protest. At the University of Queensland the movement soon became a broadly-based protest against the state government's refusal to permit unauthorized demonstrations of any kind, whereas at Monash the university administration was the main target of noise and violence.[10] This spirit of confrontation flowed back into off-campus anti-Vietnam demonstrations. In July 1968 the American Consulate in Melbourne was stoned. In April 1969 Students for a Democratic Society took over the federal attorney-general's office in Sydney, provoking a rough reaction from the police. A year or two later Arthur Calwell remarked: 'I haven't taken part in demonstrations in recent times because an anarchist crowd of students have taken over and it's no use appealing for peaceful demonstrations'. And he added prophetically: 'most of them who are performing so badly in their teens will finish up as petty bourgeoisie and highly respectable lawyers, and maybe judges!'.[11] At the time, Vietnam seemed likely to become the most divisive issue to strain the fabric of Australian society since the conscription crisis of 1916–17, but where the earlier controversy had split Australians on long-lasting lines of class and sectarianism, the Vietnam dispute was taking on something of the character of a conflict between the generations.

Wider public sympathy was retrieved for the anti-Vietnam movement by the government's inept handling of conscientious objectors. Although national service regulations, more generous than during the two world wars, allowed exemption of young men belonging to a recognized pacifist religious group such as the Society of Friends or Jehovah's Witnesses, there was no provision for non-believers, nor for those who objected solely to the Vietnam War. Groping for a solution, a cabinet minister, Bill Snedden, suggested that objectors might be conscripted for civilian projects at under-award rates of pay, but his colleagues rejected the idea. Some reluctant recruits showed great ingenuity in faking psychological symptoms which would disqualify them from service. Others went into hiding, and their sympathizers enjoyed defying the authorities' attempts to find them. Often the government was slow to prosecute, wishing to avoid contention.[12] But some objectors stood their trial for refusal to undertake national service and became liable for two years' imprisonment.

Only one objector is known to have served the full two years. He was Brian Ross, who after sentence in October 1969 was imprisoned at Sale, in Gippsland, from where he managed to send a story to the *Australian* describing the winter cold, petty regulations, inadequate food, criminal company, and sheer boredom of his surroundings.[13] He would have received a milder penalty for putting lives at risk through drunken driving. The case which embarrassed the government most was that of Simon Townsend, a recalcitrant conscript who after induction defied the army authorities so provocatively that he was sentenced to forty-eight hours on bread and water in an 8-square-metre cell. During his sentence he was awoken every half-hour. When the matter was brought before the House of Representatives the minister for the army, Phillip Lynch, a smooth young man without military experience of his own, simply stated that it was part of the normal code of military discipline, was meant to ensure that Townsend refrained from suicide, and in any case had been discontinued.[14] Lynch had previously made heavy weather of fending off earlier allegations that Australian troops had administered a form of water torture to a suspected Viet Cong woman guerrilla. After such a debut it was only four years before he was his party's deputy leader.

Such episodes helped to build up disillusion with the war. Public opinion polls, never biased in favour of the protest movement, continually showed that a majority of Australians opposed sending conscripts to Vietnam. However, until mid-1969 the presence of Australian armed forces in Vietnam kept majority support, and so did the two-year national service scheme, particularly among males and younger people.[15] By late 1967 Holt was resisting strong pressure from President Johnson to increase Australia's force in Vietnam, and his successor John Gorton early in 1968 made a public commitment to that effect. The North Vietnamese Tet offensive of January—February 1968, although a military failure, was a psychological success which helped to drive Johnson into stepping down from the American presidency. His successor, Richard Nixon, in 1969 proclaimed the Guam doctrine indicating that American forces would gradually scale down their overseas commitments, leaving the South Vietnamese to self-help. Australian opinion was probably also influenced by vivid television portrayals of devastation in Vietnam. In no previous war had civilians been brought so immediately into contact with front-line realities. Those with teenage sons could have few illusions about what was involved. During 1968 and 1969 the movement to end Australia's involvement in the war gathered strength.

Its foremost spokesman was Dr Jim Cairns, a former Melbourne policeman turned economist and federal politician, of curiously uneven judgement but great moral courage.[16] Cairns won many sympathizers among the young by his passionate sincerity for the moratorium movement, although his Labor colleagues were torn between those who distanced themselves from him and those who thought him a fitter leader for the party than the more cerebral Whitlam. Although the victim of a violent bashing in his own home in August 1969 by thugs whose motives were never divulged, Cairns persisted in focusing protest on the Vietnam question, and disturbed the government considerably by urging workers and students to occupy the streets of Melbourne to proclaim their views. Encouraged by a federal election in October 1969 which slashed the Gorton government's majority, the anti-Vietnam movement planned street marches in every major city for the weekend of 8—10 May 1970. Although the movement was committed to non-violence Snedden, with his gift for elephantine metaphor, likened the organizers to 'political bikies who pack-rape democracy'.[17] The march drew a turnout of over 75 000 in Melbourne alone, and probably 200 000 in the whole of Australia. It seemed as if the tide of events was flowing in favour of the moratorium movement. Two further demonstrations, neither quite so well attended, followed at six-month intervals on a nation-wide basis.

However heartening as a manifestation of social conscience, even the biggest anti-Vietnam protests had no impact on government thinking. Australia's decisions to commit or withdraw forces in Vietnam continued to be influenced by American initiatives, modified by considerations of cost. The real importance of the moratorium movement lay elsewhere. As put by Ian Turner, a veteran radical who applauded the large participation of youth in 'peaceful objections to the war in Vietnam', this was a moment when:

a culture and sensibility are being transformed before our eyes. And along with that goes the attempt to transcend the old political norms. Representative democracy, as run by the old bureaucrats of the tribe, will no longer do. Politics takes on new dimensions: the young no longer see themselves as apprentices to the old power structures; they demand policies and institutions which are responsive to their needs. Happily they are as little given to wielding authority as they are to being on the receiving end; they are as likely to transform democracy rather than to supersede it.[18]

Bliss was it in that dawn to be alive . . . Perhaps Turner looked at things with the idealistic eye of a Melbourne intellectual. There were still many young men who went off to Vietnam unquestioningly, as well as those other cheerfully insensitive youngsters who could be heard in beer-gardens on Saturday afternoons singing to the tune of 'The Nickelodeon Song':

> Put another Buddhist in,
> In the Buddhist burning bin,
> Light him up with kerosene,
> And burn him, burn him, burn him.[19]

Nevertheless the Vietnam moratorium movement was an instructive model for protest for a large number of under-appreciated Australians, among them Aborigines, women's groups, ecologists and others previously lacking an outlet for their grievances. The anti-Vietnam movement drew strength from an awareness, stimulated by television coverage and other media, that Australians were not confined to narrow and parochial issues but could form part of a world-wide movement of moral protest. Thus it became a school of political education for many who despaired of finding redress through the conventional mechanisms of politics, particularly after twenty unbroken years of Liberal–Country Party rule. When the parliamentary system appears to be the monopoly of one faction its credibility suffers. It was not surprising that the late 1960s and early 1970s saw a ferment of alternative movements seeking to broaden the terms of political dialogue, and these might have dwindled into futility if Labor under Whitlam had not offered a feasible alternative to the old coalition. By seeming an instrument which might enable the reformers' hopes to become reality Labor enhanced its prospects of winning office, but only by carrying an impossible burden of high expectations.

It was both the greatness and the misfortune of Gough Whitlam that he appeared to be, and considered himself to be, one of the few Australian politicians capable of translating high expectations into achievement. Son of a senior federal public servant, and a lawyer by training, Whitlam was a cultivated man of metropolitan background. He knew at first hand, as no previous aspirant to the prime-ministership knew, the needs and frustrations of dwellers in the new working-class suburbs of Australia's big cities. Yet he could never take the rest of Australia quite seriously, and often behaved as if the sun rose over Sydney and set over Canberra. A large, self-confident, dominant personality, he was compared by some with Menzies both for his capacity to provoke antagonism and then to overcome it by rhetoric and repartee. But he was unlike Menzies in one most important respect. Where Menzies had seen the art of government as largely consisting of inaction until the pressure of events dictated otherwise, Whitlam viewed political power as an instrument for social change based on intellectual analysis.[20] For his opponents who headed the Liberal–Country Party coalition between 1966 and 1972 it would be a test of statesmanship to modernize the practices which had served them so well under Menzies, so as to accommodate the demands for social change which could no longer be ignored.

Harold Holt, prime minister from January 1966 to December 1967, suffered from the expectation that, like Anthony Eden after Churchill, he would prove to have been too long the crown prince to develop a style and policies of his own. Having inherited the Vietnam War, he is often remembered as its uncritical apologist: 'All the way with LBJ'. In the conduct of parliament he was sometimes inept, notably in October 1967 when, uncritical of faulty departmental advice, he misinformed the house about the availability of records detailing the flights taken by senior politicians in the RAAF's VIP squadron of aircraft, until corrected by the government leader in the Senate, John Gorton. On the other hand he was a liberalizing influence in fields such as Aboriginal policy, immigration and support for the arts, and he was prepared to experiment with constitutional innovation at the modest level of authorizing a referendum to break the convention that the Senate must be half the size of the House of Representatives. Although supported by both sides in federal parliament the proposal was defeated in every state. The majority of voters evidently feared that the move would lead to a huge expansion of the lower house and the erosion of state rights. Few noted that in the same year a rare combination of ALP and DLP senators had rejected a government proposal to increase postal charges, thus establishing the first small precedent for the assertion of the Senate's long-dormant claims to dispute the budget put forward by the government of the day.

Holding office developed a certain toughness in the normally affable Holt. He resisted President Johnson on the issue of more Australian forces for Vietnam, and he braved the wrath of the Country Party and his formidable deputy prime minister, McEwen, by refusing in November 1967 to devalue the Australian dollar at a time when only primary producers stood to benefit. But he was a man embattled, and when the half-Senate election in late 1967 showed a 7 per cent swing against the government he knew his performance to be under question. During a weekend holiday on 17 December he insisted on swimming in a strong sea off Portsea, Victoria, and was swept away. His body was never recovered. Despite gossip about suicide and a bizarre tale seeking to prove him a Chinese secret agent[21] his death can be seen as no more than the result of a middle-aged Australian male's attempt to shake off the cares of the workplace by strenuous physical activity — coupled with a no less Australian impatience with the concept that a prime minister must be accompanied at all times by heavy security.

McEwen was sworn in as prime minister until the Liberals decided on a new leader. He at once stated that he would not enter a coalition if the Liberals chose William McMahon, who as federal treasurer had been most associated with the controversial refusal to devalue, and whom McEwen mistrusted personally.[22] Of the remaining possibilities the two foremost were the minister for foreign affairs, Paul Hasluck, and the government leader in the Senate, John Gorton. Hasluck was known to be favoured by Menzies; he was a hard-working intellectual, controversial because of his dogged advocacy of the Vietnam War, and disdainful of public relations. Gorton, although Oxford-educated, was down-to-earth, gregarious, and a Victorian—and Victoria was the heartland of the Liberal Party. He had made a good impression by his candour over the VIP aircraft affair, and was thought to have the potential to match Whitlam in terms of public image. The party chose him. Hasluck retired from politics in April 1969 and became governor-general.

What the party did not realize about Gorton—who moved to the House of Representatives in Holt's old seat—was that he wanted to be an active reformer. He was one of the considerable number of Second World War ex-servicemen who, although strongly anti-communist and convinced of the need for a sustained defence effort, were gripped by a vision of Australian nationalism which transcended the pettiness of state loyalties, while at the same time avoiding the excessive deference to great and powerful allies which had been too much an Australian characteristic under Menzies and Holt.[23] He combined these unorthodoxies with a free-and-easy personal touch and an impulsive outspokenness, at times bordering on the larrikin. If his policies had been more conventional he might have got away with his cavalier style, and if his style had been conventional he might have carried through his policies. Once again a Liberal prime minister would have survived by stealing Labor initiatives. As it was, although hard-working and even far-sighted in his goals, he gave the impression of being careless and unsafe.

His beginnings were promising. Labor's fortunes were still flagging. South Australia was lost in 1968 to a young, reform-minded Liberal premier, Steele Hall, and when the Liberals won Tasmania for the first time in thirty-five years in May 1969, there followed twelve months when Labor was out of office everywhere in Australia. Whitlam was in trouble with his party because of his power struggle with the federal executive, and in April 1968 survived a leadership challenge from Cairns by a narrow margin.[24] Whitlam also had to contend with the hostility of the Victorian branch of the party, and it took him until 1970 to secure federal intervention in the affairs of that branch. The Gorton government could be excused for believing that Labor's old habits of self-mutilation would keep the party on the Opposition benches. But it was not long before mutters of perturbation were heard on the Liberal side as well.

Gorton's worst publicity came from sexist tittle-tattle about trivial breaches of decorum. The most damaging incident resulted from Gorton's conduct on a night in November 1968 when the American ambassador, concerned because Gorton had not been given prior information about American plans to halt bombing in Vietnam, invited him to visit the embassy at a late hour. When Gorton eventually arrived he was accompanied by his press secretary and a young woman journalist, daughter of a Labor senator, to whom they were giving a lift. Her presence was no cause for scandal, but a Liberal back-bencher, Edward St John, created a fuss. Gorton made a slovenly defence in parliament, and discrepancies emerged about the timing of his visit. St John was not supported and quit the Liberal Party, but the episode damaged Gorton, largely because of his slapdash handling of American relations. Sections of the media continued to present him as a playboy with an eye for a pretty girl. Yet he might have survived all these calumnies if he had been perceived as sound on the question of overseas investment.

During the last years of the Menzies era Australia had borne an enviable reputation as a safe haven for investment. In 1964 the London *Financial Times* declared Australia the healthiest economy on earth.[25] Encouraged by a tax investment allowance of 29 per cent for capital equipment for manufacturing industries, private overseas investment had grown by 250 per cent from 1958 to 1959, to reach $644 million by 1965–66. American investors were everywhere. Even that most traditional of outback pursuits, the north Australian beef industry, was attracting the attention of Texas ranchers after the success of the King ranch in acclimatizing tick-resistant Brahman-cross cattle during the 1950s. In 1964, 20 per cent of Australian manufacturing industry had American ownership, in 1965, 27 per cent. 'It is probably fair to say', wrote Donald Brash early in 1968, 'that most Australians would have difficulty naming a breakfast food, a cosmetic, or a toilet article *not* produced by the local subsidiary of some American company'.[26] By that year Australia was the fifth largest field for American investment anywhere in the world. There can be little doubt that much of this investment was encouraged by Australia's reputation as a stable and loyal ally of the United States, democratic yet anti-socialist, and more welcoming than much of Latin America or Africa. This reputation had been powerfully enhanced by Australia's participation in Vietnam.

Swollen by this tide of investment, the mineral boom surged ahead between 1966 and 1969.[27] Following several discoveries of natural gas off the Gippsland coast in Victoria, Australia's largest and most profitable oilfield was located by off-shore drilling by Esso-BHP in 1967, so that Australia could now hope to provide about 60 per cent of domestic oil and petroleum needs from local sources. In March 1966 the first shipment of iron ore from Mt Newman left Western Australia; in August Hamersley Iron began shipments through the new port of Dampier. During the same year manganese contracts were signed for the deposits on Groote Eylandt. The United Kingdom Atomic Energy Authority agreed to take 1000 tons of Australian uranium each year between 1971 and 1980. Nickel, previously unknown in payable quantities, was found during 1966 at Kambalda, south of Kalgoorlie, and at Greenvale in the north of Queensland. Of all the lures for speculators nickel seemed the most beguiling, and capital poured in for every share issue. Primed by the mineral boom, private capital influx into Australia topped $1000 million for the first time in 1967–68. By 1971–72 the figure reached a peak of $1867 million which would not be exceeded for the rest of the decade. This bounty came not only from the traditional providers such as the United States and Britain, but increasingly from Japan and other foreign nations. These sources accounted for more than one-third of the bonanza of 1971–72. It was as well that Eddie Ward had not survived to see this happy enmeshment of the Australian economy in the web of international finance.

Many trade unionists expected the North American companies to prove tough employers. They pointed at the six-month dispute at Mount Isa during the summer of 1964–65, an extraordinarily confused affair from which few emerged with credit.[28] By far the longest established of the big American-owned mining companies in northern Australia, Mount Isa Mines was locally managed and had cultivated a favourable image as a firm aware of the human needs of its workforce. Mount Isa was presented as a model 'company town'.[29] During the early 1960s, however, bonus payments for working miners fell behind comparable communities in

'Burly with the ingestion of too many carbohydrates . . .':
three Victorian politicians, mid-1950s

Prime Minister Robert Menzies and John McEwen, imperturbable after
a cliff-hanger federal election, December 1961

Suburbia in the bush: Mount Isa shopping mall, 1960

Open-air markets, like this one at Salamanca Place, Hobart, were another sign of European influence

Mary Kathleen and Broken Hill. In reprisal the men refused to undertake contract work, insisting on time wages. The president of the Queensland Industrial Court, a judge whose wife was a shareholder in Mount Isa Mines, declared their action a strike. The settlement of the problem was bedevilled by at times violent rivalry between two groups of unionists, the conservative Australian Workers' Union and a grass-roots movement led by an enigmatic North American radical, Pat Mackie. The arbitration authorities were vacillating and dilatory; the management refused to compromise and sacked many of the strikers, including Mackie; the Queensland government, always excitable about industrial disputes, barged in with draconian interventions against picketing and sent in large numbers of police. Eventually the strike petered out with the company largely victorious, but the dispute showed how easily tempers could fray and intransigent attitudes be struck in the hot and thirsty environment of a northern mining community.

Experience in the new mining communities of Queensland and Western Australia revealed many social problems. Because most workers knew they would spend only a few years at their jobs they did not become involved in community affairs but tended to expect the employing company to provide facilities. Many women felt themselves to be isolated, under-occupied, and oppressed (despite the increasing use of air-conditioning) by the summer heat. There was a lack of grandparent figures or mature sources of support (the average age in some northern mining towns was under fourteen), and an excess of males. Marital problems were rife. The proportion of migrants was usually much higher than the Australian average, and this led to problems of assimilation and culture conflict.[30] Intelligent managements grew concerned about these difficulties and attempted social planning. When Hamersley Iron decided in 1969 to establish a new town at Karratha in the Pilbara, the firm joined with the Western Australian government in approaching the Australian Inland Mission to act as an agency in setting up community facilities and self-help projects. Within four years Karratha had several churches and twenty-seven community groups, ranging from a Catholic sodality to Weight Watchers, and was also the local co-ordinating centre for external university courses. If only from enlightened self-interest, it seemed that the multinationals could learn to be good employers. Mount Isa Mines, for instance, having recovered strongly from the trauma of the great strike, embarked on a new phase of expansion in the early 1970s, but took care at the same time to finance new housing estates with many amenities and to provide the town with a cultural complex completed in 1974 at the cost of $3 million.[31]

Some prominent Australians nevertheless reacted uneasily to the increasing dominance of overseas investors. According to H. C. Coombs, who retired as chairman of the Reserve Bank in 1968, the growth of overseas ownership:

entrusted decisions on matters which may become of increasing national concern to men whose purposes are not ours, whose allegiances are elsewhere, who are not exposed to the social pressures which influence Australians, and whose interests in our economy may therefore be limited to the short or long-term profits they can derive from it.

That staunchest of economic nationalists, John McEwen, persuaded the government in 1970 to set up the Australian Industries Development Corporation (AIDC) as a kind of government-owned merchant bank which could contribute loan capital or equity for predominantly Australian-owned firms planning new projects in the mineral processing and manufacturing sectors. This initiative was his last victory in his long feud with the federal Treasury, whose senior officials welcomed the resources boom as reconciling growth with stability, and mistrusted as futile most proposals for purposeful government intervention in economic planning. The advent of the AIDC also created some uneasiness among businessmen, who wondered what use a socialist government might make of such an instrument.[32] Nor was this fear unrealistic. McEwen's aim of 'buying back the farm' struck a responsive chord among many of his Labor opponents, none more so than the blunt, bulky veteran from Wollongong, Rex Connor who, although a latecomer to federal politics, had already impressed his colleagues by his largeness of vision and a tough entrepreneurial drive not totally unlike that of such captains of the mining industry as Lang Hancock.

Nor was Gorton, although prime minister for much of the boom, at all deferential in his public utterances:

Until very recently it has seemed to me that the posture of Australia in seeking overseas capital has been the posture of the puppy lying on its back with all legs in the air and its stomach exposed saying 'Please, please give us capital. Oh, tickle my tummy. Oh, on any conditions'.[33]

In September 1968, when British financiers seemed likely to take over the large Canberra-based MLC insurance company, Gorton announced that the federal government would not allow it. Neither cabinet nor the treasurer had been consulted in advance, and even those who applauded Gorton's economic nationalism were dubious about his precipitancy. A by-product of this nationalism was a renewed interest in atomic energy. States without adequate coal reserves, such as Western Australia, were already looking to alternative sources of electricity generation such as oil. In its 1968 report the Australian Atomic Energy Commission stated that because of shifting costs nuclear energy was becoming competitive with other energy forms in New South Wales and Victoria. Some of Gorton's back-benchers were enthusiastic; Dr Malcolm Mackay in 1968 said Australia should stockpile plutonium and 'cut corners in programmes for nuclear power stations'.[34] The federal government called for tenders for a 500-megawatt nuclear reactor at Jervis Bay, the Australian Capital Territory enclave on the New South Wales coast. There the scheme stalled. With coal production increasing annually, and with the first significant oil production coming on line, it was too much to contemplate the capital cost of a nuclear power station. Planning was postponed, then suspended indefinitely in 1971. In the light of later debate about nuclear energy it would have been a curious monument to the Gorton era.

Gorton's interest in nuclear energy was thought by some to foreshadow new directions in Australian defence policy. Reliance on great and powerful allies had led to some unfortunate planning decisions. The F-111, trumpeted in 1963 as a major gain, was as far off delivery as ever, its costs escalating until, to paraphrase one commentator, it seemed the armed forces' rejoinder to the Sydney Opera House. It was thought that Gorton's view of Australian defence policy was shifting away from fighting as America's ally in distant wars such as Vietnam in favour of a concept of 'fortress Australia', a nation building up capacity for self-defence against aggression which might not come from a major nuclear power such as the Soviet Union. Right-wing Liberals and the DLP were displeased when Gorton failed to repudiate a new minister for external affairs, Gordon Freeth, who stated that the presence of Russian shipping in the Indian Ocean was not necessarily cause for Australian panic.[35]

At the House of Representatives elections in October 1969 the

Gorton government's majority was reduced from thirty-eight to seven. Freeth was one of the casualties. Open doubts began to be voiced about Gorton's administrative style, and McEwen discreetly let it be known that he withdrew his objections to McMahon as leader. Undeterred, Gorton plunged into the troubled waters of Commonwealth–state relations. His first initiative should have been relatively uncontentious. For many years the states had imposed stamp duty on receipts until the High Court ruled that this was an excise which could be levied only by the Commonwealth. The Gorton government prepared legislation empowering Canberra to collect receipts duties on behalf of the states. This was rejected by the Senate in 1970, the DLP joining the Opposition on the grounds that such duties mainly hit the less affluent. Whitlam and the Labor leader in the Senate, Lionel Murphy, made much of this rebuff, claiming that a government whose financial legislation was rejected by the Senate should go to the polls. It was a long time since the Senate had been so assertive of its powers, and a dangerous game for Labor to play. The time was not far distant when a Whitlam Labor government would have to contend with a hostile Senate.[36]

Gorton was provoking far more hostility from within his own party by his centralism. In 1970 legislation was prepared for federal control of the seas and submerged lands around Australia. State governments, eager for the revenues which would come from successful offshore mineral exploration, found it hard to stomach the assertion of Commonwealth authority, and complained that Gorton had disregarded a promise to consult further with them before submitting proposals to parliament. A former cabinet minister, David Fairbairn, supported them. McEwen devised a formula which acquitted Gorton of bad faith, but the issue was shelved and Gorton's reputation further shaken. This mishandling meant that it was now very difficult for a Liberal–Country Party government to create a national policy on offshore development, and virtually impossible for any future Labor government.

Yet such offshore legislation was a necessary component of minerals and energy policy, and the need for a national approach grew plainer every year. Australia was enjoying a spectacular boom in mineral exports. Coal, iron ore and bauxite increased their share of Australia's export income between 1966–67 and 1970–71 from 4 to 15 per cent. Admittedly the mainstay of

Australia's export performance was still the traditional rural trinity, wool, cereals and meat, making up over a third of the total in 1970–71, but wool prices were falling, and wheat was plentiful on world markets. The most important shift in Australia's trading pattern during those years was the collapse of the United Kingdom as a market, especially after its long-delayed entry into the EEC was negotiated for 1971. By 1971–72, although the United Kingdom would still provide 20 per cent of Australia's imports, it would take only 9.2 per cent of exports. Japan stood out as Australia's best customer, taking 27 per cent of exports in 1971–72; another 12 per cent went to South-East Asia, and the same to the United States. The old British Commonwealth connection based on investment and migration was yielding to the compulsions of geography. Australia was becoming part of the Pacific economy.

Trade conquered ideology in Australia's quest for markets. The Soviet Union was a steady buyer of wool. China provided a market for wheat, and the Islamic nations of the Middle East were taking meat and livestock. This ingenuity in finding new trading partners was not matched by diversification of export products. Nor was enough attention paid to new technologies such as electronics, or to the pattern of industrialization emerging in countries such as Singapore, South Korea and Taiwan province. All of these, like Japan, were increasing their GDP at a rate faster than Australia's 6 per cent, but Australia continued to outstrip the United States and Britain, and caught up with the German Federal Republic. During the twentieth century there was never a five-year span when Australian productivity grew faster. Population also grew by 1.5 million between the censuses of 1966 and 1971. Of these people about 40 per cent were migrants. Continental Europeans were fewer because prosperity was improving at home and jobs could be found in the EEC, but significant numbers were beginning to arrive from the Muslim countries of the eastern Mediterranean: Turkey, Lebanon, Egypt. British migration revived so strongly that in 1971 it was considered feasible to abandon the £10 subsidized fare. Australia still seemed the lucky country which could find jobs for all.

The habit of affluence persisted. Between 1966–67 and 1970–71, although the consumer price index inflated by 15 per cent, wage rates rose by 39 per cent and spending on private consumption by 45 per cent. Between 1966 and 1971, 750 000 new dwellings were built for Australian home-buyers. This confirmed a trend building up since the early 1950s. Australian families were paying more of their incomes into mortgage repayments or rent, and proportionately less on food, clothing, liquor or tobacco. This emphasis on home-buying drew criticism from two very different quarters. Advocates of industrial growth complained that excessive investment in housing directed Australian capital from more productive uses in industry. Socialists asserted that workers were tied to the capitalist system by mortgage payments and advertising pressures to fill their homes with consumer goods.[37] Unperturbed, most Australians went on investing in housing and, beyond that, in travel. Motor vehicles on Australian roads increased from 3 million to 4 million in the five years after 1966. Motor-cycles, after dwindling in popularity since the early 1950s, came back from a minimum of 64 000 in 1966 to 173 000 in 1971, a response to Japanese marketing and American iconography in films such as *Hells Angels* and *Easy Rider*. The number of television licences grew from 2 million to 3 million, exceeding the number of people who stayed faithful to radio. In one year (1969–70) the income tax authorities harvested a 20 per cent increase on the year before.

These flourishing times came to an end partly because of the Vietnam War. Trying to finance the war without cutting back on welfare and economic growth, the Johnson and Nixon administrations in the United States launched a series of deficit budgets. These built up inflationary forces which released much speculative capital for which Australia's mineral sector offered the warmest of welcomes. Promoters floated increasingly risky propositions. The nickel boom roared to a halt after the summer of 1969–70, when stock-market punters talked up the shares of a Western Australian exploration company, Poseidon, to ridiculous heights before a sudden collapse. In the Northern Territory in 1970 Queensland Mines boasted the potential of its uranium prospects at the Aboriginal reserve at Nabarlek before admitting that original estimates were much exaggerated, thus causing many investors to lose money. In February 1971 Mineral Securities Australia, an investment group previously well regarded on the stock exchange, went bankrupt overnight. Other collapses followed. A subsequent Senate inquiry chaired by Senator Peter Rae found that much of the investment raised for mineral exploration during the boom was wasted and mismanaged, serving only to increase the level of foreign equity in Australian mining.[38]

Confronted by such prodigality among the moneyed classes, the trade unions pressed their own demands without compunction. By abandoning margins awards in 1967 the Arbitration Court lost a set of procedures which at least set guidelines for inflation. More and longer industrial disputes resulted. In 1967 only 750 000 working days were lost through strikes. By 1971 the number increased to over three million. The figures might have been more but for the frenetic activity of Bob Hawke, president of the ACTU from 1969, who in three years won television coverage and headlines as last-minute mediator in a number of disputes which seemed poised to swell into major confrontations between labour and capital. No believer in irreconcilable class antagonisms, Hawke took initiatives to bind the trade union movement into closer partnership with Australian business, and even experimented with control and ownership. The establishment of the ACTU-Solo petrol stations, providing cut-price competition for the large oil companies, was one of his successes; the part-purchase of a retail store in central Melbourne proved otherwise. Even through his failures Hawke was a portent that the trade union movement was moving from the resistance to change which had ossified it during the Menzies era.[39]

Industrial unrest aroused fears among employers and Liberal politicians lest overseas investment should be discouraged. They demanded the implementation of penal clauses against strike leaders. But the futility of paper penalties was demonstrated in 1969 when a militant Victorian union official, Clarrie O'Shea, refused to pay fines imposed on his union by the Industrial Court. The case was heard by Mr Justice Kerr, soon to be Sir John, who condemned O'Shea to prison. In imposing this sentence, albeit reluctantly, he valued a literal-minded legalism above convenience or popularity — a trait which he would reveal in more dramatic circumstances in 1975. Half a million trade unionists went out on strike. Then, as happened several times in those years, the issue was defused by the payment of the outstanding amount by an anonymous benefactor. The excitements of industrial action on this scale were something which even Hawke did not scorn. In August 1970 the ACTU led 750 000 workers on a one-day strike in protest against a federal budget which was considered too unsympathetic to pensioners and low-income earners. Government supporters retorted that tighter budgeting was required because of the inflationary pressures stimulated by wage increases. It would have been more to the point to argue that wage rises protected the adult unionized worker at the expense of the unskilled young, who were already finding it difficult to get jobs.

Wage demands were largely a response to the world-wide inflationary forces released by the Vietnam War and steadily undermining the American financial system as a bulwark of western capitalism. This darkening of the economic horizon provided an ominous backdrop for the crisis of leadership in the Australian government. By the beginning of 1971 Gorton's days were numbered. McEwen, who had shielded him in several scrapes, retired from politics in January, and was succeeded as Country Party leader by Douglas Anthony, a generation younger. Late in February the *Bulletin* brought forward allegations claiming a breakdown in relations between the army authorities and the minister for defence, Malcolm Fraser, a grazier from the Western district of Victoria who at forty was already forecast as a future leader of the Liberal Party. Fraser resigned on the grounds that Gorton had failed to support him. At a party meeting on 10 March the Liberals divided evenly on a vote of confidence in Gorton. He gave his own casting vote in favour of his resignation, then successfully ran for deputy leader against Fraser and Fairbairn. The new prime minister was William McMahon, who at sixty-three was older than any of his predecessors since federation at their time of first appointment. An efficient treasurer, Australia's first with formal training in economics, McMahon was by no means a bad choice since, as well as seeking a prime minister of impeccable orthodoxy, the governing parties required financially experienced leadership to cope with the increasing turbulence of a boom economy which was starting to come apart.

Unfortunately McMahon lacked the substance to match the increasingly confident Whitlam, who sneered at him as 'Tiberius on the telephone'. An inveterate lobbyist, McMahon felt unable to rely on more than half his cabinet colleagues, and within a few months dropped Leslie Bury as foreign minister and Gorton as minister for defence. His media appearances were sometimes ill-starred; he was not verbally dexterous, though unfailingly fluent, and was remembered for such phrases as 'there comes a time in the life of a man in the flood of time that taken at the flood leads on to fortune'.[40] Although his government's first budget in 1971 attempted to curb inflation by holding back government spending and raising taxes, it was not well received because of its effect on unemployment. The proportion of jobless in the workforce was beginning to slip past the 2 per cent which had proved almost fatal to the Menzies government. Much depended on the capacity of the United States to stabilize the western economy. In 1971 Washington bowed to inflationary pressures by suspending the convertability of the dollar into gold. The Bretton Woods Agreement, mainstay of the world's free enterprise economies for the past quarter-century, began to totter. By the end of 1971 a respite was gained by the so-called Smithsonian Agreement for a controlled devaluation of the American dollar relative to the yen and major European currencies. The McMahon government nearly split at this point, since the Country Party, representing hard-pressed rural interests in search of overseas markets, wanted Australia to devalue in step so that Australia's mineral and rural exports would remain competitively priced. Manufacturers hoping to improve their stake in the home market favoured keeping the Australian dollar tied to sterling, which would have had the effect of an upward revaluation of over 8 per cent. In the end a compromise was worked out which favoured urban interests more than rural. Once again McMahon was left with the appearance of diminished authority.

Nor was the McMahon government helped by changes in American foreign policy. Following his proclamation of the Guam doctrine, President Nixon had authorized the withdrawal of 150 000 American troops from Vietnam, and at the same time a thousand Australians were sent home. In November 1970 it was agreed that Australian troops would not serve in Cambodia (Kampuchea), and during 1971 nearly all Australia's remaining forces in Vietnam were withdrawn. Unlike every previous Australian expeditionary force, their homecoming saw little celebration or welcome, and many of the men felt understandable resentment at this lack of recognition. It was beyond the capacity of the McMahon government to explain what they had been fighting for. The old certainties were shifting. China, so long the object of Australian fear, was taking steps to improve its relations with the non-communist world. One of the first western politicians to visit China was Gough Whitlam, who with a small party of colleagues was hospitably received in July 1971.[41] Predictably McMahon scoffed, only to be dumbfounded when the American secretary of state, Henry Kissinger, visited China immediately after Whitlam. By October Mao Zedong's regime was admitted to the United Nations as the legitimate representative of China. The communist threat which had served the Liberal–Country Party so well was unaccountably failing them.

While helplessly accompanying the Americans in the phased withdrawal from Vietnam, the McMahon government deliberately stepped up the prosecution of young men resisting national service. Where only 12 per cent of those failing to register were summonsed in 1971, the figure for the first half of 1972 was 71 per cent. Thus the government won the most odium for harassing objectors at the moment when there was least need to do so for the nation's defence. Having embittered the tenor of Australian political life for seven years, having drained Holt's energies and provided a catalyst for Gorton's downfall, the Vietnam involvement was now dragging the last of the Liberal dynasty into unpopular measures which could only contribute to defeat. In the states Labor was beginning the long haul back to office. In 1970 South Australia fell to Labor under Don Dunstan, followed in 1971 by Western Australia and in 1972 by Tasmania. With mounting relish Whitlam and his colleagues in the federal Labor Party pitched their appeal to the many groups who had felt excluded from decision-making during the long hegemony of the Liberal–Country Party coalition and who had been taught by the Vietnam experience that protest might in time be converted into new policies for Australia.

8

NEW DIRECTIONS?

ALTHOUGH THE VIETNAM moratorium movement schooled a considerable number of Australians in the techniques of protest, these protests mostly fed on grievances which had been growing years before the Vietnam movement began. Opposition to censorship and the death penalty, and the environmental movement, were causes whose origins could be detected as far back as the early years of the century. Long-standing Australian stereotypes about gender produced the sense of oppression behind the emergence of the new feminist and homosexual groups which transformed sexual politics around 1970.[1] But it was the group with the oldest grievances of all, the Aborigines, whose demands for change were to arouse greatest discomfort among more fortunate Australians and whose methods of protest, while at times influenced by American models, drew most strongly on authentic local tradition.

The Pilbara movement of 1946–49, which had taken several hundred Aborigines from pastoral work into co-operatives, remained for more than a decade an isolated portent. Following a luckless attempt to attract outside investment its members split into several separate groups. Never completely a failure, the co-operatives sustained the self-respect of their members but found few imitators. Following the appointment of Paul Hasluck as minister for territories in 1951 the authorities were encouraged to hope that Aborigines would find fulfilment under a policy of assimilation, with equal access to education and job opportunities. Assimilation has recently been reviled as a plan to wipe out Aboriginal identity; in fact it was intended as an improvement on the old practice of classifying the Aborigines as, in Hasluck's words, 'within a legal status that has more in common with a born idiot than of any other class of British subject'.² For the first time official policy accepted Aborigines as entitled to full citizenship, although the gesture was tarnished by restrictions on those who in the eyes of authority were incapable of getting through life without care and protection. Thus Northern Territory legislation from 1957 admitted all 'half-castes' (as mixed-race Aborigines were then termed) to citizenship, together with such other Aborigines as were deemed able to look after themselves and their families. But such legal niceties placed great strains on Aboriginal communities where some members had citizenship and some not. Albert Namatjira, a senior Arunta artist whose water-colour landscapes had a considerable vogue in the 1950s, was imprisoned for six months (later reduced to three) for supplying liquor to a kinsman who was not a citizen. 'It must be clear', commented the *Northern Territory News*, faithful mouthpiece of white Territorians, 'that it was a mistake to give Namatjira his citizenship passport, despite the fact that he had proved he could "walk with kings", even more than most whites, and had dignity and ability . . . Assimilation can only come through the young'.³ In a region with Australia's highest consumption of alcohol the capacity to handle liquor became the hallmark of citizenship.

All too gradually the legal barriers came down. In 1959, after twenty years of discussion, Aborigines without citizenship became eligible for pensions and maternity allowances. In 1960 a conference of federal and state ministers agreed to end the segregation of Aborigines in reserves, although Queensland failed to act on this agreement. In 1962 the federal government admitted Aborigines to the franchise, although not insisting on the compulsory registration and voting required of other Australians. It was only in 1969 that New South Wales ceased the practice of separating Aboriginal children from their parents, and not until 1972 that the clause allowing the exclusion of Aborigines from primary schools was cut out of the teachers' handbook. Recently these reforms have been criticized. 'Through social security', complains one writer, '. . . Aborigines were processed from a people who were central in a marginal culture to a group who became marginal in a central culture . . . only eugenics logic can explain these procedures. The "black" culture was the antithesis of wartime and postwar capitalism'.[4] At the time it was those who tried to exclude Aborigines from social services who seemed the reactionaries. Nor was it true that Aboriginal culture was submerging in the dominant Australian mass.

In parts of rural Australia Aboriginal groups adapted the teachings of Christian missionaries to their own evolving traditions. Thus on the north coast of New South Wales descendants of the Bandjalang developed a form of Pentecostalism which, unlike the Old Rule, was accessible to both women and men, but followed the old ways in placing great emphasis on initiation, healing rites and taboos on certain foods, and was a source of self-respect in asserting the worth of the poor. In the West Kimberley region a movement followed the cult of Jinimin, a version of Jesus Christ who was both black and white and who taught that the land would belong to all.[5] Urban Aborigines were less given to revivalist religion, and their sense of identity was sometimes sustained by long-standing feuds based on family or regional loyalties from three or four generations back. In such communities in Melbourne, Diane Barwick found that 'Older women of strong personality usually displace their menfolk in managing family affairs and in determining family status'.[6] In Sydney an outstanding figure among the Aboriginal quarter at Redfern was the social worker 'Mum Shirl' (Colleen Shirley Perry) who, when she was awarded the MBE, thought back to her girlhood at Cowra when she and others like her were chased by white children yelling 'Nigger, nigger, pull the trigger'.[7] Australia's Aboriginal communities were grossly disadvantaged, but despite this their survival and adaptation were not achieved at the cost of loss of identity.

In order to generate self-confidence for the future it is useful to take pride in the past. Aboriginal Australia before white settlement in 1788 had usually been seen as 'a timeless land', sparsely inhabited by hunter-gatherers who left little trace on their environment. From the mid-1950s archaeologists and historians began to reveal that Aborigines had profoundly influenced the shaping of Australia. Carbon-dating pushed back the earliest evidence of human occupancy at least 40 000 years. At Lake Mungo in western New South Wales the remains were found of the world's earliest cremation. Researchers looked at the Aboriginal custom of burning off large tracts of country in order to flush out game and rejuvenate the grasslands, and concluded that this 'firestick farming' had done much to create the attractive pastures which were the making of the modern pastoral industry. By 1961 enough scholars were in the field to justify the convening of a conference in Canberra on the future of Aboriginal studies, and in 1964 the federal government set up an Australian Institute of Aboriginal Studies. If it had done no more than to show that, as John Mulvaney asserted, 'the discoverers, explorers, and colonists of . . . Australia were its Aborigines'[8] the institute would have influenced Australian attitudes significantly. As it was, the findings of scholars reinforced the process of self-assertion in the Aboriginal community and gave them encouragement. Intellectual weight was given to the views of the increasing number of Aborigines who were beginning to question assimilation. In 1963 the National Missionary Council issued a statement urging that assimilation should not be forced; it would not be detrimental to national well-being if some Aboriginal groups wished to retain a distinctive identity.

In this concept of a distinctive identity lay the germ of future debate about land rights. The rise of the mining industry in Queensland, the Northern Territory and Western Australia was a major catalyst for change. Christian missions to Aboriginal communities were usually situated on reserves of country considered worthless for economic development. With the aluminium boom of the early 1960s developers grew covetous. In 1963 the Presbyterian Church sold its mission site at Mapoon, near Weipa on the west coast of Cape York Peninsula, to the Commonwealth Aluminium Corporation (Comalco). The Queensland government closed the Royal Flying Doctor Service and in November 1963 sent in the police, who herded the inhabitants onto the beach and destroyed most of the buildings. (In 1970 Comalco made a share issue, offering parcels of shares to cabinet ministers in Queensland and elsewhere at a profitable discount. The Aborigines were not offered any shares.) In the same year at Gove in the Northern Territory another investor, Nabalco, sought land occupied by a Methodist mission to the Yirrkala people, who objected. They sent the House of Representatives a petition pasted to a traditionally-painted bark sheet, requesting a select committee to hear their views before authorizing the transfer. This committee recommended the payment of royalties to the Yirrkala community during the lifetime of the Nabalco lease, thus recognizing a moral right to compensation. Some committee members were moved to demand the repeal of those sections of the Commonwealth Constitution excluding Aborigines from the census and from the Commonwealth's power to spend money. It was the first time that Aboriginal land rights came into public awareness, although in the United States and Canada the North American Indians had for some time demanded a stronger recognition of their ancestral claims, already better protected than those of Australia's first inhabitants.

American influence on the forms of Aboriginal protest came through the first generation of Aborigines to achieve tertiary education with its access to wider sources of information. One of the earliest Aboriginal graduates from the University of Sydney was Charles Perkins, whose Arunta background was mingled with the genes of two British grandfathers and Kalkadoon ancestors from north-western Queensland whose resistance to white invasion was among the fiercest on record.[9] A talented sportsman and student, Perkins concerned himself with conditions in the country towns of New South Wales, where police harassment of Aborigines was on the increase between 1955 and 1965.[10] Where the older generation of male Aborigines had been skilled itinerant workers with a recognized niche in rural society, their sons and daughters found fewer employment opportunities. Unemployed young people tended to stay in one town, where any episodes of fighting or drinking built up an accumulation of prejudice. Unofficial barriers went up. At Walgett Aborigines were not allowed into the RSL club and at Moree they were banned from the municipal swimming-pool. Basing the idea on the American civil rights workers who took buses with passengers of mixed race into the most segregationist areas of the Deep South, Perkins and a number of university students organized a 'freedom ride' into rural New South Wales in the summer of 1965. At Moree an angry grazier fired a shot in the direction of the bus, and nowhere were the 'freedom-riders' able to end informal segregation. But they raised the awareness of urban Australians and started the process of educating public opinion to favour change.[11] Perkins, a fiery speaker though subtler in negotiation, came to prominence through this episode.

In May 1967 the Holt government held a referendum proposing

that Aborigines should be included in the national census and empowering the Commonwealth parliament to legislate on their behalf. These modest proposals were supported by a 'Yes' vote of over 90 per cent, a record for an Australian referendum, although rural Australia was less enthusiastic than the middle-class suburbs of Melbourne and Sydney. In anti-centralist Western Australia and North Queensland the 'Yes' vote fell to 80 per cent, and was considerably lower in outback areas where friction between whites and Aborigines was common.[12] Emboldened, Holt in November 1967 set up a Council for Aboriginal Affairs chaired by H. C. Coombs, whose experience of helping the disadvantaged through the post-war reconstruction programme of the 1940s provided an instructive model for tackling the problems of disadvantaged Aborigines. Holt, who in this as in several other respects showed promise of shaping into a reforming prime minister, was supported by few of his cabinet colleagues, and although he intended to give the council a charter of defined responsibilities, his undertakings were not honoured after his death in December 1967. Instead under Gorton the council met with bureaucratic hostility and ministerial apathy.

Ably supported by the anthropologist W. E. H. Stanner, the wily and tenacious Coombs managed to initiate a number of major changes, notably the provision of a capital fund for Aboriginal enterprises, a scheme for secondary education grants, and a legal service of great value in safeguarding the rights of individual Aborigines. The council had an ally in Gorton's minister for Aboriginal affairs, W. C. Wentworth, previously noted as an implacable anti-communist, but in his new role a valiant but unavailing fighter against unhelpful senior colleagues. When McMahon succeeded Gorton in 1971 he dropped Wentworth from the ministry in deference to pressure from Queensland, and replaced him with the polished but slow-moving Peter Howson who mistrusted Coombs profoundly.[13] It was a recipe for inaction.

The Aboriginal movement would not wait. Land rights were to come to the forefront of demands but in the early years wage rates had greater prominence. Equal pay for equal work had long been a main plank of the Council for Aboriginal Advancement formed in 1958. In 1960 the Northern Territory authorities introduced a licensing system for employers of Aboriginal labour and prescribed a regular cash wage of about 10 per cent of the average Australian worker's weekly earnings. For many years Aboriginal stockmen and station-hands in northern Australia had worked for meagre wages, compensated to some extent by access to the Royal Flying Doctor Service and other amenities and by the reluctance of pastoralists to interfere with their life-style off-duty, so that traditional cultural practices and disciplines could continue with little disturbance. During the 1950s and the early 1960s absentee companies consolidated their hold on the beef-cattle industry, taking over from resident owners. In reaction the North Australian Workers' Union applied to the Arbitration Commission in 1965 for a wage award which would cover Aborigines and others uniformly.[14] This was granted, though exemptions were allowed and operation was deferred for three years to enable the pastoral industry to adjust. Disaster followed. Many pastoral companies declared that they could no longer afford to maintain Aboriginal camps on their properties, although in those years the strong American demand for hamburger beef was stimulating the export trade. Aboriginal communities were ousted from the cattle stations, in many cases from land which they had occupied for generations before white settlement. Most settled in ill-prepared camps around the northern townships. There, disoriented and lacking occupation, many took to drink, lost the influence of traditional authority, fought among themselves, and met the antipathy of white settlers and tourists.

Some fought back. Wave Hill in the western part of the Northern Territory was the biggest cattle run in the world, since 1914 the Australian headquarters of Vesteys, a British firm with an unsurpassed record as grudging investors and tax evaders. In 1967 the Gurindji decided to withdraw their labour from the property and established a settlement on 20 square kilometres of their traditional lands. They asked that this area should be excised from the Wave Hill pastoral lease. Wentworth gave his support but the Gorton cabinet rejected the idea as a dangerous precedent. The Gurindji stayed there nevertheless, and their example enheartened the Yirrkala, still contending that Nabalco's bauxite development of Gove invaded their proprietary rights. Nabalco had attempted to involve members of the Aboriginal community in their project, and even to accommodate their prejudices. A 19-year-old Aboriginal clerk-typist fell in love with a white youth, thus incurring the censure of Yirrkala elders, and the firm obligingly sacked her. But it was one thing to yield to the patriarchal traditions of Aboriginal society; Nabalco drew the line at land rights. Milirrpum and other senior Yirrkala petitioned the Supreme Court of the Northern Territory for recognition of their prior title to the land in question. The case was heard by a thorough and scholarly judge, Richard Blackburn, who after hearing much anthropological and constitutional argument decided, not without reluctance, against the Yirrkala.[15] This entrenched the legal fiction of *terra nullius*, which alleged that Australia had no social institutions or concept of land ownership before white settlement. In nearly two decades this judgment was never overturned. If Aborigines were to secure from their fellow-Australians any recognition of their presence in the land before 1788 and their right to compensation for dispossession, they must somehow extract that recognition from the politicians, the law courts and the general public of the 1970s and 1980s.

It would not be easy. The mining companies and similar investors could be expected to resist, although whereas some Australian-born mining executives denounced the principle of land rights as socialistic and probably unchristian, firms with North American experience were accustomed to coming to terms with the claims of indigenous groups. Stronger opposition would be encountered from the state governments, particularly Queensland and Western Australia, ever fearful that investors would be deterred by the least restriction. Only federal intervention could coerce them into acceptance of Aboriginal land claims, and federal intervention depended to some extent on the pressure of urban middle-class consciences. In most of the communities where Aborigines and whites lived at close quarters— the struggling outback townships, the State Housing Commission suburbs, inner-city districts such as Sydney's Redfern—respectability was too hard-won to allow tolerance of Aboriginal failure to conform.

The federal government fumbled. In an Australia Day speech in 1972 McMahon set his face against Aboriginal land rights. In response a group of Aborigines pitched a tent on the lawn outside Parliament House, Canberra, declaring it their embassy. It was allowed to remain for five months, attracting national and international attention, before the police were sent to break up the 'tent embassy' in July—too late for the government to seem resolute, too domineering for decency. It took two attempts and twenty-six arrests to effect the removal. Then and only then, the federal government convened a meeting of Aboriginal advisory councillors, who called for the restitution of the 'tent embassy' before debating further. The Labor leader, Whitlam, made much of the issue. In his policy speech later in 1972 he told his hearers: 'Australia's treatment of her Aboriginal people will be the thing upon which the rest of the world will judge Australia and Australians—not just now but in the greater perspective of history'.[16]

Racism was an issue which sat lightly on many Australians in those years. Even after Menzies retired Australia was seen as less hostile towards South Africa than almost any other nation. When Rhodesia made its unilateral declaration of independence in 1965 Australia gave increasingly open moral and economic support to the breakaway regime, though not dissenting from resolutions by British Commonwealth heads of government favouring economic sanctions.[17] When an all-white South African rugby team, the Springboks, toured Australia in the winter of 1971 most followers of sport took the view that the games should be enjoyed without thought of South Africa's system of apartheid.[18] At almost every match the team encountered noisy demonstrations from strenuous opponents of apartheid and police reaction. At Melbourne the police, having been pelted with rocks, fireworks and fruit, arrested over 150 demonstrators. As ever going one better, the Queensland government declared a state of emergency during the team's visit to Brisbane. Coming after several years of anti-Vietnam demonstrations, these confrontations between police and protesters seemed to deepen the divisions in Australian society, but at least may have raised the level of awareness of race as one of those contentious issues which Australia had been too long in confronting. The McMahon government deplored the fuss, but otherwise did nothing effectual.

It could not be taken for granted that Australia would handle its own colonial responsibilities in Papua New Guinea with becoming sensitivity. Two setbacks followed Hasluck's departure from the Department of Territories. In September 1964, to the dismay of the administrator, Sir Donald Cleland, the Australian government ruled that indigenous teachers and public servants must be paid lower salaries than Australian expatriates. C. E. Barnes, the new minister, did not want to saddle the Papua New Guinea of the future with an expensive bureaucracy, and one of his senior advisers airily assumed that high pay was not required by men who could wear lap-laps. Nothing could have politicized the professional classes more quickly. At the same time a lively trade union movement grew up in the private sector where, as Gough Whitlam remarked, 'nearly every employer was an Australian and nearly every employee a New Guinean, and therefore every individual dispute was potentially a racial dispute'.[19] Public service employees, aided by the ACTU with Hawke as advocate, took their complaints to arbitration in 1967, but met with a disappointing judgment. Teachers and public servants then teamed with the trade unions to form Pangu Pati, a political movement working for independence and mobilizing support in every part of the country. Because Pangu Pati was a nation-wide organization the likelihood of fragmentation based on tribal or ethnic background was to some extent reduced, and many inhabitants of Papua New Guinea began for the first time to take the prospect of independence seriously.

This was important because there were divisive possibilities in the problem of indigenous land rights. In 1963 the New Guinea courts had found in favour of the traditional rights of the Tolai people for land confiscated from them many years earlier. The Australian government successfully appealed to the High Court to reverse the decision. The Tolai were incensed. A series of protests led in 1969 to the formation of the Mataungan Association demanding local autonomy. Meanwhile in 1967 Conzinc Rio Tinto began work on large deposits of copper at Bougainville Island. This activity not only raised the question of appropriate compensation for local communities, but had ominous potential to stir up a secessionist movement. If Bougainville seceded from the mainland any one of the numerous ethnic or geographical sub-groups making up the mosaic of Papua New Guinea might claim the same right. Nobody would benefit from such fragmentation. In the face of these complexities some Australian politicians, among them Gorton, concluded that chaos and bloodshed would result if Australia withdrew from Papua New Guinea. On his first visit in July 1970 Gorton was vociferously heckled at Rabaul, and reacted by taking authority to call out the Pacific Islands Regiment. Against the advice of cabinet colleagues he did not revoke the call-out, although it was never necessary to activate it.

More constructive counsels eventually prevailed. The rise of Pangu Pati showed the Papuan capacity to organize politics on a national scale, while fears that a newly independent Papua New Guinea would be taken over by Indonesia receded after Sukarno's downfall. Gorton was persuaded to appoint the reforming director of education, Les Johnson, as administrator in 1970. Australia ceased to withhold its vote from United Nations resolutions demanding a speedy timetable for independence for Papua New Guinea. The pace of change quickened early in 1972, when Andrew Peacock replaced Barnes as minister. In April of that year new elections were held. Michael Somare, at the head of a Pangu-dominated coalition, became chief minister of Papua New Guinea. The way was now clear for the eventual declaration of independence in 1975. Where seasoned European powers often failed to transfer authority to their ex-colonies without re-crimination, bloodshed and the early breakdown of authority, Australia and Papua New Guinea had somehow succeeded. Despite, or perhaps because of, Australia's lack of an ingrained tradition of colonial administration, despite the crass and self-seeking racial attitudes of some Australian expatriates, despite the recency of contact between Papua New Guinea and the rest of the world, and despite the diversity of its scattered population, Papua New Guinea was to survive its first decade and a half of independence without lapsing into anarchy or dictatorship.[20]

Racism was not the only form of discrimination under challenge. Another term which gained vogue in the early 1970s was sexism: the devices by which a male-dominated society imposed re-strictions on women. During the Menzies era Australian women's standing in public life improved only slowly by comparison with other western nations. Many would have agreed with B. A. Santamaria when he claimed that 'married women in the work-force struck a major blow at the reproductive base of the Australian community'.[21] It was 1967 before women were entitled to serve as jurors in all parts of the Commonwealth—South Australia and the Australian Capital Territory being the last to fall into line. As late as 1969 there were only two women in the federal parliament, both non-Labor senators, and very few in the state legislatures. Queensland, Tasmania, Western Australia and the Victorian Legislative Council had none. This state of affairs mirrored power relations in the wider community.

The foremost issue was equal pay. An International Labour Organization convention of 1951 adopted by Australia (though not ratified until 1974) prescribed equal pay for work of equal value, and although even conservatives such as Menzies and Santamaria expressed some support for it, the trade union movement was slow to press the issue. Meanwhile the proportion of women in the workforce increased from 22.8 to 31.7 per cent between 1954 and 1971. The private sector accounted for nearly the whole of this increase. The proportion of women in the Commonwealth Public Service, almost entirely in the lower ranks, was the same in 1974 as it had been in 1947. By the early 1970s married women made up more than half the female workforce. Whether it was because a two-income family could more readily pay mortgages and buy consumer goods or because mothers of small families had greater time and energy once the children were at school, whether it reflected improved educational qualifications for women or a growing dissatisfaction with a suburban life isolated by poor public transport, married women were becoming an increasingly significant part of Australia's workforce, and naturally they campaigned for financial justice.

New South Wales, as so often the trend-setter, legislated in 1958 for a limited equal pay Act to come into effect from 1963, but the rest of Australia held back. It was not until 1967 that the Arbitration Court, in the process of adopting a total wage in lieu of basic wage and margins, deliberately awarded the same increase to adult males and females. Heartened by this hint, a coalition of women's organizations backed a test case in 1969 seeking acceptance of equal pay in the federal meat industry award. The ACTU and its advocate, Bob Hawke, supported this move. Employers predictably grizzled that the claim was theoretical, doctrinaire, and ruinously expensive. The commission found in favour of equal pay, but with the important qualification that it should not be provided in jobs customarily performed by females. Slightly more than half of Australia's working women were in occupations such as typing, nursing and cleaning, where women outnumbered men. They would remain underpaid until the advent of a government prepared to back their claims. Women also held very few positions of seniority or responsibility. Fewer than 10 per cent of working women in 1971 were employers or self-employed. In private banking fewer than 4 per cent of the staff were women, nearly all juniors in their late teens and early twenties. Only 1 per cent of Australia's university professors were female. Not one woman headed a department in either the federal or state public services.[22]

The state of mind which brought Australian women to acquiesce in these inequalities was trenchantly attacked in 1971 by Germaine Greer in an international best-seller, *The Female Eunuch*.[23] Greer argued that women were prevented from exploring their capacity by male-dominated cultural practices. Her book followed insights developed by other contemporary American feminists, but its impact bit sharply in Australia because the author drew on a Melbourne Catholic background. Here at last was personified the challenge to family values which writers such as Santamaria had long expected from advocates of women's rights. Soon Greer was joined by historians such as Anne Summers, Beverley Kingston and Miriam Dixson who from differing perspectives showed that women's role in Australian history had long been underexplored and undervalued.[24] Meanwhile, during 1970 and 1971 at least forty Women's Liberation groups came into being in Australian cities, and the first of many feminist publications, *Mejane*, attained a print-run of 4000. In February 1972 a group of Melbourne women launched the Women's Electoral Lobby (WEL) with the aim of identifying and lobbying parliamentary candidates who were likely to sympathize with feminist issues. WEL quickly generated support on a nation-wide basis, especially among professional women. Its members found Labor Party candidates most likely to prove responsive, Liberals largely half-hearted, and the Country and Democratic Labor parties unsympathetic.[25] Traditionally the women's vote had tended to favour the conservative parties. This could no longer be taken for granted.

The women's movement drew some support from two markedly different radical groups which were coming to the fore. One was the New Left, representing a coalition of young university-educated urban-dwellers, many of them radicalized by experience of anti-Vietnam protest, who were endeavouring to breathe new life into the bones of Marxism after its eclipse in the 1950s. In contrast to the strongly political approach of the Left in the 1940s, the newcomers drew ideas from European Marxists such as Gramsci who saw the ruling classes as exercising hegemony through their control of information and popular culture. In an Australia where control of the media was concentrated in a few hands, especially since the coming of television, this approach had some plausibility. With the rapid influx of overseas capital in the late 1960s and early 1970s Australian national identity seemed further threatened. Stimulated by these developments, the New Left intensely debated issues of class and gender in their journals *Arena* and *Intervention*. The strongest public impression was probably made by Humphrey McQueen, whose *A New Britannia*, published in 1970, denounced the old radical nationalism celebrated by historians such as Russel Ward as bourgeois romanticism, ignoring the unpleasant elements of racism and jingoism in Australian culture.[26] Outside the universities the influence of the New Left was limited, but many of its members looked to the ALP as an instrument which might be turned to the restructuring of Australian society.

A wider cross-section of young Australians seeking an alternative vision of society were attracted to what became known as the 'counter-culture'. This movement rejected the conventional patterns of household and family in favour of forms of communal living which might hope to avoid what many saw as the destructive power relations fostered by capitalist consumer society. Some groups attempted to form communes in large inner-suburban houses, but many were attracted to rural life, growing their own food by organic methods, sharing responsibilities by consensus and scorning the profit motive. In many respects, as in so much during those years, the counter-culture followed American models, but in Australia it had the effect of unexpectedly enlivening a number of small farming districts which had been falling into decay. The biggest concentration of seekers after alternative life-styles settled in the region around Byron Bay and Nimbin in northern New South Wales. Other concentrations included several pockets in the far north of Queensland and the south-west of Western Australia. Although their philosophy of self-help was often tempered by reliance on unemployment benefits, the newcomers on the whole encountered less friction with the local residents than might have been expected. By 1972 the alternative movement had established a number of information exchange services, food co-operatives, short-lived periodicals and encounter groups. Plans were afoot for a national festival of the alternative society at Nimbin in May 1973.[27]

Disapproval of the alternative movement often took the form of allegations that its adherents were drug addicts. Undeniably the use of habit-forming drugs had increased during the later 1960s, partly through the influence of American servicemen from

Vietnam visiting Sydney for rest and recreation leave, and partly in imitation of world-wide trends. None of these imports came anywhere near tobacco and alcohol in endangering the lives and health of Australia, but they caused considerable public alarm, especially when addicts who could not supply themselves legally took to robbery and prostitution in order to raise the means. Police reactions were at times excessive, as when the Queensland police staged a commando-type raid on a hippie commune at Cedar Bay in 1976. By far the mildest and the most widespread of the new drugs was marijuana, a form of Indian hemp said to produce a state of unaggressive euphoria. By 1971 crops were grown commercially, if illegally, in several parts of Australia, notably the Murrumbidgee irrigation district centred on Griffith. A substantial number of young people admitted to smoking 'dope'. Its use was widespread among surfers. Some politicians, such as Don Dunstan and John Gorton, believed that its possession should not be a criminal offence. But the police, supported by majority public opinion, opposed any relaxation of the laws, so that marijuana became yet another issue dividing the younger generation from the status quo.[28]

Often allied with the counter-culture were the 'greenies', environmental conservationists who criticized capitalism because they saw its practices as wasteful of finite natural resources and responsible for industrial pollution. While their critique drew on American models, it also gained considerable momentum from older established sources. One was the bush-walking and wilderness movement, which since the earliest decades of the century had campaigned for the protection of flora and fauna and the reservation of national parks of 'natural bush'. Others threw their energies into the series of state branches of the National Trust set up after the Second World War to ensure the preservation of colonial buildings. From these acceptably respectable pressure groups developed the Australian Conservation Foundation, set up in 1965 as an independent corporation with Sir Garfield Barwick as president.

Granted federal funding from 1968, the foundation soon proved an efficient propagandist. Its early concerns were mainly with the preservation of the natural environment, but this soon brought it into conflict with developers for whom profit and economic growth were priorities, as well as challenging development-minded state governments. With the aid of a sustained campaign by the Melbourne *Age* the foundation succeeded in 1969 in forcing the Victorian government to back down from a plan to subdivide for farming the pristine wilderness of the Little Desert in the Wimmera district. They got nowhere with the Tasmanian government when its powerful Hydro-Electric Commission proposed to flood the notably beautiful Lake Pedder for a dam to meet the state's energy needs. Despite six years of pressure, from 1967 to 1973, the dam went ahead.[29] Like Queensland and Western Australia, Tasmania was hungry for economic growth. It was all very well for the maturely industrialized regions based on Sydney and Melbourne to nourish an environmental conscience, but not if it thwarted the hopes of less advanced regions to catch up. Queensland was especially sensitive to federal intervention on the Great Barrier Reef, despite the triple threat of over-use by tourists, exploitation for oil-drilling and the ravages of the crown-of-thorns starfish. Nevertheless between 1969 and 1974 each of the states set up an environmental planning authority, though their powers varied widely.[30]

While the environmental movement confined itself to the preservation of natural scenery and wildlife it could be seen as politically unthreatening and, in the boom years before the early 1970s, affordable. But for the great majority of Australians their day-to-day environment was urban, the creature of highly political decisions by municipal councils and real-estate developers. The National Trust could exercise only a moral influence to shield old buildings from the wrecker, and the rest of the built environment was almost entirely unprotected. The trade union movement offered little support, preferring jobs to aesthetics. But in 1970 the secretary of the New South Wales branch of the Builders' Labourers Federation (BLF), Jack Mundey, forged a remarkable alliance between his militant union and an environmental movement of impeccably middle-class credentials. Kelly's Bush, a 5-hectare tract of open land in the prosperous suburb of Hunters Hill, was threatened with subdivision for housing. The protests of local residents were fruitless until they were reinforced by the BLF, whose members refused to work on the project. This 'green ban', as it was called, saved Kelly's Bush and encouraged Mundey's plans for an alliance of environmentalists and radicals. The techniques pioneered at Hunters Hill were next used to prevent the construction of high-rise apartments on one of the few open spaces in the working-class suburb of Eastlakes. By 1973 twenty-seven green bans had been success-fully imposed, and many districts had residents' action groups to keep an eye on the activities of developers. Mundey may not have managed to radicalize Australians, but the green bans movement certainly raised the level of grass-roots participation in decision-making processes.[31]

Issues of social conscience assumed greater prominence in political debate. Possibly this was just the result of a quarter-century of affluence enabling voters to look a little beyond economic factors; perhaps it owed something to the increasing number of university graduates in the community. Unfortunately party discipline had become so strongly encrusted in Australian politics that even sensitive issues such as capital punishment were largely determined by party bias rather than on moral principles. Labor parliamentarians were pledged by their party platform to abolish hanging, a fate which usually befell only members of the working class. Country Party members and rural Liberals, al-though unpledged, habitually voted as if society could only be safeguarded by executions. The balance was sometimes tipped by 'soft' urban Liberals and DLP members who, because they upheld the right to life for the unborn, felt that they could not con-sistently support the state's power to take life judicially. But progress was uneven.

Labor abolished hanging in Queensland in 1923 and in New South Wales in 1955, and held office for so long in Tasmania that the effect was the same. In other states executions became rarer, and when they happened provoked increasing protest. South Aus-tralia did not send anyone to the gallows after the Stuart case of 1960, when Max Stuart, an Aboriginal convicted on contentious evidence of the rape and murder of a schoolgirl, was reprieved only after bitter controversy.[32] Western Australia, after a quarter of a century with only one execution, revived hanging between 1959 and 1964, but then, although retaining the mandatory death sentence on the statute book until 1984, regularly commuted to life imprisonment. In Victoria it became a matter of prestige for the Bolte government to uphold its right of execution after public agitation brought about the reprieve of a demented sexual psychopath in 1962. Accordingly, in February 1967, Ronald Ryan, convicted of shooting dead a prison warder while escaping from Pentridge gaol, became the last Australian to go to the gallows. Protest was so widespread that no later Victorian government insisted on the right to hang, although the penalty remained on the statute book until 1975. In the federal territories abolition came two years earlier.

Concern for the sanctity of human life sharpened debate over the question of abortion. For many years legal penalties against backyard abortionists had been in force in every state, but abortion was a common method of terminating pregnancy. Between 1920 and 1935 the Royal Women's Hospital in Melbourne showed a ratio of one abortion to every two live births, and supporting evidence suggests that Australian figures were higher than either British or American.[33] With the widespread adoption of the contraceptive pill during the 1960s the risk of unwanted pregnancies might have been expected to diminish but, possibly because of greater sexual activity among teenagers, the demand continued and increasingly was met by qualified medical practitioners. As these activities were illegal, Melbourne abortionists were in the habit of bribing the police, until in 1969 the controversial Dr Bertram Wainer, who openly advocated the right to abortion and operated an abortion clinic, threw the spotlight of publicity on them. The legal situation then remained dubious until in 1971 a judgment in the New South Wales courts ruled that a doctor need not fear prosecution for an abortion carried out to safeguard the physical or psychological health of the mother. This definition, which in practice allowed a fair degree of latitude, was matched by a similar ruling in Melbourne a few months later. Meanwhile in 1969 a Liberal government in South Australia had allowed members a conscience vote to define the conditions under which pregnancies might lawfully be terminated. On the other hand Western Australia and Queeensland, socially in most matters the most conservative of states, continued for some years to threaten prosecution to doctors who performed illegal operations, and counselling services which advised pregnant women about abortion. Even on a question of such intimately personal morality Australian attitudes were riddled with parochial diversity.

It was even harder to lighten the laws making homosexuality between consenting adult males a criminal offence. Until well into the 1960s police in all Australia's major cities went to considerable lengths to entrap homosexuals in parks and public conveniences. Once again following an American prototype, homosexuals and their sympathizers formed a movement in 1970 known as CAMP (Campaign Against Moral Persecution). They were ranged against a very strong tradition of cultural prejudice dating from Australia's convict origins. South Australia, which under the Dunstan government was making a name for social experiment, was the first state to discontinue the prosecution of adult, consenting homosexual acts, but the move only came in 1972 after a university lecturer had been murdered in an Adelaide park by a group of unidentified men. Even then the legislation originated not with Dunstan, who had been discouraged by the unreadiness of some of his Labor colleagues, but with a Liberal real-estate developer in the Legislative Council.[34] It was again a Liberal, John Gorton, who in 1973 successfully moved in the House of Representatives for the decriminalization of the offence in the Australian Capital Territory. Elsewhere in Australia, however, the Liberals were often foremost in intolerance, and Labor uninterested. As with the abolition of capital punishment, the public at large was probably even less ready for change than members of parliament. Opinion polls early in 1968 showed that although a majority of those questioned favoured the legalization of abortion in some circumstances, nearly two-thirds wanted to continue the ban on male homosexuality.[35]

Capital punishment, homosexuality and abortion could all be seen as issues unlikely to affect the majority of voters personally. Social welfare was the traditional index by which a government's sense of compassion could be measured. Where Menzies had shown a discerning anticipation of welfare demands his successors were often left behind by Labor and the minor parties. Not that Australia's social welfare was over-lavish during the prosperous 1950s and 1960s, despite the comments of recent advocates of low government spending. Under Menzies the proportion of gross national product (GNP) spent on cash social benefits, after rising from 5 per cent in the early 1950s to nearly 6 per cent in the early 1960s, began to recede towards its former level. Adjustments to pension rates and child endowment failed to keep up with inflation. Most advanced nations spent substantially more. By 1969 only Japan devoted a smaller proportion of GNP to social welfare, with the United States and Israel on a level with Australia. In 1966 Professor Ronald Henderson led a team of researchers to investigate poverty in Melbourne. They proved that even in that era of affluence poverty was not unknown in Australia. At least 4 per cent of those interviewed, and probably more, eked out an existence at a level lower than the basic wage. Not surprisingly, most poverty was found among the aged, widows, invalids, recent migrants, single parents and families with many children. Henderson calculated that the problem could be contained by increasing government spending on social welfare to the 6 per cent level. The federal authorities failed to respond. It was only in 1972, under Opposition prompting and with an election looming, that the McMahon government commissioned Henderson to head a nation-wide inquiry into poverty. Also in preparation for the election the treasurer, Snedden, announced that the government would progressively abolish the means test with which Australia, unlike most advanced nations, screened applicants for old-age, invalid and widows' pensions. The main objection to the means test was that it allegedly discouraged thrift. However, as Henderson showed, it was a device for concentrating social expenditures where they were needed, offering a major instrument for redistribution of income in favour of those in need.[36] The means test had not created hardship for pensioners, but Labor, pandering to popular prejudice, had been demanding its abolition for nearly twenty years, and the coalition could no longer hold back.

Health care also found the government floundering. For too long they had assumed that Sir Earle Page's voluntary hospital and medical benefits scheme represented the last word in social security. Largely from wariness of antagonizing the powerful medical lobby, nothing was done to correct the diseconomies of scale resulting from the over-provision of competing health funds. While the affluent benefited from tax deductions on their contributions, low-income earners often lacked cover and were disadvantaged by the complexities of the voluntary system. When these defects were exposed by two academics in the *Economic Record*[37] Whitlam was quicker than the government to take up their criticisms. In 1968, backed by the minor parties, the Opposition found the numbers in the Senate to force through the appointment of a select committee into health costs—a good cause, but once again a reminder to the Senate of its under-exercised powers. Gorton responded by setting up another committee, under Mr Justice Nimmo. Its report called for free insurance for families near and below the poverty line.[38] In 1970 the government partially accepted this recommendation, but in a manner which stored up trouble for the future.

In reducing the gap between the rate of medical benefits and the fees charged by practitioners, the government introduced the concept of a 'most common fee' for use as a benchmark. Without waiting for the government to compile a list of schedules and tables, the Australian Medical Association (AMA) unilaterally increased fees in February 1971 by 15 per cent. Even this failed to deter many specialists from raising their fees by greater amounts, so that from that time onwards general practitioners experienced a sense of grievance. As put by one of their spokesmen, 'The period 1969–70 devastated general practice, reducing it to office medicine of stunningly boring intellectual content'.[39] In 1968, even before these events, general practitioners had formed a separate association, which now took a harder line than the AMA in lobbying against any form of government intervention in health care. So the medical profession appeared self-seeking and the government inept, whereas the Labor Opposition offered the public attractive promises of a simple scheme which would benefit all.

In education the Liberal–Country Party government's record was more generous, but again it appeared to respond haphazardly to the pressures of demand rather than proceeding towards specific goals. There was a rapid growth of colleges of advanced education after 1965, and new universities were approved in Queensland and Western Australia, thus providing alternatives in every state except Tasmania. From 1967 federal subsidies supported teachers' colleges and from 1968 kindergarten colleges. In the same year school libraries became eligible for federal grants. Labor continued to accuse the government of excessive kindness to private schools, but until 1970 carried the handicap of a Victorian branch that refused to abandon the old faith of total opposition to state aid. It was left to a middle-class lobby, Defence of Government Schools (DOGS) to nip at the heels of the Liberals. A more compelling critique was made in 1970 by the state ministers of education, who commissioned a nation-wide survey which found that educational funding for the next five years would be deficient by more than $1700 million without increased federal aid. But the federal government refused to bail out the states, and even in 1972, with an election coming, would go no further than promising federal assistance to child-care centres. Thus education provided the Labor Party with another opportunity for promising systematic reform in place of the coalition's patchwork.[40]

The non-Labor governments of the later 1960s showed some

taste for cultural patronage. Menzies, who combined a long-standing if conservative taste in art with real enthusiasm for Canberra's potential as national capital, gave the green light for planning a National Gallery in 1965. Holt, with a life-long interest in theatre and the ballet, listened receptively when H. C. Coombs argued that arts funding required a government agency of wider scope than the successful Australian Elizabethan Theatre Trust. Shortly before his death in 1967 he authorized the creation of an Australian Council for the Arts to co-ordinate government support policies, with Coombs presiding. Gorton went ahead with this initiative. Although not personally a great patron of the arts, he was one of the first politicians to see electoral value in arts funding. He also shared, even more keenly than Holt, the latter's wish to give the new council a role in encouraging the making of films 'not directed primarily at the commercial feature film market'.[41] In 1970 his government legislated for the establishment of a Film and Television Development Corporation to invest in Australian film-making. Further stimulus was promised by the creation of an experimental film fund and the planning of a national film school. Progress slowed because of personality clashes during the McMahon administration of 1971–72, so that the role of pioneer passed to South Australia, where the Dunstan government set up a film corporation in 1972. Its first feature, *Sunday Too Far Away*, based on the Queensland shearers' strike of 1956 and starring Jack Thompson, was an early indication of Australia's capacity to make films which would appeal to international as well as local audiences. Soon the federal body followed suit with films such as *Picnic at Hanging Rock*, *The Cars That Ate Paris* and *The Last Wave*. Australian film-making, largely stifled since the creative 1920s by American and British competition, seemed on the point of renaissance.[42]

These were the years in which Australia shed much of its reputation for literary censorship. McMahon's minister for customs, Don Chipp, was mainly responsible, following a fairly widespread shift in educated middle-class opinion. Until his time literature dealing too frankly with sexual matters had been banned from Australia by a heavy-handed customs bureaucracy. Before 1958 the public lacked access even to an authoritative list of prohibited works, though James Joyce's *Ulysses* and Aldous Huxley's *Brave New World* were known to have figured on it. Some decisions were ludicrous. Import of a children's book entitled *Fun in Bed* and Martin Buber's theological study *Between Man and Man* were both held up while officials scanned them for salaciousness. During the early 1960s works whose sale was permitted in the United States and Britain, among them D. H. Lawrence's *Lady Chatterley's Lover*, Vladimir Nabokov's *Lolita*, James Baldwin's *Another Country*, and T. E. Lawrence's *The Mint*, were kept out of Australia.[43] If the federal authorities relented, a book might still be banned in one or more of the states. On its arrival in 1964 Mary McCarthy's *The Group* was banned by a Victorian attorney-general who feared for its impact on his hypothetical teenage daughter. The gesture lost much of its effect after he quoted the offending pieces in the Legislative Assembly, thus making the next Hansard a best-seller.[44] Although Chipp's liberalization drew fire from some churchmen and DLP supporters, his policies could not have cost his party many votes.

For some of Australia's most publicized clergy morality seemed to begin and end with denunciation of the permissive society. This viewpoint found a focus in 1973 with the launching of the Festival of Light by the Sydney evangelical clergyman Fred Nile, who subsequently won frequent headlines and a minor parliamentary career by painting gloomy pictures of Australia's surrender to crime and sexual deviance. But the very longevity of such a crusade suggested that the churches as institutions no longer exercised much influence over Australian consciences. Congregations fell away in almost every branch of the faith. Though Catholics, because of post-war migration, were starting to overtake the Anglicans as numerically the strongest creed, their faith was no longer the monolith of old. Nuns were abandoning their habits for secular dress; the Latin Mass gave way to the bare vernacular. Pope Paul VI's uncompromising stand in 1968 against any form of birth control encouraged traditionalists but alienated many younger Catholics. The newly created Catholic Commission for Justice and Peace, like the Anglican Brotherhood of St Laurence, offended some because of an unseemly zeal for social justice. Australians in search of a morality found divided counsels in the churches.[45]

Most traditional sources of authority were on the wane. Anxious conservatives equated the decline of moral standards with the decadence of national power. When the federal parliament decriminalized homosexuality old Sir John Cramer was heard to say: 'Keep on the way we are going, you can wrap

Australia up in a neat little package and hand it over as a gift to our enemies'.[46] With the recognition that the United States was withdrawing from Vietnam and mending its fences with China came an end to Australia's confident reliance for protection on great and powerful allies. The dazed McMahon government could not adapt to this change; it was left to the DLP's Senator Vincent Gair to declare roundly that 'Australia can't rely on allies'.[47] Nor was there much to the British connection except nostalgia.[48] Australia had not heeded Britain's requests in 1968–69 to curb the outflow of London portfolio investment, nor had Britain taken care of Australian interests during the 1971 negotiations for entry into the EEC. Admittedly Australian tourists were flocking to Britain in greater numbers than ever before, especially after the introduction of cheap return air fares in 1972. The number passed 100 000 in 1970 and reached 190 000 in 1974. But in 1971 the United Kingdom, wishing to curb the flow of immigrants from the Afro-Asian nations of the British Commonwealth and unwilling to endorse racial discrimination, tightened its entry laws so that only Australians with at least one British-born grandparent would be admitted without restriction. As Germans and Italians—Britain's foes during the Second World War—were admitted without restriction this caused irritation, and it could be expected that Australia might soon retaliate. The days were finished when Australia drew status from the British connection.

Since God and the British Empire were fading as sources of authority, conservatives were left with few alternatives. The business morality of the mineral boom seemed to favour those who could enrich themselves through manipulating the stock-exchange and the property market, rather than those who built up a firm or busied themselves with old-fashioned productivity. This tendency was fostered by the tone of the High Court under Sir Garfield Barwick. Probably acting from libertarian principle rather than a desire to protect wrong-doers, Barwick guided his court into a series of judicial interpretations which cramped the powers of government legislation to curb tax evasion and regulate business. The effect was to discourage the federal authorities from intervention.[49] A generation of young entrepreneurs grew up considering it right to pay as little tax as possible. After more than twenty years of prosperity it was easy to imagine that opportunity was open to all, that social welfare merely pampered the undeserving, and that the distribution of resources should be organized on the 'user pays' principle. As a seasoned political journalist, Mungo McCallum, saw it:

The new conservatives are disturbingly young, and disturbingly cynical; there is a real air of authoritarianism about them . . . They don't believe the slogans they chant about socialism and the destruction of freedom under Labor, but they have no compuction about using them to scare the wits out of the undereducated, the confused, and—especially—the migrants.[50]

On the other side of the political spectrum sat the groups that had gained purpose and cohesion through the defiance of established authority: the anti-Vietnam protesters, the feminists, the seekers after Aboriginal rights, the counter-culture. Some among them, while prepared to work with the Labor Party for the defeat of the Liberal–Country Party government, saw this as a mere preliminary to the transformation of society.[51] Representative parliamentary democracy would yield in time to a more truly co-operative and consultative order of things, where power would be shared and capitalism would no longer rule people through their acquisitiveness. The majority of Australians could not remember a time when a federal Labor government had held office, and for them it would be a sufficient experiment to vote Whitlam into power. If a Whitlam government was given a mandate for change it would be for change within the current parameters of Australia as a property-owning democracy, most of whose voters valued security above experiment.

The election came at the last possible moment, in December 1972. Tired, mediocre and over-familiar though the McMahon government was, it had endeavoured not unintelligently to meet many of the demands for change. In moving towards Papuan autonomy, setting up the Henderson Inquiry into poverty, easing censorship and attempting, however ineffectually, to enter into dialogue with Aboriginal spokespeople, the coalition was at least making a piecemeal attempt to win back the confidence of swinging voters, and in the upshot came closer to success than many would have predicted. But on the big issues there was little vision. Foreign policy could no longer consist of anti-communist cliches. Unemployment was rising beyond the 2 per cent level which had almost proved fatal to the Menzies government in 1961. Inflation was fuelled by a swelling tide of overseas investment which the government seemed incapable of controlling. In retrospect Gorton, with his unabashed nationalism and his readiness to take chances, had a certain nostalgic appeal. A leader who could affirm national aspirations and legislate with a sense of considered direction might succeed where Gorton had failed.

Like many of his generation Whitlam had been inspired when young by the example of Franklin Roosevelt and the American New Deal, and this was a model for which Australia seemed ready in 1972. Running the most professional campaign so far mounted by the ALP, Whitlam and his colleagues courted the voters with the slogan 'It's time!'. If Labor could not win this election, muttered the old hands, they could never win. Under the pinch of rural recession the outer states—Western Australia, South Australia and Queensland—were already showing the first signs of shifting towards a renewed conservatism. But the suburban households of Sydney and Melbourne were ready for Whitlam's message, and late on the evening of 2 December the television cameras crowded into the lounge-room of a typical Cabramatta residence where, surrounded by euphoric followers who could not quite believe the reality of their triumph, tall Gough Whitlam and his equally tall wife Margaret stood at the apex of their fortunes.

A SHINING ABERRATION

WHITLAM CAME IN LIKE a lion. Within three days of the election he set up himself and his deputy, Lance Barnard, to form with the governor-general Australia's smallest executive council. He explained that Labor's impetus would otherwise be frustrated, since a cabinet could not be chosen until just before the Christmas—New Year shutdown. The two-man ministry suited Whitlam's proconsular style as well as his penchant for unorthodox constitutional devices. He probably never appeared to better advantage. Between 5 and 18 December 1972 Whitlam and Barnard touched every major issue of policy. They promised Papua New Guinea independence, and gave diplomatic recognition to communist China. Draft defaulters were pardoned and imprisoned protesters released. National service was terminated, albeit with promise of a bonus to encourage existing trainees to complete their term of service. Australia made a commitment to ratify international conventions on nuclear arms, labour and racism. Racially biased sports teams were banned from visiting Australia, and the Rhodesia Information Office in Sydney was obliged to close. For the first time in twenty-three years there was an element of unpredictability about Australian foreign policy.

At home, Aborigines were promised special schools, and a stop was put to the leasing of mineral lands on Aboriginal reserves in the Northern Territory. Where the McMahon government had stood aloof from an application before the Arbitration Court for equal pay for women, the case re-opened with the Whitlam government's support. Sales tax was lifted from the contraceptive pill. Those who fretted about the spread of permissiveness noted that in the same week the excise was removed from wine, as was a ban on the import of the novel *Portnoy's Complaint*. The imperial honours list was scrapped, foreshadowing a more assertive Australian nationalism. Economically this took the form of a directive for preference to Australian-owned firms in government purchasing and the freezing of some overseas take-over bids. On the other hand, local inefficiency was not to be pampered, and the Tariff Board was directed to take a close look at some manufacturing industries. Grants were guaranteed to the disadvantaged outer states, South and Western Australia. A new centre for regional growth was planned for Albury—Wodonga as a blueprint for the promotion of decentralization. An Australian Schools Commission was initiated, at last bringing the Commonwealth completely into educational policy.[1]

On the fourteenth day Gough rested. The Labor caucus presented him with the expected names for his cabinet: Barnard became minister for defence, Frank Crean treasurer, and Senator Lionel Murphy attorney-general. Among ministers who for one reason or another would stand out among the Whitlam cabinet Jim Cairns took on overseas trade and secondary industry, Kim Beazley education, and (one of the very few members of non-British family origin) Al Grassby immigration. Except for one or two such as Beazley, all had spent their entire parliamentary careers in Opposition, and none had experience of ministerial office. Some ministers expected to meet hostility from public servants inured to twenty-three years of conservative rule. All were in a hurry to make changes. Within the party there was a widespread feeling that it was against the nature of things for Labor to hold office in Canberra, and they must make the most of their opportunity in the three years which were all they could expect. The mirror-image of this belief was held by many Liberal and Country Party supporters, who could not accept the legitimacy of an election which their side lost.[2]

Over Whitlam's victory loomed the powers of the federal Senate, always ready to plume itself on its symbolic role as protector of states' rights, and taught in recent years by Whitlam himself and by Lionel Murphy to assert its long dormant right to block a government's financial measures. Machiavelli, whom Whitlam was fond of quoting, remarked that the prince should combine the qualities of the lion and the fox. Whitlam was a lion who deluded himself into thinking he could also play the fox. One of the most creative thinkers ever to hold high office in Australia, he scorned the arts of political survival, if indeed he ever learned them. The maxim 'crash through or crash' served him well as leader of an Opposition in need of new heart, but was a dangerous precept for someone who wished to change Australian society at a time of economic uncertainty.

To Whitlam and his colleagues the first priority was social justice—the government must use its powers to improve the opportunities of the disadvantaged and to narrow the gap between the affluent and the underprivileged. To avoid alarming the middle-class supporters whose votes gave Labor its margin of victory, it must however avoid the road of radical socialism or confiscatory taxation. Instead, noting the steadily rising returns from federal taxation in a period of high employment and steady inflation, the government expected to fund its reforms from the growth in tax revenue without having to increase rates.[3] Since this presupposed that business confidence would hold up, and that overseas investors would not choose to punish a Labor government by withholding their capital, it was thus necessary to establish a name for sound economic stewardship. With the post-war weakening of the United States's supremacy in the world economy and the continuing inflationary tendency of nearly all currencies this would be no easy task.

The McMahon government, having failed to damp down the boom in 1971, reverted to an expansionary budget before the 1972 election, thus leaving its successors an annual inflation rate of 7 per cent. The recent massive inflow of overseas capital, together with price rises in internationally-traded foodstuffs, contributed to the problem. In common with many western nations Australia was having its first experience of 'stagflation', a combination of low economic growth, increasing unemployment and accelerating inflation. No Australian government drawing on the experience of the previous thirty years could have been prepared for this. For Labor stagflation would provide a particularly malign background for reform and experiment. So many expectations were pinned on the Whitlam government that in the early months of 1973 delay would have been unthinkable;

as Whitlam put it, 'We did not use recession as an alibi against reform'.[4]

The pressure to introduce overdue changes meant that many of the Whitlam government's new programmes were not adequately costed and could easily be blamed for Australia's financial difficulties.[5] The Treasury was unsympathetic and, as Liberal prime ministers also complained during the 1970s, unhelpful. During 1973 it was especially easy to misread the omens since manufacturing and the building industry were prospering; the recession of 1971–72 seemed just another hiccup in the inexorable spread of post-war prosperity. It was only in October 1973, when OPEC (the Organization of Petroleum Exporting Countries) decided to cut oil production as an answer to American support of Israel, that the industrial world temporarily lost control of inflation. By the middle of 1974 Australia, already hit by the boom in commodity prices, was facing the highest inflation since the 1951 wool boom, and the Whitlam government was floundering financially. Its performance was a drama in two acts: the first, from the end of 1972 to the early months of 1974, was one where it seemed able to reconcile Australia's most sweeping post-war programme of social reform with adequate economic management; the second, covering the remainder of 1974 and the first half of 1975, was one of almost unrelieved catastrophe. A third act was cut short by an unprecedented interruption.

In endeavouring to bring order to the economy the Whitlam government revalued the Australian dollar upward three times during its first year in office. The flood of overseas capital was stemmed by requiring importers of capital to deposit a proportion of their borrowings interest-free with the Reserve Bank. These measures had something in common with the economic nationalism of Gorton and McEwen, but the Whitlam government went further in seeking actively to expose Australian manufacturers to the competition of exports. Advice was sought from the chairman of the Tariff Board, G. A. Rattigan, who with his colleagues had been attempting for some years to nudge the coalition government away from McEwen's policy of courting numerous pressure groups in primary and secondary industry by the lavish use of protective tariffs.[6] Rattigan chaired a committee which recommended a 25 per cent across-the-board cut in tariffs, and Whitlam and Cairns announced this as government policy in July 1973. This seemed a well-chosen moment, as unemployment was falling, consumer demand was buoyant and retailers were reporting a wide range of shortages at a time when Australians had money in their pockets. Even if the import of consumer goods increased, the Australian economy could stand it. In the long run lower tariffs would strengthen Australia's bargaining position internationally. As Rattigan later wrote: 'It was only the unilateral 25 per cent cut in the Australian tariff by the Whitlam government which enabled the Liberal–Country Party government in 1978 and 1979 to secure . . . concessions which benefited our exports of agricultural products'.[7] But in the short run the tariff cuts were blamed for every increase in unemployment during the ensuing years. Trade unions joined manufacturers in howls of protest. Unabashed, the Whitlam government went on to expand the Tariff Board into an Industries Assistance Commission and entrusted it with numerous inquiries ranging from the performing arts to dairy-farming.

The easy availability of imports did nothing to hold back consumer prices, and by the end of 1973 inflation was running at 13 per cent. Price control was a matter for the state governments, which showed no sign of acting in the matter, and in August 1973 the federal government established a Prices Justification Tribunal before which companies would be required to explain any proposed increases. The tribunal had no legal power to enforce its findings, but business firms showed an unexpected readiness to abide by its suggestions, even when this meant repudiating sweetheart deals concocted with trade unions to cover an increase in wages. No doubt voluntary compliance was thought preferable to any risk of stronger coercion. The federal government later in 1973 went on to seek authority to regulate prices and wages, but this required the endorsement of a national referendum. Predictably the Opposition and most of the state governments opposed the idea, and so did the trade unions, which claimed that a conservative federal government might misuse such powers. In December 1973 the referendum was decisively defeated. This meant that there was now no curb on the stronger trade unions with the industrial muscle to demand steep wage increases as a counter to price inflation. Over this issue, as with a number of others, Whitlam had failed to consult adequately with the trade union movement. It was his habitual failing, and one from which the president of the ACTU, Hawke, was to draw a lesson for the future.

Whitlam's energies were concentrated on forcing social

reforms on all fronts. It was probably a fair criticism when a newspaper poll in December 1973 reported that 74 per cent of respondents agreed that the government was trying to do too many things at once.[8] And it was important to set priorities because the government's effective powers were limited. The Senate was still in hostile hands, with the DLP holding the balance of power, but Whitlam resisted advice to force a double-dissolution of parliament while his government was fresh in office. He greatly underestimated the Senate's powers of obstruction and the extent to which Labor in recent years had revived that chamber's pretensions. Nor could the co-operation of the state governments be taken for granted; even the three Labor states were suspicious of centralism. Whitlam and his supporters were wont to boast that they had introduced much more legislation than any previous government. Perhaps this profusion was stimulated by the knowledge that not all their initiatives would survive.

For Whitlam 'the most enduring single achievement of [his] government was the transformation of education in Australia'.[9] With Kim Beazley as minister an interim Schools Commission was set up in December 1972 under Professor Peter Karmel. Its first task was to chart the inequalities still lurking within the Australian school system. Its report confirmed that children of Aborigines, migrants and the working class in general, stood less chance than the rest of the community of enjoying schooling of a quality which would equalize their opportunities in life. The permanent Schools Commission was planned with a mandate for remedial action. The poorer state and Catholic schools would be favoured more than the prosperous private schools and state schools in affluent suburbs. This was at first resisted by the Opposition majority in the Senate, but under prompting from the churches the Country Party swung round to supporting the legislation.[10] Fees for universities and colleges of advanced education were abolished, and a support scheme was set up for needy tertiary students. Whitlam saw education as 'the great instrument for the promotion of equality'[11] and his government was well aware that Australia had fallen behind many other countries in the proportion of GNP spent on education. His hopes were to be dashed. The shift towards equality of opportunity did not outlive the Whitlam government.

It took longer to deal with the problem of universal health

insurance. This was the responsibility of one of the ablest of the younger Labor ministers, the gritty Queenslander Bill Hayden.[12] By April 1973 his advisers had put together the concept of Medibank, a scheme under which hospital treatment would be free, medical benefits would total at least 85 per cent of the cost of services, and patients could exercise free choice of doctor or hospital. The medical profession, already unsettled by the Gorton government's intervention, attacked the scheme with the same ferocity as the Chifley government had encountered many years earlier. Always unhelpful in suggesting alternatives, the AMA and the General Practitioners' Association claimed that the quality of care would be gravely damaged by any government intrusion which weakened the traditional fee-for-service nexus.

It took until July 1974 for Medibank to be authorized by parliament, and then the Senate delayed its operation further by refusing to approve a levy on taxable incomes designed to finance the scheme. By September 1975 Medibank was at last operating. Commonwealth funding of public hospitals also increased substantially, and a start was made with the provision of community health centres. Among other social welfare measures were a supporting mothers' benefit payable at the same rate as the widows' pension for female single parents; a discretionary benefit for lone fathers; allowances for the guardians of orphans and severely disabled children; and increases in the old-age pension and repatriation allowances, coupled with the removal of the means test for those over seventy years of age. An Australian Assistance Plan was created to provide social welfare services at a grass-roots level. It was an imaginative concept designed to encourage citizens to participate in decision-making without that over-reliance on bureaucracy for which, the political scientists assure us, Australians have an inclination.[13] Administration of the scheme was entrusted to thirty-seven regional councils, federally funded and representing local government and voluntary organizations. State governments were alarmed, since they were bypassed by the scheme and feared that the federal authorities were using social welfare to promote centralism. The High Court upheld the scheme, but it was an unpromising start to what could have been a constructive innovation.

Federal–state co-operation was essential if the Whitlam government were to influence urban and environmental policy. Whitlam put a colleague from a neighbouring part of Sydney's western suburbs, Tom Uren, in charge of a new Department of Urban and Rural Development, which aroused unfriendly comment from the deliberately unbureaucratic nature of its procedures.[14] As a new department competing with others it failed to gain Treasury support, but was associated with some commendable initiatives. An early concern was the old issue of decentralization. With Sydney and Melbourne approaching the 3 million population mark, and with Brisbane, Adelaide and Perth each reaching towards their first million, it was arguable that new provincial cities must be fostered, as Canberra had been, so as to provide economic and social opportunities and an enhanced quality of life for Australians who might not achieve them in the crowded state capitals. Most of the states were prepared to co-operate. The front-runner was Albury–Wodonga on the New South Wales–Victoria border, where a growth centre was founded in 1973. By 1981 its population had increased by 50 per cent and its workforce nearly doubled. Other experiments were less impressive. A proposed growth centre between Bathurst and Orange in New South Wales made little headway. A more promising prospect was Monarto, 80 kilometres east of Adelaide. The South Australian capital was thought incapable of expanding much beyond its present size without encroaching on some prized scenic and wine-growing country, as well as presenting serious problems of water supply.[15] The Dunstan government envisaged 'a shady, compact, walkable, easy-to-live-in city' incorporating the latest concepts of town-planning. But the Whitlam government was never excited about the project, and when population forecasts suggested that Adelaide might not grow as quickly as anticipated the Monarto scheme was scaled down and, in 1977, abandoned. Several more proposed growth centres, such as Salvado in Western Australia and Tamar in Tasmania, did not even reach the drawing-board.

A more immediate question was the price of land in state capitals. With the building boom of the early 1970s land for housing was in short supply and many would-be home-owners were discouraged by soaring prices and interest rates. In November 1973 the federal government introduced legislation for the establishment in each of the states of a land commission with authority to buy up tracts of urban land which might be subdivided for release to purchasers at moderate prices, which would provide competition for profit-motivated private developers. South Australia gave the only positive response to this scheme. During the next five years its land commission bought out several unsuccessful developers, and by 1977 provided more than two-thirds of the housing allotments on the market. Adelaide thus enjoyed some of Australia's lowest prices for land and housing. The federal government also contributed substantially to the rehabilitation of historic inner-city areas such as Glebe and Woolloomooloo in Sydney and Emerald Hill in Melbourne, though the benefit went to young professional couples rather than the traditional working-class inhabitants of those suburbs. Many more benefited from the Whitlam government's funding of a national sewerage programme. Although few votes were to be gained from such an initiative, none could gainsay its usefulness. Neville Wran, premier of New South Wales, coined the epigram: 'It was said of Caesar Augustus that he found a Rome of brick and left it of marble. It can be said of Gough Whitlam that he found Sydney, Melbourne, and Brisbane unsewered and left them fully flushed'.[16]

Whitlam wished also to be remembered for less humble monuments. It was only a coincidence that the long-delayed Sydney Opera House was completed during his term of office, in October 1973, but he left his mark unmistakably on Canberra. Under his government, work was commenced in 1973 on the national art gallery authorized eight years previously but subsequently sunk in procrastination. More controversially, he authorized a bold purchasing policy, drawing a storm of criticism when more than a million dollars was paid for the painting *Blue Poles* by the American abstract expressionist artist Jackson Pollock. *Blue Poles*, admittedly a work of minority appeal, was criticized as a symbol of the spendthrift habits of the Whitlam government; in fact it turned out to be a good investment. Of considerably greater cost to the taxpayer was the new High Court building, also commenced under the Whitlam government after long delays. The expense to the public was partly due to the chief justice, Sir Garfield Barwick, who showed great skill in persuading the federal authorities, both during and after Whitlam's time, to stint nothing in the building's amenities or materials. The 'Gar Mahal' was later to be outdone by a new parliament house, constructed on Capitol Hill. Although the site was decided under the Whitlam government, the responsibility for its final appearance and cost belonged to his successors.

Money spent on Canberra was begrudged by the state governments, but the strains of federal—state relations went a good deal
deeper. Zealous for a programme of reform which of its nature
should be masterminded from Canberra, the Whitlam government inherited a situation where states' rights were resurgent. For
more than twenty years since the Second World War the conventional wisdom had held that the Commonwealth would continue
gradually to accumulate power at the expense of the states
because of its financial leverage.[17] The mineral developments of
the 1960s and early 1970s reversed this tendency by enriching the
large underpopulated states of Queensland and Western Australia
and launching them on programmes of economic expansion
whose aims clashed with those of the manufacturing south-east.
With the rapid growth of overseas investment it was tempting
for the states to believe that they could make better bargains for
themselves without the restraints of Canberra. This attitude was
nowhere more strongly held than in Queensland, where from
1968 it was upheld by the sole Country Party premier, Johannes
Bjelke-Petersen. An ungenerous fundamentalist, but financially
shrewd, Bjelke-Petersen from shaky beginnings had consolidated
himself in office with the aid of skilled media advisers.[18] He now
found the perfect populist catchcry in defending Queensland
against the inroads of an unsympathetic and wasteful Canberra.
He was gravely underestimated by Whitlam, who saw only that
he had the provincial's narrowness, and not that he also possessed
the provincial's tenacity and sure sense of local emotions.

Two of the most contentious issues to sour federal—state
relations were minerals and energy policy and environmental
control. Out of office, the federal Labor Party had contended
that the only sure means of countering excessive overseas ownership of Australian mineral exploitation was planning and participation by the federal government. Rex Connor, as federal
minister for minerals and energy, commissioned Tom Fitzgerald,
an experienced financial journalist, to compile a report on the
contribution of the mineral industry to Australian welfare.[19] The
Fitzgerald Report suggested that the federal government had
spent more money on the mining industry than it had received in
the form of taxation, that the states in the six years ending
1972—73 had collected only $263 million in royalties, and that five
times that amount had been expatriated overseas as profits for the
parent companies. Without waiting for the publication of the

Fitzgerald Report Connor went ahead with two measures aimed at strengthening the Commonwealth government's grip on mineral development. Gorton's abortive legislation proclaiming the federal government's title to the seas and submerged lands around Australia was resurrected and strengthened. A proposal was also made for a Petroleum and Minerals Authority which should promote exploration and development of Australia's mineral resources as well as providing the venture capital for which reliance had previously been placed on overseas investment. Neither proposal got past the Senate in 1973, and the state governments, including those with Labor ministries, protested loudly. Environmental issues were not yet at a sensitive pitch, but by the end of 1973 the Tasmanian Labor government had already rejected Commonwealth plans to stop the flooding of Lake Pedder, and the Queensland government was eyeing uneasily the activities of a federal royal commission into oil-drilling near the Great Barrier Reef. Meanwhile the federal government set up a committee of inquiry into the national estate under Mr Justice Hope.

In defence of the federal system the states found themselves polishing up the constitutional armour of the past. Barely a month after coming to office the attorney-general, Senator Lionel Murphy, went to London to negotiate the repeal of Britain's surviving authority over Australian matters, including judicial appeals to the Privy Council. Before long this apparently theoretical issue roused the states to protest, Queensland loudest among them, because they feared that the Australian High Court would be less sympathetic to states' rights than the Privy Council had shown itself to be in the past. By the time Whitlam began consulting the state premiers Queensland was already on the point of consolidating its own right of appeal, and the other states failed to co-operate. Bjelke-Petersen and others like him also smelt the brimstone of republicanism in Whitlam's attempts to shelve 'God Save the Queen' as Australia's national anthem in favour of 'Advance Australia Fair', and in 1974 had his parliament proclaim Elizabeth II queen of Queensland. For his part Whitlam discarded the term 'Commonwealth of Australia' as an anachronism, thus giving rise to allegations that Australia would soon lose the federal character implicit in the term 'Commonwealth' and become a unitary state ruled from Canberra. None of these trivialities would have mattered, but they increased the difficulty of rational dialogue between the federal government and the states. When, as a result of an initiative taken by the McMahon government, a constitutional convention met in September 1973 for the first systematic overhaul of the federal Constitution since its origins in 1897–98, it ended in stalemate. Agreement could not even be reached on the simple principle that the state and federal governments might exchange powers. During the next few years of political turmoil several commentators were to complain that 'The makers of Australia's constitution botched the job'.[20] At least the founding fathers had been able to sink their differences and create a federation of some kind; all the evidence suggests that the task would have been completely beyond the statesmanship of the 1970s and 1980s.

In foreign policy also the Whitlam government's performance during its first year was stronger in style than content. Like Menzies before him, Whitlam felt capable of acting as his own foreign minister. While in Washington in July 1973 he took pride in informing President Nixon: 'We are not a satellite of any country. We are a friend and partner of the United States, but with independent interests of our own'.[21] This was a somewhat belated declaration, as within a few days of taking office members of the Whitlam government had given Washington some offence by the vigour with which they denounced the renewed bombing of North Vietnam. The plain fact was that Australia's defences were inadequate for any foreign policy which did not include the American alliance. The Whitlam government recognized this by adhering steadily to the ANZUS agreement. The wider obligations of SEATO were no longer at issue, as with the proclamation of Nixon's Guam doctrine that treaty was being allowed to decay quietly. Nor was the Whitlam government willing to listen to the peace movement or to the left wing of its own party in seeking the removal of the American communications bases at North West Cape, Pine Gap and Nurrungar. Face was saved early in 1974 by the negotiation of improved Australian access to the management of these bases, but there was no thought of removing them.[22]

At the meeting of British Commonwealth Heads of Government in July 1973 Whitlam showed himself concerned to strike up friendship with the Third World nations among the members and took some pride in his role in encouraging Jamaica, Guyana and others to join with Australia in setting up an international bauxite association which would maintain prices on the world market in the interests of producers.[23] But Australia could also be at the receiving end of such tactics. The decision of the OPEC countries to treble the price of crude oil in a few months after October 1973 found the Australian economy unprepared. This gave a further stimulus to the inflationary pressures within the Australian economy, but because of Australia's self-sufficiency in alternative fuel sources the full impact was not expected until mid-1974. A half-Senate election was due in May, after which the government in power could anticipate rough weather. It was unlikely that Labor would pick up enough seats to dominate the Senate unless extra vacancies were created. In March 1974 Whitlam tried to engineer such a vacancy by appointing the deposed leader of the DLP, Senator V. C. Gair, as ambassador to Ireland. The operation was bungled, for although Gair accepted he did not resign until the Queensland government had been alerted to the manoeuvre and could issue the writs for the half-Senate election without waiting for the Gair vacancy.[24] Whitlam looked ridiculous, and the DLP was so incensed that it joined with the other Opposition parties in the Senate in blocking supply. This was an unprecedented exercise of Senate authority, but instead of challenging it Whitlam decided that there would never be a better opportunity of securing a renewed mandate before the time came for making hard economic decisions, and obtained a double-dissolution of parliament.

It would have been a good election to lose. No Australian government could have weathered the inflationary spiral of the next twelve months without losing popularity. The Liberal leader, Snedden, however, was unequal to the challenge, and the Whitlam government was returned with a reduced majority in the House of Representatives and still without control of the Senate. The only consolation was the total eradication of the DLP. It had outlived its usefulness, proving unable either to prevent the coming to office of a Labor government nor the fashioning of peaceful co-existence with Communist China, and its role as custodian of morality was easily accommodated within the larger conservative parties. After ineffectually trying to ally itself with the Country Party the DLP withered away until in 1978 the Victorian branch, its original power base, went into liquidation. Meanwhile the Country Party, encouraged by the example of Queensland into hoping to extend its activities into the suburbs and towns, gradually transformed itself into the National Party. Rural Australia was no longer an adequate base, although after 1974 it was almost entirely a non-Labor fief. By wiping out the government bounty on superphosphate, cutting the subsidy on petrol for rural areas and pointedly ignoring rural pressure groups Whitlam had so antagonized the country vote that it was almost entirely lost to Labor. It was probably realistic to calculate that there were few bush workers, railway employees and other traditional Labor supporters left in the bush, but in deciding to concentrate on the cities Whitlam unnecessarily flouted rural susceptibilities.[25]

Among the victims of this trend was the minister for immigration, Al Grassby, who lost his Riverina seat after a nastily racist campaign and was soon appointed Australia's first commissioner of community relations. He was associated with a major shift in policy towards multiculturalism, a concept of slippery definition, usually taken as indicating that ethnic diversity should be preferred to the old concept of assimilation to an Anglo-Australian ideal.[26] Facilities for the schooling of migrant children were improved, and ethnic radio stations were established at Sydney and Melbourne. Multiculturalism in government policy tended to mean positive discrimination in favour of minorities of non-British origin. This concept was queried by, among others, the former Czech migrant Frank Knopfelmacher, who argued that Australia was what he termed an 'anglomorph' society and that full opportunity within that society was unavailable to those who stayed within a minority cultural tradition.[27] Government policy, however, deprived British migrants of their preferred status. Although more than 30 per cent of the 1973 intake were British the proportion fell afterwards. From the beginning of 1975 Britons entering Australia were required to obtain a visa, allegedly to deter the influx of criminals, but almost certainly as a reprisal against the stiffening of British entry regulations. Assisted passages were made available to non-European migrants, thus ending the last remnant of the White Australia Policy. As yet the numbers entering were not high enough to arouse much public controversy.

Although the Whitlam government failed to satisfy feminist grievances or eradicate Australian male chauvinism, some progress was made. In April 1973 Whitlam appointed Elizabeth Reid as special adviser on women's issues. During the next two years the federal and state public services cleared themselves of discriminatory practices against women. Private enterprise was also moving; during the 1970s the percentage of women employed in private banks increased from 4 to 27, though as yet overwhelmingly in the lower echelons. Odd pockets of prejudice survived. As late as 1979 Sir Reginald Ansett was refusing to allow women — 'old boilers' he termed them — to train as airline pilots.[28] But even he was eventually overcome. The most tenacious resistance to change came from some trade unions. When in 1975 the Melbourne tramways admitted women conductors as trainee drivers it ended nearly twenty years of obstruction by the relevant union. The BLF believed that employers would use female employees to bring down wages. In 1965 a rising official, Norm Gallagher, boasted that in no circumstances would women be admitted to the union. In a 'macho' industry where labourers invested their raw strength Gallagher's law tended to win out over federal policy.[29]

In May 1974 the Court of Conciliation and Arbitration at last granted women the full adult minimum wage. This belated act of justice was blessed by the federal government, but was soon blamed for fuelling inflation and unemployment, although the evidence is at best inconclusive. During the 1974 election campaign the sole fresh item of major expenditure to which the government pledged itself was the provision of child-care centres for working mothers. Other innovations included the establishment of women's health centres and refuges in most major cities, although the Queensland government refused to pass on some of the funds allocated for women's shelters. Counselling centres were founded for victims of rape. Abortion remained a contentious subject; in 1973 a House of Representatives debate decisively rejected a proposal to legalize the practice but endorsed a suggestion for a royal commission into the social, legal and educational aspects of human relationships. This was amended so as to include an endorsement of the value of responsible parenthood, and in that form was accepted by the House by a large majority.[30] Chaired by a judge, Elizabeth Evatt, the royal commission was to constitute a searching examination of Australian personal values and to form one of the most illuminating legacies of the Whitlam era.

Nor were cultural values neglected.[31] It gave a felicitous boost to the new nationalism when in 1973 Patrick White became the first Australian to receive the Nobel Prize for literature, thus matching the earlier recognition of the scientists Sir Macfarlane Burnet and Sir John Eccles. Whitlam was not backward in figuring as a patron of the arts. Holt's Australian Council for the Arts was upgraded in 1975 to form the Australia Council, under whose aegis literature, drama, ballet and a variety of arts and crafts received regular sustenance. Of no less value to authors was the establishment in 1974 of Public Lending Right, assuring them of a payment for the use of their books in public libraries. The Australian Film and Television School was established in 1973, and support was given to a lively and burgeoning Australian drama. Theatre companies such as La Mama in Melbourne and the Nimrod in Sydney produced the work of new Australian playwrights such as Alexander Buzo, David Williamson, Jack Hibberd and many more. The wider public owed to the Whitlam government the introduction of FM radio and colour television, together with an insistence that both radio and television should ensure a specified percentage of Australian content in their programmes. This did something to break the rather deadening hegemony of American material on commercial television. Viewers soon showed that they watched 'soap operas' such as 'Number 96' and 'Prisoner' with at least as much relish as they viewed overseas imports. The quality of Australian-produced material owed a great deal to some unknown public servant who, when television was first introduced, stipulated that advertise-ments for commercial stations must be made in Australia, thus building up a school of experienced scriptwriters and producers who could turn their hands to bigger assignments when oppor-tunity arose.[32]

If Australian households found it possible to buy new colour television sets it was perhaps because most of them had never had so much money to spend. Many housewives would have denied this. They would have complained of shopping prices which rose almost every week, and which helped to precipitate the downfall of at least one chain of supermarkets—Tom the Cheap Grocer, the creation from the late 1950s of the lord mayor of Perth, Sir Thomas Wardle.[33] Official statistics would have confirmed that food prices rose by nearly 19 per cent in 1973–74 and 9.7 per cent in 1974–75, clothing by 13.7 and 21 per cent respectively, and housing by over 30 per cent in those two years. But during the same two years household incomes rose by over 50 per cent in aggregate, thus staying well ahead of inflation. It was one of those rare periods in Australian history when wages were increasing faster than profits, and when the spending power of wage and salary earners rose ahead of the cost of living. Partly this could have been due to the militancy of the trade unions. In 1974, 6.292 million working days were lost in industrial disputes, an all-time peak.[34] These tactics were largely a response to rising prices. Employers made terms, passed on the extra costs to consumers, and blamed the Whitlam government and the arbitration system for failing to control the situation. The government's popularity continued to fall even though most households, and even old-age pensioners, had more in their purses than ever before.

And spend they did. In 1972–73 Australians spent $2.085 million on household durables; during the next three years the amount doubled. It was no coincidence that in 1974–75 net expenditure on gambling showed its biggest rise ever, from $2.891 million to $3.706 million.[35] In addition to wages and salaries, hire-purchase offered an easy source of credit, and another source of temptation appeared late in 1974 when the banks began to promote credit cards, charging higher than average rates of interest but offering fresh opportunities to those who chose to buy now and pay later. All these forces helped to fan the flame of inflation and thus promoted uneasiness in that desperately fickle factor, business confidence. Interest rates jumped and created liquidity problems which forced several major property developers into receivership and eventually forced the closure of a major stockbroking firm, Patrick Partners. Several building societies were shaken. One authority writes that 'September 30, 1974 was the blackest day on Australian stock exchanges this century'.[36] High interest rates at least revived overseas investment during 1974–75 after two low years, but very little of it was going into the mining industry or into other major export-earners. Unemployment was also rising, and although at 4 per cent it fell far short of what would be considered acceptable in the 1980s, it was worse than any but the middle-aged could remember.

Perhaps temporarily exhausted by the effort of winning another election and pushing some of its delayed legislation through the first joint sitting of both houses of parliament, the Whitlam government was not coping well with the challenges. Graham Freudenberg describes the winter of 1974 as 'some of the unhappiest weeks of the Labor government'.[37] The Treasury recommended anti-inflationary measures including a 10 cent increase in petrol excise, higher postal and telephone charges and tax increases on higher-income groups. But Whitlam was unable to persuade his colleagues to take such harsh medicine, and although the 1974 budget saw notable increases in urban affairs and the provision of child-care centres it failed to come to grips with the long-term problems of economic management. Instead, in December 1974 Cairns, who had led the revolt against the Treasury line, became federal treasurer. His star seemed to be on the ascendant, since he had displaced Barnard as deputy leader after the May elections and had gained grudging approval from some sectors of the business community for his performance as minister for trade. His appointment completed the alienation of the Treasury officials, and he had no clear financial philosophy of his own to impose.

One man who believed he had the answer to Australia's financial problems was the minister for minerals and energy, Rex Connor. He thought the oil crisis could be met by hastening the development of alternate sources of energy within Australia, particularly natural gas and the conversion of coal to motor spirit. Connor's programme included a transcontinental natural gas pipeline, a petrochemical plant, three treatment plants to convert uranium into yellowcake, electrification of major railways, redevelopment of coal ports, and the purchase of a year's supply of Middle East oil to be stored against future emergencies.[38] To find the massive capital outlay for these projects Connor looked to the oil-rich Arabs themselves. He found a contact in the unlikely form of a Pakistani middleman, Tirath Khemlani, who informed Connor in November 1974 that he could raise US$4000 million from Arab sources. Khemlani was an unknown, and the servicing of interest on the loan would be a formidable commitment. Treasury officials were deeply unhappy at the prospect of being by-passed, and warned that the Australian government would damage its extremely high standing in international capital markets by using such unorthodox channels. Their attitude persuaded the Commonwealth Bank Board to stay aloof. Ignoring bureaucratic caution Connor convinced Whitlam and, less easily, Cairns. The loan was approved at a meeting of the executive council at the prime minister's Lodge on the night of Friday, 13 December. In order that parliament and the federal Loan Council could be by-passed the loan was classified as temporary. It was symbolic of the rushed and informal nature of what should have been a major undertaking that the minute of authority was signed while resting on the Lodge refrigerator.

The executive council could be used in this way only with the concurrence of the governor-general. This was no longer the meticulous and politically experienced Hasluck, but Sir John Kerr, previously chief justice of New South Wales. Kerr had already shown his readiness to use formal powers despite the cost in personal popularity. In 1969 he had braved industrial strife by sentencing Clarrie O'Shea to imprisonment. He was not present at the meeting authorizing the loan. He added his signature nevertheless, but resented not having been briefed before the discussion. Whitlam made no attempt to mend matters, apparently confident that the governor-general accepted an entirely ceremonial view of his role. He departed on an overseas trip, leaving Cairns as acting prime minister. When a week went by with no word from Khemlani Cairns decided that there should be no more dealings with him, and Connor's authority was revoked shortly after.

Whitlam's overseas trip was unproductive and unlucky in its timing. On Christmas Day 1974 the town of Darwin was devastated by the tropical cyclone Tracy. Cairns gained widespread approval by his prompt and sympathetic appearance on the scene of the disaster and his support of Major-General Alan Stretton who cut through red tape to effect relief operations.[39] A few days later a freighter collided with Hobart's Tasman Bridge, severing the city's main traffic artery. Whitlam laid himself open to media criticism by superficial off-the-cuff comments. A little later the media turned against Cairns as stories circulated of his close relationship with his office co-ordinator Junie Morosi. A striking personality of Filipino background, Morosi interfered too much in the management of the treasurer's office and lacked the art of avoiding publicity. She was a woman, she was attractive, she was Asian, and Cairns talked to the media with fearless candour about the warmth of his feelings for her. Both were pilloried. Morosi was eventually transferred to another job, the victim of Australian sexual hypocrisy and Australian emotional reticence, but also of her own insensitivity to public decorum. Cairns remained treasurer for a while—alienated from his senior advisers, his mind only half on the job at a time when the economy was in dire crisis. Meanwhile Connor persuaded his colleagues at the end of January to renew his authority to prospect for overseas funds, though on a smaller scale. Obsessively he waited for word from Khemlani. It was an odd way to run an economy.

The parliamentary turmoil of 1975 tended to overshadow Whitlam's last year in office and undoubtedly distracted a good deal of the ministry's energies from its essential tasks of bringing the economy under control and maintaining its impetus in social reform, yet considerable progress was made in both directions. While Cairns remained treasurer public sector expenditure continued to increase as a device for stimulating the economy, but this did nothing to damp down inflation. That problem was tackled in April, when the Arbitration Commission restored the indexation of wages in line with official consumer prices, giving employers, the government and the ACTU some chance of holding the line against bigger claims. Early in June Whitlam removed Cairns from the Treasury and Clyde Cameron, the patron of higher public service salaries, from the ministry for labour. The new treasurer, Bill Hayden, made a good impression. Hayden's budget cut public sector spending, reduced company tax and increased duties on liquor and tobacco, thus offering incentives to investment. By the second half of 1975 the rate of inflation was slowing, company profits were recovering, and capital inflow seemed to be improving. The return to financial orthodoxy looked as if it would assist economic recovery.

Left-wing commentators have complained that these trends marked a retreat from the Whitlam government's earlier commitment to social justice and reform.[40] But the increase in real wages during 1974 had been possible only at the cost of throwing some employees out of work, and it would be some time before the trade union movement squarely confronted the dilemma that, with the ending of the long post-war boom and the acceleration of technological change, the majority who remained in work would improve their pay and conditions only at the expense of the unemployed. Nor were the Whitlam ministers behaving like reactionaries who had lost their faith in social democracy. Funding was found for Medibank, and plans were in preparation for the federal government's entry into the field of insurance by setting up a corporation which would compete with private companies for life and property insurance, as well as providing cover against natural disasters such as bushfires or cyclones. In 1975 also a start was made on the construction of a standard-gauge railway from the transcontinental line to Alice Springs; the federal government by consent took over the country railways in South Australia and Tasmania; and plans were initiated for the federal construction of an outer-circle suburban railway in Sydney. The divorce laws were simplified so that an unsatisfactory marriage could be dissolved after twelve months' separation, and an attempt was made to rob the process of divorce of some of its trauma by setting up specialist family courts. In challenging entrenched business and professional interests, in issues of human relationships, and in developmental projects the Whitlam government had lost little of its creative energy.

It was harder to devise a satisfactory new Aboriginal policy. Just as the Whitlam government was favouring multiculturalism in place of the old rubric that migrants must conform to some predetermined Anglo-Australian norm, so too Aborigines were no longer pressed to seek fulfilment in assimilation. Every state government except Queensland agreed to transfer Aboriginal policy to the federal government. Late in 1973 a National Aboriginal Consultative Committee was formed, with forty-one elected members, including some Torres Strait Islanders. The Aboriginal Legal Service was expanded and Aboriginal majorities placed on the governing bodies of its offices. An Aboriginal medical service was established to work through community clinics, and a start was made on reducing the infant mortality rate, which among Aborigines in northern Australia remained unacceptably high. These reforms did not avert a little activism. During a royal visit in February 1974 the Queen and Whitlam were booed by Aborigines outside Parliament House, and three armed Aborigines bailed up some public servants in their office. But federal spending on Aboriginal needs rose by 64 per cent in the 1974 budget, mainly on housing, education and health.

In 1974 a royal commissioner, Mr Justice A. E. Woodward, formerly counsel for the Yirrkala of Gove, reported on land rights in the Northern Territory. He recommended the creation of Aboriginal land trusts holding reserves in inalienable communal freehold, backed by community-based land councils and by a government fund for the repurchase of traditional lands. Entry for mining, tourism and other purposes would be subject to the consent of the local community, although an Aboriginal veto on mining could be overruled if the federal government thought that the national interest required it. In the spirit of these findings Whitlam in August 1975 handed over a tract of land to the Gurindji people of Wave Hill whose walkout in 1967 had catalised the land rights movement. Woodward's recommendations became law only after the fall of the Whitlam government. They were supported by both sides in federal politics, but among the states only South Australia followed this example. Aboriginal land reforms, however overdue, ran the risk of rousing the envy of the poorer farmers and graziers of rural Australia, who were also contending with isolation, heat and limited opportunities. Nor could the mining industry be expected to welcome legislation limiting its right of exploration in favour of Aboriginal possession.[41]

An opportunity to clarify the legal position was missed in February 1975 when, on the motion of the Aboriginal Liberal senator Neville Bonner, the Senate passed a resolution affirming that the people now known as Aborigines and Torres Strait Islanders had been in prior occupancy of Australia, that this priority had been unduly ignored by Australian law, and that remedial measures were required. If the House of Representatives had concurred in this motion it would have established Aboriginal claims on a politically acceptable basis instead of leaving the issue to become a source of constitutional and antiquarian debate.[42] Suspicious of Liberal motives in putting forward such a motion, the government took no action. It was a reflection of the embittered temper of party politics in 1975.

The Senate was the cockpit. Its appetite for rejecting or emasculating the Whitlam government's legislation grew with experience, and the only unresolved question was whether its members would repeat the threat of early 1974 to hold up the passage of the government's budget. The question sharpened after February 1975, when Murphy left the Senate to become a judge of the High Court and was replaced, not as convention dictated by another Labor nominee from his state of New South Wales, but by an elderly independent. He, as it turned out, never used his vote against the Whitlam government on crucial issues; but the breach of precedent was too much for Bjelke-Petersen to resist when another vacancy occurred through the death of a Queensland Labor senator at the end of June. He demanded that Labor should put forward three names from whom the Queensland parliament might choose a new senator. Predictably but foolishly the request was refused, so that Bjelke-Petersen felt free to nominate an obscure Labor renegade who made no secret of his wish to bring down the Whitlam government. Legal action ensured that this man never took his seat, but the Whitlam government was now totally unable to control the Senate.

In the House of Representatives Whitlam remained dominant—perhaps all too dominant, as in Canberra it is easy to succumb to the illusion that mastery of the parliamentary arena implies mastery of the nation. Snedden, already under a cloud as Opposition leader after his unsuccessful lunge for power in May 1974, was reduced to inanity. After he had interrupted one of Whitlam's speeches with 'Woof, woof!' his colleagues speedily replaced him with the more substantial figure of Malcolm Fraser. A principled conservative, Fraser seemed to represent a clear alternative to Whitlam. He stood for reduced government spending, the restoration of powers from the Commonwealth to the states (with the obligation for the states to find their own funding), the limitation of social welfare to the obviously disadvantaged, and an end to experiments in government initiative. He stated that the Opposition would not use its numbers in the Senate to block the budget except in 'extraordinary and reprehensible circumstances'.[43] Before the end of the year he would claim to have found these extraordinary and reprehensible circumstances. It must be allowed that in many respects the Whitlam government made it easy for him.

Among Labor circles it has been customary to blame the Whitlam government's calamitous reputation on the bias of hostile media.[44] Australia's press and television were concentrated in the hands of a small group of magnates, all of them mindful that their advertising revenue depended on the goodwill of the business community, and all usually anti-Labor in their editorials.[45] The major owners were Consolidated Press, which under Sir Frank Packer was cheerfully and consistently anti-Labor; the Herald and Weekly Times chain, whose conservatism was more tempered; the Fairfax family, owners of the *Sydney Morning Herald* and the *National Times*, who were negotiating themselves into alliance with the Syme family's *Age*, all of them 'quality' newspapers which, although usually moderately pro-Liberal, had on occasion temporarily backed Labor; and Rupert Murdoch, son of the founder of the Herald group who, having cut adrift from the old firm, built up his own thriving media empire. Its most influential newspaper was the *Australian*, which with partial success attempted the role of Australia's only nation-wide daily, pitching its appeal largely to the business community. In good years Labor could expect support from at least one of these media barons, and in 1972 and 1974 Murdoch's *Australian* was their friend, if often a candid friend. But by 1975 the Murdoch press had swung into vicious opposition. Some have tried to explain this as the consequence of Murdoch's thwarted ambition, others as sheer manipulative king-making. This pre-supposes that Australians are swayed in their voting habits by what they read in their newspapers. It is more likely that the Murdoch press sensed that the Whitlam government was doomed to defeat and shifted its policies accordingly.[46] It was certainly the case that by 1975 every major Australian newspaper, with the partial exception of the *Newcastle Morning Herald*, was editorially hostile to the Whitlam government. During the first nine months of 1975 opinion polls showed the government slipping ever deeper into unpopularity.

Public perceptions of the Whitlam government were shaped by a series of ineptitudes which even the most benevolent of media would have found hard to present sympathetically. In February 1975 the Speaker of the House of Representatives resigned after Whitlam refused to support his rulings, abusing him in the process. Early in April, as the war in Vietnam neared its end, Whitlam sent messages to both sides urging negotiation. He informed parliament that the texts of the two messages were substantially the same. When it emerged that there were minor differences the *Sydney Morning Herald* carried a scalding editorial categorizing the Whitlam regime as 'the government we cannot trust' and describing the discrepancy, with huge exaggeration, as 'the gravest political scandal since Federation'.[47] At the end of April Saigon fell. Many South Vietnamese attempted to flee. Fraser demanded that Australia, as a party to the war, should offer to take 50 000 refugees, but the Whitlam government was not over-eager to welcome so many Asians, and in 1975 took only a thousand. In comparison with some nations which had not participated in the war this seemed niggardly, but it was not the kind of issue that would bring down governments.

Far more lethal were the government's self-inflicted wounds brought about in the quest for overseas investment from un-orthodox sources. In May Connor's authority to prospect for

Arab money was finally rescinded, but he was by now infatuated by the possibility and, unknown to his colleagues, continued to keep in touch with Khemlani. Meanwhile Cairns signed a letter offering a Melbourne businessman, George Harris, a commission for locating overseas loan funds. Challenged in parliament in early June, he denied all knowledge of signing it, probably truthfully as his office was chaotic. Two days later Whitlam decided to replace him with Hayden and to demote Cameron. When the latter refused to resign Whitlam got the governor-general to remove him. At the same reshuffle Lance Barnard also resigned to take up a diplomatic posting. The ensuing by-election dramatically underscored Labor's unpopularity. Whitlam had mortally offended a vocal section of the migrant community by giving diplomatic recognition to the Soviet Union's sovereignty over three formerly independent Baltic states: Lithuania, Latvia and Estonia. Unemployment had passed 5 per cent and was still rising. After thirty years with the Barnard family the seat emphatically swung to the Liberals.

At the end of June it emerged that Cairns had misled parliament when he denied signing the Harris letter. He refused to resign. Once more Whitlam had to ask Sir John Kerr to dismiss a minister. No prime minister had ever given a governor-general so much practice in the use of the prerogative. Nor had any prime minister had such apparent difficulty in imposing loyalty and discipline on senior colleagues. A special session of parliament was called on 9 July to justify the government's approach for Arab loan monies, though without adequately explaining the executive council's hole and corner methods. Connor made a spirited defence; nobody could have guessed that he was still playing with fire.[48] But the Whitlam government's reputation sank even lower in the public eye. In South Australia Don Dunstan's state government survived an election only by firmly dissociating itself from its Canberra colleagues.

The mischief came out early in October during the budget sitting of parliament. The Melbourne *Herald* revealed that Connor had continued to communicate with Khemlani after the time when he had assured parliament and cabinet that dealings had ceased. He resigned. Now the press was in full cry against the Whitlam government. Editorials demanded that the Senate should use its numbers to rid Australia of such incompetents. Fraser announced on 16 October that the reprehensible circumstances when the Senate would decline to pass the budget had now come about. Whitlam accepted the challenge, arguing that the Senate was acting in breach of convention. So it was, but Whitlam had flouted so many conventions that the point was almost irrelevant. The question was whether some of Fraser's own back-benchers in the Senate would come to share that view and break ranks to enable the budget to pass. If they held firm the federal government would start to run short of money by the end of November. Many thousands of Commonwealth employees would find their pay in jeopardy; Canberra might sink into paralysis; funding for pensions might cease; and the effect on Australia's international credit was unthinkable. To add to the generally apocalyptic atmosphere of that spring, civil war had broken out in East Timor after the withdrawal of Portuguese authority. The likely outcomes were either victory to a Marxist-influenced independence movement or occupation by Indonesia, neither of them compatible with Australia's declared interests. It was understandable that many Australians were tiring of the parliamentary sideshow and looking for stability in government.[49]

But these events were not turning to Fraser's advantage. As October gave way to November every week's public opinion polls told the same story: the pendulum was swinging back to the Whitlam government. The veteran political journalist Alan Reid reported that, having crossed his Rubicon, Whitlam had seldom seemed in better form.[50] He toured the country orating, denouncing his enemies, exuding confidence, energized by the intense enthusiasm of cheering audiences. Perhaps the voters thought that there would be an improved performance from a Whitlam government purged of its most controversial elements; perhaps they were impatient with the Opposition's spoiling tactics, considering that the state of the world economy did not allow much latitude to any Canberra politicians. Dourly stonewalling, Fraser on 3 November gave a little ground by offering to pass the budget if Whitlam promised to call another double-dissolution no later than June 1976. Whitlam refused. By this time rumours were flying fast. The National Party leader Doug Anthony was known to have rented a Canberra house to an officer of the Central Intelligence Agency (CIA). Were there other links? And would Whitlam offend the Americans by revealing the names of CIA officials in Australia? Khemlani came and went, bringing a large number of documents, but nothing of which the Opposition could make use.

Beneath all the hullabaloo the critical factor was finance. The private banks could not be counted on to bail out the government if it ran short of funds, and although the government was exploring several ingenious alternatives none was obviously workable. Sir John Kerr, the governor-general, was deeply exercised by this possibility, and convinced himself that if the crisis was not resolved by the second week of November it would be too late for corrective action, especially if an election was called. He persuaded himself further that Whitlam would accept no compromise short of total defeat of his opponents. Less justifiably he also accepted Fraser's assurance that the Opposition phalanx in the Senate was unshakeable. In fact four or five Liberals were ready to desert. By 9 November Kerr had taken a fateful decision. He decided that he had no choice but to dismiss Whitlam, and to dismiss him without warning so that Whitlam had no time to persuade the Queen to oust Sir John himself from Government House. Hundreds of thousands of words have been expended on the validity of this decision, but the issues are simple. There can be no doubt that theoretically the governor-general has power to appoint and dismiss prime ministers. In deciding to dismiss Whitlam he exercised his judgement validly but mistakenly. It is not necessary to write him down as a stooge of American or British intelligence agents.[51] His reading of the situation was faulty and was too much influenced by his concern to cling to office. Having determined on the divisive step of dismissing an elected prime minister he should have foreshadowed his intention to resign immediately after the next federal election whatever the outcome. By remaining in office he made himself a partisan.

Whitlam was also much to blame for the impasse. He had not communicated adequately with Kerr about the constitutional implications of the crisis. In regarding the governor-general as a mere figure-head he failed to recognize that Kerr's vanity was almost equal to his own, and that ever since the loans affair in December 1974 Kerr had not considered himself sufficiently consulted. Apart from Whitlam, Kerr had no other proper source of advice to whom he could turn in a crisis. He decided to consult Sir Garfield Barwick, remembering only that he was chief justice and not that he was a former Liberal attorney-general and once Whitlam's political opponent. Barwick fortified Kerr in all he intended to do. On the morning of Remembrance Day, 11 November, Kerr telephoned Fraser. Words passed which led

Fraser to expect that he would soon be called on to form a caretaker government.[52] Shortly before lunchtime he went to Government House and waited in a reception room while Whitlam arrived to recommend a half-Senate election. Kerr did not wait for this advice. He informed Whitlam that as he (Whitlam) would neither resign nor recommend an election for the House of Representatives he would dismiss him. After Whitlam departed Kerr commissioned Fraser to form a caretaker government until elections were held on 13 December.

In his over-confidence Whitlam had made not the flimsiest plan for any such contingency. He might have used his formidable eloquence to talk Kerr around to a face-saving compromise. He might have instructed his ministers in the Senate to postpone or withdraw the supply bills, leaving Fraser with the task of getting a new budget through a hostile House of Representatives.[53] He might have threatened to challenge Kerr's action in the High Court. Instead he accepted his government's dismissal, trusting that in the ensuing election a continuing surge of public support would sweep him triumphantly back to office. The Senate passed the budget early in the afternoon of 11 November. At the same time the new Fraser government was given a vote of no confidence in the House of Representatives and the Speaker was sent to Government House to communicate this formally to Kerr. Kerr took no notice. Much more than his original dismissal of Whitlam, this was a gross breach of constitutional practice, but by this time nobody was worrying much about technicalities. Kerr's official secretary was despatched late in the afternoon to read from the steps of Parliament House a proclamation dissolving parliament. He faced an excited crowd, and behind him loomed Whitlam, stony-faced, exhorting his followers to maintain their rage until after the election and making angry quips against Kerr and Fraser. But eventually everyone went home.

Intellectuals excitedly took sides. Manning Clark asked his fellow-Australians: 'Are we a nation of bastards?' and observed that perhaps the trade unions and the students would not allow Fraser to govern. The psychologist Ronald Conway claimed that parts of Whitlam's proposed legislation would 'strike at the very roots of free enterprise, free contract, and free public speech in Australia', and imagined he heard echoes of Hitler's Nuremberg rallies in the crowds enthusing over Whitlam's oratory.[54] But most Australians read the crisis in homelier metaphors. As Kerr

Debutantes at Graduation Ball, University of Western Australia,
early 1960s

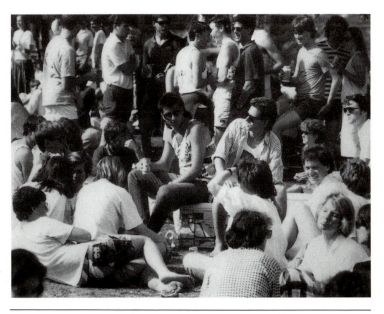

An end to formality: university students in the early 1980s, Perth

Feminist demonstrators, University of Queensland, early 1970s

Time of hope: anti-Vietnam war protest, Brisbane, 1970

himself later put it, he was 'the umpire in the roughest political match in Australian history'.[55] A sporting nation could understand this concept more readily than constitutional niceties; Kerr was an umpire of Whitlam's own choosing and he had decided against Whitlam, who had to go. The Whitlam government's gains in public opinion polls melted away. The management of the economy was a more potent issue for most voters than the rules of the parliamentary game. On 13 December there was a uniform swing of 6.5 per cent against Labor; they lost all their House of Representatives seats in Tasmania, all but one in Western Australia and Queensland, and most of their gains in the middle-class suburbs of Sydney and Melbourne. The Liberal—National Party coalition won 91 of the 127 House of Representatives seats and commanded an absolute majority in the Senate. Whitlam's Australia had rejected him crushingly.

Whitlam remained leader of the Labor Party for two more years, retiring after the next elections in December 1977 when his party suffered a no less ignominious defeat. He outlasted Kerr, who resigned in July 1977 after enduring much abuse. By now he was an embarrassment to Fraser, who replaced him successively with two appointees who brought 'a touch of healing' to the post: Sir Zelman Cowen and Sir Ninian Stephen. After an abortive attempt by Fraser to appoint Kerr to the largely honorary job of ambassador to UNESCO, Kerr and his wife left Australia for some years, quietly returning when the advent of another Labor government softened old rancours.

Whitlam became ambassador to UNESCO from 1983 to 1986, revered by many Australians but mistrusted by others. Stephen Alomes argues that Whitlam offered Australia new national goals with which many Australians could not identify.[56] Certainly his government effected many overdue reforms and could largely claim to have rewritten Australia's political agenda. Many of the issues which preoccupied Australian politics in the decade and a half after 1975 could trace their ancestry to Whitlam's policies and the conservative reaction against them. But his government had not been able to stem the increase in unemployment and inflation or to calm the anxieties generated by these two factors. Australia was a society of children of the 1930s Depression and post-war migrants, both groups who sought security and modest prosperity and were accordingly apprehensive of too much change. It was unfortunate that the Whitlam government's record suggested that social change could be achieved only at the expense of level-headed political leadership and sound economic management. This was to some extent unfair, as the Whitlam ministry had experienced ill-fortune with the international economy, but it raised the possibility that Australia would be found essentially a conservative nation in whose history the Whitlam interval would seem a shining aberration.

Part IV

And It Works—Kind Of
1975–1988

For better or for worse, Australia today is very much what the rest of the world will be like tomorrow. Its life may at times lack style, but its heart may be as close to gold as mere mortals can aspire to. I have seen the future and it works, kind of.

Richard Walsh, 'Australia Observed', *Daedalus*, 114, 1 (Winter 1985), p. 437

10

ON THE MAKE

FRASER WAS TO REMAIN in office for seven years and four months, achieving by a narrow margin the second longest term of any Australian prime minister. For the first five years his government enjoyed the rare combination of a majority in the Senate and domination of the House of Representatives. But it was not a stable team. Don Chipp broke away and formed the Australian Democrats, a consciously middle-of-the-road party which after 1980 held the balance of power in the Senate. Philip Lynch was obliged to resign as treasurer after involvement in tax avoidance schemes. Reg Withers, an architect of victory in 1975, was ousted for a minor impropriety over electoral redistribution. Others quit after disagreements with Fraser. Although these altercations fed the media's tendency to present politics as theatre, they also showed Fraser's grip on his cabinet to be unchallengeable. No federal government in three decades enjoyed such freedom to impose its own mark on Australian society.

Where the Whitlam government would have welcomed such freedom to impose changes in the name of greater equality of opportunity, Fraser and his colleagues had other goals. It was not that in practice they wished to undo all the innovations of the previous three years—their bark was much worse than their bite. The individualism prominent in Fraser's earlier speeches gave way to a conservative humanism.[1] But the Liberals and the National Party viewed society as essentially competitive.

247

Individual profit and reward were the necessary spurs to progress. Their first priority was the restoration of economic growth and the creation of conditions that would rouse business confidence, stimulate investment and bring back the cheap credit and low unemployment of the 1960s. They believed that the surest instrument for this policy was government spending cuts. The axe, the razor, the knife figured often in the journalistic metaphors of the late 1970s. Inflation must be curbed by reducing government expenditure, reducing budget deficits, reducing the growth of money supply, and reducing of necessity the overhang in real wages from which most workers had benefited in 1974–75. In the process several election promises had to be broken. Tax deductions failed to appear, and unemployment benefits were cut, but not pensions or child endowment.

Recovery was nevertheless sluggish. It took the trade cycle more than two years to recover from the trough of November 1975. During that time inflation continued to mount at an annual average rate of 13 per cent as measured by the consumer price index. Wage indexation ensured that pay packets grew as fast, but only just. The trade union movement, which had behaved so fractiously under Labor, calmed down considerably. Even when strikes were called they were often against unpopular government policies, such as the partial dismantling of Medibank, rather than industrial issues. By 1977 the number of working days lost through industrial disputes fell to a quarter of the 1974 figure. This did not stop Liberal politicians from blaming the unions for most of Australia's economic ills. Ian Sinclair, a senior National Party minister, was particularly upset about the mischief done by 'Pommy shop stewards'.[2] But the Fraser government hardly interfered with the unions beyond extending the provisions for secret ballots on strikes and creating an Industrial Relations Bureau to investigate complaints by rank-and-file union members. The state governments were less patient. Victoria in 1976 passed legislation against the disruption of work on vital state projects. Western Australia in the same year required demonstrators to obtain a police permit before assembling in public, and in 1979 provoked a national one-day general strike by arresting trade unionists in the Pilbara for failing to comply. In the same year Bjelke-Petersen, as usual going to extremes, legislated to ban strikes in essential industries in Queensland, and even to make it illegal for union members to be quoted in the media as supporting a strike. None of these laws seemed to make much difference to industrial relations.

Even the most docile of labour unions could do little to alter the international economy in which Australia had to operate. Fraser went back to using the tariff to protect manufactures and upbraided the Industries Assistance Commission when it balked at cushioning the textile industry.[3] But Australia was losing ground with its trading partners, even in rural products. The EEC's protected farmers were past satisfying local markets and were dumping their ever-increasing surpluses on overseas markets competitively with Australia. The United States was anxiously questing for wheat and beef markets. By 1977–78 wool had fallen behind coal and cereals as Australia's major export item. Meat exporters were making the most of the livestock export trade to the Middle East, so that in 1978–79 meat accounted for one-eighth of Australia's export income. But the main hope lay in minerals. By 1978–79 iron ore was earning Australia nearly $1000 million, coal over $1500 million, and other metals a like amount. If only as a quarry for Japanese and South-East Asian manu-facturers Australia might yet trade its way to continued solvency.

The Fraser government had to coax a mining industry badly ruffled by its experience of Whitlam and Connor. To encourage exploration and development, taxation concessions were restored and extended and Treasury proposals for a resource tax on the petroleum and uranium industries were rejected. Where the Whitlam government had insisted that new uranium projects must be 100 per cent Australian-owned, and that foreign par-ticipation must not exceed 50 per cent in other mining projects, Fraser in 1978 softened the rule to a 25 per cent Australian equity but with a majority of Australian citizens on the board of management. The revival of uranium mining proved less trouble-some than expected. Whitlam had set up a commission of inquiry chaired by Mr Justice Fox to inquire into the environmental consequences of uranium mining, and in September 1975 the ACTU had resolved that all export and mining of uranium should cease until the commission reported. But during 1976 the unions progressively weakened their opposition, so without wait-ing for the final report of the Fox Inquiry Fraser was emboldened to go ahead and permit uranium exports to nations which had signed the Nuclear Non-Proliferation Treaty. The Fox Report found that although uranium mining might provide scope for terrorists and might add to the world's stock of nuclear weapons, Australia's safety procedures were strict enough not to necessitate a ban on exports.[4] Accordingly, uranium mining resumed. The ensuing protests included a Brisbane street-march in October 1977 which led to the arrest of 418 citizens in one afternoon—a record figure.

But it was not *carte blanche* for the mining lobby. They were now constrained by environmental considerations. Fraser had inherited from the Whitlam government a batch of legislation based on the Hope Inquiry, and this was passed with the support of all parties. Valued portions of the built and natural environment, such as nature reserves, historic buildings and major scenic areas were to be brought into the Australian national estate. A Heritage Commission would compile a register of the national estate and recommend grants for its preservation. The mining industry voiced alarm lest the Heritage Commission override the use of an area wanted for mineral exploration, and also grumbled at separate legislation requiring companies to prepare environmental impact statements. But after some delay Fraser decided to keep this legislation, although depriving the Heritage Commission of some of its funding powers. In some respects his government outdid Whitlam. Where Connor had been prepared to condone the mining of mineral sands on Queensland's Fraser Island, in the teeth of opposition from nearly half the Labor caucus, the Fraser government in 1976 accepted the advice of a commission of inquiry to ban the operation completely. This pleased neither the Queensland government nor the overseas-based company. In 1978 the minister for minerals and energy, Doug Anthony, upset the mining companies further by imposing guidelines for negotiating contracts with overseas buyers. The aim was to present a united front in bargaining with overseas customers, especially the tightly organized Japanese steel mills. But several state governments, Queensland and Western Australia in particular, complained at what they saw as interference by Canberra.[5]

Mineral development had been one of the main bones of contention between Canberra and the states when Whitlam was prime minister and Connor the most formidable of his barons, but the state governments found Canberra under Fraser no easier to ignore. In what has been called 'one of the few attempts by the conservative parties to formulate a coherent practical policy for a major portion of public sector activity'[6] the Fraser government soon after coming to office proclaimed a 'new federalism'. Reversing the Whitlamite trend, the 'new federalism' was intended to decentralize responsibility by defining more tidily the respective authority of Commonwealth and states and by delegating greater taxing powers to the states. The states would cease to receive general revenue grants from Canberra, and would instead be guaranteed a specified share of federal income tax receipts. They could also levy supplementary income tax and other charges. There would be a council for inter-governmental relations, thus improving consultation between Canberra and the states. But the states preferred Canberra to carry the odium of tax collection, so that although the new federalism enabled more efficient housekeeping it did not materially change the balance of power between the Commonwealth and the states.

Suspicion of Canberra also thwarted Fraser's hopes of clarifying the Senate's status by providing for an election for half the Senate at each election for the House of Representatives. Jealously guarding the prerogatives of the states' house, Queensland, Tasmania and Western Australia voted against this change at a referendum in May 1977, so that although the proposal gained a 62 per cent 'Yes' vote Australia-wide, it could not be approved because a majority of states had not accepted it. Several minor reforms, however, were passed at the same referendum, and 'Advance Australia Fair' gained endorsement as the national song by a two-to-one margin over 'Waltzing Matilda'. Queensland and Western Australia also quarrelled with the Commonwealth over Aboriginal policy. When Fraser maintained the Whitlam government's practice of granting land rights to Aboriginal communities in the Northern Territory, the states complained that this precedent raised expectations among their own Aborigines which they did not want to meet. Early in 1978 Canberra suffered a rebuff over the Queensland Aboriginal reserves of Aurukun and Mornington Island in the far north. Wishing to encourage a French–American mining company, the Queensland government resumed these reserves from the Uniting Church against the wishes of the Aboriginal community. After inconclusive negotiations with Bjelke-Petersen, Fraser passed Commonwealth legislation to give Aboriginal communities on Queensland reserves the option of managing their own affairs, overriding the state government. But Bjelke-Petersen promptly abolished all Queensland reserves, set up a local government authority for Aurukun and Mornington Island, then dismissed the councils and sent in administrators from Brisbane. The federal government was equally ineffectual in 1980 when Sir Charles Court's government in Western Australia excised 4 hectares from the Yungngora people's federally funded station at Noonkanbah in the Kimberleys to permit drilling for oil near a sacred site. Despite strong protest the Court government rebuffed federal urging to reach an accommodation with the Noonkanbah Aborigines and enforced the company's right to drill with a strong police presence. No oil was found and the incident served mainly to reveal the Commonwealth's inability to defend Aboriginal rights against a determinedly development-minded state government.[7]

The Fraser government continued to work at improving relations with the states. In 1979 Anthony withdrew the federal guidelines on iron-ore negotiations while retaining those on coal and bauxite. With the revival of offshore exploration for oil and natural gas came another opportunity for conciliation. In 1975–76 the High Court confirmed the validity of the Whitlam government's legislation ending state jurisdiction at the low-water mark and vesting control of the surrounding seas in the Commonwealth. In 1980 the federal government by delegation restored offshore powers to the states, thus offering the fiscal benefits of new discoveries, as well as facilitating the development of such resources as the natural gas of the North West Shelf. Such concessions did not mollify the iron-ore magnate Lang Hancock, who since 1974 had been wasting effort and money trying to encourage Western Australian secession. He found an ally in Bjelke-Petersen, who in 1982 informed a surprised Japanese press conference that 'we are not Australians—we are Queenslanders'.[8] But the federal government ignored this posturing, confident that it was taken seriously neither by the Australian public nor by foreign investors.

In 1978–79 private capital inflow from overseas reached $1713 million, the second highest recorded figure. During 1979 the OPEC exporting nations cranked up the price of oil further, stimulating demand for coal exports from Queensland and New South Wales. To protect local producers and explorers the government imposed a levy on Australian crude oil so as to equalize its price with the current level on the world market, thus boosting the federal Treasury with an unexpected windfall. Meanwhile gold was responding strongly to the freeing of the international market in 1976. Bauxite was also in demand. Natural gas showed promise for exploitation. From 1977 Sydney drew gas by pipeline from Moomba in South Australia, and offshore deposits in the north-west of Western Australia were tapped in the hope of attracting overseas buyers as well as a domestic market. During 1979 and 1980 politicians, journalists and business leaders talked with swelling confidence of a resources boom which would restore Australia to its rightful status as 'the lucky country'.

But lucky for whom? By slowing down wage rises through indexation the arbitration system, with the federal government's blessing, was managing to hold real wages for most employed Australians at 1975 levels or a little below. For two years from mid-1977 inflation was held at under 9 per cent, and the number of unemployed settled steadily at 6 per cent.[9] Since 1975 households were spending more on food and considerably more on rent or mortgage repayments, but were economizing on cigarettes, liquor, clothing and most of all on household durables. This was unwelcome news for Australian manufacturers, whose home market had already shrunk since the decline of immigration under the Whitlam government, and who were experiencing fierce competition from Japanese and South-East Asian exporters. By the late 1970s Holden's share of new vehicle registrations was less than a quarter of the total; in 1958 they had held half. Foreign imports, mainly Japanese, had risen from commanding less than one-third of the market in 1971 to nearly half by 1978. Some of Australia's worst pockets of unemployment were to be found in industrial cities such as Newcastle and Wollongong.[10]

Fraser's Australia in its distribution of rich and poor, jobless and securely employed, was coming to resemble the Australia of the 1920s more than the Menzies era, but there was considerable regional diversity. It is instructive to look at the findings of the 1981 census, held during his sixth year of office, particularly since on first coming to power Fraser had been so unimpressed by accurate statistics that he almost cancelled the 1976 census. In 1981 there were 14.5 million Australians, twice as many as there had been in 1945. Nine million of these were concentrated in New South Wales and Victoria; 6 million in the cities of Sydney and Melbourne. But the outer states were growing faster.

Western Australia's population had risen by 8 per cent since 1976 and would shortly overtake that of South Australia. Queensland's figure rose by nearly 10 per cent; the Northern Territory's by over 25 per cent, including some Aborigines who had not been counted previously.

Tasmania had the highest proportion of Australian-born, and Queensland the next, supporting the view that the Sunshine state drew many of its newcomers from colder climates interstate, especially elderly citizens seeking an agreeable retirement. In an endeavour to capitalize on this trend Queensland became in 1976 the first state to abolish death duties and probate, but within five years all the other states followed suit. About 20 per cent of Australian residents were born overseas, mainly in Britain and Ireland; Western Australia, with 27.4 per cent, had the highest proportion, suggesting that unlike Queensland the West drew less on internal migration and more on newcomers who made it their first port of call. This may explain why Lang Hancock's short-lived secession movement found its main spokesmen in British migrants. Demography fails to explain, however, why Western Australia and Queensland were often the last states to adopt innovative social reforms.

After more than thirty years of substantial non-British migration the Australian-born generation was beginning to take over. No more than 4.5 per cent of Australian residents in 1981 were born in the Mediterranean nations such as Italy and Greece. Except for some Italian and Spanish settlers around Broken Hill and in the sugar-growing districts of North Queensland, nearly all lived in the cities. In the inner suburbs of north and west Melbourne they formed between 18 and 20 per cent of the residents, and in some parts of inner Sydney between 12 and 14 per cent. Politics, especially at the municipal level in such suburbs, began to reflect the influence of migrant communities, often brokered by senior officials of the various ethnic clubs. These communities had nothing of the ghetto about them. Families tended to move out as they prospered. In many new suburbs Italian families who had done well built with selective memories of European opulence, with balustrades, stone steps and perhaps a pair of lions flanking the front gate. As they moved out they were replaced in the inner suburbs by more recent migrants: Turks, Lebanese and a small but growing number from South and South-East Asia, especially Vietnamese.

After the fall of Saigon in 1975 anti-communist Vietnamese continued to flee their homeland. Some unauthorized parties made their way in small boats to landfalls in northern Australia: by 1977 twenty-five boats, containing 723 people, with more coming. Despite anxiety about Australia's capacity to absorb unlimited numbers of 'boat people' the Fraser government accepted the responsibility of housing these refugees, the largest number arriving in 1979.[11] Between 1976 and 1980 about one-third of Australia's immigrants were Asians. The largest concentration was to be found in the western suburbs of Sydney, with a strong Vietnamese presence at Cabramatta. Very few settled in Tasmania or in rural districts. The federal constituency of Hume, covering the sheep and wheat country around Canberra, had the fewest foreign-born voters anywhere in Australia. It also had the most consistent church-goers: a mixture of non-conformist Protestants and staunch Catholics of Irish origin of the kind commemorated by Father John Hartigan in *Around the Boree Log*.

Religion was now ceasing to play such a prominent part in Australian life. Over 10 per cent of the population described themselves as not practising any faith, with Tasmania, rural New South Wales and Queensland containing the fewest atheists and agnostics. Catholics and Anglicans were almost equal in number, each around 3.8 million. Catholics considerably outnumbered Anglicans in the Australian Capital Territory and Victoria, but were noticeably under-represented in Tasmania and South Australia. In rural south-eastern South Australia Catholics and Anglicans were both much outnumbered by Methodists and other Protestants, though the Australia-wide tendency was for the Protestant churches to lose ground. In 1977 many Methodists, Presbyterians and Congregationalists joined to form the Uniting Church, losing in the process a minority of conservatives who continued, much diminished, under their old names. Hans Mol, the historian of religion in Australia, estimated that no more than 26 per cent of Australians could be described as even moderately regular church-goers, though he also noted a growth of new and experimental forms of religious experience.[12] American cultural influence was reflected in a revival of fundamentalist Protestantism, respectful of material success but deeply mistrustful of science and the intellect. The Mormons, Jehovah's Witnesses and various Pentecostalist faiths all reported increasing support, and within the older churches a minority of congregations were drawn to the charismatic movement. A smaller number of Australians found themselves attracted to religions of Indian origin, and the shaven heads of the Hare Krishna movement and the orange robes of Bhagwan Rajneesh's followers soon ceased to excite much attention in Australian city streets. Unlike North America, Australia generated few new varieties of religion but remained, as in so much else, an importer of culture.

Religious pressure groups made their presence felt in Australian public life, though not always consistently. The Catholic Commission for Justice and Peace produced a series of critiques of social inequality and the problems of the powerless, until in 1986 the Hierarchy decided that it was becoming too political and restricted its responsibilities.[13] In the Anglican Church the Brotherhood of St Laurence similarly stirred consciences, with the result that its leading spokesman, Peter Hollingsworth, was passed over in 1984 as too contentious for the archbishopric of Melbourne. Other church people, among them the dominant party in the Anglican diocese of Sydney and a number of fundamentalist Protestant groups in Queensland, considered that moral conservatism came first. They used their influence to urge politicians to stand fast against permissive values. In Queensland Rona Joyner successfully led two pressure groups against what they saw as 'anti-Christian, anti-family socialist-humanist cells active within the education department',[14] so that in 1978 a primary school course of social studies taught to 11-year-olds throughout Australia was banned in Queensland schools. Some, including one state minister for education, endorsed the demand that the view of Creation set out in the Bible's first book of Genesis and evolutionary theory should be taught with equal emphasis. Once again Australians were showing themselves all too faithful to American precedents.

Concern about the stability of the traditional family was understandable. Following the passage of Lionel Murphy's Family Law Act in 1975 the number of divorces rose sharply to a peak of 63 230 in 1976. This number was doubtless due to the backlog of cases taking advantage of the new rules, but when in later years the number stabilized at around 40 000 it could be seen that the ideal of lifetime marriage no longer applied to at least a quarter of Australia's adult population. By 1986, 19 per cent of adult women were living in de facto relationships, and among both women and men in the 25–29-year age group the conventionally married were outnumbered by those who had taken a mate without the formalities of church or state. Such relationships lasted an average of two years before ending in either marriage or separation. Marriage was no longer essential for parenthood; the number of children born out of wedlock rose from 8 per cent in 1966 to 18 per cent in 1986.[15]

Traditional families survived most strongly in the country and in the newer suburbs of the state capitals. South Australia's population contained relatively fewer children and more old people than any other state. South Australia also had the fewest affluent families, then defined as those earning over $26 000 a year. Canberra had the most well-to-do families, and also by far the highest proportion of graduates and diploma-holders—nearly 20 per cent of the adult population. Education certainly seemed a passport to affluence. The 'silvertail' suburbs of Sydney and Melbourne shared with Canberra the largest number of adults with higher education. The Maranoa district of Queensland had the highest percentage of adults entirely lacking trade or professional qualifications, with Port Adelaide and rural South Australia next. The fewest graduates were found in the inner city suburbs, although the next ring of suburbs tended to hold large numbers with trade qualifications. Most intellectuals were suburban commuters. As late as the 1980s the move from the migrant working class through the ranks of artisans and clerks to the professional classes often involved moving further and further from the old heart of the cities.

Patterns of work and unemployment reflected educational background, but there were some deviations that at first sight seemed surprising. There were more poor in the Northern Rivers district of New South Wales than in any of the cities' inner suburbs, but this was largely due to the dropouts and followers of the counter-culture who chose to settle down in that benign climate and to manage without the formal cash economy, except perhaps for dole cheques. Registered unemployment was greatest in Port Adelaide, followed by the Northern Rivers of New South Wales and the districts around Newcastle. Unemployment was usually greatest in traditional Labor-voting blue-collar areas, although the low employment rate on Queensland's Gold Coast was partly due to its large population of retired people. Western Australia and Queensland had less than the average amount of unemployment, South Australia and Tasmania more; there were more impoverished families in Tasmania than in any of the mainland states, a factor which did much to explain the Tasmanian preoccupation with using its hydro-electricity to attract new industry without concern for the environmental consequences. High-income earners were most numerous in the North Shore suburbs of Sydney and—confirmation of those who spoke enviously of public service salaries—in Canberra. A calculation of 1978 showed that the richest 10 per cent of adult Australians shared more than half the total wealth of the nation. The poorest 10 per cent had less than 1 per cent. And the gap was widening.

The Fraser government was early provided with two authoritative surveys which depicted the destructive effects of poverty on family life. Professor Henderson's report on Australian poverty, commissioned in 1972 by the McMahon government and extended in its scope by Whitlam in 1973, showed a deteriorating situation. Nearly 18 per cent of Australian income units were living on the margin of poverty or beyond it.[16] As in his previously published surveys Henderson found the aged, large families and single parents to be most at risk of penury. The poor paid higher interest for their credit and had less access to information which might enable them to plan thriftily. Although the Fraser government continued to devote about the same proportion of government spending to social welfare as Whitlam had done, unemployment benefits continued to demand a larger allocation and this meant that most other forms of welfare were gradually scaled down. Fraser had promised not to abolish Medibank, but in 1976 his government provided that taxpayers must either be levied a charge on income to fund the scheme or else cover themselves with private insurance, Medibank being permitted to compete in this field. As health costs escalated Medibank was progressively dismantled, and then abolished, at least for the time being, in 1981. This restored the pre-Whitlam arrangements under which pensioners and those who passed a means test could receive free public hospital treatment and payment of most of their medical bills but it did nothing to address the problems that Medibank had been set up to resolve.[17]

More valuable evidence on the condition of the Australian poor was provided at the end of 1977 when the Royal Commission on Human Relationships submitted its final report.[18] Although

Fraser had personally sponsored this inquiry his government had cut down its funds and the amount of time available to it, and when some of its more controversial findings were leaked to the media he did not wait to make a detailed examination but simply claimed that some parts would fill every family in Australia with horror. His cavalier reaction to a thoughtfully researched report was intelligible, if ignoble, in the middle of an election campaign against Whitlam, who could be attacked as the friend of fashionable permissiveness. Perhaps it was a classic strategy of beating the messenger who brings bad news, because the report showed that for many Australians, especially women and children, the family was failing in its purpose of supplying support and emotional nourishment. Where the family was deficient the report urged that the community, which in practical terms meant government funding, must help the needy. This ran counter to the Fraser government's preference for stressing the virtues of self-help and self-reliance.

Even the equality of the sexes could not be taken for granted. The commission found plenty of evidence to show that it was harder for women to achieve financial independence because banks and other lending institutions displayed a totally unreasonable bias against advancing money to women, restricting their credit and insisting wherever possible that a male relation should underwrite them.[19] They also found that teenage girls were leaving school with a much lower self-esteem than boys of the same age. This was especially marked with regard to their mechanical and mathematical aptitude. (Despite this, far fewer girls than in 1951 saw marriage as their sole ultimate goal.) Yet there may have been a major cleavage in class attitudes. Girls from working-class families still looked to marriage and the family as their best hope of self-fulfilment. 'Work's no fun', they said. Susan Koch, a process worker at the Queensland Can Company in Brisbane, said that there were no child-care facilities or flexibility in working hours. The union held its meetings at night, when married women could not attend, and management was discriminatory: 'Men can maybe turn off the machine five minutes or ten minutes early and nothing is ever said, but if a woman walks up and turns off her machine, the foreman would come up and say, "You had better watch out, the boss is looking"'.[20] Home with a supportive husband and children might well seem preferable to factory life of this kind.

Unfortunately husbands were not always supportive. An Anglican clergyman who knew the housing commission suburbs of western Sydney described the cycle. Young people lacking love and sympathy at home sought it in early marriage. Incomes were usually low, and when children came the temptation to plunge into debt through hire-purchase and credit cards could seldom be withstood. Coming from backgrounds which saw no great value in the education system, such families often failed to develop elementary skills:

In the parish in which I work, we have families where the children are under two years of age and they are put to bed without nappies because the parents have never thought of putting a nappy on a child when it goes to bed, with consequent lack of hygiene. We have parents who have no idea of normal ways to prepare meals. The problem is that in early stages of the relationship the children fit in very well, but as they grow older they see that the parents do not provide the things they look for and long for, and thus the relationship breaks down.[21]

Such pressures sometimes led to violence. Husbands escaping their troubles in the camaraderie of the pub came home to tired wives and fretful children, quarrelled and battered them. Often the women put up with it. If they left home they had to depend on relatives or women's shelters, and while the Fraser government continued to finance shelters it was at a reduced level; Queensland continued to refuse this form of help. The police did not like becoming involved in domestic violence. Work was very hard to find for housewives who had been out of the labour market for some years. Journalists in those years were fond of quoting Fraser's aphorism that life wasn't meant to be easy. Many abused wives would have agreed.

None of these matters should have earned Fraser's condemnation, nor the scandalized reactions of citizens who wrote letters to their newspapers describing the report as 'sick and misguided' and likely to develop 'a promiscuous irresponsible attitude in the community'.[22] Sex was, as so often, *the* taboo. The commission wanted to lower the age of consent to fifteen, repeal the laws against homosexuality between consenting adults, and permit abortion up to the twenty-second week of pregnancy in cases where the mother's life or health were gravely at risk or where the child would be seriously disabled. All three recommendations were vehemently attacked, but it was the last which aroused most heat. Catholic theology and the tenets of the Right to Life Association taught that life began at the moment of fertilization, and that the laws of the state must not allow for differences of opinion on this delicate and contentious issue. Although the commission insisted that nobody with conscientious objections to abortion should have any involvement with the practice, the opposition lost none of its vigour. Consequently the problem surfaced during 1978 in the federal parliament.

The first controversy occurred in the Senate over regulations for the Australian Capital Territory disallowing private abortion clinics. Three attempts to modify this ruling were defeated by a fair margin, and Canberra's public hospitals were left in sole control.[23] In the House of Representatives, S. A. Lusher, a Catholic back-bencher who was the Country Party member for that stronghold of church-going native-born Australians, Hume, estimated that in 1977–78, 60 000 abortions were performed annually in Australia. If his figures were correct they would have represented one in five of all known pregnancies, though it was not known whether this indicated a marked increase on past years. Lusher believed that abortion was granted on increasingly flimsy pretexts, and stated that in South Australia, the only state where the practice was legalized, no more than forty-nine of the 3590 abortions performed during 1977 were due to medical disorders. He accordingly moved that Commonwealth medical benefits should not be paid for abortions unless a physician certified that the mother's life was endangered.

The debate took place in March 1979.[24] As it was in effect a judgement on the ethics of abortion, party leaders agreed that members should be free to register a conscience vote on the motion. Consequently the debate which followed was uncommonly full, thoughtful and restrained, though its quality was inevitably weakened by the fact that there was not one woman in the House of Representatives. In the end the House rejected Lusher's proposal in favour of a more permissive amendment providing that abortions must be carried out consistently with the laws of the appropriate state or territory in order to secure medical benefits. The Liberal who proposed this amendment at once aroused the wrath of the Right to Life Association, which contributed to his defeat at the next election. But the subject was not re-opened and with one exception state governments were prepared to tolerate abortion without harassment, if without enthusiasm. The Queensland government in 1980 brought forward a bill forbidding abortion except for women with suicidal tendencies and imposing fourteen years' gaol with hard labour for doctors performing abortions, with shorter terms for counselling or attempting to perform one's own abortion. The resulting protest was reinforced by the AMA because of the threat to doctor–patient relationships. Having reduced its status to a private member's bill, the Queensland government made no attempt to resurrect the measure when it was narrowly defeated in May 1980.[25]

Other methods of family limitation were by now widely accepted. More than half of all women in couple relationships, and probably three-quarters of other sexually-active women, used the contraceptive pill despite reports of undesirable side-effects in some cases.[26] A growing number of Australian women, often those who had the desired number of children, were committing themselves to sterilization. Vasectomy was also available (though there were legal difficulties in Queensland) but men, on a variety of pretexts, were less ready to accept sterilization than women. The Australian birth rate fell steadily during the 1970s, reaching its lowest recorded point of 15.7 per thousand in 1978. Such a trend ran counter to the thinking of earlier generations who had seen the nation's well-being as dependent on a steadily increasing population. It reflected not only the easy availability of efficient contraception, but also the increasing presence of married women in the workforce, whether from choice or necessity. Couples may have been influenced by uncertainty about the future. Though many found a nuclear war too unimaginable to contemplate, all were aware of the end of full employment.

And yet the family ideal still flourished. Professor John Caldwell, a respected demographer from the Australian National University, conducted a survey in Melbourne on behalf of the Royal Commission on Human Relationships. He found that 88 per cent of his respondents had been reared by both biological parents until leaving home and only 10 per cent regarded their parents' marriage as truly unhappy. Over half still visited their parents at least once a month. Two-thirds were perfectly happy to remain in the house where they were currently living, an interesting figure since official statistics showed that each year about 16 per cent of Australians changed their place of residence.

Rather than imagine that a large majority of satisfied home-owners co-existed with a significant minority of itinerants, it is simpler to note that most of those who moved stayed in the same state capital. Many must have been moving because of family circumstances to a larger, or a smaller or a more prestigious dwelling. About four out of seven of those who moved house were aged between 20 and 35. Some may have been travelling around Australia to see something of the world before settling down. Most would have been couples saving for a home in which to raise children or, less happily, those whose marriages had broken up and were moving out. Older householders shifted with reluctance; fewer than 10 per cent in any year. Most remarkable of all, Caldwell reported: 'We found to our utter astonishment that only 7 per cent described themselves as very dissatisfied about the family financial situation and only a quarter as being even somewhat dissatisfied . . . It is not a terribly dissatisfied society'.[27] This is one of the most profound statements that has been made about contemporary Australia and has been largely ignored by historians and sociologists.

If further proof was required of the survival of family values among the Australian public it could be found in two highly publicized events of the early 1980s. At Monash University Professor Carl Wood and his colleagues became one of the first medical teams in the world to conduct *in vitro* fertilization, a procedure enabling some previously infertile married couples to have a child through the assistance of sophisticated medical technology. After the first successful experiments in 1981 criticisms surfaced. Some religious groups condemned the procreation of children by any method other than conventional sexual intercourse between wife and husband; others thought the expense disproportionate; and beyond lay a deeper, though less well-formed, fear lest the same techniques eventually could be used for cloning or the production of hybrid monsters. Opinion polls suggested that the majority of Australians were prepared to accept any scientific breakthrough that enabled couples to enjoy the good fortune of parenthood. In 1984 a Victorian committee of inquiry recommended that *in vitro* fertilization should be permitted with certain safeguards. The right to parenthood still seemed a paramount Australian priority.[28]

Popular attitudes to religion, morality and the family were thrown into sharp relief by the Chamberlain case.[29] A Seventh

Day Adventist pastor and his wife, Michael and Lindy Chamberlain, were camping one evening in 1981 near Uluru (Ayers Rock) when their baby daughter Azaria disappeared—taken by a dingo, said Lindy Chamberlain. The baby's remains were never found, but at an inquest in Alice Springs a seasoned coroner found in favour of the dingo theory. By this time the dramatic nature of the tragedy had provoked a good deal of media coverage, which in turn led to a prodigious amount of nation-wide gossip, ranging from tasteless dingo jokes to lurid speculations about black magic. Because the Chamberlains belonged to a minority fundamentalist sect and failed to conform to stereotypes of appropriate grief it was easy for many to believe that justice was done when Lindy Chamberlain was arrested for the murder of her child. She was jailed after conviction by a jury influenced by what seemed a convincing array of expert witnesses. A higher court confirmed the sentence. It was only after vigorous agitation that in 1986 a royal commission was appointed to review the case and found that Lindy Chamberlain should never have been convicted. Much of the expert testimony had been seriously faulty. Some commented that even a largely secular society such as Australia could come perilously close to witch-hunting when family values were involved.[30]

It took longer to rouse public disquiet over the ethics of business and professional life. One of the unintended side-effects of Australia's involvement in the Vietnam War was a marked upturn in the traffic in illegal drugs, bringing greater opportunities for corruption, especially in Sydney where senior police officers had long been suspected of involvement with those who did well out of illicit gambling, prostitution and liquor.[31] Crime assumed international dimensions. The Mafia allegedly entered Australia in 1969, and during the 1970s was credited with influence among marijuana growers and dealers. Nugan Hand, a newly formed merchant bank with intriguing American connections, was also suspected of involvement in the illegal drug trade during the 1970s, but its activities came to light only after the death or disappearance of the managing partners. The shadows touched politics. Sir Robert Askin, who from humble beginnings became Liberal premier of New South Wales from 1965 to 1975, and died in 1981 the richest man ever to hold that office, turned a blind eye to malpractice. In 1973—74 Askin was obliged to appoint a royal commission under Mr Justice Athol Moffitt to investigate allegations of organized crime in the operation of poker machines in clubs, but the inquiry was fed contradictory testimony by the police and was inconclusive. In 1977–79, following the assassination of a Griffith businessman who had campaigned against the local marijuana industry, two further royal commissions were appointed.[32] Both stressed the need for action on a federal level. But when the Fraser government received the report of its own royal commissioner, Sir Edward Williams, in March 1980, it simply transferred the work of its Narcotics Bureau to the Federal Police.

Even this was an acknowledgement that the work of policing could not be conducted adequately at the state level. Some state governments indeed found it difficult to strike a proper balance in the relationship between a government and its police force. In Queensland in November 1976 an honest commissioner of police, Ray Whitrod, resigned because of excessive interference in police affairs by the premier and cabinet ministers. At the other extreme the South Australian government in January 1978 dismissed Harold Salisbury as commissioner because he refused to allow the premier access to the police force's files, in which it turned out that the Special Branch kept dossiers on all Labor Party members and candidates but not on their political opponents. Such episodes reinforced arguments for the reform of police powers and responsibilities but there was little agreement on the desirable changes. Meanwhile the federal government found itself obliged to move further into the enforcement of commercial ethics. Between 1976 and 1979 repercussions of the property slump of 1974–75 continued, bringing down several more investment companies, and in 1979 forcing the Bank of Adelaide to seek refuge in a takeover by a larger competitor.[33] In Victoria the state housing commission was shown to have paid too much for several tracts of outer-suburban land, and although a royal commissioner reported in 1978 that this showed poor judgement rather than corruption, the responsible cabinet minister thought it best to resign. As part of the rehabilitation of the share market the federal government successfully negotiated with the states to set up a regulatory body, the National Companies and Securities Commission, which after a slow start in 1980 was to establish itself as a watchdog of the public interest.

Despite such reforms the media in the late 1970s and early 1980s depicted a society in which politicians, trade unions, business and law were all tainted with a corruption bred of a perverted competitiveness, personal gain and the urge to win driving out any remnant of the 'fair go' tradition.[34] Even sport was affected. During the 1960s and 1970s commercial television, joined by the ABC, found big money for the rights to screen major sporting events, and this in turn led successful players to demand greatly increased pay and transfer fees. Games such as the Victorian Football League's Grand Final were transformed:

In 1977 Barry Crocker was flown from London by the VFL to sing 'The Impossible Dream' before the assembled Grand Final crowd . . . In 1979 it was a cast of thousands—pop singers, parachutists, brass bands and choirs, a live television coverage, pop star Johnny Farnham singing 'Waltzing Matilda' and singer/writer Mike Brady doing his very own hit of 1979 'Up There, Cazaly' . . .[35]

Politicians vied for the Number One ticket of leading football clubs. Cricket also moved with the times. In 1977–78 the media magnate Kerry Packer dismayed traditionalists by promoting a world series tailored for television cameras, with colourful clothing, night cricket, and a much enhanced professionalism.[36] Crowds urged on gladiatorial bowlers such as Denis Lillee with cries of 'Kill! Kill! Kill!', and Lillee flirted with unorthodox tactics such as the use of a metal bat. As captain, Greg Chappell thwarted his New Zealand opponents in a close match by instructing his brother to bowl underarm so that the batsmen had no chance of hitting boundaries.

Sport, of course, transcended politics. Malcolm Fraser, a convinced believer in the multi-racial character of the British Commonwealth—in 1979 he played a crucial role in persuading Margaret Thatcher to accept the arrangements by which Rhodesia became the African-dominated nation Zimbabwe—had been in 1977 a willing signatory of the Gleneagles Agreement, under which Commonwealth heads of government disavowed sporting contacts with a nation such as South Africa which practised apartheid. This did not prevent several prominent golfers and cricketers from defying reprisals and playing in South Africa. Fraser had no more success at the beginning of 1980 when the Soviet Union sent in troops to prop up a communist regime in Afghanistan. Believing this 'the most dangerous crisis since World War II',[37] Fraser asked the Australian Olympic Federation to withdraw from participation in the Olympic Games scheduled for Moscow later in 1980. But it became clear that several individual athletes intended to compete anyhow, and after long thought the Federation in June rejected Fraser's plea for a boycott. During the games the government's popularity dropped sharply for a while, but by the time the federal elections were held in October 1980 the Fraser government was able to secure a third term of office, albeit with a reduced majority.

By now the ministerial team was somewhat jaded. Peacock resigned as foreign minister in 1981, and a year later challenged Fraser unsuccessfully for the leadership. Lynch retired, mortally ill; others such as Staley and Garland got out though still in their forties, evidently deeming ministerial office no longer worth the pressures. Increasingly reliant on the congenial advice of senior National Party ministers—Anthony, Sinclair, Peter Nixon—Fraser confronted a new deterioration in the economy. The resources boom of 1979–81, on which hopes had ridden high, turned out to be an illusion. By increasing Australia's overseas reserves and causing the Australian dollar to appreciate on the world's exchanges, mineral exports had the effect of crowding out rural and manufacturing exports on overseas markets.[38] Much of eastern Australia was afflicted by drought during 1981 and 1982, culminating in south-eastern Australia's worst bushfires for over forty years on Ash Wednesday, 1983. Farm incomes fell sharply with the drop in rural exports. Meanwhile a second round of increases in world oil prices had stimulated steep inflation in the United States in 1979 and 1980, thus pushing up interest rates as well as causing inflation in Australia once more to rise past 10 per cent.

At the end of 1981 the Fraser government received a report, three years in preparation, from a Committee of Inquiry into the Australian Financial System. Chaired by Sir Keith Campbell, chairman of the property-developing Hooker Corporation, the committee offered several bold suggestions.[39] The Australian dollar, whose exchange rate was controlled closely by the Reserve Bank, should be allowed to find its own level on foreign exchange markets. More controversially, foreign banks should be admitted to compete with the handful of large private banks operating in Australia. These banks—the Australia and New Zealand, the National Australia, and the Bank of New South Wales (which in 1982 hid its honourable name under the plastic neologism of Westpac)—controlled the market after a series of amalgamations in the 1960s and 1970s and also had a stake in many finance companies. They already faced competition for the custom of small investors from a great expansion of building societies, credit unions and property trusts. When it came to operating on the international money market, the case for deregulation was superficially attractive as providing further competition. But the initiative came at a time when improvements in communications technology were enabling overseas investors to shift huge sums between countries at short notice, so that the currency of a trading nation dependent on exports, such as Australia, would run the risk of instability. Treasury caution ensured that no action was taken on the Campbell Report during the remaining term of the Fraser government. Already the capital inflow was beginning which, during the rest of the 1980s, would hugely swell Australia's foreign debt.

Fraser's other strategy for reining in the economy took the form of renewed confrontation with the trade unions. After about four years of relative calm, industrial disputes increased during 1980 and 1981 as wage indexation came under stronger challenge. The unions threw much of their energy into reducing the working week from 40 to 35 hours. In March 1981 Fraser tried to stem the 35-hour movement by threatening ICI Australia with company tax and a reduction of tariff protection unless it disavowed negotiations for a shorter working week. But in July the Conciliation and Arbitration Commission, under pressure from both the government and the ACTU to alter the guidelines of wage indexation, decided to abandon the system altogether. Strong unions and compliant managements could now negotiate 'sweetheart' deals unfettered. Several industries agreed to a 38-hour week, and real wages rose by 4 per cent in 1981–82, but only at the cost of accelerated unemployment. On the initiative of the Western Australian ex-premier, Sir Charles Court, the Fraser government eventually managed in December 1982 to negotiate an agreement with all the state governments for the imposition of a six-month pause in wage claims. It was the first step towards consensus. But by this time inflation, encouraged by an expansionary federal budget for 1982–83, was past 11 per cent.

In 1982 a former quiz champion turned back-bench Labor member of parliament, Barry Jones, published a book[40] forecasting continued economic decadence and rising unemployment if Australia failed to pay more attention to the research and development required to come to grips with the new technology. Since the Second World War the main effect of new technology had been the phasing out of openings for the working class. As improved gas-stoves gave way to microwave ovens, and freezers and dishwashers came into general use, demand ceased for full-time domestic servants, although many migrant women earned some useful dollars by part-time cleaning for professional families. As mechanization and containerization came to the waterfront, as postcoding facilitated the automatic sorting of mail, as bull-dozers and cherry-pickers replaced the use of human muscle, many of the traditional working-class occupations declined. Mining, once a prolific employer of hands who could always go prospecting in hard times, was now the epitome of a capital-intensive industry requiring comparatively little labour. On the railways and the waterfront an ageing workforce bargained for the conservation of jobs until they reached pensionable age.

White-collar workers were also challenged by technological change. Since the late 1950s scientific laboratories and financial corporations had been using computer technology, but it was only with the introduction of microprocessors in the early 1970s that a mass market was opened. Most members of the Australian public at first encountered the portents of change in the form of new consumer goods: pocket calculators and digital watches for adults, and interminable games of Space Invaders for the young. Soon secretaries and typists found themselves obliged to upgrade their skills as word-processors began to replace electric type-writers, and visual display units proliferated in stockbrokers' and newspaper offices. White-collar unions sharpened their bargaining skills, but the percentage of workers in unions overall was beginning to decline. Although Jones did not say so, the ALP increasingly would depend for its survival on recruits from the educated middle class such as himself, while its traditional working-class supporters grew fewer.

Hoping to embarrass the trade union movement, Fraser in 1980, in conjunction with the Victorian government, set up a royal commission to inquire into the activities of the Federated Ship Painters and Dockers' Union (FSPDU). This Melbourne-based union had fallen into the hands of an unseemly clique that had expanded from conventional graft and pilfering into a variety of criminal pursuits, including murder.[41] The royal com-missioner, Frank Costigan, identified a number of irregularities which needed correction, but then caused consternation by putting his finger on a major form of racketeering which shifted attention away from the waterfront. He found that a considerable number of very important businessmen had been systematically avoiding taxation by stripping assets from companies in which they had an interest and then selling them to dummy or fictitious purchasers, among them members of the FSPDU. In mid-1982, prompted by revelations of malpractice in Western Australia, the Fraser government tabled Costigan's interim reports, thus whistling up a high wind of controversy. Prominent individuals were named and issued indignant denials. To many it seemed particularly offensive that the rich should be profiting from loopholes in the taxation laws while unemployment was passing 8 per cent of the workforce and among some sectors, such as youth under twenty-one and recently-arrived migrants, stood as high as 20 per cent.[42] Fraser promised corrective action; he was probably encouraged by the knowledge that since Sir Garfield Barwick's retirement as chief justice in 1980 the High Court under the guidance of Sir Harry Gibbs was less permissive towards ingenious taxpayers who fought their assessments. But Costigan's revelations of what were called 'bottom-of-the-harbour' schemes must have encouraged some voters to feel it was time for a change in federal politics.

The omens were mixed. During 1982 the Liberals had won Tasmania from its long-standing Labor allegiance but had lost South Australia and Victoria and were about to lose Western Australia. On the other hand, the federal Labor Party late in 1982 failed to win an important by-election. Bob Hawke, who had entered the House of Representatives in 1980, had already once challenged Hayden for the leadership of the Labor Party and was likely to do so again. A country man, Fraser persuaded himself that the drought would continue to have a debilitating effect on the Australian economy and decided to call an election in March 1983. On the very day that Fraser asked the governor-general to grant him a double-dissolution Hawke successfully made his move. But instead of indulging in cut-throat feuding the Opposition united behind its new leader, Hayden contenting himself with the remark that even a drover's dog could lead Labor to victory. He was right. Fraser fought a lack-lustre campaign, resorting at times to the outmoded anti-socialism of the 1950s. It was no longer credible to inform the voters that if Labor came to power their savings would be safer under the bed than in the banks. At the election Labor won a comfortable lead in the House of Representatives, although the Democrats held the balance of power in the Senate. As they were pledged never to use the Senate's authority to force an election, Hawke could rest easier than Whitlam in his time.

In Perth a young poet contemplating the election and mindful of an underrated virtue in Australian society wrote some lines:

> On the weekend there was a change
> of government. New men with new motives
> will make new laws
> to maintain, mould, and move us.
>
> This morning, I drove through Perth
> Along Stirling Highway to Fremantle,
> And I tell you this: I saw
> no blood dried in the gutters,
> no bodies strewn on the pavement,
> no tanks stationed in the streets.
> I swear: as usual, there were
> girls in the malls,
> cars on the carriage-ways,
> ships in the port.
>
> There is a new Government
> but no-one has gone
> into hiding . . .[43]

There was little of the heady jubilation which greeted Whitlam's victory in 1972, for a decade of economic difficulty had taught Australians not to expect too much of their politicians. Yet there was a portent of change, a hint of a significant shift in the emotional temperature of Australian society. Hawke had been noted among his contemporaries as a man not ashamed to bare his emotions in public, and some had questioned whether one who so spontaneously revealed his anger, his humour and his tears would make a fit leader for his nation. But in the moment of giving up the leadership of his country and his party it was the austere Malcolm Fraser whose eyes filled with tears and who yielded to the consolation of his son's arm around him. Nothing became Fraser in public life more than his leaving of it, for in his open acknowledgement of strong feeling the Australian people might learn that beyond the virtues of stoicism and rationality, beyond the quest for the equitable distribution of resources and the advancement of every individual there was a need to accept and find a public place for that generosity of human emotion which at times during their years of prosperity they had seemed in danger of losing.

11

TOWARDS THE BICENTENARY

THE HAWKE ADMINISTRATION entrenched itself more securely than any previous peacetime Labor government. Unlike Chifley and Whitlam, Hawke was not ousted from office by hostile pressure groups mobilized against what they perceived as radical threats to their interests and, unlike the earlier Labor governments of Hughes and Scullin, the party did not split asunder under the force of great controversies. Using the double-dissolution Hawke went to the polls in 1984 and again in 1987, each time gaining a sufficient though scarcely overwhelming majority over the Liberal–National Party coalition. Each time the Democrats and independents were left with the balance of power in the Senate, thus continuing to provide a check on government legislation without pushing towards a repetition of the deadlock of 1975. Australian voting patterns were fairly stable. None of the incumbent state governments, whatever their party, lost an election from 1983 until the defeat of the New South Wales Labor government in 1988, although the margin of victory was often extremely close.

Federal Labor's success was due partly to the disarray of its opponents. Totally unaccustomed to a prolonged spell in opposition, and deprived by resignation of the experienced leadership of Fraser and Anthony, the coalition parties found it hard to throw loyal support behind front-benchers who failed to seize the reins of power. Andrew Peacock, who with apparent ease reflected every shade of opinion within his party's ranks, was leader from 1983 to 1985. He was replaced by the tenacious ex-treasurer, John Howard. The National Party was led by the hardened veteran Ian Sinclair, who lacked obvious heirs. Hawke meanwhile was able to surround himself with a mixture of experienced survivors from the Whitlam regime such as Bowen (deputy leader), Hayden (foreign affairs) and Keating (treasurer) and able newcomers. Fraternal strife within the party was contained by formalizing its three major factions (Broad Left, Centre Left, and Right) and ensuring the balanced distribution of portfolios and key positions between each group. While Australian federal politics continued to pay formal obeisance to the two-party Westminster model, in practice parliamentary politics began to resemble those looser coalitions of interest groups which made up majorities in Washington and some European capitals.

Having guarded against the factional quarrels which had damaged Labor's prospects in the past, Hawke all too effectively sought to lay the ghost of Whitlam's reputation for economic mismanagement. No past Labor leader had gone to greater lengths to secure co-operation from business as well as the trade unions. Within two months of taking office Hawke convened a national economic summit of government, business and labour. To enhance the seriousness of the occasion the conference met in Parliament House—the first time in over half a century of its history that the chamber was used for a non-parliamentary purpose. The delegates endorsed a prices-and-incomes agreement, including the restoration of wage indexation, as the cornerstone of a generally cautious approach to economic policy.[1] It heralded six years of durable if at times uneasy industrial calm. Hostile critics commented that the Hawke government had surrendered itself to corporatism. Apart from reviving Medibank under the name of Medicare, funded by an income tax levy, there were no innovations in welfare. Veterans of the excitements of the Whitlam years complained that Hawke's pragmatism offered too pointed and deliberate a contrast to the idealism of 1972. Hawke retorted that he was 'not about . . . divorcing myself and my party from the opportunity of Government'[2] and urged 'those who would advocate change to temper their fervour with a sense of gradualism'. He added that 'This constraint sits happily with me'.[3] It also seemed to sit happily with the public. For many

*11 November 1975: Gough Whitlam watches the reading of the
proclamation dissolving Parliament*

*11 November 1975: Malcolm Fraser leaves Parliament House after
appointment as caretaker Prime Minister*

Old men ranged against the world: Nobel laureate Patrick White and artist Lloyd Rees in protest against the dismissal of 11 November 1975

months Hawke enjoyed greater popularity than any modern prime minister, at times registering 70 per cent approval in the opinion polls. Even the press was largely disarmed; thus at the 1984 general election the Brisbane *Courier-Mail* for the first time in its long career editorially supported Labor.

Part of the legacy from the Fraser years was the effort to clean up official corruption. The Costigan royal commission made its final report in 1984, and this was followed by the creation of a National Crimes Authority and a more aggressive policing of business ethics through the National Companies and Securities Commission. In New South Wales a chief stipendiary magistrate and a former cabinet minister found themselves serving prison sentences for corrupt practices. The shadows even touched the federal High Court, where Mr Justice Lionel Murphy found himself fighting for his reputation because of a telephone conversation in which he was alleged to be improperly protecting the interests of a highly controversial Sydney lawyer. He was prosecuted, found guilty and sentenced to a gaol term; appealed and was acquitted; and then became the subject of a parliamentary inquiry whose party spirit was sharpened by rancours surviving from Murphy's term as Whitlam's attorney-general. The case looked like awakening serious difficulties about the relationship between parliament and the judiciary until it was found that Murphy had terminal cancer. Having insisted on his right to sit once more on the High Court bench, he died in 1986. When the news was announced in federal parliament he received a greater number of obituary tributes from members of all parties than any other individual has ever received.[4] It was a peculiarly Australian tragedy, seen both from the vindictiveness with which the hunt against Murphy was pursued and the quick readiness to forget unpleasantnesses in the presence of death. Murphy himself, in his carelessness and spaciousness, had much of that quality which Les Murray has defined as 'sprawl'.[5]

It is by economic management rather than incorruptibility that Australian governments survive or fall. During its first two years the Hawke government and its treasurer Paul Keating built up a strong reputation for economic management. Good luck played a part in this achievement because the drought broke shortly after Labor came to office, so that in 1983–84 the productivity of Australian farms jumped by 37 per cent and farm incomes by 360 per cent—an extreme example of the swinging fortunes of families on the land. Between mid-1983 and mid-1985 GDP rose each year by 5 per cent, a figure which compared favourably with the leading OECD nations and more than favourably with the average of under 2 per cent for the last six years of the Fraser regime. The rate of inflation, which during the last four Fraser years had been running at an annual average of 10 per cent, was nearly halved by the early months of 1985. Unemployment, having risen from 5.8 to 9.3 per cent between 1980–81 and 1982–83, peaked at 10 per cent in the first year of the Hawke government before receding gradually over the next two years to around 8 per cent, where it tended to remain.[6]

People with leisure to write letters to the newspapers or to participate in 'phone-in' sessions on commercial radio stations inclined to damn the unemployed, particularly the young unemployed, as 'dole bludgers'. More than a quarter of the teenage labour market were without jobs in 1983, and although the Hawke years saw some improvement the figure never dropped below 20 per cent. Among the workforce as a whole the proportion of the long-term unemployed rose from about 20 per cent under Fraser to stabilize at around 30 per cent under Hawke. Put another way, between 180 000 and 200 000 Australians, brought up in a society where work defined personal worth, faced an indefinite future without a job. Many more would undergo up to a year of uncertainty. Those who became unemployed remained unemployed for longer — on average about 46 weeks in the Hawke years as against 32 in the last three Fraser years. It seemed that the post-war vision of full employment was gone for good, to be succeeded not by the rampant poverty of the 1930s but the creeping inequalities of the 1920s.

The rich grew richer; a 1986 estimate credited Australia with about 30 000 millionaires.[7] In Sydney, Perth and the Gold Coast the very rich lived, built and enjoyed themselves with a lack of social conscience comparable to the 'Gilded Age' in the United States. Ten per cent of Australia's families owned 60 per cent of its wealth. World Bank statistics suggested that Australia had the most unequal distribution of wealth of any Western nation. While the middle classes and skilled workers in regular employment continued to manage comfortably despite the standstill in real wages and incomes, younger couples trying to establish their first home were hard-pressed by high interest rates. The proportion of households living in poverty rose from 11.5 to 12.4 per cent between 1981–82 and 1985–86, the greatest impact falling on large families, the aged, and the single.[8] Australia's juveniles included probably 25 000 homeless, as well as deprived groups such as Aborigines with high rates of disease and mortality. In the 1987 election campaign Hawke grandiosely promised to abolish child poverty within three years. This did not happen, but by mid-1989 many low-income families benefited from the reform and indexation of family allowances, so that although about one million Australians lived below the poverty line, this was half the number of three years previously.[9] But there was little hope for the poor in Australia. Social security outlays had fallen as a percentage of GDP since 1983. No major political party wanted to increase government welfare spending, nor to tax the rich any harder.

The majority of Australians still had cash or credit. Retail spending and expenditure on personal consumption in general took some time to recover from the 1982–83 slump, but there was a strong recovery in residential building in 1983 and the early months of 1984, followed by an equally strong surge in the purchase of new cars and station wagons. Although the rate of wage increase was less than half that of the last Fraser years, so was the cost of living, and Hawke's accord with the unions seemed to head off industrial militancy over bread-and-butter issues. In Fraser's last three years an average of 2.8 million working days was lost in industrial disputes. During the next four years the figure never rose above half that number.[10] Unlike the experience of the Whitlam years, when Hawke as president of the ACTU had led the union movement in some embarrassingly lavish demands for pay increases, the trade union movement was behaving with remarkable moderation.

Encouraged by the Hawke government's amicable relations with sections of the business community, overseas investors looked at Australia with returning confidence. From the financial year 1984–85 new capital expenditure increased strongly, at first mainly in the manufacturing and mining sectors but with finance, insurance, real estate and business services coming into greater prominence from 1986. Unfortunately these years also saw a massive expansion in Australia's overseas debt. Venturing where the Fraser government had hesitated to go, the Hawke government unpegged the exchange rate of the Australian dollar and lifted the restrictions on the entry of foreign banks into Australian finance. Borrowing throve. In mid-1982 Australia's net external debt stood at 8.6 per cent of GDP, of which more than two-thirds represented borrowing in the private sector. During the next four years the figure nearly quadrupled, passing 31 per cent by mid-1986 before a short-lived pause. Although critics were quick to blame the federal government, Canberra's borrowing was effectively restrained from 1985–86. But state government instrumentalities ran up debts, and the private sector took large sums for property speculation, take-over bids and other high-profile activities which did very little to improve Australia's productivity and export income.

By 1985 Keating was ominously declaring that Australia was at risk of becoming a 'banana republic', and a few months later a leading New York financial house whose word was venerated in such matters reduced Australia's credit rating from the highest level of good standing to the next rank. As two observers commented: 'Policy strategy, both social and economic, will increasingly have to be framed with regard to the perceptions and reactions of foreign opinion'.[11] The Australian dollar in three years from January 1985 shed more than one-third of its value on the world's money markets, eventually stimulating exports so that, with strong improvement in wool and beef prices in 1987, the economy stabilized for a while. Little credit was due to Australia's most prominent business leaders who, often using the foreign capital which fattened Australia's overseas debt, threw their energies obsessively into bigger and greedier take-over bids.[12]

Perhaps the greatest media interest was provoked during 1986 and 1987 by the attempts of two rival tycoons, John Elliott of Elders-IXL and Robert Holmes a Court, to secure a controlling interest in Australia's largest company, BHP. Such men, and their competitor Alan Bond, stretched their ambitions beyond Australia and fought for control of businesses in Britain and the United States. From his early beginnings with the *Australian* Rupert Murdoch by the late 1980s grew not only into Australia's biggest media magnate but also became owner of the London *Times*, its very popular idiot half-brother the *Sun*, and many other newspapers throughout the English-speaking world, as well as owning half of Australia's major non-government domestic airline. Eventually, to facilitate ownership of American assets, he became an American citizen. Unlike some of the very rich,

Murdoch at least recognized that wealth should be philanthropic. The stock-market slump of October 1987 chastened a number of entrepreneurs, though without persuading many that their energies would be better spent on improving Australian research, development and productivity. To many unsophisticated Australians the rich provided an admirable role-model. When in 1985 Alan Bond's daughter was married amid great pomp, a young working-class woman of Southern European parentage was heard to comment that 'These people are our royalty'.[13]

But if capitalists were admired, the political parties of capitalism failed to profit by it. Despite the fluctuating economy, the Liberal–National Party coalition for the first time since 1949 found it impossible to persuade the voters that Australia's finances would be safer in their stewardship than under Labor management. Considering that Labor under Hawke had seized the middle ground in politics, the Opposition under Howard, looking— as so many previous Australians had looked—overseas for inspiration, decided that the success of Thatcher in Britain and Reagan in the United States demonstrated that the public would respond to a toughly-stated right-wing alternative. There was some tendency to disparage Menzies and Fraser as leaders who had allegedly chosen to stay in power by taking soft options when it came to maintaining welfare spending and propitiating pressure groups such as the manufacturers and the trade unions. Market forces should be allowed unrestricted play, the welfare state should be largely dismantled, and the rich rewarded by lower income tax. But it was hard to reach agreement about the areas of welfare and tariff protection which should be eliminated, and several factions battled for the conscience of the Right.

Journalists spoke of this phenomenon as 'the rise of the New Right' and identified as its spokesman the former secretary of the Treasury, John Stone, who to the surprise of some remained with the Hawke government for eighteen months but then resigned with acid criticisms of its aims and performance.[14] In 1985 a group of businessmen formed a society in honour of H. R. Nicholls, a former editor of the Hobart *Mercury* who had been a radical journalist at the time of the Eureka Stockade but in old age became an implacable foe of the Arbitration Court. One or two members of the H. R. Nicholls Society won considerable publicity through their crusading zeal against the trade unions. But although John Howard sometimes spoke sympathetically of such initiatives, he was too measured and cautious to win the hearts of the populist Right. For those who craved simpler leadership a more promising standard-bearer stood up in the North. Wily, well publicized, undeniably successful in his own state of Queensland, Sir Joh Bjelke-Petersen (he had been knighted in 1984 with a citation of unparalleled sycophancy) offered himself for election as prime minister.

Bjelke-Petersen's remedies had the great gift of simplicity: cut income tax to a flat rate of 20 or 25 per cent, discipline the unions, prune government spending and capital would flow freely to Australia. His record in Queensland looked formidable. Not only had the Labor Party been reduced to squabbling impotence after thirty years in the wilderness, but the urban Liberals had been squeezed from the governing coalition in 1984 and the Nationals now governed in their own right. This followed two years in which the Liberals had lost office in every state except Tasmania. In 1985 Bjelke-Petersen had used his government's strong anti-union laws to break a strike of electricity workers in south-eastern Queensland. That Bjelke-Petersen in his eagerness to attract foreign investment often committed his state to bad bargains and alienated irreplaceable natural resources, that Queensland's unemployment rate was one of the highest in Australia, and that the amount spent on education and Aborigines tended to be Australia's lowest per capita, made no difference to the old chieftain's admirers. During the summer of 1986–87 a vocal 'Joh for Canberra' movement mounted a publicity campaign. Speculation flourished about the extent of its backing by the long purses of the new breed of Queensland millionaires. The *Australian* and the rest of the Murdoch press began to treat the new portent seriously.

But from the end of February the push faltered. Bjelke-Petersen's Nationals did poorly in the Northern Territory elections. The *Australian* backed off. The Queensland Nationals withdrew from the federal party, formally splitting the Opposition coalition, but Bjelke-Petersen decided against chancing his fortunes in the federal parliament, contenting himself with dumping one of his staunchest supporters to make room for John Stone in the Senate (where he soon proved himself a formidable critic of the government, but from within the main Opposition). Bjelke-Petersen's intemperate criticisms of the coalition leaders Howard and Sinclair almost certainly cost them the federal election in July 1987. Once seen as losers, both were deposed from the leadership of their parties in May 1989, and Peacock was given a second chance as the head of the Opposition. Bjelke-Petersen also met his nemesis. During his plunge into federal politics his colleagues set up a committee of inquiry into the Queensland police force. An honest commissioner, Tony Fitzgerald, found that the premier in his bucolic cronyism had been, at best, singularly blind to the widespread presence of corruption. Bjelke-Petersen promised to step down in August 1988 after twenty years as premier, then tried to sack several cabinet ministers, and in December 1987 was obliged to retire after the unanimous desertion of his following. It was less than a year since the 'Joh for Canberra' push was at its zenith. Perhaps his career showed, as Jack Lang on the Left had shown in the 1930s, that a populist politician based on a single state courted disaster if he tried to storm the federal heights. But there is an enduring populist streak in the Australian community and Bob Hawke was one of its beneficiaries.

Himself an enthusiastic golfer and once a cricketer of some prowess, Hawke was never happier than when associating with sport and popular entertainment. It was a happy coincidence that in 1983, the same year that Hawke came to office, the Western Australian mining, property, brewing and television magnate Alan Bond brought to Australia the world's leading ocean-going yacht trophy, the America's Cup. Bond's victory came by the narrowest of margins after a contest in which his crew seemed underdogs fighting more than a century of unbroken American victories. The triumph was seen not only as a tribute to Bond's readiness to risk his money, but to the technological craft of Ben Lexcen, the skills of helmsman John Bertrand and his crew, and the capacity of Australians to give an acceptable amount of cheek to senior allies.[15] Hawke identified himself with this triumph, encouraging bosses to give their employees a day off to celebrate and, although now a teetotaller, featured in the media drenched in other people's champagne. The *Sydney Morning Herald* described the day as Australia's greatest since the coming of victory in the Second World War.[16] In no other nation would one of the most conservative and respectable newspapers have made this claim of a sporting event. But undoubtedly the *Herald* and Hawke showed a sure instinct for Australian priorities.

It could not be expected that Australia would hold the Cup

indefinitely (the Americans won it back at the replay in 1987) or that equally glorious sporting victories could come every year. Instead the Hawke government wanted to celebrate Australia's Bicentenary on 26 January 1788, the two hundredth anniversary of the day when Captain Arthur Phillip and the First Fleet of convicts and marines had come ashore at Sydney Cove and founded Australia's first city. Even this national occasion may have owed some inspiration to the American bicentenary of 1976; the decision to produce a multi-volume national history for the Australian bicentenary in 1988 was certainly stimulated by the American example. The Fraser government had set up an Australian Bicentennial Authority to plan the celebrations, and in 1982 announced a Bicentennial roads project which led to the upgrading of many major Australian highways. But the Bicentennial Authority ran into difficulties, and it was far from certain that the rest of Australia would enthuse over what could be seen as merely the birthday of New South Wales. Aboriginal Australians in particular, recently reminded by scholars of the antiquity of their past and chafing under the experience of poverty and residual racism, were disposed to see 1788 as the origin of their troubles and to demand that the Bicentenary should be regarded as a day of mourning.

The coming of the Hawke government was viewed hopefully by some Aboriginal campaigners. The High Court delivered a new instrument into the federal government's hands in 1982 through its verdict in Koowarta's case.[17] Ironically, this blow to states' rights resulted from the Bjelke-Petersen government's obstinacy. The Queensland cabinet refused to allow the sale of a pastoral lease to an Aboriginal community on the Cape York peninsula. As the government would not relent, the Aborigines appealed to the High Court, which found that the federal government was entitled to overrule Queensland because of its power in foreign affairs, having ratified an international covenant on civil and political rights. This use of the foreign affairs powers sustained the Hawke government in 1983 when the Tasmanian government planned to dam the Franklin River, a region of wilderness much valued by environmentalists. Because of the river's World Heritage listing (an international agreement) and environmental considerations the dam was vetoed.

Having scored this second success the Hawke government showed itself very reluctant to put further pressure on the states by exercising the powers conferred on it through international treaties. To the disappointment of Aboriginal activists nothing was done to override the refusal of several states to enact land rights legislation. This inaction also reflected the influence of sections of the mining industry. Although the Hawke government went against many of its followers in permitting the export of uranium in some circumstances, and although mineral exploration was seldom inhibited by environmental legislation, some spokesmen for the mining industry were apt to complain at the slightest restriction on their entrepreneurial activities, and saw a threat in the campaign over Aboriginal land rights. Press and television advertisements condemned the concept of land rights as a wasteful form of apartheid, and no sympathy was given to those academics and writers who followed the elderly H. C. Coombs in urging a formal compact—a Makarrata—between Aborigines and white Australians acknowledging Aboriginal dispossession and the need for acts of reconciliation.[18]

Consequently as the Bicentennial celebrations drew nearer more was heard of the prospect of Aboriginal protest in contradiction to the national festivities. The Tasmanian Aborigines found a publicist in Michael Mansell, a lawyer with the Tasmanian Aboriginal Legal Aid Service, who brought fear to some white Australians by threatening negotiations with Libya's Colonel Gaddafi for aid for the Aboriginal cause. Nervous citizens circulated rumours about caches of communist-bloc arms landing on remote Kimberley coasts for future Aboriginal use.[19] Hawke, aware of the divisive potential of racial issues, made a comment which could be seen as an undertaking for some kind of compact of reconciliation with the Aboriginal community but its details remained unclear.[20] By the beginning of January 1988 it was evident that Sydney's celebrations would be marked by an Aboriginal counter-demonstration, but few could forecast its effect.

Since the public holiday for 26 January 1988 fell on a Tuesday most Australians, not being a people on whom the work ethic held a compulsive grip in high summer, took a four-day long weekend.[21] The approach to the Bicentenary was marked by portents. Bushfires raged in south-eastern Australia, though they were contained from repeating the tragedies of 1939 and 1983. Tennant Creek in the Northern Territory was shaken by one of Australia's strongest earth tremors, though with remarkably little damage. But on the day of the Bicentenary itself, except for some seasonable thunderstorms at Darwin, every state capital enjoyed fine weather.

After all the forebodings Australia-wide celebrations took place. Flags were raised and speeches made in the timber country of the south-west, the hay-and-apple towns of southern Tasmania, the cane-growing centres of North Queensland. At Heavy Tree Gap tavern, near Alice Springs, people tried to break the national piano-smashing record. At Jerilderie in the Riverina, famous for Ned Kelly's raid in 1879 and uneventful since, the local Apex Club mocked up a boat constructed of fencing droppers, wire, hessian marquee poles and old house-blinds, floated it on the artificial lake in the town park, drilled eight young men carrying replica muskets, and re-enacted Phillip's landing to the delight of several hundred bystanders. At night in Perth crowds sat in Kings Park to watch a chrysanthemum choreography of fireworks, leaving an astonishing quantity of empty bottles and cans for the rangers to clean up next morning. But the national focus of celebrations was Sydney Harbour.

For some time it had been evident that a maritime motif would dominate the Bicentenary. Among the birthday gifts donated to Australia by other nations the United States gave a wing to the national maritime museum; the British sent a sail training vessel, the *Young Endeavour*; and New Zealand presented a century-old ocean-going yacht. Largely through the enthusiasm of a descendant of Phillip's junior colleague, Governor King, a replica of the First Fleet, having retraced its original route across the Atlantic, Indian and Southern Oceans, was scheduled to tie up at Farm Cove near the Opera House late in the morning, to be greeted by a distinguished official party. The proceedings began with a prayer for the nation from the Anglican archbishop of Sydney (a man chiefly notable for his belief that the female half of humanity were unfit to be clergy), his Catholic colleague having earlier been entrusted with the prayer for the state of New South Wales. These were almost the only explicitly religious elements in the entire day's ceremonies. One American habit not yet absorbed by Australian public figures was that of identifying God's purposes with the nation's well-being. But there was a Bicentennial hymn, 'Lord of Earth and all Creation', backed by the Sydney Symphony Orchestra. Better still, the singing of 'Advance Australia Fair' was reported to have produced an unpredicted surge of emotion, which apparently communicated itself to many people watching the proceedings on television at home. This was perhaps the moment when a mediocre tune with mediocre words, adopted grudgingly over the protests of many who still hankered after 'Waltzing Matilda' or 'God Save the Queen', suddenly won acceptance as a national anthem, endearing through familiarity if no other cause.

Speeches followed: from B. Unsworth, Labor premier of New South Wales, subdued by a forthcoming election and determined that all should go well enough at the ceremony to expunge the somewhat shopsoiled appearance that a state government of nearly twelve years' standing was apt to acquire; Hawke, somewhat overcome by the genuine emotion of the day; and, representing the sovereign, Charles, Prince of Wales, whom some credited with a readiness to serve as governor-general after the retirement of the present appointee, the ex-High Court judge Sir Ninian Stephen.

But after the events of 1975 only an Australian could fill that potentially contentious office; and since that event the number who favoured a republic was slowly increasing. Few felt as strongly as Patrick White, who considered that Australia had not much to be proud of in its past, disliked the whole Bicentenary concept, and was shocked by the presence of 'the royal goons'. More sympathized with Donald Horne when he argued that monarchy was a link with only the British portion of Australia's multicultural inheritance, and must be discarded as a curb on the development of a decently self-confident Australian nationalism. This still failed to convince those who feared that a republican Australia must be a centralized Australia, and meanwhile most hearers conceded that Charles, during whose lifetime these issues must be resolved, made an unusually impressive speech.

After a state luncheon the Prince and Princess of Wales joined HMAS *Cook*, from which they were to watch the sail-past of two hundred Tall Ships (the media always awarded them capitals). Gathered from every quarter of the world, so many sailing ships creating a spectacle for which the harbour on a fine afternoon made an admirable background. The Tall Ships were flanked by countless smaller craft; on a raffish, hedonistic holiday afternoon in much greater numbers than usual. A boatload of bare-breasted young women exchanged greetings with the prince, and his wife in mock retaliation took particular note of some bronzed young surfies. But although the sailing fleet led by Britain's *Young Endeavour* presented a fine sight, comment was caused by the biggest ship, the *Soren Larsen*, conspicuously and unashamedly flying the Coca-Cola ensign. Nothing could have symbolized more clearly the presence of multinational capitalism in Australia.

Australians had not been able to agree on a flag of their own. They could neither persuade themselves that, despite any anachronism, the old Commonwealth flag with its Union Jack from Britain and its Australian Southern Cross was sufficiently hallowed for cherishing, nor resolve to adopt the icon of republicanism, the Southern Cross in the form of the Eureka Stockade flag. Competitions in recent years had produced designs as innocent of elegance as of sound heraldry; it was a mark of vestigial colonial immaturity that Australians were not yet ready to make a choice.

Elsewhere in the city more than 20 000—perhaps 40 000—Australians marched that morning to another flag: the black, scarlet and gold of Aboriginal protest. Some had come in convoys of buses from as far away as Darwin and Port Hedland, still encountering barmen at Coober Pedy who refused them service and waitresses at Port Augusta who looked as if they wished they could. Others were urban Aborigines from Sydney and Brisbane. On the morning of 26 January they and their sympathizers converged in two parties from Redfern, their stronghold in the inner suburbs, across the length of the city to Mrs Macquarie's Chair. Here, across the bay from the Opera House and the official party, the Aboriginal demonstrators made camp. It was the biggest protest march that Sydney had seen since the height of the anti-Vietnam demonstrations twenty years previously. Unlike the Vietnam protests, and despite some heartfelt oratory, there was no violence by either marchers or police. Instead, those who stayed around Mrs Macquarie's Chair after the march could listen to the energetic sounds of Galapagos Duck, the Dancehall Racketeers, and in the evening Georgie Fame.

In the days before the Bicentenary celebration expatriate Australians overseas and the ABC at home had taken some pains to publicize the wrongs suffered by Australia's original inhabitants by the coming of European settlement, and in its editorial of 26 January the *Sydney Morning Herald* observed truly enough that because of 'this great unsettled issue . . . Australia . . . has yet to make peace with itself'. If white Australians had needed reminding of the need to agree quickly with their opposites, they received a strong hint a few days before the Bicentenary when the inhabitants of the Torres Strait Islands gave notice of intent to secede from Australia unless their grievances were remedied. Nor was it cheering that on the day after the celebrations a royal commission opened in Adelaide on the large number of Aborigines found hanged in their prison cells, nor that three state governments were refusing to contribute to the costs of the inquiry. Yet there was room for hope in the Sydney demonstration. In how many other great cities of the world, in how many nations, could such a protest have been heard unmolested, accorded publicity, and ended up with its participants listening to rock groups?

Charles Perkins, the Aboriginal Australian who had risen to prominence in the Aboriginal protest movement of the 1960s, was at this time a senior public servant, head of the Department of Aboriginal Affairs. Shortly before the Bicentenary he launched an attack on the admission of Asian migrants to Australia, claiming that too many were arriving for easy absorption. He showed an unerring instinct for trouble. By this time about one-third of Australia's immigrants were of Asian origin, including refugees from Kampuchea and Vietnam. In 1984 an eminent historian, Geoffrey Blainey, had created a storm by means of a talk to the Warrnambool Rotary Club expressing views similar to those of Perkins. From an original position of judicious caution about the rate of intake of Asian migrants Blainey had been tempted by media controversy into stronger assertions which dismayed many of his academic colleagues but pleased simpler souls.[22] While the debate was an interesting test of the special responsibilities of academics in public controversy, it had contributed little to migrant policy, except to show that as the latest wave of migrants South-East Asians were meeting the same prejudices from older Australians as Europeans had met forty years previously. In reviving the debate Perkins showed how ethnic rivalries might thwart the ideal of multiculturalism which had been official policy since Whitlam's time. At the same moment multiculturalism was being assailed by the Australian Chamber of Commerce, which wanted integration into some commonly accepted Australian stereotype such as Liberal ministers had commended twenty years previously, yet might have given short shrift to Aboriginal claims to separate identity. Nor was it easy to reconcile the dubious reception accorded Asian migrants with the acknowledged dependence of Australia's future in trade and investment on Japan and other nations of South-East Asia and the Western Pacific.

Thus even in 1988 there was a good deal of confusion about what it meant to be Australian. Some such as Blainey and the Australian Chamber of Commerce seemed to think that the national character had been decisively moulded in the nineteenth century, or at latest by Gallipoli, and that later comers could be expected to assimilate to this model. Blainey indeed would claim that the post-1945 migration of Europeans into Australia could be seen as a success precisely because the ethnic differences of the Old World had been eroded to a considerable extent in Australia. Others followed Donald Horne in rejoicing that the British and Irish domination over Australian folk-ways had at last been overthrown in favour of a receptive pluralism; Australians might draw on many sources to fashion some new amalgam of humanity, shaped by their distinctive environment.[23] Those who pinned their faith on multiculturalism were often loudest in downplaying the significance of British input to the Australian ethos and thus ran the risk of distortions which the conservatives were not slow to point out. Yet Australia's geography, remote from Europe, neighbourly to East and South Asia, left no long-term alternative. Change might be painful but, as the example of South Africa suggested, staying still would be worse.

The symbols of Australian nationhood were still hard to discern. It had taken so long to agree on a national anthem, let alone a flag. An astute historian, Richard White, pointed out that many of the symbols of Australian nationality had been fostered to promote social consensus and acceptance of the status quo.[24] Most modern slogans and symbols were the creation of journalists and advertising agents. The Australian 'Marseillaise' commemorated a sporting event:

> You've been training all the winter
> And there's not a team that's fitter
> And that's the way it's gotta be;
> 'Cause you're up against the best you know,
> This is Supertest you know
> And you've got to beat the best the world has seen.

C'mon Aussie c'mon c'mon
C'mon Aussie c'mon c'mon
C'mon Aussie c'mon c'mon
C'mon Aussie c'mon.[25]

The equivalent of 'Rule Britannia' was probably the rock group
Men at Work's paean to the America's Cup:

I come from a land down-under . . .
Where beer does flow and men chunder . . .
Where women glow and men thunder . . .[26]

Sport was the fundamental metaphor of Australian public life:
Elliott and Holmes a Court vying for BHP like two kids playing
Monopoly; Sir John Kerr umpiring the roughest game in Australian political history; the Springbok tour and the Moscow
Olympics as moral comments on tyranny overseas . . . The
tradition continued. Pat Cash, winner of the men's singles at
Wimbledon after a long period of Australian eclipse, was heckled
during his attempt on the Australian title in January 1988 by
anti-apartheid campaigners who disapproved of his visiting South
Africa. Perhaps there was a deeper significance to the Australian
preoccupation with sport. In a generation that saw so much militarism throughout the world, and when even the urban British
had become a byword for football hooliganism, it was no mean
achievement for Australians to channel the universal impulses of
competition and aggression into sporting activities which, however
commercialized and trivialized, were basically a form of play.

This interest in sport helps to explain why capitalists who
complained of Australian unwillingness to work hard, and Marxists who protested against Australian readiness to accept multinational influence in the economy, may have been equally wide
of the mark. Both criticisms assumed that economic gain was the
hallmark of success for Australians. Undoubtedly most Australians
enjoyed the material things of life—the house and the car were
the proper rewards of the migrant virtues of thrift and planning.
But they were means to an end: the enjoyment of leisure. To
choose increased leisure in preference to harder work was an
intelligible decision in a community largely descended from those
whom Les Murray has described as 'the poor who got away'.[27] It
was true that Australia, having enjoyed in the late nineteenth
century perhaps the world's highest per capita income, was
slipping down the international ladder and in 1988 may have

stood no higher than fourteenth. But it has been pointed out that 'this particular statistical measure does not take into account such aspects of the quality of life as climate, the environment, leisure, housing standards, low social friction, and political freedom and stability'. As Professor Caldwell had observed, Australia was not a terribly dissatisfied community.

Such a community might not place too high a value on the pursuit of excellence lest it shade over into élitism. Yet an Australian philosopher of international stature, John Passmore, spoke up for his compatriots as seekers after the classic ideal of the golden mean, *aurea mediocritas:*

It is our historic task to show the world what can be created by a resolute pursuit of mediocrity. I mean mediocrity in the original sense of that word—the full recognition that we are all human beings, with all the limitations of human beings. . . our mediocrity is our saving grace.[28]

A nation of European origins in an Asian neighbourhood could do worse than pursue the Middle Way which was a great theme of Chinese classical civilization as well as ancient Greece. If it chose to divert much of its energy, its enthusiasm and its aggression into sport and recreation this made it a less threatening and more engaging neighbour than countries with a strenuously developed sense of national mission. If Australians showed little aptitude for the public expression of religious experience they had a strongly developed tradition of equity which tempered many of the harsher manifestations of modern capitalism in difficult times.

This tradition of equity seemed in danger of eroding during the 1980s. As the gap grew between poorer Australians and the very rich no major political party seemed able or willing to curb the process. This was in part a reaction to the uncertainties in the world economy since the early 1970s, which had impelled corporations into multinational growth and nations into more strongly organized trading blocs. Australia's traditional economic strengths and skills no longer seemed sufficient to ensure relative security. Unable to deliver prosperity, many public figures contended that Australia could no longer afford the redistributive policies which created greater equity: the less well-off must practise restraint in order that the powerful might succeed better in their attempts to create wealth. Once again this was a doctrine imported from overseas. Neither the Second World War, nor its prosperous aftermath, nor the challenges of the 1970s and 1980s could dispel the view that wisdom lay in the United States, or in the United Kingdom or in Japan—anywhere but in the rational and compassionate application of Australian intelligence to Australian needs and opportunities. Australia must import its political philosophy as it imported so much of its technology and its research.

Some of the fault lay with the intellectuals, too many of whom still raged at their fellow citizens for their derivative culture, their lack of high standards of excellence, their protective cynicism which enabled them to shrug off the follies and injustices of public life. It still seemed that many Australians found it difficult to communicate emotional warmth of any kind or to articulate the satisfactions which came of being Australian. Yet from the shared experiences of the Australian-born, coming as they did from an increasingly mixed ancestry, there might in time arise a decent self-confidence in national identity. It was a migrant writer, David Martin, knowing both the Australian foreground and the European past, who observed:

Foreigners easily—too easily—assume that Australia is a crude habitat. They do not understand that, on the contrary, it is a subtle one, home of a subtle people.[29]

NOTES

SUP   Sydney University Press
UNSW   University of New South Wales
UQP   University of Queensland Press
UWAP   University of Western Australia Press

CHAPTER 1: THE PEOPLE AT WAR

1   H. M. Shannon, MHA, director of the South Australian Farmers Union; quoted by B. Muirden, *When Power Went Public: A Study in Expediency*, Monograph No. 21, APSA, Sydney, 1978, p. 56.

2   A. D. Hope, 'Australia', in *Collected Poems 1930–1970*, Angus & Robertson, Sydney, 1972, p. 13; E. Dark, *The Timeless Land*, Angus & Robertson, Sydney, 1941.

3   Personal experience.

4   For these and biographical details quoted elsewhere, see L. F. Crisp, *Ben Chifley*, Longmans, London, 1960; A. Fadden, *They Called Me Artie*, Jacaranda, Brisbane, 1969; A. Hasluck, *Portrait in a Mirror*, OUP, Melbourne, 1981; P. Hasluck, *Mucking About*, MUP, Melbourne, 1977; C. Hazlehurst, *Menzies Observed*, Allen & Unwin, Sydney, 1979; L. Ross, *John Curtin*, Macmillan, Melbourne, 1977; K. Tennant, *Evatt, Politics and Justice*, Angus & Robertson, Sydney, 1970; W. J. Hudson, *Casey*, OUP, Melbourne, 1986.

5   W. Osmond, *Frederic Eggleston*, Allen & Unwin, Sydney, 1985, p. 158.

6   G. Blainey (ed.), *If I Remember Rightly*, Cheshire, Melbourne, 1967; *The Steel Master*, Macmillan, Melbourne, 1971; K. Buckley & K. Klugman, *The Australian Presence in the Pacific: Burns Philp 1914–1946*, Allen & Unwin, Sydney, 1983; Colonial Sugar Refining Ltd, *South Pacific Enterprise*, Sydney, 1956.

7   W. K. Hancock, *Country and Calling*, Faber, London, 1954; S. Cockburn & D. Ellyard, *Oliphant*, Axiom Books, Adelaide, 1981; D. Watson, *Brian Fitzpatrick*, Hale & Iremonger, Sydney, 1979; K. S. Inglis & J. Brazier, *This Is the ABC*, MUP, Melbourne, 1983.

8   S. Macintyre, *The Oxford History of Australia*, vol. 4, *1901–1942: The Succeeding Age*, OUP, Melbourne, 1986, ch. 14 (for the Japanese campaign of 1941–42). See also L. Wigmore, *The Japanese Thrust*, Australian War Memorial, Canberra, 1957; T. Hall, *The Fall of Singapore 1942*, Methuen, Sydney, 1983; for the experience of prisoners of war: H. Nelson, *P.O.W.: Australians under Nippon*, ABC Publications, Sydney, 1985; S. Arneil, *One Man's War*, Alternative Publishing Co-operative, Sydney, 1981; E. E. Dunlop, *The War Diaries of Weary Dunlop*, Nelson, Melbourne, 1986.

9   D. Lockwood, *Australia's Pearl Harbour*, Cassell, Melbourne, 1966; T. Hall, *Darwin 1942: Australia's Darkest Hour*, Methuen, Sydney, 1980.

10 I. D. Chapman, *Iven F. Mackay, Citizen and Soldier*, Melway, Melbourne, 1975, p. 285.

11 P. M. C. Hasluck, *The Government and the People 1939–1941*, Australian War Memorial, Canberra, 1952, pp. 519–20. On Curtin, see Ross, *John Curtin*; H. C. Coombs, 'John Curtin—A Consensus Politician?', *Arena*, 69 (1984), pp. 46–59.

12 W. J. Hudson & H. J. W. Stokes, *Documents on Australian Foreign Policy 1937–49*, AGPS, Canberra, 1982, vol. 5, pp. 521–54, 559–66; D. Day, 'Anzacs on the Run: The View from Whitehall, 1941–2', *Journal of Imperial and Commonwealth History*, 14, 3 (1986), pp. 187–202.

13 D. M. Horner, *High Command: Australia and Allied Strategy 1939–1945*, Australian War Memorial and Allen & Unwin, Canberra, 1982, chs 9–12; J. Edwards, 'The War Behind the War', *National Times*, 30 Jan.–3 Feb. 1978.

See also P. M. C. Hasluck, *The Government and the People 1942–1945*, Australian War Memorial, Canberra, 1970, pp. 55–69, 115–33, 149–58; P. Spender, *Politics and a Man*, Collins, Sydney, 1972, p. 76.

14   J. Edwards, 'The Battle for Australia', *National Times*, 6–11 Feb. 1978, based on files of the Operations Planning Division and the Military Intelligence Division (G2) of the American War Department. On the invasion threat, see J. Robertson, *Australia at War 1939–1945*, Heinemann, Melbourne, 1981, ch. 12. On the welcome to the troops, see H. Gullett, *Not as a Duty Only*, MUP, Melbourne, 1976, p. 94. On MacArthur and the Australian generals see D. M. Horner, *Crisis of Command: Australian Generalship and the Japanese Threat*, ANU Press, Canberra, 1978 (pp. 88–90 for comments on the CMF). In recent years this period has received interesting fictional treatment in Thomas Keneally, *The Cut Rate Kingdom*, Wildcat Press, Sydney, 1980, and in David Williamson's television series 'The Last Bastion'.

15   J. C. McDonald to Millice Culpin, 7 May 1943 (letter in possession of Mrs Frances Mackeith, Winchester, England); Hasluck, *The Government and the People 1942–1945*; S. L. Carruthers, *Australia Under Siege: Japanese Submarine Raiders, 1942*, Solus Books, Sydney, 1982.

16   Hasluck, *The Government and the People 1942–1945*, pp. 718–42; B. Muirden, *The Puzzled Patriots*, MUP, Melbourne, 1968; J. Wegner, Hinchinbrook: The Hinchinbrook Shire Council, 1879–1979, MA thesis, James Cook University, Townsville, 1984.

17   Personal information; *CLR*, 67 (1943), pp. 116 *et seq*. See also P. Strawhan, 'The Closure of Radio 5KA, January 1941', *HS*, 21 (1985), pp. 550–64.

18   Hasluck, *The Government and the People 1942–1945*, p. 272.

19   Robertson, *Australia at War 1939–1945*; M. McKernan, *All In! Australia during the Second World War*, Nelson, Melbourne, 1983 (chs 4–6 are the best sources for the home front).

20   G. Blainey, *Mines in the Spinifex*, Angus & Robertson, Sydney, 1961; S. J. Butlin & C. B. Schedvin, *War Economy 1942–1945*, Australian War Memorial, Canberra, 1977, pp. 453–8; and for the economy in general, chs 3–4 and 7–8.

21   Butlin & Schedvin, *War Economy*, chs 2 and 6.

22   R. Hall, 'Aborigines, the Army, and the Second World War in Northern Australia', *Aboriginal History*, 4 (1980), p. 80 and pp. 73–95; *Sydney Morning Herald*, 15 Jan. 1944 and 3 Jan. 1945; T. Wise, *The Self-Made Anthropologist: A Life of A. P. Elkin*, Allen & Unwin, Sydney, 1985, pp. 164–8; R. M. & C. Berndt, *End of an Era*, AIAS, Canberra, 1987.

23   Hasluck, *The Government and the People 1942–1945*, pp. 711–17; E. Spratt, *Eddie Ward: Firebrand of East Sydney*, Rigby, Adelaide, 1965.

24   L. Turner, 'The Crisis of Japanese Strategy, January–June 1942', *RMC Historical Journal*, March 1972, pp. 100–19.

25   D. Dexter, *The New Guinea Offensives*, Australian War Memorial, Canberra, 1961. For the enlisted man's point of view, see Gullett, *Not as a Duty Only*, pp. 95–130; G. Johnston, *War Diary 1942*, Collins, Sydney, 1984.

26   Ross, *John Curtin*, ch. 23; P. Love, 'Curtin, MacArthur and Conscription, 1942–43', *HS*, 17 (1977), pp. 505–11.

27   *Courier-Mail*, 24 March 1942. See also E. D. Potts & A. Potts, *Yanks Down Under*, OUP, Melbourne, 1985, ch. 7; J. H. Moore, *Over-Sexed, Over Paid, and Over Here: Americans in Australia 1941–1945*, UQP, St Lucia, 1981; McKernan, *All In!*, ch. 7; D. Phillips, *Ambivalent Allies*, Penguin, Ringwood, 1988; R. Campbell, *Heroes and Lovers*, Allen & Unwin, Sydney, 1989; J. Wright, 'Brisbane in Wartime', *Overland*, 100 (1986), pp. 64–8; M. Sturma, 'Loving

the Alien: The Underside of Relations between American Servicemen and Australian Women in Queensland, 1942–1945', *JAS*, 24 (1989), pp. 3–17. For the Brisbane incident see R. Fitzgerald, *From 1915 to the Early 1980s: A History of Queensland*, UQP, St Lucia, 1984, p. 109; *National Times*, 10–15 Feb. 1975. For American views on Australians, see *National Times*, 30 Jan.–4 Feb. and 6 Feb.–11 Feb. 1978.

28   P. Charlton, *The Unnecessary War: Island Campaigns in the South-West Pacific 1944–1945*, Macmillan, Melbourne, 1984.

29   H. Gordon, *Die Like the Carp*, Cassell, Sydney, 1978; see also the novel by Seaforth Mackenzie, *Dead Men Rising*, Jonathan Cape, London, 1951.

30   Quoted by G. Long, *The Final Campaigns*, Australian War Memorial, Canberra, 1963, p. 554. See also the *Sydney Morning Herald*, *Age*, and *West Australian*, all for 16 August 1945; J. Reynolds, *Launceston: History of a City*, Macmillan, Melbourne, 1969, p. 177.

31   Alison Patrick, quoted in P. Grimshaw & L. Strahan, *The Half-Open Door*, Hale & Iremonger, Sydney, 1982, p. 207.

32   J. Hetherington, *Blamey—Controversial Soldier*, Kingfisher, Melbourne, 1983; N. D. Carlyon, *I Remember Blamey*, Melbourne, 1980; P. Charlton, *Thomas Blamey*, UQP, St Lucia, 1988; Hasluck, *The Government and the People 1942–1945*, pp. 572–3; Horner, *Crisis of Command*, pp. 207–15; Keneally, 'The Cut Rate Kingdom', p. 85.

33   McKernan, *All In!*, p. 271.

34   Hasluck, *The Government and the People 1942–1945*, pp. 253–60, 388–96; A. Walker, *Coaltown*, MUP, Melbourne, 1945, esp. pp. 89–90; R. A. Gollan, *The Coal Miners of New South Wales*, MUP, Melbourne, 1963; E. Ross, *A History of the Miners Federation of Australia*, Australasian Coal and Shale Employees' Federation, Sydney, 1970, chs 14–15.

35   B. A. Santamaria, *The Price of Freedom*, Campion Press, Melbourne, 1964, ch. 2; A. Davidson, *The Communist Party of Australia*, Hoover Institution Press, Stanford, Calif., 1969, p. 84. For a realistic appraisal of the influence and limitations of a communist union official, see S. Macintyre, *Militant: The Life and Times of Paddy Troy*, Allen & Unwin, Sydney, 1984.

36   A good study of popular anti-communism in Australia has not been attempted and is needed. For North Queensland see D. Menghetti, *The Red North*, Studies in North Queensland History No. 3, James Cook University, Townsville, 1981.

37   For these two paragraphs see R. Haese, *Rebels and Precursors*, Viking, Ringwood, 1981; A. N. Jeffares, 'The Ern Malley Poems', in G. Dutton, *The Literature of Australia*, Collins, Melbourne, 1964; L. Strahan, *Just City and the Mirrors: Meanjin Quarterly and the Intellectual Front, 1940–1965*, OUP, Melbourne, 1984, ch. 2; Ian Turner, 'My Long March', *Overland*, 59 (1974), pp. 21–40.

38   C. Ferrier (ed.), *Point of Departure: The Autobiography of Jean Devanny*, UQP, St Lucia, 1986; E. Ryan, 'Jean Devanny', *Australian Feminist Studies*, 4 (1987), pp. 189–94; D. Modjeska, *Exiles at Home: Australian Women Writers 1925–1945*, Angus & Robertson, Sydney, 1981; W. Mitchell, 'A Pilgrim's Progress', in M. Dawson & H. Radi, *Against the Odds*, Hale & Iremonger, Sydney, 1984, p. 212; *Sydney Morning Herald*, 11 Nov. and 23 Nov. 1942.

39   C. Larmour, *Labor Judge: The Life and Times of Alfred William Foster*, Hale & Iremonger, Sydney, 1985, ch. 16.

40   E. Ryan & A. Conlon, *Gentle Invaders: Australian Women at Work, 1788–1974*, Nelson, Melbourne, 1975; K. Daniels & M. Murnane, *Uphill all the Way*, UQP, St Lucia, 1980; M. McMurchy, M. Oliver & J. Thornley, *For Love or Money*, Penguin, Ringwood, 1983; S. Eccles, 'Women in the Australian

Labour Force', in D. Broom (ed.), *Unfinished Business: Social Justice for Women in Australia*, Allen & Unwin, Sydney, 1984; G. Reekie, 'Industrial Action by Women Workers in Western Australia during World War II', *LH*, 49 (1985), pp. 75–82; P. Johnson, 'Gender, Class, and Work: The Council of Action for Equal Pay and the Equal Pay Campaign in Australia during World War II', *LH*, 50 (1986), pp. 132–46.

41 Butlin & Schedvin, *War Economy*, p. 346, and see ch. 13 generally.
42 Wright, 'Brisbane in Wartime'; G. Reekie, 'War, Sexuality, and Feminism: Perth Women's Organisations, 1938–1945', *HS*, 21 (1985), pp. 576–91; K. Saunders & H. Taylor, '"To Combat the Plague": The Construction of Moral Alarm and State Intervention in Queensland during World War 2', *Hecate*, 14 (1988), pp. 5–30.
43 P. Hetherington, *The Making of a Labor Politician*, [the author], Perth, 1982, p. 105.
44 *Australian Women's Weekly*, 25 August 1945, quoted by A. Wright, 'The Women's Weekly: Depression and War Years, Romance and Reality', *Refractory Girl*, 3 (1973), p. 12; A. Game & R. Pringle, 'Sexuality and the Suburban Dream', *ANZJS*, 15 (1979), pp. 4–15; C. Allport, 'Left off the Agenda: Women, Reconstruction, and New Order Housing', *LH*, 46 (1984), pp. 1–20.

CHAPTER 2: THE PLANNERS

1 Quoted in L. F. Crisp, *Ben Chifley*, Longmans, London, 1961, p. 183.
2 R. Maddock, 'Unification of Income Taxes in Australia', *AJPH*, 28 (1982), pp. 354–66; P. Hasluck, *The Government and the People 1942–1945*, Australian War Memorial, Canberra, 1970, pp. 316–21; *Bulletin*, 29 July 1942; A. Barnard, Taxation, Insurance, and Australian Welfare Provisions 1920–45, Seminar Paper, Department of Economic History, ANU, Canberra, 3 Dec. 1982.
3 W. J. Waters, 'Labor, Socialism, and World War II', *LH*, 16 (1969), pp. 1–9; see also 'Australian Labor's Full Employment Objective, 1942–45', *AJPH*, 16, 1 (1970), pp. 48–64.
4 H. C. Coombs, *Trial Balance*, Macmillan, Melbourne, 1981, p. 60, and part I in general; J. Whitwell, 'The Social Planning of the F & E Economists', *AEHR*, 26 (1985), pp. 1–15. Of great importance are the conference papers presented to the Postwar Reconstruction Seminar, ANU, Canberra, 31 Aug.–4 Sept. 1981.
5 D. H. Merry & G. W. Bruns, 'Full Employment: The British, Canadian and Australian White Papers', *ER*, 21 (1945), p. 232; C. Forster & C. Hazlehurst, 'Australian Statistics and the Development of Official Statistics', *Year Book Australia*, 71, Australian Bureau of Statistics, Canberra, 1988, p. 76.
6 A. W. Martin & J. Penny, 'The Rural Reconstruction Commission: 1943–47', *AJPH*, 29 (1983), pp. 218–29.
7 S. J. Butlin & C. B. Schedvin, *The War Economy 1942–1945*, Australian War Memorial, Canberra, 1977, pp. 752–62; G. Crough & T. Wheelwright, *Australia: A Client State*, Penguin, Ringwood, 1982, p. 3. An autobiographical account from General Motors-Holden's side is given in Sir Laurence Hartnett, *Big Wheels and Little Wheels*, Lansdowne, Melbourne, 1964.
8 C. Lloyd & P. Troy, 'The Commonwealth Housing Commission and a National Housing Policy', Postwar Reconstruction Seminar Papers, ANU, Canberra, 1981.
9 Commonwealth Housing Commission, Ministry of Postwar Reconstruc-

tion, *Final Report*, Canberra, 25 August 1944, p. 8; quoted by Lloyd & Troy, 'The Commonwealth Housing Commission'.

10   *CPD*, vol. 184 (1945), p. 6265.

11   Crisp, *Ben Chifley*, p. 195.

12   D. Dymock, *Adult Literacy Provision in Australia: Trends and Needs*, Australian Council for Adult Literacy, Armidale, 1982, p. 12; F. Alexander, *On Campus and Off*, UWAP, Nedlands, 1987, pp. 22–8; C. Packer, *No Return Ticket*, Methuen, Sydney, 1984, p. 64.

13   D. Horne, *Confessions of a New Boy*, Penguin, Ringwood, 1986, p. 158.

14   R. Wild, *Social Stratification in Australia*, Allen & Unwin, Sydney, 1978, p. 36.

15   *Daily Telegraph*, 17 April 1944.

16   The case for Calwell is put in C. Kiernan, *Calwell*, Nelson, Melbourne, 1978, p. 98; A. A. Calwell, *Be Just and Fear Not*, Lloyd O'Neil/Rigby, Melbourne, 1972.

17   K. S. Inglis & J. Brazier, *This is the ABC*, MUP, Melbourne, 1983; G. C. Bolton, *Dick Boyer*, ANU Press, Canberra, 1967, ch. 5; A. W. Thomas, *Broadcast and Be Damned*, MUP, Melbourne, 1980, chs 4–6.

18   *CPD*, vol. 177 (1944), p. 521; T. Hunter, 'Pharmaceutical Benefits Legislation 1944–50', *ER*, 41 (1965), pp. 412–25; Sir Earle Page, *Truant Surgeon*, Angus & Robertson, Sydney, 1961, pp. 372–82.

19   J. R. Hay, 'The Institute of Public Affairs and Social Policy in World War II', *HS*, 20 (1982), pp. 198–216.

20   J. Brett, 'Menzies' Forgotten People', *Meanjin*, 2 (1984), p. 260.

21   Coombs, *Trial Balance*, p. 67.

22   J. Wilson, 'The Pilbara Aboriginal Social Movement: An Outline of its Background and Significance', in R. M. & C. M. Berndt, *Aborigines of the West: Their Past and Present*, UWAP, Nedlands, 1979, pp. 151–68; K. Palmer & C. McKenna, *Somewhere Between Black and White*, Macmillan, Melbourne, 1978.

23   C. D. Rowley, *Outcasts in White Australia*, Penguin, Ringwood, 1972, pp. 391–4.

24   *Alfred Conlon 1908–1961*, Benevolent Society of New South Wales, Sydney, 1963; 'The Master Puppeteer', *Nation*, 1, 1 (26 Sept. 1958), p. 12; Sir John Kerr, *Matters for Judgement*, Macmillan, Melbourne, 1978, chs 7–8; Sir Paul Hasluck, *Diplomatic Witness: Australian Foreign Affairs 1941–1947*, MUP, Melbourne, 1980, p. 132; B. Jinks, 'The Directorate of Research and New Guinea Policy', Postwar Reconstruction Seminar, ANU.

25   H. Nelson, 'From Kanaka to Fuzzy-Wuzzy Angel', in A. Curthoys & A. Markus, *Who are our Enemies?: Racism and the Working Class in Australia*, Hale & Iremonger, Sydney, 1978, pp. 172–88.

26   J. R. Murray, 'In Retrospect: Papua–New Guinea 1945–1949 and Territory of Papua New Guinea 1949–1952', *AJPH*, 14 (1968), p. 320; I. Downs, *The Australian Trusteeship in Papua-New Guinea 1945–1975*, AGPS, Canberra, 1980, pp. 3–89.

27   G. Sawer, *Australian Federal Politics and Law: 1929–1949*, MUP, Melbourne, 1963, p. 216.

28   A. A. Calwell, 'Introduction to Essays in Honour of Sir Douglas Copland', *ER*, 36 (1963), pp. 2–3.

29   P. Love, *Labour and the Money Power: Australian Labour Populism 1890–1950*, MUP, Melbourne, 1984.

30   Quoted in Crisp, *Ben Chifley*, p. 205.

31   M. Beresford & P. Kerr, 'A Turning Point for Australian Capitalism: 1942–52', in E. L. Wheelwright & K. Buckley (eds), *Essays in the Political Economy of Australian Capitalism*, ANZ, Sydney, 1980, vol. 4, pp. 148–71; but

see also P. Robertson, 'Official Policy on American Direct Investment in Australia, 1945–52', *AEHR*, 26 (1986), pp. 159–84.

32   The case for Chifley is made by Coombs, *Trial Balance*, pp. 113–19.

33   R. Ward, *A Nation for a Continent*, Heinemann, Melbourne, 1977, p. 292. See also A. L. May, *The Battle for the Banks*, SUP, Sydney, 1968, and G. Blainey, *Gold and Paper*, Georgian House, Melbourne, 1958; S. J. Butlin, 'Australian Central Banking, 1945–59', *AEHR*, 23 (1983), pp. 95–192.

34   J. Mills, *The Timber People*, St George, Perth, 1986, pp. 100–2.

35   Evatt's selected speeches are in H. V. Evatt, *Foreign Policy of Australia*, Angus & Robertson, Sydney, 1945; G. Greenwood & N. D. Harper, *Australia in World Affairs 1950–1955*, Angus & Robertson, Sydney, 1946. See also Sir A. Watt, *The Evolution of Australian Foreign Policy 1938–65*, CUP, Cambridge, 1967, chs 3–4; Sir P. Hasluck, *Diplomatic Witness*, MUP, Melbourne, 1980; K. Tennant, *Evatt: Politics and Justice*, Angus & Robertson, Sydney, 1970; A. Renouf, *Let Justice Be Done: The Foreign Policy of Dr H. V. Evatt*, UQP, St Lucia, 1983; P. G. Edwards, *Prime Ministers and Diplomats*, OUP, Melbourne, 1983, ch. 5; also 'Evatt and the Americans', *HS*, 18 (1979), pp. 549–60; W. Crocker, 'The Riddle of Herbert Evatt', *Overland*, 94/95 (1984), pp. 69–74; D. Day, 'H. V. Evatt and the "Beat Hitler First" Strategy: Scheming Politician or Innocent Abroad?', *HS*, 22 (1987), pp. 587–603.

36   W. M. Ball, *Japan, Enemy or Ally?*, Cassell, Melbourne, 1948; A. Rix (ed.), *Intermittent Diplomat: The Japan and Batavia Diaries of W. Macmahon Ball*, MUP, Melbourne, 1988; R. N. Rosecrance, *Australian Diplomacy and Japan, 1945–1951*, MUP, Melbourne, 1962; T. R. Reese, *Australia, New Zealand, and the United States 1941–1968*, OUP, London, 1969, ch. 6; R. Bell, 'Australian–American Disagreement over the Peace Settlement with Japan, 1944–46', *Pacific Historical Review*, 30, 2 (1976), pp. 239–62.

37   Ball, *Japan, Enemy or Ally?*, pp. 112–33. See also the review by Delmer Brown in *Pacific Historical Review*, 18, 4 (1949), pp. 535–6.

38   H. S. Albinski, 'Australia and the China Problem under the Labor Government', *AJPH*, 10 (1964), pp. 149–72; E. Andrews, 'Australia and China, 1949: The Failure to Recognise the PRC', *Australian Journal of Chinese Affairs*, 13 (1987), pp. 29–50; G. W. Bell, 'Some Australian Responses to the Establishment of the People's Republic of China in 1949', *RMC Historical Journal*, 3 (1974), pp. 47–50.

39   P. Edwards, 'The Australian Commitment to the Malayan Emergency, 1948–1950', *HS*, 22 (1987), pp. 604–16.

40   R. Lockwood, *Black Armada*, Hale & Iremonger, Sydney, 1982.

41   Watt, *The Evolution of Australian Foreign Policy*, pp. 249–57; G. Greenwood & N. Harper, *Australia in World Affairs 1950–1955*, Cheshire, Melbourne, 1957, pp. 256–9, 378–86.

42   L. Pearson, *Memoirs*, Gollancz, Toronto, 1973, vol. 1, p. 277.

43   Sir P. Spender, 'The View from External Affairs', *Quadrant*, 50 (Nov.–Dec. 1967), pp. 40–54.

44   J. O'Brien, 'Australia and the Repeal of the External Relations Act', Paper delivered at the Australian–Irish Bicentenary Conference, Kilkenny, 20 October 1983.

45   W. Millis (ed.), *The Forrestal Diaries*, Cassell, London, 1952, p. 496, quoted by Watt, *The Evolution of Australian Foreign Policy*, p. 99; see also Geoffrey Sawer's comments in Greenwood & Harper, *Australia in World Affairs 1950–1955*, p. 113; M. Burgmann, 'Evatt and the Russians', in A. Curthoys & J. Merritt (eds), *Australia's First Cold War 1945–1953*, Allen & Unwin, Sydney, 1984, vol. 1, pp. 80–108.

46   *Cairns Post*, 15 June 1953; C. Clark, 'Land Settlement in Queensland', *Economic News*, 19, 7–8 (1950), pp. 1–8.

47 *CPD*, vol. 184 (1945), pp. 4911–15; A. Markus, 'Labor and Immigration: Policy Formation 1943–45', *LH*, 46 (1984), pp. 21–33.

48 National Health and Medical Research Council, *Interim Report on the Decline of the Birthrate*, Canberra, 1944, p. 91; B. Cass, 'Population Policies and the Australian Welfare State: The Legitimation of Redistributive Policies', in C. Baldock & B. Cass (eds), *Women, Social Welfare and the State*, Allen & Unwin, Sydney, 1983, p. 176.

49 A. A. Calwell, *How Many Australians Tomorrow?*, Reed & Harris, Melbourne, 1945; Kiernan, *Calwell*, chs 5–6.

50 O. A. Oeser & S. B. Hammond, *Social Structure and Personality in a City*, Routledge & Kegan Paul, London, 1954, p. 55.

51 A. Markus, 'Labor and Immigration: The Displaced Persons Programme', *LH*, 47 (1984), pp. 73–90.

52 ibid., p. 78; N. W. Lamidey, *Partial Success: My Years as a Public Servant*, [the author], Sydney, 1970.

53 A. T. Yarwood & M. J. Knowling, *Race Relations in Australia*, Methuen, Sydney, 1982, p. 285; H. I. London, *Non-White Immigration and the 'White Australia' Policy*, SUP, Sydney, 1970, p. 186; *CPD*, vol. 202 (1949), pp. 72–92, 147–9.

54 Sir W. McKell, oral history interview, 29 April 1971, NLA TRC 121/19.

55 G. Johnston, *Clean Straw for Nothing*, Collins, London, 1969, p. 99. But see also the more critical account in B. Collis, *Snowy: The Making of Modern Australia*, Hodder & Stoughton, Sydney, 1989.

56 McKell, interview, 29 April 1971; W. K. Hancock, *Discovering Monaro*, CUP, Cambridge, 1972, pt 4, ch. 2.

CHAPTER 3: PRAGMATISM ASCENDANT

1 T. Sheridan, 'Labour vs. Labor: The Victorian Metal Trades Dispute of 1946–47', in J. Iremonger, J. A. Merritt & G. Osborne, *Strikes: Studies in 20th Century Australian Social History*, Hale & Iremonger, Sydney, 1978, pp. 176–224; 'Aspects of Decision-Making in a Monopoly: BHP and the 1945 Steel Strike', *AEHR*, 22 (1982), pp. 1–27; 'The 1945 Steel Strike: Trade Unions, the New Order, and Mr Chifley', *LH*, 42 (1982) pp. 1–26.

2 J. Hagan, *The History of the ACTU*, Longman Cheshire, Melbourne, 1981, pp. 118–19 and 189; T. Sheridan, 'Planners and the Australian Labour Market', *LH*, 53 (1987), pp. 99–113.

3 Hagan, *History of the ACTU*, p. 191, quoting Albert Monk.

4 C. Larmour, *Labor Judge: The Life and Times of Alfred William Foster*, Hale & Iremonger, Sydney, 1985, p. 208.

5 M. Page, *The Flying Doctor Story 1928–78*, Rigby, Adelaide, 1977, p. 198; *Australian*, 29 April 1989.

6 The official total for 30 June 1947 was 7 579 378; but as this excludes Aborigines I have rounded the figure to 7.7 million.

7 Quoted in *Daily Mirror* (Sydney), 31 October 1988.

8 Alice, Duchess of Gloucester, quoted in N. Frankland, *Prince Henry, Duke of Gloucester*, Weidenfeld & Nicolson, London, 1980, p. 110.

9 The material in this paragraph is extracted from a notebook kept by my mother, Mrs W. M. Bolton of Mt Lawley, WA, and inherited from her after her death in 1985.

10 G. T. Caldwell, Leisure Co-Operatives: The Institutionalization of Gambling and the Growth of Large Leisure Organizations in New South Wales, PhD thesis, ANU, Canberra, 1972; B. D. Haig, *Gambling in Australia 1920–21 to 1980–81*, Working Papers in Economic History, No. 20, ANU,

Canberra, 1984; 'Luck for Sale', *Nation*, 15 July 1961; P. N. Grabosky, *Sydney in Ferment: Crime, Dissent, and Official Reaction 1788–1973*, ANUP, Canberra, 1975, p. 133.

11   *CPD*, vol. 210 (7 Nov. 1950), pp. 2016–20.

12   M. Boyd, *Day of My Delight*, Lansdowne, Melbourne, 1965; P. White, *Flaws in the Glass*, Jonathan Cape, London, 1981, p. 126.

13   Boyd, *Day of My Delight*, pp. 237–8.

14   *Farrago*, 11 May 1949, quoted in P. Deery (ed.), *Labour in Conflict: The 1949 Coal Strike*, Occasional Publications in Labour History, No. 1, Australian Society for the Study of Labour History, Canberra, 1978, p. 24.

15   *Courier-Mail*, 23 July 1948; *Sydney Morning Herald*, 24 July 1948.

16   R. D. Rivett, *David Rivett, Fighter for Australian Science*, [the author], Hawthorn, 1972; *CPD*, vol. 198 (30 Sept. 1948), pp. 1028–49.

17   *CPD*, vol. 199 (4 Nov. 1948), pp. 2478–528.

18   M. Cribb, 'State in Emergency: The Queensland Railway Strike of 1948', in Iremonger, Merritt & Osborne, *Strikes*, pp. 225–48.

19   Hagan, *History of the ACTU*, p. 129; *Communist Review*, April 1949, pp. 112–16.

20   The phrase 'boots and all' was Chifley's; see *Argus*, 4 July 1949. See also R. A. Gollan, *The Coal Miners of New South Wales*, MUP, Melbourne, 1963, pp. 230–5; E. Ross, *A History of the Miners Federation of Australia*, Australasian Coal & Shale Employees' Federation, Sydney, 1970, ch. 17; P. L. Coleman, 'The 1949 Coal Strike in New South Wales', *Victorian Journal of History*, 52, 1 (1981), pp. 58–71.

21   L. Haylen, *Twenty Years Hard Labour*, Macmillan, Melbourne, 1969, pp. 88–9.

22   R. Murray & K. White, *Ironworkers: A History of the Federated Ironworkers' Association of Australia*, Hale & Iremonger, Sydney, 1982; J. Merritt, A History of the Federated Ironworkers' Association of Australia, 1909–1952, PhD thesis, ANU, Canberra, 1967.

23   P. Osmond, *The Movement*, Penguin, Ringwood, 1972; E. Campion, *Rockchoppers*, Penguin, Ringwood, 1982, ch. 4; D. Blackmur, 'The ALP Industrial Groups in Queensland', *LH*, 46 (1984), pp. 88–108; G. Henderson, *Mr Santamaria and the Bishops*, St Patrick's College, Manly, 1982.

24   *CPD*, vol. 199 (9 Nov. 1948), p. 2592; G. C. Bolton, *Dick Boyer*, ANUP, Canberra, 1967, pp. 169–73.

25   *CPD*, vol. 204 (14 Sept. 1949), pp. 189–242.

26   A. Fadden, *They Called Me Artie*, Jacaranda, Brisbane, 1969, pp. 107–8.

27   There is no good analysis of the 1949 elections. See L. F. Crisp, *Ben Chifley*, Longmans, London, 1960, ch. 22; C. A. Hughes, 'The 1948 Redistribution and the Defeat of the Chifley Government', *LH*, 34 (1978), pp. 74–86.

28   L. L. Robson, reviewing W. J. Hudson & J. North, *My Dear P.M.*, AGPS, Canberra, 1980, in *Australian Book Review*, May 1981.

29   R. Ward, *A Nation for a Continent*, Heinemann, Melbourne, 1977, p. 300. He verified this story with both Fadden and Coombs.

30   R. O'Neill, *Australia in the Korean War 1950–53*, AGPS, Canberra, vol. 1, 1981; vol. 2, 1985.

31   The text of ANZUS is at F. K. Crowley, *Modern Australia in Documents, 1939–1970*, Wren, Melbourne, 1973, pp. 248–50. See also T. R. Reese, *Australia, New Zealand, and the United States*, OUP, London, 1969, chs 7–8; R. N. Rosecrance, *Australian Diplomacy and Japan 1945–1951*, MUP, Melbourne, 1962; P. C. Spender, *Exercises in Diplomacy*, SUP, Sydney, 1969; Sir A. Watt, *The Evolution of Australian Foreign Policy 1938–1965*, CUP, Cambridge, 1967, pp. 117–42.

32   *CPD*, vol. 207 (9 May 1950), p. 2251.
33   S. P. Stevens, 'The Importance of Wool in Australia's National Income', *ER*, 26 (1950), pp. 217–38.
34   Fadden, *They Called Me Artie*, p. 116.
35   A. Johnson, *Fly a Rebel Flag*, Penguin, Ringwood, 1986, p. 194.
36   L. C. Webb, *Communism and Democracy in Australia: A Survey of the 1951 Referendum*, Cheshire, Melbourne, 1954; F. Cain & F. Farrell, 'Menzies' War on the Communist Party, 1949–1951', in A. Curthoys & J. Merritt (eds), *Australia's First Cold War 1945–1953*, Allen & Unwin, Sydney, 1984, vol. 1, pp. 109–34. For a reasoned statement of the 'Yes' case, see N. Cowper, 'Action Against Communism', *AQ*, 22, 1 (1950), pp. 5–12.
37   H. Arndt, *Labour and Economic Policy* (Chifley Memorial Lecture), MUP, Melbourne, 1956; *Age*, 28 July 1956; K. S. Inglis & R. H. Wallace, 'Professor Arndt and the Labor Party', *AQ*, 28, 4 (1956), pp. 55–64.
38   Crisp, *Ben Chifley*, conclusion. Note also the characterization of Chifley in the 1988 television series 'The True Believers', and comment by J. Walter, 'The Dark Side of the Moon Party', *Cinema Papers*, 74 (1989), pp. 36–41.
39   R. Watts, *The Foundations of the National Welfare State*, Allen & Unwin, Sydney, 1987.
40   T. C. Truman, 'The Press and the 1951 Federal Elections', *AQ*, 23, 4 (1951), pp. 33–44.

CHAPTER 4: GETTING AND SPENDING

 1   D. Cottle, 'A New Cure for the Old Disorder: The State, Class Struggle and Social Order 1941–45', in R. Kennedy (ed.), *Australian Welfare History: Critical Essays*, Macmillan, Melbourne, 1982, p. 273.
 2   I. W. McLean & J. J. Pincus, *Living Standards in Australia 1890–1940*, Working Papers in Economic History, No. 6, ANU, Canberra, 1982; E. F. Gillen, 'Social Indicators and Economic Welfare', *Economic Papers*, 46 (June 1974); R. Broom & F. Lancaster Jones, *Opportunity and Attainment in Australia*, ANUP, Canberra, 1976.
 3   A. Game & R. Pringle, 'Sexuality and the Suburban Dream', *ANZJS*, 15 (1979), p. 15.
 4   R. F. Henderson, A. Harcourt & R. J. A. Harper, *People in Poverty: A Melbourne Survey*, Cheshire, Melbourne, 1970, p. 7.
 5   D. Horne, *The Lucky Country*, Penguin, Ringwood, 1964.
 6   Two contemporary surveys are J. G. Crawford, *Australian Trade Policy 1942–1966*, Longmans, Melbourne, 1968, and J. O. N. Perkins, *Australia in the World Economy*, Sun Books, Melbourne, 1968.
 7   F. L. Hitchens, *Tangled Skeins*, Robertson & Mullens, Melbourne, 1956.
 8   K. Tsokhas, *Beyond Dependence*, OUP, Melbourne, 1986.
 9   *CPD*, vol. 217 (28 May 1952), pp. 961–4.
10   Quoted in R. Milliken, *No Conceivable Injury*, Penguin, Ringwood, 1986. See also T. Sherratt, 'A Political Inconvenience: Australian Scientists at the British Atomic Tests, 1952–53', *Historical Records of Australian Science*, 6, 2 (1985), pp. 137–52.
11   *West Australian*, 16 Aug. 1956, 1 Jan. 1988; Fadden's quotation is given in Millikin, *No Conceivable Injury*, p. 369.
12   S. Cockburn & D. Ellyard, *Oliphant*, Axiom Books, Adelaide, 1981, esp. chs 16–17.
13   *CPDS*, vol. 12 (19 March 1958), p. 256.
14   A. Kerr, *Australia's North-West*, UWAP, Nedlands, 1975.
15   B. Galligan, *Utah and Queensland Coal*, UQP, St Lucia, 1989.

16   J. Warhurst, *Jobs or Dogma? The Industries Assistance Commission and Australian Politics*, UQP, St Lucia, 1982.

17   R. V. Jackson (ed.), *John McEwen* (transcribed tapes), NLA, Canberra, 1983, p. 61. See also H. G. Gelber, *Australia, Britain, and the European Economic Community, 1961–63*, OUP, Melbourne, 1966.

18   L. G. Melville, 'Tariff Policy', *ER*, 43 (1967), pp. 193–208.

19   T. Griffiths, *Contemporary Australia*, Croom Helm, London, 1977, p. 39.

20   A. McKay, *Science and Enterprise: Fifty Years of Science for Australia*, CSIRO, Canberra, 1976.

21   H. Bloom, 'The Changing Pattern of Academic Research: 8, The University of Tasmania', *Proc. Royal Aust. Chem. Inst.*, 28 (1961), pp. 437–40.

22   B. J. Bok, 'The Future of Astronomy in Australia', *Aust. Jl Sci.*, 25 (1963), pp. 281–8; Sir F. White, 'Administrative Problems in the Development of Scientific Research', *Aust. Jl Sci.*, 27 (1965), pp. 113–40; T. Pearcy, *A History of Australian Computing*, Chisholm Institute of Technology, Caulfield, 1988.

23   A. E. Alexander, 'Survey of Higher Graduates from Australian Universities, 1946–62', *Proc. Royal Aust. Chem. Inst.* 31 (1964), pp. 27–9.

24   J. P. Allen, 'Scientific Innovation and Industrial Prosperity', *Proc. Royal Aust. Chem. Inst.*, 30 (1963), pp. 377–400.

25   S. H. Bastow, 'Research in the Manufacturing Industry in Australia', *Journal of the Institute of Engineers, Australia*, 36 (1964), pp. N37–N40.

26   Commonwealth of Australia, *Report of the Committee of Economic Enquiry* (J. Vernon, Chairman), Melbourne, 1965; see also reviews of the report in *Economic Record*, 42, 1 (1966); P. Samuel, 'Politics for Economic Growth: The Vernon Report, A Review', *AQ*, 37, 4 (1965), pp. 11–25.

27   F. G. Castles, *The Working Class and Welfare: Reflections of the Political Development of the Welfare State in Australia and New Zealand 1890–1980*, Allen & Unwin, Wellington, 1986, esp. pp. 29–43.

28   *National Times*, 27 May–1 June 1978.

29   P. Cochrane, 'Company Time: Management, Ideology, and the Labour Process, 1940–1960', *LH*, 48 (1985), pp. 54–68.

30   J. Hill, *From Subservience to Strike*, UQP, St Lucia, 1982; N. F. Dufty, *Unions and Politics — The Five-Day Week Campaign for Western Australian Bankers*, Discussion Paper in Industrial Relations, No. 7, Department of Industrial Relations, University of Western Australia, Nedlands, 1985.

31   See two biographies by B. d'Alpuget: *Mediator: A Biography of Sir Richard Kirby*, MUP, Melbourne, 1977; *Hawke: A Biography*, 2nd edn, Schwartz, Melbourne, 1983.

32   K. Gravell, *Professional Incomes in Victoria*, MUP, Melbourne, 1957.

33   Quoted in L. Foster & D. Stockley, 'Multiculturalism in the Australian Context', *ANZJS*, 16 (1980), pp. 109–14.

34   N. Culotta [J. O'Grady], *They're a Weird Mob*, Ure Smith, Sydney, 1958.

35   D. R. Cox, 'Pluralism in Australia', *ANZJS*, 12 (1976), pp. 112–17; R. Taft, *From Stranger to Citizen*, UWAP, Nedlands, 1965.

36   *Age*, 24 March 1986.

37   T. A. G. Hungerford, *A Knockabout in a Slouch Hat*, FACP, Fremantle, 1985, p. 153; R. Bosworth, 'Conspiracy of the Consuls? Official Italy and the Bonegilla Riot of 1952', *HS*, 22 (1987), pp. 547–67.

38   *Bulletin*, 30 Sept. 1986.

39   *Sunday Australian*, 25 April 1971.

40   Information N. Honner, Murdoch University.

41   R. D. Francis, *Migrant Crime in Australia*, UQP, St Lucia, 1981.

42   S. Lindsay Thompson, *Australia Through Italian Eyes*, OUP, Melbourne, 1980, p. 106.

43   R. Huber, *From Pasta to Pavlova*, UQP, St Lucia, 1977, p. 43.
44   J. I. Martin, *The Migrant Presence*, Allen & Unwin, Sydney, 1978; *The Ethnic Dimension*, Allen & Unwin, Sydney, 1981.
45   Quoted by A. Jakubowicz, M. Morrissey & J. Palser, *Ethnicity, Class, and Social Policy*, Social Welfare Research Centre, UNSW, Kensington, 1984.

CHAPTER 5: BEING AUSTRALIAN

1   L. Ritter, 'Toilet Training in Postwar Australia', *Oral History Association of Australia Journal*, 8 (1986), pp. 88–94.
2   Commonwealth Statistician, *Commonwealth Year Book, 1964*, Bureau of Census and Statistics, Canberra, 1964, p. 708.
3   G. Caiger (ed.), *The Australian Way of Life*, Heinemann, London, 1953, p. 42; A. W. Black, 'Religious Studies in Australian Public Schools', *Australian Educational Review*, 7, 3 (1974), p. 3. The experience of schooling in this period is described in K. Skelton & J. Barrett, 'When Teacher Ruled: Two Views', *JAS*, 24 (1989), pp. 99–105.
4   J. Mundey, *Green Bans and Beyond*, Angus & Robertson, London, 1981, p. 12.
5   J. Arnold, *Mother Superior, Woman Inferior*, Dove, Melbourne, 1985.
6   H. Praetz, *Building a School System*, MUP, Melbourne, 1980.
7   E. Campion, *Rockchoppers: Growing Up Catholic in Australia*, Penguin, Ringwood, 1982.
8   B. Dawe, 'Life-Cycle', in *Sometimes Gladness: Collected Poems, 1954–1978*, Longman Cheshire, Melbourne, 1978.
9   K. Forster, 'Advantage Australia — Davis Cup Tennis 1950–1955', *Meanjin*, 45, 2 (1984), pp. 273–85.
10   D. Fraser, *Gold Medal Girl*, Nicholas Kaye, London, 1965.
11   A. Barcan, *A History of Australian Education*, OUP, Melbourne, 1980, pp. 301–4.
12   ibid., pp. 302 and 311.
13   S. Encel, *Equality and Authority*, Cheshire, Melbourne, 1970, p. 157; J. McCalman, 'Old School Ties and Silver Spoons: A Statistical Footnote from Darkest Victoria', *Australian Cultural History*, 8 (1989), pp. 78–83.
14   R. Connell, 'Class and Personal Socialization', in *Ruling Class, Ruling Culture*, CUP, Cambridge, 1977; R. Connell *et al.*, *Making the Difference: Schools, Family, and Social Division*, Allen & Unwin, Sydney, 1982; G. Maslen, *School Ties*, Methuen, Melbourne, 1982; see also J. R. Darling, *The Education of a Civilized Man*, Cheshire, Melbourne, 1962; S. Braga, *Barker College: A History*, John Ferguson in association with Barker College, Sydney, 1978.
15   *Observer* (London), 3 April 1983.
16   *West Australian*, 29 Oct. 1956.
17   J. Roe, '"First Matriculate . . ."', in H. Radi & M. Dawson, *Against the Odds*, Hale & Iremonger, Sydney, 1984, p. 69.
18   Sir Keith Murray *et al.*, 'Report of the Committee on Australian Universities', *Commonwealth Parliamentary Papers*, Government Printer, Canberra, 1958, vol. 7.
19   W. H. C. Eddy, *Orr*, Jacaranda, Brisbane, 1961.
20   R. Ward, *A Radical Life*, Macmillan, Melbourne, 1988.
21   D. Hilliard, 'Popular Religion in Australia in the 1950s: A Study of Adelaide and Brisbane', *Journal of Religious History*, 15, 2 (1988), pp. 219–35.
22   J. Stratton, 'Bodgies and Widgies — Youth Cultures in the 1950s', *JAS*, 15 (1984), pp. 10–24; D. Dunphy, *Cliques, Crowds and Gangs: Group Life of Sydney Adolescents*, Cheshire, Melbourne, 1969; S. Alomes, 'An Australian Culture? Australian Rock from Johnny O'Keefe to Jimmy Barnes', *Island*,

30 (1987), p. 58; R. Evans, 'Heroes Often Fail: Johnny O'Keefe and Another Australian Legend', *Cinema Papers*, 71 (1989), pp. 37–42.

23   K. Pearson, *Surfing Subcultures of Australia and New Zealand*, UQP, St Lucia, 1979.

24   D. R. Lewis, *Oral Contraception in Melbourne*, ANUP, Canberra, 1975.

25   G. Kelly, 'Portrait of a New Community', *Meanjin*, 18, 4 (1957), pp. 399–406; P. Spearritt, *Sydney Since the Twenties*, Hale & Iremonger, Sydney, 1978, p. 104.

26   T. van Dugteren (ed.), *Rural Australia: The Other Nation*, Hodder & Stoughton, Sydney, 1978, p. 167; J. Barrett, 'A Defence of the Ward Thesis', *Historian*, 25 (1973), p. 5.

27   *Observer* (London), 7 August 1982.

28   R. Boyd, *Australia's Home*, MUP, Melbourne, 1952; *The Australian Ugliness*, Cheshire, Melbourne, 1960.

29   C. McGregor, *People, Politics, and Pop: Australians in the Sixties*, Ure Smith, Sydney, 1968, p. 52.

30   H. Stretton, *Ideas for Australian Cities*, Orphan Books, Melbourne, 1970, pp. 16–17 (later editions by Georgian House, Melbourne).

31   H. Mol, *Religion in Australia*, Nelson, Melbourne, 1971; D. McCaughey, 'Churches, Sects, and Culture', in J. McLaren (ed.), *A Nation Apart: Essays in Honour of Andrew Fabinyi*, Longman Cheshire, Melbourne, 1983.

32   For the Masons, see B. Stannard, 'Are the Masons a Menace?', *Bulletin*, 11 April 1989; for Rotary, H. Hunt (ed.), *The Story of Rotary in Australia 1921–1971*, Rotary International, Sydney, 1971.

33   I. Manning, *The Journey to Work*, Allen & Unwin, Sydney, 1978.

34   R. W. Gibbins, 'American Influence on Commercial Practice', in R. A. Preston (ed.), *Contemporary Australia*, Duke University Press, Durham, NC, 1969, p. 503.

35   *Australian Book Review*, Feb.–March 1983, p. 3.

36   D. Halpin, *Consumers Choice: 25 Years of the Australian Consumers Association*, Australian Consumers Association, Sydney, 1984.

37   J. E. Richardson, 'Australian Antitrust and the Decline of American Influence', in Preston, *Contemporary Australia*, pp. 454–97.

38   A. Curthoys, 'The Getting of Television: Dilemmas in Ownership, Control and Culture', in A. Curthoys & J. Merritt (eds), *Australia's First Cold War 1945–1959*, vol. 2, *Better Dead than Red*, Allen & Unwin, Sydney, 1986, pp. 123–54.

39   F. G. Clarke, The Democratic Labor Party in Western Australia: Its Origins and Early Years, MA thesis, University of Western Australia, Perth, 1969.

40   Spearritt, *Sydney Since the Twenties*, p. 234.

41   *Australian Financial Review*, 24 Sept. 1963; D. Mort, Economics of Scope and Corporate Diversification in Australia, Paper presented to Business History Workshop, University of Melbourne, 1–2 June 1983.

42   G. T. Caldwell *et al.*, *Gambling in Australia*, Croom Helm, Sydney, 1985; J. O'Hara, *A Mug's Game*, NSWUP, Kensington, 1987.

43   'Luck for Sale', *Nation*, 15 July 1961.

44   F. Salter, *Borovansky: The Man who Made Australian Ballet*, Wildcat Press, Sydney, 1980; E. H. Park, *Ballet in Australia: The Second Act 1940–1980*, OUP, Melbourne, 1981.

45   *Sydney Morning Herald*, 26 April 1961.

46   *CPDHR*, vol. 12 (29 August 1956), p. 8.

47   D. Dunstan, *Felicia*, Macmillan, Melbourne, 1981, p. 23.

48   G. Dutton, 'Under Old Management', *Nation*, 19 Oct. 1963.

49   D. Adler, 'Matriduxy in the Australian Family', in A. F. Davies & S. Encel, *Australian Society*, Cheshire, Melbourne, 1965, 1st edn, pp. 149–55.
50   *Australian Women's Weekly*, 16 May 1979.
51   *ibid.*, 27 June 1979.
52   Obituary, 1984, provided by the Australian–American Association, Sydney.
53   S. Macintyre, *Militant: The Life and Times of Paddy Troy*, Allen & Unwin, Sydney, 1984, pp. 194–6.
54   R. Conway, *The End of Stupor?*, Sun Books, Melbourne, 1984, p. 75.
55   Quoted in G. Whitlam, *The Whitlam Government 1972–1975*, Penguin, Ringwood, 1985, p. 354. See also C. Russell, *The Aging Experience*, Allen & Unwin, Sydney, 1982.
56   G. Griffin & D. Tobin, *In the Midst of Life*, MUP, Melbourne, 1982; M. Crouch & B. Hüppauf (eds), *Essays on Mortality*, Faculty of Arts, UNSW, Kensington, 1985 (see essays by D. B. Waterson and S. Tweedie).

CHAPTER 6: THE POLITICS OF AFFLUENCE

1   *West Australian*, 6 July 1977.
2   In January 1954, when Menzies wished to have the visiting delegates to the Commonwealth Finance Ministers' Conference admitted to temporary membership of the Royal Sydney Golf Club, he asked Owen to arrange it. (Menzies MSS, NLA; unclassified at time of consultation.)
3   B. Milliss, *Serpent's Tooth*, Penguin, Ringwood, 1984. R. Manne, *The Petrov Affair*, Pergamon, Sydney, 1987, attacks the view that Menzies had advance knowledge of Petrov's defection but is too kindly about the subsequent management of the inquiry. Among the numerous works on the controversy are N. Whitlam & J. Stubbs, *Nest of Traitors*, Jacaranda, Brisbane, 1974; M. Thwaites, *Truth Will Out: ASIO and the Petrovs*, Collins, Sydney, 1980; D. Marr, *Barwick*, Allen & Unwin, Sydney, 1980, ch. 10; T. Hill, 'Petrov in Retrospect: Conspiracy or Cold War?', *Arena*, 69 (1984), pp. 124–32; J. Waterford, 'A Labor Myth?', in A. Curthoys & J. Merritt (eds), *Australia's First Cold War 1945–1959*, vol. 2, *Better Dead than Red*, Allen & Unwin, Sydney, 1986, pp. 99–119.
4   *Age*, 6 Oct. 1954.
5   R. Murray, *The Split: Australian Labor in the Fifties*, Cheshire, Melbourne, 1970; F. G. Clarke, 'Towards a Reassessment of Dr Evatt's Role in the 1954–55, ALP Split', *LH*, 19 (1970), pp. 55–62.
6   *CPDHR*, vol. 8 (19 Oct. 1955), p. 1695.
7   K. White, *John Cain and Victorian Labor 1917–1957*, Hale & Iremonger, Sydney, 1982, ch. 9.
8   A. A. Calwell, *Be Just and Fear Not*, Lloyd O'Neil/Rigby, Melbourne, 1972, pp. 143–4.
9   R. Fitzgerald & H. Thornton, *Labor in Queensland*, UQP, St Lucia, 1989, ch. 4; C. Hughes, *The Government of Queensland*, UQP, St Lucia, 1980.
10   C. Kiernan, *Calwell*, Nelson, Melbourne, 1978, p. 188.
11   P. L. Reynolds, *The Democratic Labor Party*, Jacaranda, Brisbane, 1974; L. F. Crisp, 'The DLP Vote 1958–69 and After', *Politics*, 5, 1 (1970), pp. 62–6; H. Mayer, 'The DLP—"Get on", "Get out" or Neither', in H. Mayer (ed.), *Australian Politics—A Second Reader*, Cheshire, Melbourne, 1969.
12   D. Mitchell, 'F. E. Chamberlain—The Trade Unionist', in L. Hunt (ed.), *Westralian Portraits*, UWAP, Nedlands, 1979, pp. 253–9.
13   N. Blewett & D. Jaensch, *From Playford to Dunstan: The Politics of Transition*, Cheshire, Melbourne, 1971; Sir W. Crocker, *Sir Thomas Playford*, MUP, Melbourne, 1982.

14 For SEATO, see Sir A. Watt, *The Evolution of Australian Foreign Policy 1938–1965*, CUP, London, 1967, pp. 143–80.

15 For Australia's role in the Suez crisis, see W. Macmahon Ball, 'The Australian Reaction to the Suez Crisis, July–December 1956', *AJPH*, 2, 2 (1957), pp. 129–50; N. D. Harper, 'Australia and Suez', in G. Greenwood & N. D. Harper, *Australia in World Affairs 1950–1955*, Angus & Robertson, Sydney, 1946, pp. 341–56; O. Harries, 'Menzies and the Suez Crisis', *Politics*, 3, 2 (1968), pp. 193–204; A. W. Martin, 'R. G. Menzies and the Suez Crisis', *HS*, 23 (1989), pp. 163–85.

16 Sir A. Eden, *Full Circle*, Cassell, London, 1960, p. 473.

17 D. Carlton, *Anthony Eden: A Biography*, Allen Lane, London, 1981, pp. 417–18.

18 Sir H. Beale, *This Inch of Time: Memoirs of Politics and Diplomacy*, MUP, Melbourne, 1977, pp. 91–2.

19 Menzies to Avon, 7 May 1975, Menzies MSS, NLA.

20 I. Downs, *The Australian Trusteeship: Papua-New Guinea 1945–1975*, AGPS, Canberra, 1980; Sir P. Hasluck, *A Time for Building*, MUP, Melbourne, 1976; L. W. Johnson, *Colonial Sunset*, UQP, St Lucia, 1983.

21 *CPDHR*, vol. 17 (5 Dec. 1957), p. 2923.

22 *Sydney Morning Herald*, 9–12 Nov. 1957; *CPDS*, vol. 11 (12 Nov. 1957), pp. 1147–82.

23 *CPDHR*, vol. 45 (23 March 1965), p. 231.

24 *CPDHR*, vol. 50 (29 March 1966), p. 701.

25 B. Grant, *Indonesia*, Penguin, Ringwood, p. 199.

26 Sir John Gorton, oral history interview, 24 March 1976, NLA TRC 121/78. An equally telling criticism comes from the then ambassador to Washington, Sir Howard Beale, *This Inch of Time*, ch. 18.

27 T. B. Millar in J. Wilkes (ed.), *Australia's Defence and Foreign Policy*, Angus & Robertson, Sydney, 1964.

28 M. Sexton, *War for the Asking: Australia's Vietnam Secrets*, Penguin, Ringwood, 1981; Evan Whitton's articles, *National Times*, 28 April–3 May, 5–10 May and 12–17 May 1975. But see also G. Pemberton, *All the Way: Australia's Road to Vietnam*, Allen & Unwin, Sydney, 1987; G. St J. Barclay, *A Very Small Insurance Policy*, UQP, St Lucia, 1988; P. Edwards, 'Vietnam — How the Menzies "Bullets" Backfired', *Sydney Morning Herald*, 6 June 1989.

29 *Australian*, 30 April 1965; *Bulletin*, 4 May 1965.

30 Menzies MSS, NLA.

31 W. Crocker, *Travelling Back*, Macmillan, Melbourne, 1981, pp. 184–7.

32 T. B. Macauley, 'Horace Walpole', in A. J. Grieve (ed.), *Critical and Historical Essays*, Everyman/Dent, London, 1907, vol. 1, pp. 346–52. Macauley adds: 'The praise to which he is fairly entitled is this, that he understood the true interest of his country better than any of his contemporaries, and that he pursued that interest whenever it was not incompatible with the interest of his own intense and grasping ambition'.

33 S. Brogden, *Australia's Two Airline Policy*, MUP, Melbourne, 1968.

CHAPTER 7: THE FAITHFUL ALLY

1 T. Burstell, *The Soldier's Story*, UQP, St Lucia, 1986, p. 7.

2 I am indebted to one of my Murdoch University students, Joanne Malone, for her 1982 survey of opinion among Vietnam veterans.

3 *CPDHR*, vol. 67 (1970), p. 1456.

4 D. McDougall, 'The Australian Press Coverage of the Vietnam War in

1965', *AQ*, 20, 3 (1966), pp. 303–10; Sir J. Plimsoll, 'Asian Issues in the Australian Press', *Current Notes in International Affairs*, 36 (1965), pp. 745–57.

5   *Australian*, 25 July 1968.

6   *ibid.*, 7 Feb. 1967.

7   Dame Z. Holt, *My Life With Harry*, Herald, Melbourne, 1968, p. 202.

8   Association for International Control and Disarmament newsletter, quoted by R. Summy, 'Militancy and the Australian Peace Movement', *Politics*, 5, 1 (1970), pp. 148–62; see also D. P. Altman, 'Foreign Policy and the Elections', *Politics*, 2, 1 (1967), pp. 57–66; C. Kiernan, *Calwell*, Nelson, Melbourne, 1978, pp. 240–59; R. Cooksey, 'Australian Public Opinion and Vietnam Policy', *Dissent*, 22 (1968), pp. 5–11.

9   R. Cooksey, 'Pine Gap', *AQ*, 40, 4 (1968), p. 12.

10 C. Rootes, 'The Development of Radical Student Movements in Australia and their Sequelae', *AJPH*, 34 (1988), pp. 173–86.

11 A. A. Calwell, oral history interview, 20 May 1971, NLA TRC 121/7.

12 M. E. Hamel, The Resisters: A History of the Anti-Conscription Movement', in P. King (ed.), *Australia's Vietnam*, Allen & Unwin, Sydney, 1982, pp. 100–28.

13 *Australian*, 17 July 1970.

14 *CPDHR*, vol. 59 (1968), pp. 1981–2003; *Canberra Times*, 25 May 1968.

15 M. Goot & R. Tiffin, 'Public Opinion and the Politics of the Polls', in King, *Australia's Vietnam*, pp. 129–64; Cooksey, 'Australian Public Opinion and Vietnam Policy'.

16 P. Ormonde, *A Foolish Passionate Man*, Penguin, Ringwood, 1981; I. Dowsing, *Jim Cairns MHR*, Acacia Press, Melbourne, 1971; G. Summy, 'The Revolutionary Democracy of J. F. Cairns', *Politics*, 7, 1 (1972), pp. 55–66.

17 *CPDHR*, vol. 67 (1970), pp. 1783, 2010.

18 I. Turner, 'The Vietnam Moratorium', *Meanjin,*, 29 (1970), pp. 233–4; also B. York, 'Police, Students and Dissent: Melbourne 1966–1972', *JAS*, 14 (1984), pp. 58–77; R. Nichols, 'These People', *Chauntecleer*, 2 (1970), pp. 1–10; M. Saunders, 'The ALP's Response to the Anti-Vietnam War Movement', *LH*, 44 (1983), pp. 75–91.

19 Heard in the beer-garden at the Continental Hotel, Claremont, Western Australia, November 1967.

20 Of the growing literature about Whitlam a major source is his own account, *The Whitlam Government 1972–1975*, Penguin, Ringwood, 1985, with a broader scope than those years. Other useful commentaries are G. Freudenberg, *A Certain Grandeur*, Macmillan, Melbourne, 1977 (2nd edn, Penguin, Ringwood, 1987); and J. Walter, *The Leader*, UQP, St Lucia, 1979.

21 A. Grey, *The Prime Minister was a Spy*, Weidenfeld & Nicolson, London, 1984.

22 R. V. Jackson (ed.), *John McEwen,* [n.p.], Canberra, 1983, p. 102.

23 There is as yet no biography of Gorton beyond A. Trengrove, *John Grey Gorton*, Cassell, Melbourne, 1969, written in mid-career. See also M. Walsh, 'You Ain't Seen Nothing Yet', *Quadrant*, Nov.–Dec. 1968, pp. 16–23.

24 Freudenberg, *A Certain Grandeur*, ch. 2.

25 D. L. Cuddy, 'American Business and Private Investment in Australia', *AJPH*, 26, 1 (1980), pp. 45–56; quotation from p. 50.

26 D. T. Brash, 'American Investment and Australian Sovereignty', in R. A. Preston (ed.), *Contemporary Australia*, Duke University Press, Durham, NC, 1969, pp. 539–52, quotation from p. 543.

27 For 1966, the '*Annus Mirabilis*', see *Bulletin*, 7 Jan. 1967. An overall survey is

D. W. Bennett, *Minerals and Energy in Australia*, Methuen, Sydney, 1979. See also S. Harris & G. Taylor, *Resource Development and the Future of Australian Society*, Centre for Resource and Environmental Studies, Canberra, 1982.

28 Accounts may be found in D. Murphy (ed.), *The Big Strikes: Queensland 1889–1965*, UQP, St Lucia, 1983; G. Sheldon, *Industrial Siege: The Mount Isa Dispute*, Cheshire, Melbourne, 1965; B. Mulligan, 'Four Views on the Mount Isa Dispute', *AQ*, 37 (1965), pp. 87–93; E. I. Sykes, 'The Mount Isa Affair', *Journal of Industrial Relations*, 7, 3 (1965), pp. 265–80.

29 G. Blainey, *Mines in the Spinifex*, Angus & Robertson, Sydney, 1961.

30 One regional study is M. E. Stockbridge, B. Gordon, R. Nowicki & N. Paterson, *Dominance of Giants—A Shire of Roebourne Study*, UWAP, Nedlands, 1976. See also H. M. Thompson, 'Class and Gender in the Pilbara', *Arena*, 68 (1984), pp. 124–40.

31 R. Fitzgerald, *From 1915 to the Early 1980s: A History of Queensland*, UQP, St Lucia, 1984, pp. 320–2.

32 K. Tsokhas, *A Class Apart?: Businessmen and Australian Politics 1960–1980*, OUP, Melbourne, 1984, pp. 6, 101–4.

33 *Australian*, 17 Jan. 1969.

34 *CPDHR*, vol. 60 (9 Oct. 1968), p. 1740.

35 *CPDHR*, vol. 64 (14 Aug. 1969), pp. 310–17. For some critical reactions, see *CPDS*, vol. S42, pp. 645–88.

36 *CPDHR*, vol. 67 (8 May 1970), pp. 1897–901; (15 May 1970), pp. 2242–327.

37 J. Kemeny, *The Myth of Home-Ownership*, Routledge & Kegan Paul, London, 1981; *The Great Australian Nightmare*, Georgian House, Melbourne, 1983; 'The Political Economy of Housing', in E. L. Wheelwright & K. Buckley (eds), *Essays in the Political Economy of Australian Capitalism*, ANZ, Sydney, 1975–83, vol. 4, pp. 172–91.

38 Senate Select Committee on Securities and Exchange, *Report*, pt I, vol. 1, AGPS, Canberra, 1974; R. Baxt, *The Rae Report: Quo Vadis?*, Butterworths, Sydney, 1974; T. Sykes, *The Money Miners 1969–1970*, Wildcat Press, Sydney, 1978.

39 B. d'Alpuget, *Hawke: A Biography*, 2nd edn, Schwartz, Melbourne, 1983, ch. 4.

40 *Sydney Morning Herald*, 5 Nov. 1971.

41 Whitlam, *The Whitlam Government*, pp. 53–60; Freudenberg, *A Certain Grandeur*, ch. 13.

CHAPTER 8: NEW DIRECTIONS?

1 D. Altman, 'The Creation of Sexual Politics in Australia', *JAS*, 20 (1987), pp. 76–82; P. R. Wilson & D. Chappell, 'Australian Attitudes towards Abortion, Prostitution and Homosexuality', *AQ*, 40, 2 (1968), pp. 7–17.

2 P. Hasluck, *Black Australians*, MUP, Melbourne, 1942, p. 161.

3 *Northern Territory News*, 10 Oct. 1958, quoted by F. K. Crowley, *Modern Australia in Documents*, vol. 2, *1939–1970*, Wren, Melbourne, 1973, pp. 360–1; J. Beckett, 'Aborigines, Alcohol, and Assimilation', in M. Reay, *Aborigines Now: New Perspectives in the Study of Aboriginal Communities*, Angus & Robertson, Sydney, 1964, pp. 32–47; J. Miller, *Koori: A Will to Win*, Angus & Robertson, Sydney, 1985.

4 W. de Maria, 'White Welfare, Black Entitlement: The Social Security Access Controversy 1939–88', *Aboriginal History*, 10 (1986), pp. 25–39.

5 M. Calley, 'Pentecostalism Among the Bandjalang', in Reay, *Aborigines Now*, pp. 48–57; H. Petri & G. Petri-Odermann, 'Stability and Change: Present-Day Historic Aspects Among Australian Aborigines', in R. M.

Berndt (ed.), *Australian Aboriginal Anthropology*, UWAP, Nedlands, 1970, pp. 248–76.

6   D. Barwick, *Fighters and Singers*, Allen & Unwin, Sydney, 1985; J. Beckett & M. Reay, *Metaphors of Interpretation*, AIAS, Canberra, 1985.

7   B. Sykes, *Mum Shirl*, Heinemann Educational, Melbourne, 1981, p. 105.

8   J. Mulvaney, 'A Sense of Making History: Australian Aboriginal Studies, 1961–1986', *Australian Aboriginal Studies*, 2 (1986), pp. 48–56.

9   C. Perkins, *A Bastard Like Me*, Ure Smith, Sydney, 1975.

10   P. Read, 'Fathers and Sons', *Aboriginal History*, 4 (1980), pp. 97–116.

11   *Bulletin*, 20 Feb. 1965.

12   S. Bennett, 'The 1967 Referendum', *Australian Aboriginal Studies*, 2 (1985), pp. 26–31.

13   H. C. Coombs, *Trial Balance*, Macmillan, Melbourne, 1981, pp. 289–91; see also *Kulinma: Listening to Aboriginal Australians*, ANUP, Canberra, 1978.

14   W. E. Stanner, 'Industrial Justice in the Never-Never', *AQ*, 39, 1 (1967), pp. 38–55.

15   *Sunday Australian*, 2 May 1971; J. Hookey, 'The Gove Land Rights Case: A Judicial Dispensation for the Taking of Aboriginal Lands in Australia', *Federal Law Review*, 5 (1972), pp. 85–144; H. Reynolds, *The Law of the Land*, Penguin, Ringwood, 1987.

16   E. G. Whitlam, *The Whitlam Government 1972–1975*, Penguin, Ringwood, 1985, p. 466.

17   G. St. J. Barclay, 'Friends in Salisbury: Australia and the Rhodesian Unilateral Declaration of Independence, 1965–72', *AJPH*, 29, 1 (1983), pp. 38–49.

18   A. Bear, 'Demonstrations and the Australian Press', *Politics*, 7, 2 (1972), pp. 155–9; S. Harris, *Political Football: The Springbok Tour of Australia, 1971*, Gold Star Publications, Hawthorn, 1972.

19   Whitlam, *The Whitlam Government 1972–1975*, p. 85; M. Hess, '"Doing Something for the Workers"?: The Establishment of Port Moresby's Central District Workers' Union', *LH*, 54 (1988), pp. 83–98; R. Cleland, *Pathways to Independence: Official and Family Life 1951–1975*, Artlook, Perth, 1983.

20   D. Woolford, *Papua-New Guinea: Initiation and Independence*, UQP, St Lucia, 1980; I. Downs, *The Australian Trusteeship . . . 1945–1975*, AGPS, Canberra, 1980, pt 4.

21   *Age*, 5 May 1961.

22   M. Gaudian & M. Bosworth, 'Equal Pay?', in J. Mackinolty & H. Radi, *In Pursuit of Justice*, Hale & Iremonger, Sydney, 1979, pp. 160–9.

23   G. Greer, *The Female Eunuch*, Paladin, London, 1971.

24   A. Summers, *Damned Whores and God's Police*, Allen Lane, London, 1975; B. Kingston, *My Wife, My Daughter, and Poor Mary Anne*, Nelson, Melbourne, 1975; M. Dixson, *The Real Matilda*, Penguin, Ringwood, 1976.

25   E. Preddey, *Women's Electoral Lobby: Australia and New Zealand, 1972–1985*, WEL, Canberra, 1985; H. Mayer (ed.), 'Labor in Power', *Politics*, 8, 1 (1973), pp. 169–97.

26   H. McQueen, *A New Britannia*, Penguin, Ringwood, 1970; see also 'Australo-Marximus: Or Some Reactions to A New Britannia', *Politics*, 7, 1 (1972), pp. 48–54.

27   F. Moorhouse, *Days of Wine and Rage*, Penguin, Ringwood, 1980.

28   South Australia, Government, *Royal Commission into the Non-Medical Use of Drugs: Cannabis, A Discussion Paper*, Government Printer, Adelaide, 1978; F. Crowley & L. Cartwright, *A Citizens' Guide to Marihuana in Australia*, Angus & Robertson, Sydney, 1977.

29 B. W. Davis, 'Political and Administrative Aspects of the Lake Pedder Controversy', *Public Administration*, 31 (1972), pp. 21–39.

30 G. C. Bolton, *Spoils and Spoilers*, Allen & Unwin, Sydney, 1981, ch. 14.

31 R. J. Roddewig, *Green Bans: The Birth of Australian Environmental Politics*, Hale & Iremonger, Sydney, 1978; J. Mundey, *Green Bans and Beyond*, Angus & Robertson, London, 1981.

32 K. S. Inglis, *The Stuart Case*, MUP, Melbourne, 1961.

33 L. Finch & J. Stratton, 'The Australian Working Class and the Practice of Abortion, 1880–1939', *JAS*, 23 (1988), pp. 45–64.

34 D. Dunstan, *Felicia*, Macmillan, Melbourne, 1981, p. 202.

35 D. Altman, *Coming Out in the Seventies*, Penguin, Ringwood, 1980; G. Wotherspoon, *Being Different*, Hale & Iremonger, Sydney, 1986.

36 Commission of Inquiry into Poverty, *Poverty in Australia*, First Main Report (Prof. R. F. Henderson, Chairman), AGPS, Canberra, 1975; R. Henderson, *The Welfare Stakes: Strategies for Australian Social Policy*, Institute of Applied Economic and Social Research, Parkville, 1981.

37 R. F. Scotton, 'Membership of Voluntary Health Insurance', *ER*, 45 (1969), pp. 69–83; R. F. Scotton & J. J. Deeble, 'The Nimmo Report', *ER*, 45 (1969), pp. 258–73.

38 Commonwealth Committee of Enquiry into Health Insurance, *Health Insurance, Report of the Committee of Enquiry into Health Insurance* (Mr Justice Nimmo, Chairman), AGPS, Canberra, 1969.

39 Quoted in T. Hunter, 'Medical Politics: Decline in the Hegemony of the Australian Medical Association', *Australian Society*, 3, 2 (1984).

40 J. McLaren, 'The Politics of Education', *Australian Journal of Advanced Education*, 2, 3 (1971), pp. 6–10; *Bulletin*, 18 Nov. 1972, pp. 17–22.

41 H. C. Coombs, *Trial Balance*, Macmillan, Melbourne, 1981, ch. 8, esp. p. 243.

42 I. Bertrand & D. Collins, *Government and Film in Australia*, Currency Press, Sydney, & Australian Film Commission, Carlton, 1981; I. Bertrand, '"National Identity", "National History" and "National Film"', *Historical Journal of Film, Radio and Television*, 4 (1984), pp. 179–88; A. Pike & R. Cooper, *Australian Film 1900–1977*, OUP in association with the Australian Film Institute, Melbourne, 1980.

43 P. Coleman, *Obscenity, Sedition and Blasphemy*, Jacaranda, Brisbane, 1963; *Encounter* (London), Nov. 1964, p. 64.

44 Victoria, *Parliamentary Debates*, vol. 273 (18 March 1964), pp. 3246–54.

45 E. Campion, *Australian Catholics*, Penguin, Ringwood, 1987, ch. 5; H. Mol, *The Faith of Australians*, Allen & Unwin, Sydney, 1985.

46 *CPDHR*, vol. 86 (18 Oct. 1973), p. 2333.

47 *Australian*, 13 Nov. 1972; quoted by N. Meaney, 'The United States', in W. J. Hudson (ed.), *Australia in World Affairs 1971–1975*, Allen & Unwin, Sydney, 1980, pp. 178–9.

48 G. C. Bolton, 'The United Kingdom', in Hudson, *Australia in World Affairs 1971–1975*, ch. 8.

49 D. Marr, *Barwick*, Angus & Robertson, Sydney, 1980, pp. 227–31, 293–4.

50 *Nation Review*, 3–9 May 1974.

51 R. Catley & B. MacFarlane, *From Tweedledum to Tweedledee*, ANZ Book Co., Sydney, 1974.

CHAPTER 9: A SHINING ABERRATION

1 E. G. Whitlam, *The Whitlam Government 1972–1975*, Penguin, Ringwood, 1985, pp. 19–22.

2 G. Freudenberg, *A Certain Grandeur*, Macmillan, Melbourne, 1977, pp. 266–7 (2nd edn, Penguin, Ringwood, 1987).
3 Whitlam, *The Whitlam Government 1972–1975*, p. 185.
4 ibid., p. 183.
5 F. Gruen, 'What Went Wrong? Some Personal Reflections on Economic Policies Under Labor', *AQ*, 48, 3 (1976), pp. 15–33.
6 A. Rattigan, *Industry Assistance*, MUP, Melbourne, 1986, ch. 8; J. Warhurst, *Jobs or Dogma? The Industries Assistance Commission and Australian Politics*, UQP, St Lucia, 1982.
7 Rattigan, *Industry Assistance*, p. 170.
8 *Sydney Morning Herald*, 1 Dec. 1973.
9 Whitlam, *The Whitlam Government 1972–1975*, p. 315.
10 *CPDS*, vol. 58 (12 Dec. 1973), pp. 2710–19.
11 Whitlam, *The Whitlam Government 1972–1975*, p. 314.
12 D. J. Murphy, *Hayden: A Political Biography*, Angus & Robertson, Sydney, 1980, chs 5–6.
13 A. F. Davies, *Australian Democracy*, Longmans, Melbourne, 1958, p. 4.
14 P. N. Troy, *The Land Commission Programme 1972–1977*, Hale & Iremonger, Sydney, 1978; C. J. Lloyd & P. N. Troy, *Innovation and Reaction: The Life and Death of the First Department of Urban and Regional Development*, Allen & Unwin, Sydney, 1981.
15 A. Parkin & C. Pugh, 'Urban Policy and Metropolitan Adelaide', in A. Parkin & A. Patience (eds), *The Dunstan Decade: Social Democracy at the State Level*, Longman Cheshire, Melbourne, 1981, pp. 91–114.
16 Quoted in Whitlam, *The Whitlam Government 1972–1975*, p. 739.
17 G. Greenwood, *The Future of Australian Federalism: A Commentary on the Working of the Constitution*, MUP, Melbourne, 1946 (2nd edn, UQP, St Lucia, 1976); L. F. Crisp, *Australian National Government*, 3rd edn, Longman, Melbourne, 1973.
18 H. Lunn, *Joh*, UQP, St Lucia, 1978.
19 T. M. Fitzgerald, *The Contribution of the Mineral Industry to Australian Welfare*, AGPS, Canberra, 1974.
20 D. Solomon, *Elect the Governor-General!*, Nelson, Melbourne, 1976, p. 1.
21 N. Meaney, 'The United States', in W. J. Hudson (ed.), *Australia in World Affairs 1971–1975*, Allen & Unwin, Sydney, 1980, p. 189 and pp. 163–208 *passim*.
22 D. J. Ball, *A Suitable Piece of Real Estate*, Hale & Iremonger, Sydney, 1980.
23 Whitlam, *The Whitlam Government 1972–1975*, p. 246.
24 The complex manoeuvres are discussed in C. A. Hughes, 'Australian Political Chronicle', *AJPH*, 20, 2 (1974), pp. 234–5.
25 D. H. Clune, 'The State Labor Party's Electoral Record in Rural New South Wales, 1904–1981', *LH*, 47 (1984), pp. 91–9; P. R. Hay, 'Labor Vacates the Bush: The Eclipse of Working Class Values in Victoria's Western District', *LH*, 54 (1988), pp. 64–82.
26 J. Jupp (ed.), *The Australian People: An Encyclopaedia of the Nation, its People and their Origins*, Angus & Robertson, Sydney, 1988; J. Hickson, 'Assimilation or Multiculturalism: A False Dilemma', *Arena*, 67 (1983), pp. 7–11.
27 F. Knopfelmacher, 'The Case Against Multiculturalism', in R. Manne (ed.), *The New Conservatism in Australia*, OUP, Melbourne, 1982, pp. 40–64.
28 C. Ronalds, '"To Right a Few Wrongs": Legislation Against Sex Discrimination', in J. Mackinolty & H. Radi (eds), *In Pursuit of Justice: Australian Women and the Law 1788–1979*, Hale & Iremonger, Sydney, 1979, pp. 190–201.
29 M. Bevege, 'Women's Struggle to Become Tram-Drivers in Melbourne',

and M. Burgmann, 'Revolution and Machismo: Women in the New South Wales Builders Labourers' Federation, 1961–77', in E. Windschuttle, *Women, Class and History*, Fontana/Collins, Sydney, 1980, pp. 437–52 and 453–91.

30 *CPDHR*, vol. 83 (10 May 1973), pp. 1963–2001.

31 J. Davidson, 'Mr Whitlam's Cultural Revolution', *JAS*, 20 (1987), pp. 83–91.

32 B. Warnock, 'The Australian Moving Image', *Early Days*, 9, 4 (1986), p. 67.

33 T. Stannage, 'Sir Thomas Wardle, the Grocer', in L. Hunt (ed.), *Westralian Portraits*, UWAP, Nedlands, 1979, pp. 287–95.

34 L. J. Perry, 'Trends in Australian Strike Activity 1913–78', *Australian Bulletin of Labour*, 6, 1 (Dec. 1979), pp. 31–51.

35 B. D. Haig, *Gambling in Australia 1920/21 to 1980/81*, Working Papers in Economic History, No. 20, ANU, Canberra, 1984.

36 T. Sykes, *Two Centuries of Panic: A History of Corporate Collapses in Australia*, Allen & Unwin, Sydney, 1988, p. 467.

37 Freudenberg, *A Certain Grandeur*, p. 305.

38 *CPDHR*, vol. 95 (9 July 1975), pp. 3610–25.

39 A. Stretton, *Soldier in a Storm*, Collins, Sydney, 1978.

40 B. Catley & B. Macfarlane, 'Labor and Economic Crisis: Counter Strategies and Political Realities', in E. L. Wheelwright & K. Buckley (eds), *Essays in the Political Economy of Australian Capitalism*, ANZ Book Co., Sydney, 1980, vol. 4, pp. 267–310, esp. pp. 290–4.

41 T. Rowse, 'Land Rights, Mining, and Settler Democracy', *Meanjin*, 45 (1986), pp. 58–67.

42 *CPDS*, vol. S61 (19 Sept. 1973), pp. 1267–73; vol. S63 (20 Feb. 1975), pp. 367–70.

43 P. Ayres, *Malcolm Fraser*, Heinemann, Melbourne, 1987, p. 251.

44 For example, Alan Ashbolt, 'Why Whitlam Failed', *New Statesman* (London), 19 Dec. 1975.

45 K. Windschuttle & E. Windschuttle, *Fixing the News*, Cassell, Sydney, 1981; B. Bonney & H. Wilson, *Australia's Commercial Media*, Macmillan, Melbourne, 1983.

46 For Murdoch, see G. J. Munster, *A Paper Prince*, Penguin, Ringwood, 1987; M. Leapman, *Barefaced Cheek*, Hodder & Stoughton, London, 1983, esp. pp. 64–72.

47 *Sydney Morning Herald*, 30 Apr. 1975.

48 *CPDHR*, vol. 95 (9 July 1975), pp. 3610–25.

49 A narrative account of this period in politics is R. K. Forward, 'Australian Political Chronicle', *AJPH*, 22 (1976), pp. 74–82.

50 A. Reid, *The Whitlam Venture*, Hill of Content, Melbourne, 1976, p. 358.

51 This allegation was most widely publicized by John Pilger in his 1988 television programme 'The Last Dream' (pt 3); see *Sydney Morning Herald*, 25 Jan. 1988. Consult also *National Times*, 21–27 March 1982, 15–21 March 1985; S. Alomes, *A Nation at Last? The Changing Character of Australian Nationalism 1880–1988*, Angus & Robertson, Sydney, 1988, pp. 256–8.

52 Ayres, *Malcolm Fraser*, pp. 292–3. But see also Sir J. Kerr, *Matters for Judgement*, Macmillan, Melbourne, 1978, pp. 348 and 355; *Australian*, 7 Nov. 1987.

53 On this option see the comments by G. S. Reid & M. Forrest, *Australia's Commonwealth Parliament 1901–1988: Ten Perspectives*, MUP, Melbourne, 1989, pp. 327–31, 480–1; D. A. Low, 'Wearing the Crown: New Reflections on the Dismissal, 1975', *Politics*, 19, 1 (1984), pp. 18–24.

54 R. Conway, 'Why I Can't Vote for Whitlam', *Bulletin*, 6 Dec. 1975;

M. Clark, 'Are We a Nation of Bastards?', *Meanjin*, 35 (1976), pp. 215–18.
55 *Bulletin*, 3 Sept. 1985; also 10 and 17 Sept. 1985.
56 Alomes, *A Nation at Last?*, pp. 236–61; 'Ceremonial Visions of Australia', *JAS*, 20 (1987), pp. 49–58.

CHAPTER 10: ON THE MAKE

1 J. Edwards, *Life Wasn't Meant to be Easy*, Mayhem, Sydney, 1977, ch. 14; S. C. Ghosh, 'The Ideological World of Malcolm Fraser', *AQ*, 50, 3 (1978), pp. 6–28; G. Little, 'Fraser and Fraserism', *Meanjin*, 41 (1982), pp. 291–306.
2 *Age*, 9 August 1977.
3 R. Gittings, 'Crucial Decision on Protection', *National Times*, 27 July–2 August 1980.
4 Australia, Parliament, *Ranger Uranium Environmental Inquiry: Second Report*, Parl. Paper 117, Canberra, 1977. I. Lowe, 'The Uranium Industry in Australia', in *Social Issues in the 1980s*, Occasional Papers No. 4, Australian Studies Centre, University of Queensland, St Lucia, 1984, pp. 17–55; K. A. W. Crook, 'Towards a Comprehensive Uranium Fuel Management Policy for Australia', *Search*, 8 (1977), pp. 223–31.
5 H. McQueen, *Gone Tomorrow: Australia in the Eighties*, Angus & Robertson, Sydney, 1982, p. 125.
6 C. Saunders & K. Wiltshire, 'Fraser's New Federalism, 1975–1980: An Evaluation', *AJPH*, 26, 3 (1980), pp. 355–71.
7 J. P. Nieuwenhuysen, *Aboriginal Land Rights and Industry*, CEDA, Melbourne, 1980; D. Cousins & J. P. Nieuwenhuysen, *Aboriginals and the Mining Industry: Case Studies of the Australian Experience*, Allen & Unwin, Sydney, 1984; T. R. Gurr, 'The Politics of Aboriginal Land Rights and their Effects on Australian Resource Development', *AJPH*, 31, 3 (1985), pp. 474–89; S. Hawke & M. Gallagher, *Noonkanbah*, FACP, Fremantle, 1989.
8 *Australian*, 12 June 1982.
9 P. J. Sheehan & P. P. Stricker, 'The Collapse of Full Employment 1974 to 1978', in R. B. Scotton & H. Ferber, *Public Expenditure and Social Policy in Australia*, Longman Cheshire, Melbourne, 1980, vol. 2, pp. 28–76.
10 J. Schulz, *Steel City: The Human Cost of Industrial Crisis*, Penguin, Ringwood, 1985; 'The Death of the Holden', *Sydney Morning Herald*, 27 Sept. 1986.
11 L. Hawthorne, *Refugee: The Vietnamese Experience*, OUP, Melbourne, 1982; N. Viviani, *The Long Journey: Vietnamese Migration and Settlement in Australia*, MUP, Melbourne, 1984.
12 H. Mol, *The Faith of Australians*, Allen & Unwin, Sydney, 1985; D. Watkins, 'Changes in the Religious Practices and Beliefs of Students at an Australian University, 1965–77', *Australian Journal of Social Issues*, 14 (1978), pp. 211–17.
13 E. Campion, *Australian Catholics*, Viking, Ringwood, 1987, pp. 244–6.
14 R. Fitzgerald, *From 1915 to the Early 1980s: A History of Queensland*, UQP, St Lucia, 1984, pp. 603–4.
15 A. Burns, *Breaking Up: Separation and Divorce in Australia*, Nelson, Melbourne, 1980; F. Crowley, *Tough Times: Australia in the Seventies*, Heinemann, Melbourne, 1986, pp. 230–4; G. A. Carmichael, 'The Changing Structure of Australian Families, *AQ*, 57 (1986), pp. 95–106; *Sydney Morning Herald*, 3 Apr. 1989.
16 Commission of Inquiry into Poverty, *Poverty in Australia*, First Main Report (Prof. R. F. Henderson, Chairman), AGPS, Canberra, 1975.
17 R. B. Scotton, 'Health Insurance: Medibank and After', in Scotton & Ferber, *Public Expenditure and Social Policy in Australia*, vol. 2, pp. 175–219; S. J. Duckett, 'Chopping and Changing Medibank', *Australian Journal of Social*

Issues, 14 (1979), pp. 230–43, 15 (1980), pp. 79–91; G. Gray, 'The Termination of Medibank', *Politics*, 19, 2 (1984), pp. 1–17.

18   Royal Commission into Human Relationships, *Final Report*, 5 vols, AGPS, Canberra, 1977. The report's findings are summarized in A. Deveson, *Australians at Risk*, Cassell, Sydney, 1978.

19   Deveson, *Australians at Risk*, p. 31.

20   ibid., pp. 63–5.

21   ibid., p. 94.

22   ibid., pp. 16–24.

23   *CPDS*, vol. S78 (11 Oct. 1978), pp. 1204–6; vol. S79 (9 Nov. 1978), pp. 1840–920.

24   *CPDHR*, vol. 113 (21–22 March 1979), pp. 963–1126.

25   Queensland, *Parliamentary Debates*, vol. 281 (29 April–21 May 1980), pp. 3585–657, 3689–753, 3783–847; A. J. Bourne & J. D. Kerr, 'The Characteristics of Two Samples of Women Seeking Abortion in Queensland', *Australian Journal of Social Issues*, 15 (1980), pp. 207–14.

26   K. Betts, 'The Availability of Birth Control: Victoria 1971–75', *Australian Journal of Social Issues*, 15 (1980), pp. 17–29; M. G. A. Wilson, 'The Changing Pattern of Urban Fertility in Eastern Australia 1966–76', *Australian Geographical Studies*, 22, 2 (1984), pp. 202–19.

27   Deveson, *Australians at Risk*, p. 99.

28   G. Bell, 'Medical Secrets for Export', *Bulletin*, 16 July 1985; C. Crowe, 'The Reproductive Fix', *Australian Left Review*, 91 (1985), pp. 4–9.

29   J. Bryson, *Evil Angels*, Penguin, Ringwood, 1985.

30   D. Johnson, 'From Fairy to Witch: Imagery and Myth in the Azaria Case', *Australian Journal of Cultural Studies*, 2, 2 (1984), pp. 90–107; J. Craik, 'The Azaria Chamberlain Case: A Question of Infanticide', *Australian Journal of Cultural Studies*, 4, 2 (1987), pp. 123–47; S. Piggin, 'The Chamberlain Case and Australian Secularism', in B. Hocking (ed.), *Australia Towards 2000*, Macmillan, London, 1990.

31   Writers on these matters include B. Bottom, *The Godfather in Australia*, Sun Books, Melbourne, 1979, and *Without Fear or Favour*, Sun Books, Melbourne, 1984; D. Wilson & L. Murdoch, *Big Shots*, Sun Books, Melbourne, 1985; D. Wilson & P. Robinson, *Big Shots II*, Sun Books, Melbourne, 1987; A. Moffitt, *A Quarter to Midnight*, Methuen, Sydney, 1985; D. Hickie, *The Prince and the Premier*, Methuen, Sydney, 1985.

32   Commission of Inquiry Relating to Allegations of Organized Crime in Clubs, *Report* (Mr Justice Moffitt, Commissioner), Government Printer, Sydney, 1974; Commission of Inquiry into the Legalization of Gambling Casinos in New South Wales, *Report* (Mr Justice Lusher, Commissioner), Government Printer, Sydney, 1978; Commission of Inquiry into Drug Trafficking, *Report* (Mr Justice Woodward, Commissioner), AGPS, Canberra, 1979.

33   T. Sykes, *Two Centuries of Panic: A History of Corporate Collapses in Australia*, Allen & Unwin, Sydney, 1988, chs 20–1.

34   C. McGregor, *Time of Testing: The Bob Hawke Victory*, Penguin, Ringwood, 1983, pp. 35–8.

35   I. Turner & L. Sandercock, *Up Where Cazaly?*, Granada, London, 1981, p. 167, and chs 12–14 generally; S. Alomes, 'The People's Religion and the Rise of Capitalism?', *Meanjin*, 40 (1981), pp. 534–49.

36   R. Cashman, 'Crisis in Contemporary Cricket', in R. Cashman & M. McKernan, *Sport: Money, Morality, and the Media*, NSWUP, Kensington, 1981, pp. 304–12.

37   *CPDHR*, vol. 117 (19 Feb. 1980), p. 17.

38   R. G. Gregory, 'Some Implications of the Growth of the Mineral Sector', *Australian Journal of Agricultural Economics*, 20 (1976), pp. 71–91.
39   Commission of Inquiry into the Australian Financial System *Final Report* (J. K. Campbell, chairman), AGPS, Canberra, 1981; J. O. N. Perkins, *The Australian Financial System after the Campbell Report*, MUP, Melbourne, 1982.
40   B. Jones, *Sleepers Wake!*, OUP, Melbourne, 1982.
41   R. Morris, 'The Incorrigible Waterfront and its Decline: Inquiries and Royal Commissions into Ex-officio Payments and Illegal Activities, 1958–1984', *LH*, 55 (1988), pp. 71–81.
42   *Australian Financial Review*, 27 August 1982.
43   A. Lansdown, 'Australia, March 5th 1983', in *Windfalls*, FACP, Fremantle, 1984.

CHAPTER 11: TOWARDS THE BICENTENARY

1   P. J. Lloyd, *The Accord: Australia's Experience with Consensual Incomes Policies*, Parliamentary Library, Discussion Paper 3, Canberra, 1985; F. Stilwell, *The Accord . . . and Beyond*, Pluto Press, Sydney, 1986; S. Carney, *Australia in Accord: Politics and Industrial Relations under the Hawke Government*, Macmillan, Melbourne, 1988.
2   *Age*, 17 June 1983.
3   Two examinations of this shift may be found in G. Maddox, *The Hawke Government and Labor Tradition*, Penguin, Ringwood, 1989; D. Jaensch, *The Hawke-Keating Hijack: The ALP in Transition*, Allen & Unwin, Sydney, 1989.
4   *CPDS*, vol. 117 (22 Oct. 1986), pp. 1691–704; *CPDHR*, vol. 151 (22 Oct. 1986), pp. 2489–509. The House of Representatives took two hours and twenty minutes, nearly twice as long as Murphy's former chamber, the Senate.
5   L. A. Murray, 'The Quality of Sprawl', in *Selected Poems*, Carcanet, Manchester, 1986, pp. 88–90.
6   R. Castle & J. Mangan, *Unemployment in the Eighties*, Longman Cheshire, Melbourne, 1984; E. Fisher, *Occupation Unemployed: Trends in Unemployment in Australia 1970–86*, Social Security Review, Department of Social Security, Woden, ACT, 1987.
7   J. Piggott, 'The Nation's Private Wealth—Some New Calculations for Australia', *ER*, 63 (1987), pp. 61–79.
8   '1981–86: Poverty on the Rise', *Australian Society*, April 1987, pp. 34–5, quoting figures outlined by Anthony King in *National Economic Review*, April 1987; D. O'Reilly, 'The Unfair Society', *Bulletin*, 25 April 1989.
9   A. Horin, 'Surprise, Surprise, We're Better Off', *Sydney Morning Herald*, 6 June 1989.
10   J. J. Bessi & B. J. Chapman, 'An Empirical Analysis of Australian Strike Activity: Estimating the Industrial Relations Effects of the First Three Years of the Prices and Incomes Accord', *ER*, 63 (1987), pp. 46–60.
11   P. Brain & B. Gray, 'We've Found the J-Curve but Does it Matter?', *Australian Society*, May 1986, p. 26.
12   G. J. Crough & E. L. Wheelwright, *Australia the Client State*, Penguin, Ringwood, 1981.
13   *West Australian*, 18 Nov. 1985.
14   J. Stone, *Deregulate or Perish*, UWAP, Nedlands, 1985.
15   J. Bertrand, *Born to Win*, Transworld, Sydney, 1985.
16   *Sydney Morning Herald*, 28 Sept. 1983.
17   J. McCorquodale, 'Aborigines in the High Court', *AQ*, 55, 1 (1983), pp. 104–13.

18   T. Rowse, 'Land Rights, Mining, and Settler Democracy', *Meanjin*, 45 (1986), pp. 58–67.
19   Personal observation, Perth, Nov.–Dec. 1987.
20   *Australian*, 3 Sept. 1987.
21   What follows is drawn from the *Age, Australian, Canberra Times, Sydney Morning Herald* and *West Australian*, 23–27 Jan. 1988.
22   G. Blainey, *All for Australia*, Methuen, Sydney, 1984; for criticisms, see M. Ricklefs & A. Markus, *Surrender Australia?*, Allen & Unwin, Sydney, 1985; T. Jordan, 'Politics, History, Migration: The Blainey Debate', *Arena*, 73 (1985), pp. 80–94.
23   D. Horne, *The Lucky Country Revisited*, Dent, Melbourne, 1987.
24   R. White, *Inventing Australia*, Allen & Unwin, Sydney, 1981.
25   A. Johnston & A. Morris, 'C'mon, Aussie, C'mon' (WEA Records 1979), quoted by S. Murray-Smith, *The Dictionary of Australian Quotations*, Heinemann, Melbourne, 1984, p. 129.
26   'Men at Work', quoted by Murray-Smith, *The Dictionary of Australian Quotations*, p. 184.
27   *Sydney Morning Herald*, 1 June 1974.
28   J. A. Passmore, *The Limits of Government*, ABC, Sydney, 1981, p. 52.
29   D. Martin, *On the Road to Sydney*, Nelson, Melbourne, 1970, p. 148.

SOURCES OF ILLUSTRATIONS

Every effort has been made to trace the original source of illustrations contained in this book. Where the attempt has been unsuccessful the author, and publisher would be pleased to hear from the author/publisher concerned, to rectify any omission or error.

178 from Kate White, *John Cain and Victorian Labor, 1917–57*, Hale & Iremonger, Sydney, 1982

178 *Herald and Weekly Times*, December 1941

179 from G. Blainey, *Mines in the Spinifex*, Angus & Robertson Publishers, Sydney, 1960

179 Department of Immigration, *Understanding Immigration*, AGPS, Canberra, 1987

242 from B. de Garis (ed.). *Campus in the Community: The University of Western Australia, 1963–1987*, University of Western Australia Press, Nedlands, 1988

242 from B. de Garis (ed.). *Campus in the Community: The University of Western Australia, 1963–1987*, University of Western Australia Press, Nedlands, 1988

243 Fryer Memorial Library, University of Queensland

243 Fryer Memorial Library, University of Queensland

274 National Library of Australia

274 Australian Information Service

275 Fryer Memorial Library, University of Queensland

BIBLIOGRAPHIC NOTE

Contemporary history draws upon a bewildering variety of source materials, and this note merely indicates points of departure for further reading. The endnotes give suggestions towards more detailed consultation. It should also be noted that many of the sources cited by Stuart Macintyre in his bibliographic essay for volume 4 of the Oxford History of Australia are of relevance for volume 5.

Among the publications evoked by the 1988 Bicentenary, the 11-volume *Australians, A Historical Library* (Fairfax, Syme & Weldon, Broadway, 1987) includes two volumes of particular relevance: the bibliographic volume, *Australians: A Guide to Sources*, compiled by D. H. Borchardt and Victor Crittenden, and the last of the 'slice' volumes, *Australians from 1939*, edited by Ann Curthoys, Allan Martin and Tim Rowse, and including contributions by eighteen authors and ten essayists in reminiscence. Tim Rowse's account of the compilation of this volume, '. . . Fallen among gentlemen . . .' is given in *Australian Historical Studies*, 91 (1988), pp. 121–9.

Earlier general histories covering the period from the Second World War to the recent past are Fred Alexander, *From Curtin to Menzies* (Nelson, Melbourne, 1973), and Tony Griffiths, *Contemporary Australia* (Croom Helm, London, 1977). Primary source materials may be found in F. Crowley, *Modern Australia in Documents*, vol. 2, *1939–70* (Wren, Melbourne, 1973) and in the relevant parts of Humphrey McQueen, *Social Sketches of Australia 1888–1975* (Penguin, Ringwood, 1975). It is also worth consulting the relevant sections of histories covering a wider period, such as T. R. Reese, *Australia in the Twentieth Century* (Pall Mall Press, London, 1964); Russel Ward, *A Nation for a Continent, 1901–1975* (Heinemann, Melbourne, 1978); and Fred Alexander, *Australia Since Federation* (Nelson, Melbourne, 4th edn, 1980); also G. S. Reid and M. Forrest, *Australia's Commonwealth Parliament 1901–1988: Ten Perspectives* (MUP, Melbourne, 1989). F. Crowley's *A New History of Australia* (Heinemann, Melbourne, 1974) includes my chapters on 1939–51 and W. J. Hudson's on 1951–72, but much additional research has taken place since its publication. Crowley himself wrote a sequel, *Tough Times: Australia in the Seventies* (Heinemann, Melbourne, 1986), and Humphrey McQueen's viewpoint may be found in *Gone Tomorrow: Australia in the Eighties* (Angus & Robertson, Sydney, 1982).

Other valuable sources include the four-part, 22-volume series *Australia in the War of 1939–45* (Australian War Memorial, Canberra, 1952–72); *Documents in Australian Foreign Policy 1937–49*, edited by R. G. Neale, H. Kenway and W. J. Hudson, of which seven volumes have appeared (Australian Government Publishing Service, Canberra, 1975–); and the 6-volume Australian Institute of International Affairs series *Australia in World Affairs* (1951–55 to 1976–80), edited by N. D. Harper, G. Greenwood, W. J. Hudson and P. J. Boyce (Cheshire, Melbourne, and Allen & Unwin, Sydney, 1956–84). Domestic issues are covered in *Australian Quarterly, Australian Society, The Australian and New Zealand Journal of Sociology, Current Affairs Bulletin*, and the cumulative indices of the Australian Public Affairs Information Service (National Library of Australia, Canberra, 1945–). International affairs are treated in *Australian Outlook* and in the regular feature, 'Problems in Australian Foreign Policy' in *AJPH* (1955–); the latter also features very useful surveys of contemporary federal and state politics. *Australian Book Review* (1961–73; 1978–) covers a wide range of contemporary publications. Literature, culture and ideology are covered (reading from right to left) in *Quadrant, Meanjin* and *Overland*. Among the major weeklies *Nation Review* (formerly *Nation*, 1958–81) and *National Times* (in its last year *Times on Sunday*, 1971–87), variable in quality but usually at least lively, both expired from inadequate circulation, leaving as survivor the rejuvenated *Bulletin* (1880–; incorporating the *Observer*, 1958–61).

INDEX

322